Michael Schloms

W9-DDJ-272

North Korea and the Timeless Dilemma of Aid

Espinosa Library
Castilleja School
Palo Alto, CA 94301
DISCARD

Berliner Schriften
zur Humanitären Hilfe und Konfliktprävention

herausgegeben von

Prof. Dr. Wolf-Dieter Eberwein und Dr. Sven Chojnacki
(Wissenschaftszentrum Berlin für Sozialforschung, WZB)

Band 5

LIT

Michael Schloms

North Korea and the Timeless Dilemma of Aid

A Study of Humanitarian Action in Famines

LIT

Espinosa Library
Castilleja School
Palo Alto, CA 94301
DISCARD

D 188

Bibliographic information published by Die Deutsche Bibliothek
Die Deutsche Bibliothek lists this publication in the Deutsche
Nationalbibliografie; detailed bibliographic data are available in the
Internet at http://dnb.ddb.de.

ISBN 3-8258-7531-8
Zugl.: Berlin, FU, Diss., 2003

© LIT VERLAG Münster   2004
Grevener Str./Fresnostr. 2   48159 Münster
Tel. 0251-23 50 91   Fax 0251-23 19 72
e-Mail: lit@lit-verlag.de   http://www.lit-verlag.de

Distributed in North America by:

Transaction Publishers
New Brunswick (U.S.A.) and London (U.K.)

Transaction Publishers   Tel.: (732) 445 - 2280
Rutgers University   Fax: (732) 445 - 3138
35 Berrue Circle   for orders (U. S. only):
Piscataway, NJ 08854   toll free (888) 999 - 6778

Editors' Preface

The behavior of humanitarian organizations is frequently criticized in the media as well as by politicians. One of the most serious criticisms is that aid agencies unwittingly prolong armed conflicts. However justified these reproaches might be, critics of humanitarian organizations tend to neglect one core issue: Namely, that aid agencies are inevitably confronted with a dilemma when trying to care for people in need. In this book, Michael Schloms shows what this central dilemma of humanitarian aid is all about: Accepting political demands in order to reach the victims of disaster or, instead, staying loyal to principles of action that may ultimately jeopardize the access to people in distress.

The particular relevance of this study relates to Michael Schloms' conclusion that this dilemma situation is not limited to armed conflicts. He shows that it can occur in war-related famines (as in Soviet Russia 1921-23), or as a result of natural disasters and political and economic mismanagement in an ultra-stable system (North Korea).

The overall conclusion is that the aid agencies' respect for principles of humanitarian action mainly depends on the will of the political actors themselves to respect these principles. As long as this condition is not fulfilled, humanitarian organizations can only try to solve the dilemma of their action individually from case to case. However, no course of action can claim to be of higher moral legitimacy than another.

Berlin, 2004

Wolf-Dieter Eberwein
Sven Chojnacki

Espinosa Library
Castilleja School
Palo Alto, CA 94301
DISCARD

Author's Preface

In recent years, humanitarian action has increasingly become an issue of public and academic debate. Aid missions in the Balkans, Rwanda or Afghanistan have been seen as morally ambivalent operations that ultimately questioned the traditions, principles and self-perceptions of international aid agencies. This book analyzes the ongoing international famine aid effort in North Korea and seeks to put some of the recent controversies and disputes into perspective.

As a political setting, the totalitarian and dynastic North Korea is often described as a unique case. During the course of my study I therefore had to deal with the argument that an analysis of the North Korean aid operation does not allow one to draw conclusions that go beyond this particular case. I hope that this book can disprove this argument. Looking closer, the North Korean aid mission has a number of characteristics in common with famine aid operations in the past. The North Korean case therefore provides a valuable source for understanding the ethical challenge of famine relief and humanitarian action.

This book could not have been written without the help of aid workers who were, or still are, engaged in famine aid efforts for North Korea. I am indebted to all those members of non-governmental organizations and aid agencies of the United Nations in Europe, the US, South and North Korea who have given generously of their time to the benefit of this study. A list of those interviewed can be found at the end of this book.

I was able to spend time as a visiting scholar at the Social Science Research Center of Berlin (WZB) where I have benefited from the support of the International Politics Working Group and its vast experience in the area of international humanitarian action. In particular, I would like to thank Professor Wolf-Dieter Eberwein, who accompanied this study from the beginning, for his advice and encouragement.

I would also like to thank the German Economic Foundation (SDW) for its generous financial support that allowed me to visit aid agencies' headquarters as well as project sites in North Korea.

Bonn, 2004

Michael Schloms

Contents

Abbreviations

ACF	*Action Contre La Faim*
ACT	*Action by Churches Together*
ADRA	*Adventist Development and Relief Agency International*
AFSC	*American Friends Service Committee*
APPC	*Asia Pacific Peace Committee*
ARA	*American Relief Administration*
AREP	*Agricultural Recovery and Environmental Protection*
CAD	*Children's Aid Direct*
CARE	*Cooperative for Assistance and Relief Everywhere, Inc.*
CESVI	*Cooperazione e Sviluppo*
CfC	*Campus für Christus*
CFGB	*Canadian Foodgrains Bank*
CIA	*Central Intelligence Agency*
CRS	*Catholic Relief Services*
CWS	*Church World Service*
DEC	*Disaster Emergency Committee*
DPRK	*Democratic People's Republic of Korea*
EC	*European Commission*
EC DG/DEV	*European Commission's Directorate-General for Development*
ECHO	*European Commission's Humanitarian Aid Office*
EU	*European Union*
FALU	*UN Food Aid Liaison Unit*
FAO	*UN Food and Agriculture Organization*
FDRC	*Flood Damage Rehabilitation Committee*
FFW	*Food for Work*
GAA	*German Agro Action (Deutsche Welthungerhilfe)*
GAO	*US General Accounting Office*
GNP	*Gross National Product*
ICF	*International Corn Foundation*
ICRC	*International Committee of the Red Cross*
IFAD	*International Fund for Agricultural Development*
IFRC	*International Federation of Red Cross and Red Crescent Societies*
JCA	*Joint Church Aid*
JTS	*Join Together Society*

KINU	Korean Institute for National Unification
KWP	Korean Worker's Party
MCI	Mercy Corps International
MDM	Médecins du Monde
MSF	Médecins Sans Frontières
NGO	Non-governmental organization
NSC	(US) National Security Council
OCHA	UN Office for the Coordination of Humanitarian Affairs
OPEC	Organization of the Petroleum Exporting Countries
PDS	Public Distribution System
PMU Inter-Life	Pingst Missionens Utveck-lingssamarbete (development-aid branch of the Swedish Pentecostal Mission)
PVOC	Private Voluntary Organization Consortium
RELEX	EC External Relations Directorate-General (Relations Extérieures)
ROK	Republic of Korea
SIDA	Swedish International Development Cooperation Agency
UN	United Nations
UNDP	UN Development Program
UNICEF	UN Children's Fund
USAID	US Agency for International Development
USDA	US Department of Agriculture
WFP	World Food Program
WHO	World Health Organization

Introduction

Providing aid in Afghanistan under Taliban rule, knowing that the most vulnerable group of people – women – are out of reach, assisting refugees in Goma/Zaire, aware that the people responsible for genocide are among the beneficiaries, paying thousands of US dollars to militias in South Sudan for armed protection conscious that the money will be used to keep the war machinery running. These are but a few examples of how post-Cold War relief workers have to make compromises that ultimately question their mission.

It is often argued that the changed nature of the international order has generated an environment in which humanitarian work has become an increasingly risky task. Many humanitarian actions take place in the heart of conflicts and are thus directly affected by the changed nature of crises in the post-Cold War era. Phenomena described by scholars of International Relations - such as state collapse or the privatization of violence - have a direct impact on the work of aid agencies on the ground. The conclusion is that we live in a new world where aid can no longer be carried out in the same way as before. International humanitarianism and its principles of action that were coined by the Red Cross movement in the late 19th and early 20th century appear to be outmoded and politically naive. Fox concludes: "The new world clearly needs a new humanitarianism" that is "'principled', 'human rights based', politically sensitive" (2001:275).

However, ambiguity is all but a new phenomenon in humanitarian action. Boltanski (1999:182) notes that recent criticisms take up arguments that, in essence, have been known "since the start of the debate on pity more than two centuries ago". Destexhe (1993:7) adds that "if one needs to characterize humanitarian action by a single word, it would be 'ambiguity'".[1] Slim (1997a:245) argues that the very act of giving is related to moral dilemmas: "for as long as people have felt the urge to help others, they have seen risks and faced dilemmas in doing so".

Numerous examples for dilemmas of aid can be found in aid missions in the 20th century, such as famine relief in Soviet Russia in the 1920s or the work of the International Red Cross during the Holocaust, the latter

---

[1] All translations to English are mine, unless otherwise stated.

probably being the most extreme and traumatic experience in the history of humanitarian action. Other examples include Cambodia in the 1970s, Ethiopia in the 1980s or Rwanda in the 1990s. This short and incomplete enumeration already suggests that dilemmas of humanitarian action are primarily linked to dictatorship and oppression rather than to the nature of intra-state conflicts in the post-Cold War period as such.

As for the ambiguity of aid and dilemmas of action, the international famine relief effort in the Democratic People's Republic of Korea (DPRK or North Korea) is paradigmatic. The United Nations World Food Programme (WFP), like other UN agencies and non-governmental organizations (NGOs), acknowledges that the "food aid operation in North Korea is one of the most sensitive we have ever undertaken".[2] We will argue that the dilemma of humanitarian action is related to political interests and to a political actor's capacity to pursue these interests. In other words, the dilemma of aid relates to political power more than to the collapse or failure of a political system. Evidently, as a dictatorial state praising sovereignty and autarky, North Korea is exactly the opposite of a collapsed state. Although much has been written in recent years on "The End of North Korea" (Eberstadt 1999), there are only a few reports that support the assumption of an imminent and complete erosion of power of the DPRK government.[3]

In addition to the political interests of a dictatorial recipient state, aid agencies working in the DPRK also have to deal with massive political interests on the donor side. Thus, as will be shown in this study, aid organizations' working space is limited by both recipient and donors. Due to these characteristics, the North Korean operation is an important and illustrative case for the study of the ethical challenge that humanitarian action has to face.

In effect, since the beginning of the aid operation, humanitarian action in the DPRK has been accompanied by controversies and disputes

---

[2] Catherine Bertini, the former WFP Executive Director, in a letter to the US General Accounting Office, 1 October 1998 (GAO: *Foreign Assistance. North Korea Restricts Food Aid Monitoring*. Report to the Chairman, Committee on International Relations, House of Representatives. Report Number: GAO/NSIAD-00-35. Washington D.C.: October 1999, p.33).

[3] See Don Oberdorfer (1997): *The Two Koreas*. Reading/US: Addison-Wesley, p.375: "In the early fall [of 1995], the Korean People's Army Sixth Corps, in the northeastern part of the country, was disbanded, its leadership purged, and its units submerged into others, under circumstances suggesting disarray in the ranks".

between the aid agencies themselves. In essence, this discussion is well-known from other aid missions in the past and present because the challenge that humanitarian action has to face is always the same: how can the moral duty to relieve human suffering be respected when political interests that contradict humanitarian obligations determine the environment of aid? In North Korea, aid agencies have not found a unanimous answer to that question. Most agencies continue to work in the DPRK despite difficult working conditions. Some humanitarian organizations concluded that working conditions in North Korea were unacceptable and decided to withdraw.

The second reason why the North Korean mission is an important case study for the weaknesses and ethical challenges of humanitarianism is, besides the intensity of dilemmas of action, the size of the aid operation. Since the North Korean government launched an appeal for international aid in 1995, WFP alone had, until the end of 2002, delivered food aid worth more than US$1.1 billion to the country.[4] This makes the famine aid operation in the DPRK the biggest food aid mission in the history of the United Nations. In view of the magnitude of the aid effort, Catherine Bertini, the former WFP Executive Director, points out that "the UN is proud of its role in North Korea".[5] The size of this operation is thus one reason why the North Korean case may serve as an illustrative case for a study of the reality of today's humanitarian aid. It is the objective of this study to identify the causes of moral dilemmas in humanitarian action and to analyze the behavior of aid agencies in such a situation. Our analysis thus seeks to assess the humanitarian organizations' space and the effect of aid agencies' differing strategies of dealing with dilemma situations.

The primary source of empirical data is the aid agencies that were or still are engaged in the DPRK. From 1999, more than 50 interviews with NGO and UN officials, representatives from donor institutions and academic observers of the humanitarian situation in North Korea were con-

---

[4] For 2003, the WFP asked international donors for another US$197 million for food aid to the DPRK. See FAO/WFP: *Special Report. Crop and Food Supply Assessment Mission to the Democratic People's Republic of Korea*, 16 November 2000, p.7 and various issues of the *Consolidated Inter-Agency Appeal Democratic People's Republic of Korea*.

[5] Presentation of the *Consolidated Inter-Agency Appeal Democratic People's Republic of Korea 2003*, Washington D.C., National Press Club, 27 November 2001. Author's notes.

ducted in Europe, the United States, the Republic of Korea (ROK, South Korea) and in the DPRK (a list of interviewees is attached in appendix I). Thanks to the Commission to Help North Korean Refugees (CNKR), a South Korean NGO, the author also had the opportunity to interview five North Korean refugees who left the DPRK between 1997 and 2000. Finally, thanks to an invitation from German Agro Action (GAA), he was able to visit project sites and to get a practical insight into the work of aid agencies in North Korea in early 2002.

This study is divided into two parts. The first part presents the theoretical and historical context of the North Korean famine aid operation. Chapter I analyzes the ethical basis of humanitarian action and discusses the causes of, and aid agencies' possible approaches to, moral dilemmas. Chapter II focuses on the characteristics of famines and their implications for humanitarian famine relief. We will argue that due to the political factors that, at least in parts, produce famines, famine relief necessarily faces ethical challenges. Chapter III analyzes famine aid missions that have raised controversies in the past and that, in a way, can be described as historical precedents of the North Korean case. The cases studied are Soviet Russia 1921-23, Biafra 1968-70, Cambodia 1979-80 and Ethiopia 1984-85. One conclusion from the first part of the study is that humanitarianism has to deal with a structural ambiguity that leads to dilemmas of action particularly in famines.

The second part focuses on the famine aid mission in North Korea. The causes and scale of the famine are discussed in chapter IV. Chapter V analyzes the political interests at stake on recipient and donor side. The implications for humanitarian action in the DPRK are presented in chapter VI that elaborates on the operational space and working conditions of aid agencies. Due to the different characteristics of aid programs that are carried out in North Korea, the analysis focuses on food aid, nutritional and health programs and food security/agriculture projects respectively. Chapter VII analyzes how humanitarian organizations deal with working restrictions and dilemmas in the DPRK.

The last chapter discusses the lessons that can be drawn from the North Korean experience concerning the debate on the crisis of today's humanitarianism. By and large, this debate argues in favor of a 'new humanitarianism' that breaks with the traditional concept of humanitarian action in order to overcome dilemmas of action. The North Korean case, however, shows that such a break is neither desirable nor feasible. Moreover, the famine aid mission in the DPRK reveals that international humanitarian action faces a crisis of meaning to the extent that aid agencies have no consistent position regarding the purpose and the principles of aid. It is this lack of consistency that needs to be addressed in the first place.

Part A. HUMANITARIAN ACTION IN FAMINES BETWEEN THEORY
AND PRACTICE

Chapter I.

The Ethics of Humanitarian Action

I.1 Ambiguities and Dilemmas of Aid

a) Ambiguity as a Basic Characteristic of Aid

The causes of ambiguity and dilemmas of aid seem to be basic elements of humanitarian action and neither linked to state failure nor to armed conflict. Ethical problems of aid arise no matter whether political and governmental structures in the recipient state are weak or strong and no matter whether direct or structural violence is present. Essentially, as will be shown, aid agencies face the same ethical problems in North Korea as they did in Rwanda in the 1990s or Ethiopia in the 1980s.

Furthermore, ethical problems of humanitarian action stem from the tension between moral obligations on the one hand and the question of how they are translated into action on the other. Aid becomes ethically problematic when it is being used for other than humanitarian purposes and when it does not reach the people it intends to reach. In cases where moral claim and effect of aid do not correspond, several obligations and constraints that determine humanitarian action, conflict with each other.

Broadly, humanitarian action deals with three sets of actors and, accordingly, faces three sets of obligations and constraints. A population in need of humanitarian assistance is the first actor that impacts on humanitarian aid. Although, in most missions, individual recipients of aid[1] have few means to directly influence the decision-making process of humanitarian organizations, the very existence of human suffering is one

---

[1] Throughout this study the terms 'recipient' and 'beneficiary' will be used synonymously. Although these terms stress the passivity of people who receive assistance and are thus criticized by a number of authors as "odious and de-personalising" (Slim 2001:10), they are commonly used by practitioners of aid and aid organizations.

major incentive for humanitarian action. As will be argued in later chapters, the moral imperative to relieve human suffering is intrinsic to humanitarian action.

Secondly, an aid agency's course of action is influenced by its own mandate, tradition and standards of action. This ethical framework impacts on an aid organization's perception of a humanitarian crisis, and largely determines its dealing with moral ambiguity and dilemmas.

Thirdly, humanitarian actors are bound by two "dependency relationships" (Eberwein 2001:14) to donor and recipient institutions. Financial resources are defined by public and private donors while an agency's operational space (staff safety, freedom of movement etc.) depends on the government or authority of the country where the humanitarian action takes place. Figure 1 illustrates the three different sources of obligations for humanitarian actors.

Fig. 1: Sources of Obligations in Humanitarian Action

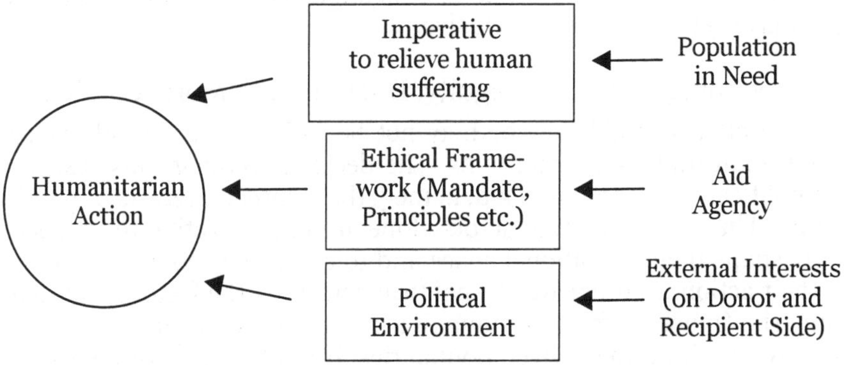

Notably, due to the geo-political changes of 1989/90, the discussion today focuses on the third set of factors, the political interests that humanitarian actors have to deal with. The end of the Cold War and the emergence of intra-state conflicts ultimately limited the freedom of action of humanitarian organizations. In armed conflicts in the 1990s, the warring parties most frequently did not respect principles of humanitarian action and deliberately manipulated humanitarian action. On the donor side, governments increasingly intervene directly in humanitarian crises. Vaux thus argues that the Cold War era was the "Golden Age" of humanitarianism (2001:43) because "the aid agencies represented the main capacity for intervention in humanitarian crises and there was a tendency for anyone concerned about humanitarian issues to defend them" (2001:76-77). But as will be shown in this study, the end of the bipolar world did not create moral dilemmas of humanitarian aid that were, as such, previously unknown to aid agencies.

When do these obligations conflict with each other? Under ideal circumstances, the political authorities on donor and recipient side are in line with the obligations binding aid organizations. Furthermore, the imperative to provide aid, as being part of the ethical framework of an aid agency, will not clash with other obligations and the aid will achieve the intended effects. When a French aid agency provides medical assistance to the victims of an earthquake in Turkey, for instance, a tension between intentions and effects that may result in dilemma situations, is most unlikely. When the political environment, however, does not correspond with or is even hostile to the ethical framework of humanitarian organizations, aid missions are likely to engender ambiguous effects. In such a situation, the three sets of obligations compete with each other, and may even be mutually exclusive.

b) Defining Terms: Ambiguity, Dilemma and Moral Conflict

The effects of aid may or may not be in line with an aid agency's moral obligations and intentions. The decisive factor in this respect is the political environment of aid, namely the external interests of political actors. Thus, humanitarian actors alone are in no position to independently shape their operational space and to completely control the effects of their action. In other words, political actors set the factors that determine the (moral) effects of humanitarian action. Aid agencies carry out their work within these given boundaries. It is a host government's decision to grant or deny free access to people in need and to accept principles of humanitarian action. Likewise, a donor institution may or may not be prepared to fund an aid project in a specific region or to pressure a recipient government into accepting humanitarian standards. This dependence of humanitarian action on political decisions, and its resulting structural incapability of determining the effects of aid, is what we call the ambiguity of humanitarian aid. Ambiguity is a structural, basic and 'timeless' characteristic of humanitarianism.

Unlike ambiguity, the term 'dilemma' describes concrete situations where aid agencies face conflicting obligations and have to take specific decisions and courses of action. While ambiguity describes a general feature of humanitarian action, dilemmas only occur when specific conditions are met, that is, whenever the three sets of obligations that bind aid agencies conflict with each other. Humanitarian organizations do not have the means to avoid these dilemma situations since, in the first place, they result from the political environment of aid and not from decisions taken by aid agencies themselves. Thus, dilemmas of humanitarian aid are inescapable. It is one focus of this study to determine the room for maneuver that aid agencies have in such a dilemma situation.

The term 'dilemma' is often used in the discussion surrounding aid operations since the end of the Cold War. Authors also use terms such as 'moral conflict', 'hard' or 'tough choices' to describe the ethical challenge faced by humanitarian organizations in numerous aid operations in recent years. However, as Slim points out, the quality or intensity of these ethical challenges differs and needs to be distinguished:

> In common parlance, the word 'dilemma' often means nothing more than a difficult decision, a tough choice. Although tough, however, a choice may not necessarily be a genuine moral dilemma. (...) By miscasting a tough choice as a moral dilemma, a relief agency could fail to see that there is in fact a right course of action in a difficult choice and so could fail to take it. (...) the tendency might be for agencies to simply label every difficult decision a moral dilemma and so become fatalistic in their programming (Slim 1997a:249, 250).

We use the term 'moral conflict' to describe a situation where humanitarian actors have to prioritize obligations of differing value. Here, an aid agency takes the risk to ultimately enhance the legitimacy of agents for the sake of its humanitarian mandate. Moral conflicts arise whenever aid agencies face a choice between obligations of differing value. In such a case, a humanitarian agency has to violate one moral principle for the benefit of another, higher and more binding, principle. The decision to interact with oppressive regimes or militias in order to reach people in need is one example of such a moral conflict. Here, an aid agency might be in a position to satisfy its obligations towards beneficiaries, donors and some of its own principles of action. Most importantly, it would be able to effectively reach the most vulnerable populations.

In a dilemma situation, however, obligations of the same value are at stake and are mutually exclusive. According to a general definition, a moral dilemma is any situation where at the same time "(1) there is a moral requirement for an agent to adopt each of two alternatives, (2) neither moral requirement is overridden in any morally relevant way, (3) the agent cannot adopt both alternatives together, and (4) the agent can adopt each alternative separately" (Sinnott-Armstrong 1988:29). Thus, aid is caught in a dilemma whenever the different sets of obligations are accorded the same moral value, and, in the given situation, are mutually exclusive. We will now discuss under what circumstances aid agencies may face such a dilemma situation.

c) Dilemma Scenarios: Aid as an Instrument and as an Accomplice

It has been argued that humanitarian organizations are bound by three sets of obligations: the moral imperative to relieve human suffering, an agency's own ethical framework (principles, mandate, tradition etc.) and, finally, the political interest of recipient and donor government or institution. Conflicts are most likely to occur between external political interests on one side, and moral obligations that derive from aid agencies' ethical framework and the suffering of a population on the other side. Thus, the political environment is the decisive factor concerning the emergence of dilemma situations. More precisely, aid agencies are likely to face dilemmas when at least two conditions in terms of the political environment of aid are met:

1. Donor institutions and governments have a strong political interest in financing aid activities in that particular crisis.
2. The political authority (government, faction leadership etc.) of the recipient country has a strong political interest in limiting the operational space of aid agencies.

The recent history of international politics provides a number of examples where either the first or the second condition was met. Humanitarian actors had to make compromises concerning their mandate and their principles of action to the benefit of donor institutions *(instrument scenario)* or to political authorities on the recipient side *(accomplice scenario)*. In both cases, the benefit for either side is not actively sought by humanitarian organizations but indirectly and unwittingly results from aid activities. The international aid operation in North Korea serves as an illustrating example for the dilemma of humanitarian action to the extent that, in that case, famine and famine aid is a politically sensitive issue for *both* donors and recipient government. As a consequence, humanitarian organizations face the *instrument* as well as the *accomplice* reproach.

In terms of the first scenario, humanitarian aid can become an *instrument* of donor governments. Donors allocate aid according to their preferences. The alleviation of humanitarian distress may play a role in that regard. But relief aid, as will be shown in later chapters, can be given because of pressure of public opinion, or because of foreign policy and national security interests. In some cases, donor policies in recent years evidently contradicted humanitarian considerations and the principles of humanity and impartiality as contained in the Geneva Conventions (see chapter II). In 1999, for instance, the European Union provided aid – officially labeled 'humanitarian' - only to those Serbian villages that were governed by opposition forces.[2] The 1999 NATO air war in Kosovo also challenged the impartiality and neutrality of humanitarian organizations on the ground. Vaux (2001:41-42) comments on Oxfam's experience at that time: "In failing to distance itself from NATO, we in Oxfam made it possible and justifiable for Milosevic to accuse us of taking sides, throw us out of Serbia and prevent us from helping the people most in need, where we had most capacity to do so". The political environment in these cases did not allow aid agencies to effectively address the needs of the most vulnerable populations. Due to the instrumentalization of aid and the discrepancy between political goals, humanitarian needs and organizational mandates and principles, humanitarian organizations were caught in a dilemma.

The subtlest use of humanitarian aid is its instrumentalization as a fig leaf in order to satisfy domestic public opinion. Aid helps to demonstrate that a government is prepared to 'do something' about a humanitarian crisis. Therefore, aid can be used as a substitute for a political engagement that addresses the underlying causes of suffering. In that respect, former UN Secretary-General Boutros-Ghali notes

> that the international community is faced with the paradox of needing ever larger resources to address the immediate survival needs of victims, while simultaneously recognizing that such action may deflect attention and support from initiatives essential to undoing the root causes of vulnerability and strife (quoted in Weiss and Collins 1996: 97).

---

[2] UNOCHA Belgrade: *Humanitarian Risk Analysis No. 11. Federal Republic of Yugoslavia.* 7 July 2000, p.4.

Secondly, humanitarian aid can become an *accomplice* of the agents on the recipient side. This scenario can become reality in a number of ways. Aid agencies can provide financial and material support to those forces whose consent is necessary for carrying out their humanitarian mission. Paying money for protection, transport, communication devices etc., such as for militias in South Sudan is a typical example. The provision of aid items to refugees in Goma, which were diverted and sold on the black market is a more subtle way of lengthening an armed conflict. The result is still the same. Aid contributes to prolonging or intensifying war and oppression. Secondly, by accepting a regime or group as an interlocutor, by accepting its policy or by taking over governmental functions (food supply, medical care), aid can bestow legitimacy. The Biafran leadership during the Nigerian Civil War, Bosnian Serbs or Somali warlords in the 1990s, it can be argued, have benefited from these legitimizing effects of humanitarian aid (for a summary, see Terry 2000:63-64).

Furthermore, aid can become an accomplice when it witnesses human rights violations committed by these political authorities that are in the position to delimit the operational space of aid agencies. Observing enforced displacements in Ethiopia in the 1980s or the exclusion of women from medical services in Afghanistan under the rule of the Taliban, confronts aid workers with a difficult choice. Publicly denouncing human rights violations may be a moral obligation but doing so is likely to jeopardize the access to people in need. Remaining silent, on the other hand, means becoming an accomplice of the perpetrators. Either course of action is risky.

Thus, the accomplice scenario can potentially create dilemma situations. When the political interest of a recipient government contradicts the humanitarian interests of its population and the principles of humanitarian organizations, the three sets of obligations of aid agencies become mutually exclusive.

Summing up, the imperative to assist people in need, an aid agency's specific ethical framework, and external political factors determine the carrying out of a humanitarian mission. Political interests on donor and recipient side can potentially jeopardize the moral obligations of aid agencies, who, as a result, face moral dilemmas. These moral obligations will be discussed in the following chapter in order to better understand the effects of external political interests on the moral integrity of humanitarianism.

I.2 The Act of Giving: Objective and Subjective Obligations

It has been argued that moral dilemmas emerge whenever at least two moral obligations are equally important and mutually exclusive. In terms of dilemmas of humanitarian action, two forces within the humanitarian ethics – described by Vaux (2001:70) as "attachment" and "detachment" – play the most important role.

What drives a man to assist others? Moral behavior, according to Hans Jonas (1977), is generally determined by two factors: rational claim and emotional responsiveness. There has to be a 'highest good', i.e. a rational claim or an ideal that appeals to human reason. This rational obligation has to go along with the second incentive, which is related to emotion. Jonas (1977:170) argues that "without our being, at least by disposition, responsive to the call of duty in terms of feeling, the most cogent demonstration of its right, even when compelling theoretical assent, would be powerless to make it a motivating force".

In terms of a humanitarian ethics, we will also have to distinguish between an objective side and a subjective side, the one being related to reason, the other to emotion. Saint Thomas of Aquin made a similar distinction with regard to the act of providing aid. He identifies reason based *(motus appetitus intellectivi)* and passion based motives *(motus appetitus sensitivi)* as those forces that lead man to assist others (Harbach 1992:91). A major difference between these two dimensions is the differing capacity to generalize. Sentiments depend on the reference to a particular case, objective motives are based upon generalization. Hannah Arendt (1963:84) opposes the sentiment of pity to the objective concept of solidarity:

> It is out of pity that men are 'attracted toward *les hommes faibles*', but it is out of solidarity that they establish deliberately and, as it were, dispassionately a community of interest with the oppressed and exploited. The common interest would then be 'the grandeur of man', or 'the honor of the human race', or the dignity of man. For solidarity, because it partakes of reason, and hence of generality, is able to comprehend a multitude conceptually, not only the multitude of a class or a nation or a people, but eventually all mankind.[3]

---

[3] For greater detail on the issue of generalization see Boltanski 1999:3-19.

Solidarity appears as one basis for the rational claim behind humanitarian action. The claim itself has to do with what Arendt described as "the common interest". One expression of this rational, general claim is religion. The Koran, for instance, contains the following passages (for further details see Wronka 1998):

> It is righteousness/...To spend of your substance,/Out of love for Him,/For your kind,/For orphans,/For the needy,/For the wayfarer,/For those who ask,/For the ransom of slaves,/To be steadfast in prayer,/And practice regular charity;/To fulfill the contracts/Which ye have made;/And to be firm and patient,/In pain (or suffering)/And adversity (Sura 2:177).

All world religions have expressed in various forms the act of helping people in need not only as a virtue, but as a religious duty. Hans Küng - in view of Jewish, Christian, Muslim, Buddhist, Hindu and Confucian traditions - summarizes: "Everywhere human well-being and human dignity are brought forward - with the categorical authority only religions possess - as the fundamental principle and goal of human ethos" (Küng 2001:81). With regard to Jewish, Christian and Muslim traditions, "the dignity of the human person (...) derives from the creation of the individual in the image and likeness of God" (Wronka 1998:38). Enlightenment philosophy deduced dignity from human reason rather than relying on the creation of man in the likeness of God. Regardless of its religious or secular justification, the concept of human dignity and equality provides the objective claim that obliges the individual to assist a person who suffers.

Following Hans Jonas, a rational claim does only lead to action when combined with the affective element of humanitarian ethics. The affective side of aid has been described by Western moral philosophy.[4] Concepts of moral behavior include terms such as "sentiment" (Cumberland, Shaftesbury, Hume), "tendency" (Kant),"intuition" (Scheler) and "pity" (Schopenhauer). Depending on the notion of "nature" and "reason" in the ethical theory concerned, the emotional elements are accorded a differing moral value. Kant, for instance, by highlighting the autonomy of reason, denies that the emotional side supplies the true motive of

---

[4] For an overview on the debate around the concept of 'pity' in moral philosophy see Boltanski 1999, Harbach 1992, Bronner 2003.

moral action (see Jonas 1977:173). Schopenhauer, by contrast, sees pity as a "basic incitement" of human behavior and argues that "only if an action derives from pity, it has a moral value" (quoted in Harbach 1992:40).

Similar to the objective claim to help, the subjective obligation was first expressed in religious terms, as, for example, in the New Testament in Matthew 22:36-40: "Thou shalt love thy neighbor as thyself". The Koran, in the Sura quoted above, also names 'love' as the basic incentive of aid. A. Ali notes with regard to the quoted passage: "Practical deeds of charity are of value when they proceed from love, and from no other motive" (quoted in Wronka 1998:42).

Enlightenment philosophy brought forward a secular foundation for the subjective incentive to help. Deduced from the concept of natural law, Rousseau argues that the subjective motive to help a suffering fellow expresses the distinct human nature. What Rousseau describes as "innate repugnance at seeing a fellow creature suffer" is, one could say, what distinguishes man from animal. Rousseau finds "compassion to be the most natural human reaction to the suffering of others, and therefore the very foundation of all authentic 'natural' human intercourse" (Arendt 1963:65,74-75).

From both a religious and secular perspective, the subjective obligation that leads the individual to help is a spontaneous, emotional and 'natural' concern for human beings in need. As such, this concern is a self-justifying cause because its justification does not derive from the effect it engenders (see Leader 2000:18, Vaux 2001:45).

In short, the ethics of aid contains an objective and a subjective dimension. It is important to note that – following Jonas' general description of ethics – "the two sides are mutually complementary and both are integral to ethics itself" (Jonas 1977:170). On the objective side, humanitarian action consists of the rational obligation to assist people in need, an obligation that derives from the overarching ideal of human dignity and equality. On the subjective side, aid results from the emotional concern for a person in need. Both dimensions are inspired by a number of moral obligations that are also expressed in religion and moral philosophy. Rational claim and emotional responsiveness combined provide the moral basis for humanitarian aid. It is not exclusively inspired by objective and general ideals, neither can it be called an 'objectless kind of ethics' (Hans Jonas) where the moral obligation only "receives its significance from the choice of our passionate concern" (Jonas 1977:173).

I.3 Implications for Humanitarian Action

The moral justification of the act of giving as the affective response to an objective ideal impacts on the ethics of humanitarian action in two ways. First, it defines its normative basis (motives and objectives). Second, the moral justification of aid determines the manner how aid should be carried out and thus defines a number of principles of humanitarian action.[5]

a) Normative Implications

The core obligation of humanitarian action lies in what is often referred to as the most fundamental principle of humanitarian aid or "the prime mover for the whole movement" (Pictet 1979:21-22): the principle of humanity. The word 'humanity' "serves to specify human nature and even the human species as a whole" (Pictet 1979:20). Evidently, the notion of a common human nature is interrelated to concepts such as human dignity and equality. These ideals are beyond dispute and have only been justified in differing – that is, religious or secular - manners.[6] It can even be argued that humanity does not require any justification because it "derives from an absolute morality that people in need should be assisted simply because that is the right thing to do" (Leader 2000:18).

---

[5] Leader (2000) distinguishes 'humanitarian principles' that are codified in international law binding state parties from 'principles of humanitarian action' that prescribe the behavior of aid agencies.

[6] Some authors see the age of Enlightenment as the turning point that separates a religiously motivated, charitable aid from the modern secular form of humanitarianism. It is argued that "under the influence of the philosophers of the Age of Enlightenment, a powerful 'humanitarian movement' was born in the 18th century" (Destexhe 1993: 15). Religious norms are seen as obstacles that had to be overcome and replaced by secular concepts such as solidarity and beneficence in order to create a new tradition of aid. This "secularization of charity" has paved the way for the emergence of modern humanitarianism and is regarded as the decisive move "from philanthropy to humanitarian action" (Brauman 1995: 27-29).

Humanity as the driving force behind humanitarian action is related to the affective, emotional element of aid. The 'Proclamation of the Fundamental Principles of the Red Cross' states that humanity is driven by the "desire to bring assistance without discrimination to the wounded on the battlefield". In a commentary on the principles of the Red Cross, humanitarian aid is described as an act deriving from "a sentiment of active goodwill towards mankind". One component of this sentiment is specified as pity, defined as "a spontaneous movement, an instantaneous affective reaction to the suffering of others" (Pictet 1979:20-21). Humanity, Pictet concludes, "is rather more a feeling than a principle" (1979:20).

Thus, what has been described as the objective ideal (human dignity and equality) and subjective responsiveness (concern for a person in need) merges in the notion of humanity as the prime mover of humanitarian action. To adhere to the ideal of humanity, with its rational and affective elements, entails that human suffering demands a response. This obligation is also named the 'humanitarian imperative'.

Humanity as the core obligation guiding the behavior of humanitarian organizations is referred to in all charters and codes of conduct of aid agencies. The 'Code of Conduct of the International Red Cross and Red Crescent Movement and Non-Governmental Organizations in Disaster Relief' from 1994 serves as an example:

> The right to receive humanitarian assistance, and to offer it, is a fundamental humanitarian principle which should be enjoyed by all citizens of all countries. (...) The prime motivation of our response to disaster is to alleviate human suffering amongst those least able to withstand the stress caused by disaster. (...) Human suffering must be alleviated whenever it is found; life is as precious in one part of a country as another.

It is controversial to what extent the overarching ideal of humanity also includes the promotion of human rights as a guiding ideal of humanitarian action. For instance, Slim notes that "human rights monitoring and reporting is now a front-line humanitarian task" (1995:116). It can be argued that a human rights conception shares the same ideals of human dignity and equality as does humanity. It has often been pointed out that a clear distinction between a human rights conception on one side and the ideal of humanity on the other can hardly be upheld (see Slim 1997b:346, Vaux 2001:67). In other words, humanitarian assistance can be seen as being an activity that protects the human right to life out of respect for the dignity of human life. However, the moral principle of humanity is intertwined with the moral justification of the act of giving and of relieving human suffering. In this regard, the promotion of human rights presents a distinct ideal and ethical framework. It is important to note that no obligation to include human rights activities (monitoring and publicly denouncing human rights violations) can be deduced from the principle of humanity as contained in the Geneva Conventions. In her comment on the notion of humanity according to international law, Mackintosh (2000:7) points out that "no more can be deduced from this term than the very basic Red Cross definition of the principle of humanity: preventing and alleviating human suffering".

Similarly, the ethics of aid and the principle of humanity do not morally oblige humanitarian organizations to promote peace. Humanity, in the first place, describes one's identification with a suffering human being. The search for a political solution of conflict and violence cannot be deduced from the principle of humanity (see Mackintosh 2000:9, Karenfort 1999:78-79).

From the perspective of traditional humanitarianism, the normative foundations of humanitarian action derive exclusively from the core principle of humanity. It is one task of this study to analyze in how far other obligations such as the protection of human rights or the promotion of peace and democracy have been adopted by humanitarian actors as an integral part of their ethical framework.

b) Implications Concerning Principles of Action

The term 'humanity' is closely related to such notions as 'the dignity of man' or 'the equality of all human beings'. Because the idea of humanity obliges us to identify with a person in need, we provide aid. Humanity by definition refers to all human beings and, consequently, humanitarian aid, as the action that derives from this ideal, has to be carried out without discrimination. Deliberately affording aid in accordance with "objective distinctions" such as nationality, race, religion, sex or wealth, contravenes the idea of humanity (see Pictet 1979:37-51). The same goes for "subjective distinctions" such as innocence or guilt, good or bad. International Humanitarian Law is unambiguous with regard to the principle of impartiality. Article 3, common to all four Geneva Conventions, proscribes "any adverse distinction founded on race, color, religion or faith, sex, birth or wealth, or any other similar criteria".

Humanity and non-discrimination do not mean providing assistance to whoever may ask for it. This would be the case if humanitarian action was only led by the sentiment of compassion, inspired solely by the moral value that lies in the act of giving. The objective idea of humanity "has its starting point in human suffering" (Pictet 1979:38). Therefore, the obligation of non-discrimination means that aid has to be given according to one exclusive criterion: need.

Examples illustrating noble humanitarian behavior often display the dedication to another person's needs and the courage not to accept any other criteria. The Samaritan is named 'good' because he only sees the needs of the injured Jew and because he does not care about the fact that the victim belongs to a hostile group of people (see Kallscheuer 1995:101-103). A nurse's behavior in the Second World War is praised because she insists on treating wounded enemies instead of complying with the order of a compatriot officer to care only for his wounded men who fought to liberate her own country. "'Over my dead body' she replied, and he realized that she really meant it as she stood barring the doorway" (Pictet 1979:37-38).

Non-discrimination and the rule 'greatest help to greatest need' are thus closely related to each other because both directly derive from humanity. In terms of humanitarian action non-discrimination and proportionality are referred to as the principle of impartiality. The Proclamation of the Fundamental Principles of the Red Cross notes that impartiality "makes no discrimination as to nationality, race, religious beliefs, class or political opinions. It endeavors only to relieve suffering, giving priority to the most urgent cases of distress." A formulation of 1955 is more precise on the principle of proportionality: "The help available shall be apportioned according to the relative importance of individual needs and in their order of urgency" (quoted in Pictet 1979: 41). The rule of proportionality is echoed in all codes of conduct in use by aid agencies. It is also firmly embedded in International Humanitarian Law (see Mackintosh 2000:8). In short, the principle of humanity describes the motivation and objective of humanitarian action. The principle of impartiality, by contrast, contains obligations that affect the manner of carrying out humanitarian assistance. Both principles are interrelated in so far as impartiality directly derives from the principle of humanity.

It is important to note that the obligation to provide proportional assistance expresses a claim that may not always be entirely fulfilled. In her analysis of principles of humanitarian action in international law, Mackintosh (2000:8) notes that

> while the principle of impartiality suggests that programmes should be designed to respond to the greatest need, they do not lose the right to be called humanitarian if for operational reasons they serve the population of just one area. The aspirations the principles represent, however, must continue to be implemented to the maximum extent.

While humanity stresses the subjective side of aid, the principle of impartiality requires one to 'detach' from the suffering of the individual and to analyze one's own doing. Assisting those in need is an act of compassion and concern. It can be perceived as a success, if one focuses on the individual recipient and his or her individual needs without trying to generalize, without trying to draw a broader picture. Assisting those in *greatest* need, however, is a matter of comparison, analysis and distance. Thus, as a humanitarian actor, "we need both attachment and detachment" (Vaux 2001:70), that is, concern for people in need on one side and "a degree of rational discipline" (Pictet 1979:34) on the other.

With regard to the carrying out of aid, two other principles are often referred to: independence and neutrality. Both can be described as "derivative principles" because they can be deduced from the "essential principles" of humanity and impartiality (Leader 1998:299). In other words, independence and neutrality serve as a means to an end, which is the impartial alleviation of human suffering. It is important to note that neither the Geneva Conventions - which do not mention either of these terms - nor the Red Cross principles oblige all humanitarian organizations to be independent or neutral. An agency may or may not keep distance from governmental donors. As long as it aspires to afford assistance according to needs only, it does not loose its character as a humanitarian organization.

In parts, the same goes for neutrality. The term neutrality primarily contains the obligation not to take sides in a conflict. The obligation not to take sides - neither ideologically nor in terms of economic support - derives from the principle of impartiality and is therefore intrinsic to the humanitarian mandate. It follows from International Humanitarian Law that a humanitarian organization must be in control of the resources it brings into a territory in order to prevent the use of the goods for other than humanitarian purposes.

According to classical humanitarianism (i.e. the principles of the Red Cross movement) neutrality also means to respect secrecy "in order to enjoy the confidence of all" as stated in the Red Cross principle. Secrecy is a self-imposed principle of the Red Cross. In his commentary on the Geneva Conventions Pictet (1958:97) explicitly notes that they do not require the Red Cross to remain silent in a conflict. Therefore, secrecy may be adopted as a useful means in order to reach vulnerable populations on all sides of a conflict, but it may also be rejected by another agency that doubts the use of this strategy. Destexhe summarizes the position of the 'sans-frontiérisme' branch of humanitarianism when he argues that "the literal application of neutrality awards the stronger and may entail that one becomes an accomplice of human rights violations" (1993:209, for further details on the neutrality debate see Leader 2000). Both views, however, are in line with the principles of impartiality and are thus covered by International Humanitarian Law (see Karenfort 1999:87).

c) Implications for a Definition of Humanitarianism

It has been argued that humanitarian action contains both a subjective element (emotional concern for people in need) and a rational, objective side (ideal of human dignity, equality). Consequently, a definition of humanitarian action would have to include both integral parts of the humanitarian ethics by referring to the normative foundations of aid as well as to principles of action.

It is surprising to see that only few definitions refer to both parts of the moral obligations of aid. The SPHERE project uses a minimalist definition in the sense that it only focuses on the task of humanitarian action that derives from the principle of humanity. Here, 'humanitarian assistance' is defined as "the provision of basic requirements which meet people's needs for adequate water, sanitation, nutrition, food, shelter and health care". This definition does not include the normative side of humanitarianism. Pictet (1958:96) highlights humanity as the basic motive of aid by defining 'humanitarian' as "being concerned with the condition of man considered solely as a human being". Such a definition focuses on the normative side but does not refer to principles of action. Brauman (1995:9) refers to both aspects, normative foundations and principles of action: "Without any discrimination and by pacifistic means humanitarian action aims at the preservation of human life in the respect of dignity and at the restoration of the individual's capacity to choose".

I.4 Conflicting Obligations in Humanitarian Action

So far, we have identified the objective of alleviating human suffering and the impartial affording of aid in proportion to needs as being those obligations that, by definition, are common to all humanitarian actors. Other obligations stem from distinct ethical and legal frameworks (e.g. monitoring and denouncing human rights violations, participation in peace-building activities).

Our focus is the dilemma of aid that occurs whenever moral requirements collide and are mutually exclusive. This results from the tension between the theoretical claim laid down in the described principles on the one hand, and reality on the other. We will now have to elaborate on this tension between theory and reality in order to detect the obligations that potentially collide with each other. Following our initial distinction, we will discuss the reality of aid in the accomplice and instrument scenarios.

a) Conflicting Obligations in the Accomplice Scenario

Moral conflicts and dilemma situations emerge when aid - by providing assistance to a population – unwittingly helps to restore the legitimacy of the governing system in place. Aid can then appear to strengthen power structures responsible for injustice and discrimination. An aid organization can feel obliged to a number of values and objectives that, in such an environment, may collide with each other.

Firstly, ultimately supporting a policy of discrimination contravenes the principle of impartiality that, as stated above, prescribes a policy of non-discrimination in order to afford aid only according to needs.

Secondly, it could be argued that the value accorded to justice can provide a distinct obligation for aid agencies. Slim explicitly distinguishes between the "basic humanitarian value, that of preserving human life" and the "principle of justice which is the moral measure of fair and equal relationships between individuals and groups". According to Slim, both objectives can compete with each other (1997a:248).[7]

Thirdly, humanitarian organizations can adhere to a human rights conception that is challenged by a policy of discrimination pursued by the governing body in place. Here, sexual discrimination is of particular relevance, since gender equity is often mentioned as an obligation in charters and sets of principles of aid organization. Oxfam, for example, adopted an agenda in 1993 which commits the agency to "develop positive action to promote the full participation and empowerment of women" and to "confront the social and ideological barriers to women's participation" (quoted in Vaux 2001:123). Confronted with the Taliban policy of gender apartheid in Afghanistan throughout the 1990s, Oxfam decided not to provide humanitarian assistance to those territories under Taliban rule. Vaux argues, as does Slim with regard to the objective of justice, that a dilemma situation emerged due to a tension between two distinct moral requirements: "Oxfam continued to grapple with its two conflicting principles – 'saving lives' and 'gender equity' – and there seemed to be no way of deciding between them" (Vaux 2001:127).

Arguably, humanitarian actors who follow a human rights motivation, have to deal with two distinct moral requirements that, in a given situation, can create dilemma situations. According to Slim (1997a:245), human rights provide one out of four "main areas of moral value" that guide humanitarian action. Vaux also distinguishes between a human rights and a humanitarian ethical framework by stating that "MSF has adopted twin objectives of 'witness' as well as humanity" (2001:63). In fact, in his speech at the Nobel Peace Prize ceremony, the MSF representative describes the protection of human rights as one distinct claim that his organizations feels obliged to: "More than offering material assistance, we aim to enable individuals to regain their rights and dignity as human beings".[8] However, as will be shown in regard to famine aid

---

[7] Slim (1997a: 248) notes that "some NGOs will have more moral dilemmas than others, depending on the range and number of their fundamental principles. (...) Different types of agencies (...) often have fundamentally different emphasis in the configuration of their core values which mean that some see moral dilemmas where others do not". Slim distinguishes between "four main areas of moral value": human life, human rights, justice, staff safety.

[8] James Orbinski, then President of the MSF International Council, Acceptance Speech, Oslo, 10 December 1999. Found at www.doctorswithoutborders.org/publications/speeches/1999/jo_nobel.shtml (21 July 2003).

missions in the past, human rights violations as such did not create moral dilemmas for humanitarian actors.

b) Conflicting Obligations in the Instrument Scenario

In cases where aid becomes an instrument for political purposes of donor governments, humanitarian action is often seen as being confronted with a further ethical challenge. Here, the moral ideal of humanity collides with the principle of independence.

Independence is accorded a different value by different actors. This is illustrated in differing policies that aid agencies adopt with regard to the allocation of public funds. While some organizations do not hesitate to accept government funds, others are not willing to accept governmental donations at all or only to a certain degree. The German NGO Cap Anamur, named after the ship that rescued Vietnamese 'boat people' in 1979, does not accept any donations from governments or intergovernmental institutions. MSF seeks to limit the amount of public funds to 50 percent of its overall budget. Both organizations argue that their policies result from an obligation to be independent from political institutions.

However, independence is not seen as an end in itself. Instead, the claim of independence clearly derives from the humanitarian obligation to assist people in need. Because political interests tend to consider other than purely humanitarian criteria, dependency on donor governments would threaten the rule 'greatest aid to greatest need'. Rupert Neudeck, founder of Cap Anamur, argues that

> we would not have been able to save a single person from Vietnam using government money – they would not have allowed us to. We have always chosen to work in places like North Korea, Sudan and Chechnya – where governments would not allow us to go.[9]

Therefore, independence appears as a tool to ensure that aid is afforded according to needs. It will have to be discussed in later chapters whether the principle of impartiality and the principle of independence are of the same moral value or whether one is of higher value than the other. In the former case, aid agencies may face the impossible choice between two equally important moral obligations (dilemma). In the lat-

---

[9] Interview in *Humanitarian Affairs Review*, published by *Reliefweb* (www.reliefweb.int, posted 16 April 2002).

ter case, it might be ethically acceptable to violate one obligation for the benefit of the other (moral conflict).

Summing up, moral dilemmas stem from the tension between moral claims and real constraints. Depending on the agenda of an aid organization, this tension can entail conflicts between a humanitarian ethics on one side (humanity, impartiality) and distinct ethical frameworks on the other (justice, human rights, democracy etc.). Or, it is a policy of discrimination (pushed through by donor or recipient side) that challenges the humanitarian obligation to provide impartial, non-discriminatory aid. In the latter case, other ethical frameworks would play a minor role. It is a matter of empirical evidence to determine which type of moral challenge prevails in practice and what strategy can help to resolve it.

After having discussed obligations that, under certain circumstances, may collide with reality, we will now have to analyze the options aid organizations have in order to deal with moral dilemmas.

I.5 Dealing With Moral Dilemmas

As argued earlier, a humanitarian organization has to deal with three factors that influence its behavior in an aid mission:

1. Humanitarian needs of the crisis-affected population.
2. Obligations stemming from organizational mandate and principles (humanity, impartiality, possibly human rights, peace etc.).
3. Interests of political authorities in recipient and donor country.

Accordingly, an aid agency that faces a concrete dilemma situations can focus on one of these factors. It can opt for exclusively considering the humanitarian needs of its target group by concentrating on the relationship between helper and individual aid recipient. Omitting the other two factors, which require a certain analytical distance from the individual 'victim' means to largely deny any conflict between claim and reality (victim-oriented or *victim-centered approach).*

Secondly, an organization can concentrate on its own mandate and principles. Here, the strategy means reconsidering an agency's guidelines, and, possibly, adapting them to the obstacles met in reality (agency-oriented or *introvert approach).*

Thirdly, a humanitarian actor can focus on the political environment of aid as being defined by political interests of donor and recipient side. Such a strategy means actively influencing these political actors (environment-oriented or *extrovert approach*).

It goes without saying that, in reality, an aid agency's strategy will be inspired by more than one approach. The following descriptions refer to ideal types that, as will be shown in later chapters, are often confused within the same organization.

a) The Victim-Centered Approach

The victim-centered approach exclusively focuses on the affective side of humanitarian action. As noted above, sentiments such as pity depend on the proximity to the victim (see Arendt 1963, Boltanski 1999). Therefore, this approach seeks to 'attach' a direct relationship between helper and helped and to focus on the individual recipient of aid. The importance of political or social factors is neglected and any political impact or mandate of aid is refused. Hence, the humanitarian imperative can be presented as the only moral obligation, so that any moral conflict or dilemma disappears. Consequently, withholding aid is never an option. "A hungry child knows no politics", said former US President Ronald Reagan. Weiss and Collins (1996:98) note that "those who feel a humanitarian imperative would argue that choosing to do nothing is never a consideration; therefore, no dilemma exists".

Evidently, this approach does not actively address the causes of the dilemma of aid. Instead, it blends out all factors that belong to the world beyond the relationship between helper and helped. In addition, the victim-centered approach does not take principles of action into consideration since they express the objective side of humanitarian action. The emotional focus on the individual person in need, however, does not allow to detach from the act of giving and thus ignores the objective side of aid.

A victim-centered focus is more a spontaneous, emotional reflex than a deliberate strategy. Nevertheless, the victim-centered approach can be most effective since it deploys simple images and stories instead of complex analysis and argument.

b) The Introvert Approach

The introvert approach focuses on an agency's own mandate, tradition and practices. The strategy is to find common standards that provide the basis for objectively good practice. Identifying objective standards of work in order to improve the quality of humanitarian aid is the overall goal of this approach. Analysis, lessons learned, accountability and coordination play an important role from this perspective.

The introvert strategy highlights the objective side of the humanitarian ethics. By contrast to the victim-centered view, this approach is in no position to avoid or put an end to moral dilemmas. External political interests are accepted as a given reality that aid agencies have to deal with. From this point of view, political interests are out of reach of humanitarian actors and cannot be changed. The pragmatic, introvert strategy thus seeks to find an arrangement with political constraints and to achieve the best possible results under given conditions. Quality, efficiency and 'best practice' provide the guiding ideals of the introvert approach.

The basic guideline of the introvert approach is expressed in the title of a conference held by ECHO and the Overseas Development Institute in 1998: "principled aid in an unprincipled world".[10]

c) The Extrovert Approach

When an aid agency faces a moral dilemma due to an unfavorable environment, it is not the humanitarian obligations that have to be changed, but the environment. This is, in essence, the conclusion drawn by the extrovert approach. It refuses to accept the ambiguity of aid that is seen as the consequence of undemocratic, oppressive, dictatorial politics.

Humanity and impartiality are not questioned as the core obligation of humanitarian aid. The conciliation of claim and reality exclusively depends on the – political – environment. Unlike the introvert approach, the extrovert strategy does not accept political constraints and a limited freedom of action as a given reality. Therefore, humanitarian action re-

---

[10] See also Slim (1997a:256): "Humanitarian aid obviously does have a dark side. Misapplied or not, the provision of help may well have negative repercussions beyond its original intention. The challenge for relief agencies is to determine the proper limits of their moral responsibility for this dark side, and then make all efforts to mitigate against it in their programmes".

lies on an "ethics of refusal"[11] and "has always been and will always be a form of revolt against the unacceptable" (Destexhe 1993:216).

The extrovert approach seeks to re-establish the legitimacy of aid through exerting pressure on political actors. Lobbying actions and co-operation with media are important tools of such an approach. In that regard, the public denouncing of human rights violations appears to be a promising means to pressure governments to change their practices. In addition, the withholding of aid can be an option in order to push through humanitarian interests. 'Be prepared to say no', is a major advice to aid agencies ("Savoir dire non", Brauman 1995:99).

The differing approaches to handling moral dilemmas in humanitarian action are presented in an overview in figure 2.

Fig. 2: Strategies to cope with moral dilemmas

Focus	*Goal*	*Instruments*	
individual recipient	dismiss criticism	- concentrate on the individual recipient of aid - refuse political agenda - withholding aid is no option - "a hungry child knows no politics" (Reagan)	*victim-centered approach*
aid agency	"good practice"/good conscience	- analysis, learning - find common principles, formulate codes of conduct - withholding some aid donations is an option - "principled aid in an unprincipled world" (ECHO/ODI)	*introvert approach*
political environment	eliminate dilemma of aid	- exert pressure on political authorities in donor and recipient country - witnessing and denouncing of human rights violations if necessary - stopping the aid program is an option - "savoir dire non" (Brauman)	*extrovert approach*

---

[11] James Orbinski, see note 8 in this chapter.

Conclusion

Moral ambiguity and dilemmas are part of the history of international humanitarianism, not only since the geo-political changes of 1989/90. Dilemmas of humanitarian action are closely related to the act of aid as a subjective, affective response to the suffering of people. Affective concern for a person in need on one side, and the principle of impartial and proportional aid on the other side provide the ethical basis of humanitarian action. Depending on the political environment of aid, both moral obligations conflict with each other or may be mutually exclusive. The latter case is what we describe as a dilemma of humanitarian action.

The principle of proportionality ('greatest aid to the greatest need') - being one component of impartiality - is of particular importance in those cases where the claim of humanitarian action collides with reality. When aid becomes an accomplice of political power in the recipient country or when it is used as an instrument by a donor government, aid organizations run the risk of delivering aid according to other criteria than needs. In such a case, three sets of constraints conflict with each other: the moral imperative to assist people who suffer, the obligation to provide assistance in accordance with an agency's mandate and principles, and, finally, the constraints that derive from external political interests (dependence in terms of freedom of action on the recipient government, dependence in terms of funding resources on donor governments). When the political environment is hostile to the impartial affording of aid, a humanitarian organization theoretically can focus on the affective side of aid *(victim-centered approach)*, it can adjust own practices and guidelines to the political constraints *(introvert approach)*, or it can seek to change the policies of recipient and/or donor authorities *(extrovert approach)*.

What influences an aid agency's ethical choice in practice, and, moreover, what is the result of these approaches on the dilemma of aid? We will seek to find answers to these questions by analyzing humanitarian actors' courses of action in historic and ongoing aid operations. For this purpose, we need to focus on an area of humanitarian action where aid agencies are most likely to face moral conflicts: famines.

Chapter II.

Humanitarian Ethics and Famine

Humanitarian actors are present in all disasters where the survival of people is at risk. Aid organizations treat the victims of war, they provide shelter, food and medical care for refugees, and they assist people who are affected by natural disasters. As argued above, the emergence of dilemmas in humanitarian action depends on the political environment of aid and the external interests of recipient and/or donor side in dealing with a humanitarian crisis. It will be shown in this chapter that famine and famine aid are closely linked to political interests. As a result, famine inevitably produces the dilemmas as described in the two ideal-type scenarios. Thus, "food distribution is without doubt the most difficult humanitarian operation in which to implement a principled approach" (Leader 2000:39-40).

II.1 Theories of Famine

What is a famine? Attempts to define the term 'famine' are numerous and all but consensual. After having listened to six famine experts on a TV broadcast, Devereux (1993:6) comments: "Six experts, twelve explanations!" In view of the variety of explanations, Nobel prize winning famine theorist Amartya Sen simply claims that "one can very often diagnose it – like a flood or a fire - even without being armed with a precise definition" (Sen 1981:39-40).

The variety of opinions, or, as Edkins (2000:19) puts it, "the hunt for definitions of 'famine'" seems to be related to the fact that famine is an interdisciplinary issue:

> If an economist writes about famine, then famine is caused by market failure or lack of purchasing power. If a climatologist writes about famine, then famine is caused by drought or desertification. When a Marxist sociologist explains famine, colonialism and international capitalism are to blame (Devereux 1993:299).

The definition of the underlying causes of famine determines the proposed remedy to overcome it. If famine emerges as a result of market failure, stimulating market mechanisms appears to be the solution; when ecological factors are held accountable, countermeasures such as embankments or agricultural improvements seem appropriate. As a result of the multitude of famine causes presented by analysts, "the boundaries between definition, description and explanation of famine are often blurred" (Devereux 1993:9).

Two aspects that characterize the famine discussion have to be mentioned. Firstly, the limited scope of theoretical approaches needs to be stressed. Alamgir (1981) argues that famines result from multiple causes that cannot be presented in one single theoretical model. He therefore notes that "it is important to realize that we can only make an approach towards a theory of famine, without really establishing *the theory*" (emphasis in original; Alamgir 1981:39). Likewise, Keen (1994:224) stresses that "it is dangerous to generalize about famines: there are probably as many causes of famine as there are famines". Secondly, very few writers include the perceptions of famine victims in their analyses. Devereux (1993:16) argues that "this ethnocentricity is responsible for much that is wrong with famine definitions and famine 'management'". We do not aim to discuss in depth the strengths and weaknesses of existing approaches.[1] We will limit our view on findings that have a direct relationship to humanitarian action in famines.

Regarding approaches that describe the causes of famine, Sen (1982:447) very broadly distinguishes between "nature-focused" and "society-focused" concepts. In general, it is fair to say that the traditionally dominant "nature-focused" school of thought has lost ground in recent decades while political and social explanatory factors have gained popularity among scholars. However, this distinction is too simple because, as will be shown, most approaches combine ecological and sociopolitical factors. In the following we will briefly discuss the differing concepts in famine theory in order to understand the challenges of famine relief. These presented concepts are food scarcity, entitlement failure, the benefits paradigm and the democracy paradigm.

---

[1] For a discussion of approaches to famine in greater detail see Devereux 1993 and Edkins 2000.

a) The Food Scarcity Paradigm

The first paradigm explains famine by a decline in food availability per capita. The basic assumption is that, due to a number of factors, food is not available in sufficient amounts in order to meet the minimum nutritional needs of a population. The result of this food scarcity is famine. Demographic and ecological factors are primarily discussed as being those forces that lead to a decline in food availability.

Thomas Malthus has presented the ratio between population growth and food production as the main explanation for famines. In a book published in 1798, he argues that "the power of population is indefinitely greater than the power in the earth to produce subsistence for man" (quoted in Devereux 1993:46). As a result, famines have to be understood as the logical consequence of limited increase in food production on the one side that cannot keep pace with uncontrolled population growth on the other. Likewise, Cox (1981:9) argues that famines occur "when the normal relationships between human population and food production have been thrown into imbalance". As a result of this paradigm, the Club of Rome states that "the only feasible solution to the world food situation requires (...) an effective population policy" (quoted in Alamgir 1980:2).

In view of historical evidence it is fair to say that the food availability per capita paradigm is factually wrong. History has shown that population growth actually leads to an increase of food output per capita. Woldemariam (1984:141), for instance, rejects the population growth paradigm:

> Many countries in Western Europe, Tsarist Russia and China have histories of famine. Now, in these same countries, in spite of much larger populations, famine does not occur. This, certainly, is sufficient to exclude population growth as the cause of famine.

Likewise, Devereux (1993:28) perceives the population paradigm as a concept that is disproved by history and has to be seen in its historical context. He argues that Malthus "lived in England at a time when it seemed inevitable that population growth on his island would eventually exceed any possible increases in agricultural output".

The second factor that, in the view of many writers, leads to food availability decline is unfavorable weather. This "most frequently cited cause of famine" (Cox 1981:7) can be due to climatic circumstances that produce regions where famines are more or less inevitable ("famine belts", Cox 1981:8). Or, temporary weather phenomena such as floods or droughts are seen as the causes of famines. Brown and Eckholm (1974:27), for instance, refer to this explanation with regard to the 1943 Bengal famine by claiming that "floods destroyed the rice crop, costing some 2 million to 4 million lives".

Political factors are not totally omitted by the food availability decline paradigm. Cox (1981:11) comments on the 1974 famine in Bangladesh:

> At face value, this famine was triggered by severe flooding which destroyed crops and displaced persons in low-lying areas. The famine, however, occurred during a year of bumper harvest – the second highest in 10 years. Hoarding and illegal smuggling of grain out of the country apparently played a role in reducing availability, but the failure of the government to respond to the aftermath of the flooding until too late seems to have been the single most important underlying cause of famine.

From this perspective, politics can be made accountable for the famine to the extent that it triggers a reduction in food availability and fails in managing this shortfall. The pivotal point is that, in this view, a decline of food availability per capita – may it be induced by demographic, climatic, political or other factors - directly causes famine. In other words, food scarcity equally affects all members of a society. In this regard the food availability decline concept contrasts with the other three paradigms.

b) The Entitlement Failure Paradigm

In the 1970s, a growing number of writers stressed the importance of political factors with regard to the emergence of famines. Lofchie (1975:553) notes that "political and economic arrangements (...), far more than changes in climate and rainfall, are at the base of human suffering and deprivation". The main argument in this respect, however, was to point at the "conditions of disaster" (Ball 1976:520) that were seen as the ultimate result of political and economic decisions such as soil degradation or the expansion of agriculture into grazing zones. In essence, declining food productivity was still viewed as the primary cause of famine.

Amartya Sen's work put an end to the dominance of the food availability argument in academic discussion. The first phrases of his pioneering work "Poverty and Famines" (1981) contain the essence of his entitlement approach:

> Starvation is the characteristic of some people not *having* enough to eat. It is not the characteristic of there *being* not enough food to eat. While the latter can be a cause of the former, it is but one of many *possible* causes. Whether and how starvation relates to food supply is a matter of factual investigation (1981:1, emphasis in original).

This factual investigation led Sen to the finding that famines can actually occur without any decline in food availability. Examples studied include Bengal 1943, Bangladesh 1974 and Ethiopia 1973 and 1974. Inversely, Kumar (1990) argues that countries that experienced a considerable decline in food availability were actually not afflicted by famine. Furthermore, Sen notes that famines took place with little or no rise in food prices. Therefore, in Sen's view, the food availability approach cannot explain why people died of starvation in these particular cases. Famines are thus primarily perceived as a matter of food demand, and not of food supply.

In Sen's perspective, the food availability per capita ratio is a helpful figure only in cases where food is equally distributed among all the members of a society. However, "we don't live in such a society, and indeed there is no such society" (Sen 1982:451). Instead,

> rich people don't starve. The idea of famines wiping out whole societies, as though the consequences of bad weather were meted out in equal measure to all, is far-fetched and can usually be traced to sensationalist history writing rather than a real record of what happened.[2]

It follows from this that famine theory has to look at an individual's ability to command food. Sen (1982:451) summarizes:

> In every society that exists, the amount of food that a person or a family can command is governed by one set of rules or another, combined with the contingent circumstances in which that person or that family happens to be placed vis-à-vis those rules.

This ability to command food is called 'entitlement'. It includes exchange opportunities, production possibilities, entitlements vis-à-vis the

---

[2] ICIHI (Independent Commission on International Humanitarian Issues), 1985, quoted in Devereux 1993:27-28.

state or other means of commanding food. In other words, a person's ability to command food depends on his 'pull' and the supplier's 'response'. In the studied cases, famines resulted from "pull failure" (Sen 1990:44) or "entitlement failure".

Put briefly, the food availability decline paradigm defines famine as a crisis of food production, the entitlement approach sees it as a crisis of *access* to food. Therefore, the entitlement approach highlights a political dimension of famine. Sen (1981:46) notes that the assessment of an individual's entitlement "will depend on the legal, political, economic and social characteristics of the society in question and the person's position in it". Consequently, famines "belong to political economy and to political science. There is, indeed, no such thing as an apolitical food problem" (Sen 1982:459). Although the entitlement approach stresses the political dimension of famine and although the term 'entitlement' carries overtones of human rights, "the entitlement approach views famine as economic disasters" (Sen 1981:162). In other words, the basic idea that famine reflects widespread failure of entitlements is somewhat narrowed down to the view that famine arises from "the general terrain of poverty" (Sen 1981:39). Furthermore, Sen limits his perspective on "those means of commanding food that are legitimized by the legal system in operation in that society" (1981:45). In his view, "the law stands between food availability and food entitlement. Starvation deaths can reflect legality with a vengeance" (1981:166).

Critics of the entitlement approach claim that this concept is overly economistic and "excessively legalistic" (Appadurai 1984:483). Or, in Devereux' words, it presents "an elegant, academic way of saying nothing more than 'people starve because they can't buy enough food'" (1993:82). More precisely, a number of writers note that Sen excludes factors that are central for an understanding of famines, namely violence, political interest, and extralegal transfers of entitlements. Edkins (2000:65), for example, concludes that in Sen's entitlement approach "famine itself has been excluded". Sen's concept received little explicit criticism from exponents of the traditional food availability school of thought. Thus, in a way, the entitlement paradigm has been reproached for stopping halfway rather than for going too far.

In sum, the entitlement approach clearly distinguishes between food scarcity on one side and people's access to food on the other. The former can be nature-induced but is not necessarily the cause of the famine. Although Sen mainly focuses on economic mechanisms, the issue of access or entitlement to food all but excludes political factors. Its basic idea is that "the food problem is not concerned just with the availability of food but with the disposition of food. That involves economics, politics and even law" (Sen 1982:459).

c) The Benefits Paradigm

The entitlement approach concentrates on legal structures that prevent access to food. It focuses on those who are deprived of this access, the victims of famine. The benefits of famine paradigm, by contrast, stresses extralegal mechanisms, namely conflict and war, and concentrates on competing political and economic interests. Rangasami (1985:1748) notes that famine "is a process in which benefits accrue to one section of the community while losses flow to the other". Therefore, analyzing famine means to focus on 'winners' and 'losers'. Advocates of the benefits paradigm remark that the food availability paradigm as well as the entitlement approach leave no space for this analysis of benefits and losses in famines. Edkins (2000:66) argues: "to see famine as either a natural disaster, in the work of Malthus, or as an economic disaster, in the work of Sen, ignores the way some people benefit from famine".

The empirical references of the benefits paradigm are the famines in the Horn of Africa in the 1980s. Keen (1994), in his analysis of southwestern Sudan, argues that neither overall food shortage nor the loss of economic assets can explain the famine. He stresses the lack of political and military power that renders a population vulnerable to famine:

> What is most striking about the victims of the famine is not that they were poor, although those who were still alive were certainly extremely poor once famine had run its course. Most evident is their near-total lack of rights or political muscle within the institutions of the Sudanese state. It was this that exposed them to the complex processes of famine (Keen 1994:211).

Benefits related to famine were numerous for both central and local interests and included the prospect of defeating rebellion and gaining access to resources. Therefore, instead of studying how poverty and lack of purchasing power in the market lead to famine, "it may be equally, or more, important to investigate how powerlessness leads to famine, as people's access to the means of force and political representation collapses" (Keen 1994:213). Similarly, Duffield describes the Horn of Africa as a region of "permanent emergency" where famine appears as the result of "the transfer of assets from the weak to the politically strong" (1993:134,135). Famines can thus be seen as the outcome of political struggle where those who benefit consciously accept the death of the less powerful, a process named "famine crimes" by De Waal (1997). Moreover, Edkins (2000:83) points out that famines not only have beneficiaries, but that "quite often these beneficiaries are the very governments that are supposed to be acting on behalf of the people who are starving". As examples she cites communist governments in Ethiopia and in China during the 'Great Leap Forward' as well as the British government in Ireland in the 1840s and in Bengal in 1944 (see Edkins 2000:80-83).

The notion of benefits of famine suggests that famine conditions can willfully be created by the politically powerful in order to repress or subjugate a population. The benefits paradigm is therefore helpful in order to explain famines where malign intent is seen as the triggering factor. Often cited examples include the Soviet famine of 1933-1934 and the Dutch famine of 1944 (see Devereux 1993:130, 140-142, 159-161).

In essence, however, it can be argued that the works of Keen, Duffield and De Waal do not refute Sen's entitlement approach. Rather, the benefits paradigm as such extends the entitlement concept by identifying political powerlessness as the decisive obstacle to access to food. Although the concepts advocated by these authors differ in a number of aspects (see Edkins 2000:129-146), their common feature is the focus on politics and power as the causes of famine. This focus on political aspects is expressed in terms like "enfranchisement" (Appadurai 1984) or "empowerment" (Watts and Bohle 1993) that were introduced in order to stress the political dimension of famine.

d) The Democracy Paradigm

Gore (1993:454-455), in view of Sen's entitlement approach, notes that

> Sen specifies the rules of entitlement in different ways in his work. Over time, there has been a progression in which, as a first step, the rules of entitlement are equated with state-enforced legal rights, and then this narrow specification has gradually been relaxed.

This progression, based upon Sen's entitlement concept, has produced a new paradigm that focuses on the role of political systems in relation to famines. The basic assumption is that, when entitlement failure lies at the basis of famines, a political system that grants a maximum of entitlements to the population should be the best prevention against famines. Sen argues that empirical evidence approves this assumption. He notes that

> we have never seen famines occur in a country that disposes over a democratic government and a free press. (...) They never afflicted an independent country that holds regular elections, that shelters critical opposition parties and newspapers which are able to freely investigate and question the wisdom of governmental strategies (Sen 1998).

Empirical data is, according to Sen, unambiguous:

> We cannot find exceptions to this rule, no matter where we look: the recent famines of Ethiopia, Somalia, or other dictatorial regimes; famines in the Soviet Union in the 1930s; China's 1958-61 famine with the failure of the Great Leap Forward; or earlier still, the famines in Ireland or India under alien rule (Sen 1999a:7).

India is an often cited example for the assumption that democratization is the most effective prevention against famine. In its history, India has been frequently afflicted by famines. Sen claims that during the last decades, widespread famines have not occurred, though he acknowledges "a remarkable continuation of endemic under-nourishment in a non-acute form" (Sen 2002). According to Drèze and Sen, the widely successful elimination of famine is not due to increases in food production under the 'green revolution' but to "the process of entitlement protection" (Drèze and Sen 1990:17).[3] In an article for the French daily *Le Monde* Sen highlights political factors and argues that successful famine prevention is the result of independence and the establishment of a multiparty system (Sen 1998). He offers the following explanation for his empirical observations:

> Famines kill millions of people in different countries on the planet, but they never kill their masters. The kings and the Presidents, the

---

[3] Drèze and Sen (1990:16) note that it is "often presumed that famines have been eliminated in independent India through a revolutionary increase in food production. There certainly has been some rise in food production per capita since independence (and the 'green revolution' has been effective in the production of wheat in particular), but the increase in food production per head has not been very large. Indeed, the average per capita food availability in India today is not substantially greater than in the late 19th century (...). The causes of success of Indian famine prevention policy have to be sought elsewhere".

bureaucrats and the chiefs, the officers and the commanders never starve. To the extent that there are no elections, no opposition parties, no space for free and public criticism, the authorities do not have to wipe off the political consequences of their incapacity and inaptitude of preventing the famine. Democracy, by contrast, would extend the price of the calamity to the leaderships and politicians.

For the politically powerful, paying the price of famine ultimately means to lose power. In democratic countries, the survival of a government would be threatened by famine, "since elections are not easy to win after famines; nor is it easy to withstand criticism of opposition parties and newspapers. That is why famine does not occur in democratic countries" (Sen 2002).

Arguably, in the course of his work, Sen increasingly considers political and human rights factors in his explanations of famine. And hence, in a way, Sen's theory lives up to the expectations that the word 'entitlement' had raised and that, in the view of some scholars, were a long time overdue.[4] Furthermore, some writers criticize the entitlement approach for creating a patronizing image of famine victims who "need welfare provision or aid, not a political voice". The democracy paradigm, by contrast, stresses the "importance of political rights" that "results from the view on human beings who are seen as individuals disposing of rights to exert, and not as passively existing 'livestock' units" (Edkins 2000:54).

Based on a differing interpretation of empirical data, other authors challenge the absoluteness of the democracy paradigm ("famine does not occur in democratic countries"). Brunel (2002) states that more than 100,000 people died of famine in India in 1965-66. Likewise, Da Corta and Devereux (1991) object to Sen's description of India as a successful example of famine prevention. They conclude that "recurrent famines have been replaced by recurrent near famines and recurrent famine relief or, at best, by institutionalized dependence on relief in normal times" (Da Corta/Devereux 1991:11). Shiva (2002) notes that democracy fails to prevent famine in India because trade liberalization and globalization

---

[4] See Edkins 2000:48,64: "Jean Drèze and Sen's work argues strongly in defense of public action, along the lines of Keynesian intervention, to eradicate hunger (...) The solution remains technical, working within (and reproducing) existing structures of (state) power. The more radical implications of Sen's work have largely been sidelined." "The word 'entitlement', which carries overtones of human rights (food for the starving, for example), turns out to do solely with buying and selling, ownership and legality, under a market economy".

policies "remove basic decisions from the democratic influence of a country's people". Yet this argument does not refute the linkage between famine prevention and a functioning democratic system. By contrast, in essence, Shiva argues that continuing starvation is due to restrictions to democracy and hence ultimately approves the democracy paradigm.

More generally, it is argued that famines have actually occurred in countries under democratic rule. Edkins (2000:64-65) cites the Irish potato famine in the 1840s and the Bengal famine in the 1940s as examples that both occurred under British rule. In a way, however, both examples seem to confirm rather than to refute the democracy paradigm since neither the Bengal nor the Irish people, as colonized peoples, were in possession of democratic rights. The fact that a colonial regime grants democratic rights in its homeland does not mean democracy in the colonies.

De Waal (2000) claims that famines have occurred in democratic countries. In his view the democracy paradigm oversimplifies matters:

> It is not the case that simply having a free press and competitive elections automatically protects a country from famine (...) we have to look at the socio-political framework whereby social ill is conquered, whereby political change is enacted and a new moral consensus emerges in a society to move forward and to make it unacceptable to have famine.

Thus, this "socio-political framework" that prevents famine evidently has a number of characteristics in common with the democracy paradigm but it extends the claim for democratization towards a broader "emancipatory movement" (De Waal 2000).

Summing up, it is notable that those approaches that see famine as the immediate effect of food shortage are increasingly refuted. An emerging consensus distinguishes between food availability decline on one side and famine on the other, the former being neither a necessary nor a sufficient condition for famine. In other words, ecological, economic or political factors cause food scarcity in a society, but *vulnerability* to these factors determines to which degree the members of this society are hit by starvation and famine. Thus, the debate surrounding the cause of famine has developed from mono-causal explanations (nature, weather) to multi-causal concepts that embrace a number of political, economic and other factors in order to explain the vulnerability of people to famines. Evidently, there is no universally applicable famine causation model.[5] However, a large consensus has been discerned which, as noted above, claims that "there is, indeed, no such thing as an apolitical food problem" (Sen 1982:459). The only paradigm that denies this and hence, dismisses the possibility of moral dilemmas for famine aid, is the food scarcity paradigm. In the light of empirical evidence, however, this school of thought, as noted above, has several major weaknesses. Above all, "it diverts attention from possibly the most salient fact of all – that famine is first and foremost a problem of poverty and inequality" (Devereux 1993:27). Causes and effects of famines cannot be analyzed without looking at the overall political setting of the country in crisis.

We will now have to discuss the implications of the aforementioned famine theories on vulnerability assessments and humanitarian action.

II.2 Famine Paradigms and Humanitarian Action

One core principle of classical humanitarian action, as noted earlier, is the provision of aid in proportion to the needs of a population. In terms of famine aid, the principle of proportionality binds humanitarian organizations to identify vulnerability in a given society and to shape their aid effort thereafter. Put differently, famine aid aims at effectively addressing people's vulnerability to food scarcity and famine. An aid agency's understanding of famine and vulnerability, however, has important implications on how the organization sees its role and mandate in a famine. An aid agency will come to differing assessments of vulnerability depending on whether it regards famine as the result of an unfavorable food availability per capita ratio, or as the consequence of entitlement failure, or as the outcome of political oppression and economic exploitation of certain population groups. As a consequence, an agency's understanding of famine and vulnerability not only determines which population groups it will try to reach. It also influences the agency's general assessment of the purpose and potential of famine aid.

Although we will discuss the implications of the famine models separately, one has to add that the different dimensions of vulnerability are not mutually exclusive but are often seen as complementary. Watts and Bohle (1993), for example, argue that the space of vulnerability is com-

---

[5] With regard to the entitlement approach, Sen (1981:162), for instance, notes that it "provides a general framework for analyzing famines rather than one particular hypothesis about their causation".

posed of lack of entitlement (command over food), lack of empowerment (state-society relations), and class relations within a specific political economy (surplus appropriation, susceptibility to crisis).

a) Food Availability Decline and Famine Aid

When famine is seen as the result of food shortfalls that hit an entire population, the overall task of famine aid is to improve the food supply situation through the immediate delivery of sufficient amounts of food. From this perspective, all population groups are equally hit by starvation and famine to the extent that the food availability per capita ratio is regarded as crucial.

Accordingly, it is assumed that all segments of the population are having equal access to food. Therefore, from this perspective, vulnerability assessment does not have to look at issues such as individual access to food or people's means to demand food. Instead, the food per capita paradigm leads to a mere physical understanding of vulnerability to famine. The principle of proportionality means focusing on those population groups with highest nutritional needs. Cox (1981:13), for instance, notes that "mortality rates are highest for the weakest and most energy-requiring segments of the population: children, the aged and infirm, and pregnant and nursing women".

A famine aid mission that is based upon such an understanding of famine and vulnerability is most unlikely to experience moral dilemmas. In this view, the delivery of food and medical assistance to people with highest nutritional and medical needs is seen as the core task for fulfilling the mandate of humanitarian organizations in a famine situation. In the long run, aid activities can seek to enhance the food output of the region currently in crisis. By doing so, aid can contribute to a long-term eradication of underlying causes of famine. The organizational mandate and humanitarian principles including the obligation to relieve human suffering are not affected in any way by the (political) crisis setting. Aid contributes to overcome starvation and addresses the root causes of the famine, namely food scarcity.

b) Entitlement Failure and Famine Aid

As for the entitlement failure paradigm, matters are more complex. In this view, "since famines reflect a collapse of entitlement, famine relief has to take the form of generating entitlements through other channels" (Sen 1982:454).

Famine aid that seeks to generate entitlements has to discover the economic causes for, and solutions to, famine. Entitlement failure hits differing population groups in differing crises. For instance, in some cases, the rural population suffers more, in other cases, this group is better off than the urban population.[6] Physical aspects hardly play a role when it comes to the definition of vulnerability. Instead, the analysis of vulnerability focuses on economic aspects such as the loss of income of specific population groups. Moreover, when famine relief seeks to generate entitlements, it does not necessarily have to deliver food or medicine. Paying food in exchange for employment (food-for-work projects, FFW) is seen as one remedy that can help to end a famine caused by the loss of income or employment.[7] Apart from free food distribution and FFW, cash relief is sometimes advocated as another appropriate means of creating additional purchasing power and to draw more food into the famine affected region (see Sen 1982:454-455).[8]

---

[6] Devereux (1993:75) argues that "cities have access to food supplies and incomes from a variety of sources, both locally and abroad, while small farmers depend on their agricultural output for both their food consumption needs and as a source of 'exchange entitlements'". See also Lipton who stresses an "urban bias" in favor of urban elites (1977:18). A different view is upheld by Desai (1984:165) who claims that "it is those who do not have to go through a purchase or sale to convert their income into consumption who are least vulnerable to a decline in real grain wage. The direct producer of grain, either as landowner or sharecropper and the worker who receives a grain wage are safer than he who receives money rent or money wage". With regard to the Chinese famine 1958-61, Kula (1989:15) notes that "starvation was most acute in the cities, partly due to the denial of famine by some district authorities and partly due to the poor coordination of transport in shifting supplies from the countryside".

[7] FFW programs are often accorded the advantage that "they are self-targeting, so that they are generally more efficient than untargeted handouts" (Devereux 1993:73). Likewise, Uvin (1994:157) praises this self-targeting effect: "People do not like to be paid in food if they can avoid it: it is unpractical and humiliating: thus only desperate people are willing to work in such projects". This view is challenged by a number of authors. Jackson and Eade (1982:38) conclude their evaluation of FFW projects by saying that "in the majority of cases, there is little or no improvement in the living and working conditions of the poor. Too frequently, people on FFW/public works projects are exploited as free labour for those who are already relatively well-off."

[8] Sen (1982:456) notes that "food does move out of famine areas when the loss of entitlement is more powerful than the decline - if any - of food supply, and such food 'counter-movement' has been observed in famines as diverse as the Irish famine of the 1840s, the Ethiopian famine in Wollo in 1973, and the Bangladesh famine of 1974".

Evidently, this understanding of famine relief goes beyond the mere alleviation of human suffering and includes a variety of short and longer-term activities. It is important to note that famine aid in this perspective will hardly encounter obstacles to an impartial and proportionate distribution of aid because vulnerability to famine is widely defined by economic impoverishment rather than by exploitation or political powerlessness.

c) The Benefits Paradigm and Famine Aid

The benefits paradigm sees famine as the outcome of a process of political struggle and poses a number of challenges to humanitarian action. When famine results from the deliberate exploitation and oppression of population groups, the eradication of these underlying political causes of famine requires aid agencies to address political issues. Thus, in contrast to the food scarcity and (economic) entitlement failure concepts, the benefits paradigm sees humanitarian agencies as playing a role in the political struggle of a country in crisis.

Vulnerability assessment means analyzing the distribution of political power within a society in order to identify the populations that have the least political power to command food. Accordingly, humanitarian work appears first and foremost to deliberately take sides in favor for the politically weak and oppressed. More than the mere provision of aid, humanitarianism includes activities such as the public denouncement of political oppression or of human rights violations.

In terms of vulnerability, humanitarian action has to assess the distribution of political power within a society in order to identify the politically weakest population groups. In this view, political powerlessness is the root cause for a lack of access to food and medical service. Humanitarian action that is shaped in order to support the politically powerless in a society can encounter a number of fundamental problems, which, ultimately, pose a serious risk to the moral integrity of aid.

Firstly, an agency's analysis of the distribution of power in a given context can turn out to be misleading or factually wrong. As will be discussed in greater detail in later chapters, the assessments by humanitarian actors of the political situation in a famine stricken country vary greatly, and, in some cases, can be called into question.

Secondly, vulnerability that is related to political powerlessness and deprivation is the most difficult to address by humanitarian aid. Thus, the purpose of a relief mission that is based upon the benefits paradigm, might in the end turn out to be illusionary. As Edkins (2000:137) argues:

> Relief operations are usually unable to tackle the processes of resource depletion that give rise to famine. It is very difficult to attract support for any program that would do this, because such a program would be redistributing assets to the weak and as such would arouse local opposition from those whose interests are threatened.

Finally, humanitarian action not only risks missing its aims, it might also lead to an aggravation of the political and humanitarian situation. Put differently, if certain groups benefit from famine, famine relief risks becoming part of the same process. Duffield (1993:140) notes:

> International emergency intervention, rather than eradicating the disaster situation, appears in many respects to strengthen it. [It] opens new avenues for the politically strong in terms of state financial support, legitimation, access to strategic resources and speculative profit.[9]

In such a situation, the effects of aid clash with the humanitarian principle to afford greatest aid to the greatest need, and, consequently aid agencies are caught in a dilemma.

d) The Democracy Paradigm and Famine Aid

Similar to the benefits approach, the democracy paradigm defines vulnerability in terms of political power and rights. However, instead of focusing on particular population groups, this paradigm applies to a political system as a whole. The solution to famine is seen in the establishment of a "socio-political framework whereby social ill is conquered, whereby political change is enacted and a new moral consensus emerges" (De Waal 2000). Such a task evidently surpasses the capacities (and mandate) of humanitarianism.

---

[9] See also Keen (1994:225) who, with regard to the Sudanese famine of 1983-85, concludes: "It is clear that precisely those groups who suffered most severely from the famine (rural people, nomads, migrants) were also those who were least well placed to stake a claim to international relief that was channeled through local political institutions and power relationships. More politically influential groups, such as merchants and prominent officials, were able to secure some benefits from famine, notably from the purchase of livestock at low prices and from the acquisition of relief food intended for the most needy".

It is often argued that internal pressure is necessary to democratize a society and that humanitarian aid, by satisfying the basic needs of a population, might undermine such a development. This disincentive argument poses a moral threat to aid because one has to ask the question: "Is it moral to 'create' misery for people, even for 'their own good'?" (Uvin 1994:165). In view of traditional humanitarianism, the answer has to be no, because the principle of humanity is accorded higher value than any obligation to promote democracy.[10] In this respect, donor interests potentially play a more influential role than the motivation of aid agencies. This aspect will be further discussed using case studies, such as Soviet Russia and North Korea.

The democracy paradigm seeks to change an entire political system. It therefore refers to the political environment of humanitarian action more than to the behavior of aid agencies. Consequently, the transition to democracy addresses the general ambiguity of humanitarianism (i.e. the incapability of humanitarian actors to determine the environment of their action). However, it does not provide any conceptual help for aid agencies who face a dilemma in a concrete situation. In other words, unlike the famine paradigms mentioned above, the democracy paradigm is not directly related to the practices of famine aid.

---

[10] Notably, some authors claim that the potential of food aid as a reform-inducing tool is often overestimated. Uvin (1994:165) argues that "suppressing food aid thus only amounts to some kind of cruel punishment for 'bad' governments or populations, but not to a policy reform inducing tool."

II.3 Famine and the Dilemma of Aid

The discussion of theoretical approaches to famine has shown that famines result from a multitude of factors including political processes and decisions. We then argued that the mandate and goal of famine relief takes a different shape depending on whether famine is seen as the result of ecological, economic or socio-political factors. These conceptual links between famine explanation, vulnerability assessment, and the role of aid have major implications on the behavior of humanitarian actors in famine situations.

As argued in earlier chapters, three "ethico-political decisions" (Edkins 2000:148) can theoretically be taken by aid agencies in dilemma situations. We will now discuss how far the conceptual approaches to famine interact with victim-centered, introvert or extrovert strategies in famine relief missions.

a) Famine Aid and the Victim-Centered Approach

The duty to provide assistance to people in need, regardless of the political interests of the suffering or the government in place, lies at the heart of the humanitarian ethical framework. The victim-centered approach understands this overarching principle of humanitarian action in a way that casts aside political factors including those that influence the operational space of aid. To understand famine as the outcome of political struggle that leaves the politically powerless prone to starvation, jeopardizes the victim-centered view. In general, humanity means identifying with a suffering person. A political definition of vulnerability that is inherent to the benefits and the democracy paradigm distracts from the relationship between helper and individual helped. Consequently, a victim-centered ethical decision will tend to regard vulnerability of people to famine in non-political terms.

Food availability decline, triggered by natural disaster, provides the most suitable argument to stress the apolitical character of the famine and hence, of famine relief efforts. However, aid agencies that adopt a victim-centered strategy run the risk of finding themselves in a coalition with those forces that are immune to starvation due to their political power and influence: "Blaming nature can, of course, be very consoling and comforting. It can be of great use especially to those in positions of power and responsibility" (Drèze and Sen 1989:47). In addition, the labeling of famine as natural disaster meets the expectations of another very influential group: private donors. Cremer (1999:52) observes that

> natural disasters are generally perceived as stemming from a *force majeure* that affects innocent victims. When it comes to evident man-made disasters, however, such as civil wars, ethnic violence and resulting mass refugee flows, donor fatigue quickly spreads.

In sum, the food availability decline paradigm gives rise to a victim-centered approach in famine relief to the extent that the political dimension of vulnerability is blinded out. This political dimension, however, as argued above, is one important, though not necessarily the exclusive cause of famine. As a consequence, the victim-centered approach ignores the nature of famine. The result can be twofold. Firstly, focusing on the individual recipient may help to uphold an aid organization's moral integrity. Secondly, however, such an approach is most prone to manipulation by political interests.

b) Famine Aid and the Introvert Approach

If an aid organization seeks to (re-) establish its moral integrity through the introspection of its guiding principles and mandate (introvert approach), then it can draw a number of possible lessons from famine theories. Firstly, following the entitlement concept, humanitarian actors may include the improvement of the economic situation of vulnerable people in their agenda. The perception of famine as an economic failure leads to the suggestion that aid should carry out activities such as income generating projects. In this perspective, aid has to shape its activities not only according to immediate humanitarian intentions but also pursuant to longer-term economic considerations. This 'relief-development-continuum' therefore seeks to solve the conflict between the humanitarian obligation to cure symptoms (relieve suffering) and the broader motivation to address the causes of famine (enhance entitlement).[11]

The benefits and democracy paradigms also invite humanitarianism to enlarge their mandate. Thus, democratization or peacebuilding activi-

---

[11] For details see Macrae (2001) and Ian Smillie (1998): *Relief and Development: The Struggle for Synergy.* Providence, RI: Thomas Watson Jr. Institute for International Studies/Brown University.

ties carried out by humanitarian actors may help to overcome moral dilemmas. Anderson (1999:146), for instance, suggests that "aid workers should try to identify local capacities for peace and connectors and design their aid programs to support and reinforce them". Such an agenda comprises, for instance, educational projects, rehabilitation programs in health and agriculture and the dissemination of International Humanitarian Law. The overall goal of this strategy is to prevent moral conflicts and dilemmas by "doing no harm" (Anderson 1999).

The enlargement of the humanitarian agenda risks setting goals that humanitarian actors are not capable of fulfilling. The Code of Conduct on Food Aid and Food Security, adopted in 1995 by EuronAid, a consortium of European NGOs, expresses this possible gap between goals and capabilities. On one side it states that "we act to minimize negative effects on food security by factors (...) such as civil conflicts, natural disasters, government and donor policies". At the same time, however, it makes clear that these factors are "outside our direct influence".

c) Famine Aid and the Extrovert Approach

The extrovert approach dismisses that political factors are outside the range of humanitarian actors. By contrast, it stresses that it is the primary task of aid to address these factors whenever it faces a moral dilemma. The benefits paradigm shares this view in so far as it identifies political power relations as the forces behind starvation and famine. Therefore, the benefits paradigm clearly suggests an extrovert humanitarianism. Both argue that to fight famine means fighting those policies that benefit from or even create famine. Consequently, "a humanitarianism that claims to be separate from and not a part of politics is no help" (Duffield 1993:148). Humanitarian actors have to take sides for an "emancipatory movement" (De Waal 2000) that seeks political and moral change and hence, is alone able to eradicate famine. Thus, political engagement is the appropriate strategy to overcome moral dilemmas.

This implies that humanitarian aid has to adopt a rights discourse that is based on International Humanitarian Law and/or Human Rights Law. The Code of Conduct on Food Aid and Food Security also serves as an example: "We affirm that access to food is a fundamental human right; we consider hunger in a world with enough food to feed all its people to be morally and politically unacceptable". The consequence of this would be that aid organizations exert pressure on political actors whenever they conclude that the "fundamental right for everyone to be free from hunger" (Rome Declaration on Food Security, 1996) is violated by the pursuit of political interests on donor and/or recipient side.

Furthermore, the benefits paradigm puts emphasis on the conditionality of aid, particularly in terms of the effective targeting of politically powerless population groups. In this context, it might be an option to withhold or withdraw aid in order to push through this demand. When Doctors Without Borders (MSF) asked Amartya Sen what to do in famine situations, the answer was: "I think the last thing to do is simply to give money or food unconditionally" (Sen 1999b).

Conclusion

Famine aid poses an ethical challenge to humanitarian action. Famine and its causes and effects are diverse and no paradigm can claim to provide an all embracing, universally applicable theory of famine. Two categories of theories have to be distinguished: one that sees famine as the immediate outcome of food availability decline and a second that defines vulnerability and access to food in relation to economic, social and/or political power. Differing approaches regard vulnerability as poverty (entitlement paradigm), powerlessness (benefits paradigm) or deprivation of democratic rights (democracy paradigm). Importantly, these famine concepts distinguish between crisis and vulnerability. On one side, it looks at factors that trigger food scarcity such as natural disaster, war or economic slump. On the other side, and more importantly, it seeks to identify the political, economic and/or social dynamics that lead to vulnerability to this food scarcity. Most notably, it is argued that famines are linked to vulnerability, not crisis. Ecological, political or economic crises are neither a necessary nor a sufficient condition of famine. This is why the academic discourse has widely refuted the food scarcity paradigm since it understands vulnerability only in physical terms.

Vulnerability to famine reflects the distribution of economic, social and political influence in a society. Famine aid is placed in this broader context because assisting the needy necessarily means assisting the (economically, socially and politically) weak. Thus, famines do not offer a technical solution. Aid cannot seek technical solutions simply because the problems addressed are not technical. The distribution of resources in a society is a political issue. This is why, as quoted at the beginning of this chapter, "food distribution is without doubt the most difficult humanitarian operation in which to implement a principled approach" (Leader 2000:39-40). The overall conclusion is that famine aid is a

> process of ethico-political decision. (...) it is not a question of formulating a more adequate theory of famine or a more sophisticated technology of relief, it is a question of politics and decision. (...) The trick is to acknowledge that the dilemmas practitioners face are inescapable, and, more than that, these dilemmas are a reflection of the importance of the activity in which they are engaged (Edkins 2000:148).

Political inequalities challenge the core principles of humanitarian action: impartiality and proportionality. Therefore, famine *by its nature* poses an ethical challenge to humanitarian action. As a consequence, famines provide an appropriate empirical reference to study the moral dilemmas that humanitarian action has to face in aid missions.

Aid agencies have to make a primarily ethical decision. That is, they have to find a way between the moral duty to help, their organizational mandate and principles, and the political realities that determine their work. Notably, there are conceptual links between famine models, the understanding of vulnerability and the ethical choice of humanitarian actors. The food scarcity paradigm largely ignores the political aspects of famine which it has in common with a victim-centered approach. Economically defined vulnerability suggests fighting poverty as a method of famine relief. Therefore, aid needs to reconsider its agenda and working principles in order to overcome moral dilemmas (introvert approach). Political vulnerability concepts, however, plead for an offensive strategy that addresses political inequalities and oppression as the main causes of famine (extrovert approach). Most importantly, all famine paradigms that impact on famine relief operations contradict, in one way or another, principles of humanitarian action. The food scarcity paradigm risks ignoring the objective obligations of aid, while the economic entitlement failure approach neglects the immediate saving of lives as the humanitarian core task. Finally, a relief operation that is based on the benefits paradigm ultimately risks losing access to people in need. In short, to address the causes of famine necessarily means violating moral obligations of aid. Therefore, dilemma situations in famine aid operations are inescapable.

We will now discuss how, in practice, humanitarian organizations deal with moral dilemmas in famines and what determines their ethical decisions.

Chapter III.

The History of Famine Aid

Humanitarian organizations deal with three sets of obligations or interests that stem from the suffering of people (humanitarian imperative), from the organization's mandate and principles, and from the political environment as defined by donor and recipient authorities. Whenever the principle of proportionality is undermined by donor or recipient interests, the moral obligations of aid may potentially conflict with each other. This scenario becomes true whenever at least one of two conditions is met: firstly, when a population's vulnerability to famine is defined by political powerlessness, and secondly, when the effective reduction of vulnerability through international famine relief runs counter to the political interests of those in positions of power and responsibility (on recipient or donor side).

The empirical analysis of ethical problems in humanitarian action therefore requires focusing on case studies where at least one of these conditions is fulfilled. In the following text we will elaborate on famine aid missions in Soviet Russia, Biafra/Nigeria, Cambodia and Ethiopia. Three sets of questions will be discussed:

1. In how far are vulnerability to famine and the attempt to reduce this vulnerability related to politics?
2. Which famine paradigm(s) do humanitarian actors adhere to and how do they deal with moral dilemmas?
3. What is the outcome of their behavior?

The four cases have been selected mainly for two reasons: Firstly, they display the dilemma of famine aid in illustrative though different ways. And secondly, all cases were accompanied by public debates, so that their respective history is relatively well documented by existing literature. Furthermore, the four case studies are essential for the analysis of today's famine aid system because they created myths, legends and traumas that still influence on today's humanitarian action. It has to be noted that international aid organizations, whose behavior is the focus of this study, were not engaged in some of the most devastating famines of the 20th century - the Chinese famine in 1958-61 and the famine in the Ukraine in 1932-33.

III.1 'Famine Fighters' and Pioneers – Famine Relief to Soviet Russia 1921-23

After World War I, a number of Central European countries faced famine as a consequence of war and economic despair. The only country that, at that time, disposed over sufficient resources to address the food crises in Europe was the United States. In a number of countries, the US provided food aid through a governmental organization, the American Relief Administration (ARA). Thus, in the period between the World Wars, for the first time, a state financed and carried out famine relief activities in a number of foreign countries.[1] When Russia, which was still caught up in an ongoing civil war between the Red Army and the 'White forces' of the 'provisional government' under Admiral Kolchak, was facing a famine in the early 1920s, it was mainly the United States that had the capacity to act. However, the situation differed to the extent that it was not a defeated former enemy state (such as Germany or Austria) in distress, but a population under the rule of a regime that was seen by some as a rising threat to the entire democratic world. Under these circumstances, humanitarian motivations were, from the beginning, dealing with a highly politicized surrounding. Some of the moral conflicts and dilemmas that appeared on the agenda of famine aid in later missions first emerged in Soviet Russia in 1921-23, which thus became somewhat of a prototype of a morally ambivalent famine aid mission.

The famine resulted from a variety of political, economic and ecological factors. War and civil war had left the economy, agriculture and infrastructure of the country in decay. With regard to the situation in the former capital Petrograd, for instance, Fisher (1927:83) notes that

> in spite of the fact that the individual workman produced in 1922 but slightly more than half of what he produced in 1912, there was such a decrease in trade and industry that the number of persons employed had dropped 57 percent.

In addition to the difficult economic situation came a drought in 1920, followed by a hard winter and a second successive drought in 1921 that resulted in massive crop failure in the Volga regions and the Ukraine. However, as Huntford (1998:503) notes, "this was nothing new.

---

[1] See McElroy (1992:59): "World War I radically altered the nature of disaster relief by creating reconstruction needs in Central Europe so great that they were beyond the ability of any nation to meet single-handedly."

A cycle of good years and lean ones was part of Russian history". Yet in 1921, two factors played a fatal role.

Firstly, the country's transport system was not capable of moving sufficient amounts of grain from surplus to famine-affected regions. Secondly, as a reaction to the government's order to deliver surplus to the state, peasants were hiding food and only tilling enough for their own needs.[2] Although the system of requisition patrols had been changed in the meantime, the peasants had no reserves in 1921. In Lenin's words, however, the famine was

> the severe consequence of Russian economic backwardness and the seven years of war, first the imperialist war and then the civil wars, which were imposed upon the workers and peasants by the landlords and capitalists of all countries (reprinted in Goldberg 1993:218).

Thus, from the perspective of the Russian leadership, the carrying out of famine relief through Western, mainly American organizations was a highly political issue. As a consequence, it was the maneuverability of international aid that was at the center of controversies.

a) Interests, Moral Obligations and Dilemmas

In 1927, H. H. Fisher of the historical department of the ARA described the political relationship between Russia and Western powers after the coming into power of the Communists in 1917 as follows (Fisher 1927:1):

> There was no call to arms, no formal blockade, none of the pomp and spectacle of the clash of nations. Yet never, perhaps, even in the very heat of the World War did the searing flames of hate blaze with more cruel intensity; seldom have men fought with such relentless, savage fury; never has a civilized land been more decisively severed from intercourse with the world.

In early 1921, the Russian government had to deal with the outbreak of a massive famine that affected an estimated 40 millions of people (Destexhe 1993:40), particularly in the Volga region. From a Western perspective, therefore, "the Soviet government faced the very type of

---

[2] See Weissman (1974:6): "The final blow was the requisition policy pursued by the Bolshevik government during the Civil War. The area under cultivation shrank to 70 percent of the average sown during the five years immediately preceding World War I. The reduction in the Volga region was even greater".

threat to its existence and legitimacy that the American government had been hoping for" (McElroy 1992:57).

The Soviet government was aware of the threat that the famine posed to its very existence. In March 1921, the head of the Soviet government and leader of the Bolshevik party, Vladimir I. Lenin warned the party congress:

> Food would have to be taken out of the mouths of the peasants. If there is a harvest, then everybody will hunger a little, and the government will be saved; otherwise, since we cannot take anything from people who do not have the means of satisfying their own hunger, the government will perish (quoted in Weissman 1974:2).

The Soviet government's interest in dealing with the famine was therefore twofold. On one side, foreign assistance was indispensable in order to avert the famine and, thus, to uphold the social and political order in place. On the other hand, this foreign assistance had to be carried out in a face-saving manner for the government. As an official of the Soviet government put it: "We will never agree to any conditions that may have the slightest effect of discrediting our government" (quoted in Weissman 1974:55).

The fact that the government was highly suspicious of aid efforts from the West was not totally unjustified. Western powers had been engaged in military activities, though on a modest scale, in the Russian civil war (see Fisher 1927:25). In addition, the United States government had provided considerable amounts of food aid through ARA to the 'White forces' in 1919.[3] Moreover, also in 1919, the ARA and her head, Herbert Hoover, declared that the provision of food aid to Hungary was impossible as long as the Communist government of Bela Kun was in power.[4] Not surprisingly, being aware of the fact that the Kun government was overthrown shortly after the declaration written by Hoover had been published, the Soviet authorities propagated "tireless watchfulness" with regard to the ARA and other foreign aid organizations.[5]

---

[3] See "Special Agreement between the American Relief Administration and the Provisional Government of Russia, 16 July 1919", reprinted in Goldberg (1993:196).

[4] According to Weissman (1974:34), "although Hoover later expressed doubt that the Red regime [in Hungary] fell because of the threat to stop food shipments, he did not deny that such had indeed been the purpose of the announcement".

[5] The passage of a pamphlet entitled "Famine and the International Situation", distributed in 1921 by the Communist Party, comments on the ARA: "In what measure there is

For the Soviet government, the very fact of having to ask for foreign assistance from capitalist states implied the risk of losing face. Therefore, not the government itself, but the internationally reputable writer Maxim Gorky issued the appeal in 1921 on behalf of the government. He asked "all honest European and American people for prompt aid to the Russian people. Give bread and medicine" (reprinted in Goldberg 1993:199).

The governments of European countries pursued differing policies with regard to famine relief to Soviet Russia. The debate centered around what we have called the accomplice scenario, i.e. the potential of aid to stabilize an unwanted regime, both through a direct, material support and through an unwitting restoration of its legitimacy. "We have to save Russia without saving Bolshevism", said the Yugoslav Ambassador to the League of Nations when discussing the matter (quoted in McElroy 1992:73). The French government was particularly reluctant to support aid efforts. Stéphen Pichon, France's Minister for Foreign Affairs, made it clear that the French government "cannot give its support to any step which might invest this tentative with a political character, the result of which would be a moral and material reinforcement of the iniquitous Bolshevik Government" (quoted in Fisher 1927:19-20). European countries largely shared this cautious approach and, within the framework of the League of Nations, pushed through the decision not to get engaged in the Russian famine relief. It was agreed with the view that was expressed by the Swiss delegate; he stressed that "only (...) charitable organizations (...) could usefully direct this kind of undertaking" (quoted in Huntford 1998:508).

The United States government, by contrast and to the surprise of the Soviet government,[6] decided to provide aid on a large scale. In 1921

---

even now behind the relief organization of the American Minister, Hoover, a definite striving to renew economic relations with Russia, in what measure through this organization the most irreconcilable interventionists are undertaking to act, and in what measure the efforts of the one are combined with the intrigues of the other, all these only experience will show. On our side are required, first the strong fulfillment of our agreements and second, tireless watchfulness in the center and the provinces. In Hungary one of the agents of this same Hoover took, according to his own printed story, an active part in the overthrow of the Soviet power" (quoted in Fisher 1927:134).

[6] See Weissman (1974:9): "Lenin did not expect assistance from the United States or any other capitalist government. In the middle of July, several days after Gorky issued his appeal to the world, Lenin told Willi Münzenberg, a member of the Executive Commit-

alone, the administration of President Warren G. Harding spent 24 million US dollars on the relief effort for Soviet Russia, an amount equal to almost one percent of the overall annual budget of that year (see McElroy 1992:58). In his analysis of this policy, McElroy (1992:86) concludes that "the only convincing explanation for US aid to Russia during the famine of 1921 is that leading American decision makers believed that the US had a moral obligation to come to the assistance of the Russian people". In his view, "humanitarian responsibility" and "Christian duty" (McElroy 1992:86) largely defined the decision to provide aid to Russia.

However, other interests may also have played an important role. Herbert Hoover, the main policy maker in the matter of Russia aid, notes that food aid should be provided under the conditions that one

> gets assurances that the Bolsheviki will cease all militant action across certain defined boundaries and cease their subsidizing of disturbances abroad. (...) If such an arrangement could be accomplished it might at least give a period of rest along the frontiers of Europe and would give some hope of stabilization. Time can thus be taken to determine whether or not this whole system is a world danger (quoted in Huntford 1998:486).

Contrary to McElroy's assessment, Huntford (1998:486) concludes from the above that the US government used "the food weapon (...) as an alternative to military action and a vehicle of high-minded influence". In any case, famine relief in Soviet Russia faced the twofold risk of becoming an instrument of Western, mainly American, political interests and, ironically, of becoming the accomplice of a Soviet regime who's survival depended on the provision of foreign aid.

b) Relief Work in Russia – Needs, Assessment and Action

International famine relief to Russia was mainly carried out by two organizations: the International Committee for Russian Relief, which organized European – largely privately funded - efforts, and the ARA that carried out aid activities funded by the US government. At that time, the ARA was the largest relief organization in the world. At the height of the Russian famine in 1922, the ARA was feeding about 8,5 million peo-

---

tee of the Communist International, that there was little hope of any substantial assistance from the capitalist powers; Russia would have to rally the international proletariat in a gigantic relief campaign."

ple compared to the 400,000 of all other organizations combined (see Huntford 1998:511). Both agencies were headed by two of the most famous personalities of their time. Fridtjof Nansen, who gained popularity as an explorer, served as an Ambassador and Minister for Foreign Affairs of Norway and as High Commissioner of the League of Nations, headed the International Committee; he was awarded the Nobel Peace Prize in 1922. Herbert Hoover, head of the US food administration during World War I, where he gained his reputation as a 'famine fighter', was Secretary of Commerce in the Harding administration during the Russian aid period and Chairman of the ARA; in 1929, he became the 31st US President. The Chairmen's multitude of functions already illustrate that neither the Committee nor the ARA were what we would today call an NGO. In 1919, the ARA Chairman himself pleaded for a neutrally organized relief mission to Russia with Fridtjof Nansen as the head, thus arguing that he was not the most suitable person to lead a neutral aid effort.[7]

In the debate surrounding the risk of aid of becoming an accomplice of the Soviet regime, both Hoover and Nansen referred to the humanitarian imperative and argued that the West has a moral obligation to provide assistance to Soviet Russia. With regard to the possible unwanted effects of aid, Nansen insisted on the priority of humanitarian concerns in front of the delegates of the League of Nations: "Suppose that it does help the Russian government. Is there any member of this Assembly who is prepared to say that rather than help the Soviet government, he will allow twenty million people to starve to death?" (quoted in McElroy 1992:74).

In fact, the Assembly still declined to provide assistance. In his Nobel lecture in 1922, Nansen explicitly comments on this event in retrospect: "But why were there some who did not want to help? Ask them! In all probability their motives were political. They epitomize sterile self-importance and the lack of will to understand people who think differently".[8] In Nansen's view, political motives have to be discarded since

---

[7] This original plan, however, failed due to the above-mentioned reluctance of Western powers to provide aid and the Soviet's refusal to consider the cessation of military activities, except at the price of recognition by the West, which, in turn, Western governments were not willing to pay. Only in 1921, when the famine situation had worsened and the Gorky appeal had reached the West, was the ARA directly negotiating with Soviet authorities (see Fisher 1927:24-27).

[8] Fridtjof Nansen: Nobel Lecture, 19 December 1922. Found at www.nobel.se/peace/ laureates/1922/nansen-lecture.html (2 July 2001).

"the struggle of the politicians amounts to little more than a struggle for power".[9] Therefore, in a situation where one has to face obligations that stem from political interests on one side, and obligations that result from the humanitarian needs of a population, Nansen only accepts considering the latter. Neither political considerations of donors or recipients nor organizational principles are taken into account. With regard to the question of food aid to Russia, Nansen clearly opts for a victim-centered view:

> When one has beheld the great beseeching eyes in the starved faces of children staring hopelessly into the fading daylight, the eyes of agonized mothers while they press their dying children to their empty breasts in silent despair, and the ghostlike men lying exhausted on mats on cabin floors, with only the merciful release of death to wait for, then surely one must understand where all this is leading, understand a little of the true nature of the question.[10]

Nansen strongly criticized the European governments for pursuing political goals even in times of humanitarian crisis. As far as American or Russian motives were concerned, however, Nansen appeared to ignore political motives on the American and on the Russian side. In 1919, for instance, when Hoover asked Nansen to offer aid to the Soviets on behalf of the Western powers and to link this offer to the cessation of military activities by the Red army, Nansen agreed in order "to show ... the Bolsheviks that there is charity which cares for suffering humanity in spite of all politics" (quoted in Huntford 1998:488). In consultations with his Ministers concerning the official Soviet reply to Nansen's offer, Lenin gave the advise to explicitly explain to Nansen that his offer of a truce contained political motives.[11]

ARA's approach differed from Nansen's perspective in various aspects. A moral duty to help as a result of human suffering was also taken into account, but it was not accorded absolute value. After receiving the Gorky appeal, Hoover notes: "I believe it is a humane obligation upon us to go in if they comply with the requirements set out; if they do not accede we are released from responsibility" (quoted in McElroy 1992:71).

---

9 See note 8 in this chapter.
10 See note 8 in this chapter.
11 "Explain to him, as you would to a 16-year-old schoolgirl, why a truce is politics. (...) one must talk frankly about politics without taking cover behind 'humanitarianism'" (quoted in Huntford 1998:488).

In other words, aid was not perceived as an absolute moral obligation because it depended on certain conditions to be fulfilled; an argumentation that strikingly contrasts with Nansen's perspective. As for the ARA, the victim-centered view played a different role since it was used by Hoover in order to create a public opinion in the US favorable to food aid for Russia.[12] Focusing on the individual victims of famine helped to raise funds but it also helped to motivate aid personnel. The aforementioned role of 'detachment' and 'attachment' in humanitarian action is illustrated in the notes of one ARA employee:

> More than once, wearied by a discussion with the government representative more futile than usual, I would drop everything and wander out to the nearest ARA kitchen just to look at the children and get back my confidence that it was worth-while trying to help them after all (Fisher 1927:104-105).

Furthermore, as a result of relief work during and after World War I, the ARA had developed a set of principles that shaped its policy of administering relief. For instance, these working standards prescribed that food must be consumed by the recipient at the ARA feeding point in order to guarantee that the food was effectively reaching the designated person (see Fisher 1927:102-103).

Finally and most importantly, political interests of the Soviet side were seen as such and were taken into account. The basic agreement with the Soviet authorities – the Riga Agreement of 1921 – contains a number of stipulations by which the ARA directly addressed some allegedly underlying motives on the Soviet side. *Inter alia*, the Soviet authorities agreed that the ARA staff has "full liberty to come and go and move about Russia" (paragraph 2); "that the relief supplies are intended only for children and the sick" (paragraph 8); "that no individual receiving ARA rations shall be deprived of such local supplies as are given to the rest of the population" (paragraph 9); and that every step will be

---

[12] See McElroy (1992:75): "Hoover feared serious opposition to the relief bills in Congress because of hostility to the Bolsheviks, an economic downturn that had hit the United States in 1921, and the fact that the Harding administration had refused to raise veteran's health benefits as part of its drive to trim the federal budget. So he arranged for the Soviet government to let US press representatives into the famine districts so that they would send home reports on the desperation of the Russian people. Soon the newspapers of the United States were filled with accounts of the famine (...)."

taken "to insure that relief supplies belonging to the ARA will not go to the general adult population nor to the Army, Navy, or Government employees" (paragraph 10).[13]

In general, the Riga Agreement granted complete operational and financial independence to the ARA. In this fundamental respect, it differed from the agreement reached between the International Committee under Nansen and the Soviet government. This agreement placed the control of the Committee's operation in Russia with a committee of two persons based in Moscow, one member was to be nominated by the Soviet government (see Fisher 1927:65, Huntford 1998:506).

c) Results and Conclusions

According to various sources, between one and five million people lost their lives in the Russian famine (see Huntford 1998:514, Destexhe 1993:44). Ten million people are estimated to have been saved from death through ARA relief supplies distributed in 35,000 feeding centers.[14] It is widely acknowledged that the ARA mission in Soviet Russia was "an outstanding success" (Weissman 1974:202) in the history of humanitarian action. Destexhe (1993:43) names the Riga Agreement "a model treaty that no organization would dare to demand today". Hoover is referred to as a legendary pioneer of famine aid under unfavorable and politicized circumstances. Natsios (2001:238) explicitly recommends the ARA mission as a model for North Korea:

> Had the United States (...) implemented an aid program along the lines of Herbert Hoover's aid to the Soviet Union in the early 1920s, it could have helped the neediest North Koreans in a way that would have precluded Pyongyang from taking any benefit.

It has to be noted, however, that a decisive factor contributing to the uncontroversial success of the ARA mission was the fact that its Chairman was a member of the principle donor government. Without the permanent high-level support from Washington D.C., a number of obstacles such as the limitation of operational space, the issue of distribution control and diversion, and the sudden arrest of Russian ARA staff,

---

[13] The Riga Agreement is reprinted in Goldberg (1993:208-211).
[14] See Weissman (1974:199): "The ARA's claim that it sustained over ten million people at the height of its effort is not open to dispute. The Soviet government, through its own agencies, verified this figure and publicly acknowledged its accuracy many times."

would have been much more difficult to overcome.[15] The independence of non-governmental humanitarian actors from governmental donors is an issue of more recent times.

With regard to the way the main actors dealt with the variety of obligations and interests, it has to be stressed that the ARA took into consideration humanitarian obligation, political interests and organizational principles. The International Committee for Russian Relief, headed by Nansen, was clearly adopting a narrower approach by focusing only on the humanitarian imperative. In both cases, however, the ambiguity of aid becomes evident. The Committee was reproached for losing its independence, to the Soviets as well as to the Americans (see Huntford 1998:501).[16] With regard to Hoover's approach, Weissman (1974:19) notes that he "transformed famine relief into a resource rivaling propaganda, diplomacy, and military force as an instrument of policy. He succeeded in harnessing politics and famine relief for the most effective promotion of each".

To sum up, the case of Soviet Russia opened the debate surrounding aid as an accomplice of an undemocratic regime and an instrument of donor interests. Importantly, however, the crucial issue of proportionality played a minor role in famine aid for Russia. In a rare coalition of interests, the humanitarian actor, the donor and the recipient government were willing to distribute international aid to the most needy.[17]

---

[15] On these issues see Fisher (1927:120, 124-125, 199-200, 204). See also the letter of Walter Lyman Brown, ARA Director for Europe, to Hoover in which he commented on the Riga negotiations (27 August 1921. Reprinted in Goldberg 1993:213-214): "It appeared to us that the best method of handling was to elicit their viewpoints, put them up to you and let you come back with the heavy artillery, which we had every reason to believe would be brought into action. The artillery came with a bang and contributed very materially toward turning the trick".

[16] A number of authors unanimously criticize the Committee's work in Russia as rather inefficient, chaotic, and, above all, politically naïve. See Huntford (1998:500-515), Destexhe (1993: 40-46), Brauman (1995:41).

[17] An ARA official notes on the Riga negotiations: "For reasons that must have been political they [the Soviet negotiators] did not desire us to work in the cities of Moscow and Petrograd, but wanted us to confine our relief to the famine areas. (...) The whole underlying idea seemed to be a desire on their part to continue to bring food to the centers in which their power lies, even from districts adjoining the famine areas and from whence the surplus foodstuffs should go to the famine areas. To cover their abandonment of these areas that to them are politically unimportant they wanted to have us undertake the feeding in those regions" (reprinted in Goldberg 1993:215).

Therefore, the Russian experience shows that dilemma situations can effectively be avoided when political interests are in line with humanitarian obligations.

Notably, this coalition between political and humanitarian interests applied to the Volga region. The Ukraine, by contrast, which was also hit by the famine received less attention from Moscow. Ten years later, when the situation in the Ukraine was even worse, neither the Soviet nor the American or any other government felt obliged to avert the famine.[18] Therefore, not an alleged donor government priority on humanitarian concerns but the congruence of political and humanitarian interests seems to lie at the heart of the success of the ARA mission in Soviet Russia.

III.2 Biafra –
Founding Myth of 'Rebellious Humanitarianism'

For a variety of reasons, the Biafran famine (1968-70) is a turning point in the history of international famine relief. It was the first African famine to mobilize massive international aid, which, in addition, was organized by the ICRC and other non-governmental actors. Moreover, in terms of the dilemma of famine aid, the Biafran case differs in one basic respect from the famine aid to Russia 45 years earlier. Instead of an all-party consensus that wanted the international aid to go to the most needy, humanitarianism in Biafra faced the violation of the principle of proportionality by the political environment. Aid agencies had to deal with divergent political interests that merged in one single aspect: the denial of access.

a) Interests, Moral Obligations and Dilemmas

Nigeria gained independence in 1960 and covered a territory who's political borders where drawn up in 1914 by British colonial rulers. Economic disparities and conflicts along ethnic and religious lines dominated the first years of the new state's existence (see Goetz 2001:2). In 1967, the Eastern region's governor, Colonel Ojukwu, declared the secession of this region and the formation of the 'Republic of Biafra'. A mili-

---

[18] On the situation in the Ukraine in 1921-23 see Fisher 1927:261-265. On the famine in 1932-33 see M. Wayne Morris (1994): *Stalin's Famine and Roosevelt's Recognition of Russia*. Lanham, New York, London: University Press of America.

tary government that seized power in the rest of the country adopted a policy of uniting Nigeria. The result was a protracted civil war that lasted 30 months and killed about two million people. The international community, however, largely ignored this conflict. Matters changed when people were not only killed by bombs and bullets, but also by starvation.

In June 1968, Nigerian federal forces took Port Harcourt, Biafra's only supply line to the external world. What followed was a blockade maintained by federal forces in order to hinder any military supplies for the secessionists. The Biafran forces still controlled a territory that was home to eight million people, including two million refugees (or 'internally displaced persons' in today's parlance, Destexhe 1993:61). In August 1968, 5,000 people were reportedly dying daily as a result of famine (Destexhe 1993:65). In addition, according to the ICRC, one million people in the territory under federal control were also in urgent need of famine relief (Thompson 1990:63). Two options theoretically existed concerning the access for aid to the Biafran population: the establishment of a humanitarian land corridor – most appropriate to carry out an aid mission of the necessary size (see Destexhe 1993:61) - or an airlift.

The federal military government's policy pursued three main goals.[19] First, the military weakening of the secessionist forces by cutting all military supply lines. Second, to demonstrate its sovereignty as the government of a country that was struggling for unity. And third, provisioning aid primarily to the territories under its control. The government generally preferred the delivery of aid to Biafra by planes that had to go via Lagos to Biafra. With this, the federal authorities tried to achieve both goals, the control of the relief supplies and the visible exercise of their sovereignty. Federal Foreign Minister Arikpo made it clear that "no humanitarian consideration can justify the violation of our airspace" (quoted in Thompson 1990:105). In addition, in order to make sure that arm supply planes could not intermingle with relief planes, the Nigerian government opposed relief flights at night.

After Port Harcourt fell under federal control, the military situation of the Biafran forces was desperate. Arms and ammunition reached Biafra only via air. Thus, from a military perspective, relief planes crossing federal territory by night seemed a helpful protection for this military sup-

---

[19] For details see Hentsch (1973:52-55).

ply.[20] In addition to military considerations, international recognition of the 'Republic of Biafra' – only granted by a number of African states – was the main goal pursued by the Biafran leadership. In this respect, the famine played a crucial role. The Biafran famine was "the first televised famine in history" (Brauman 1995:59); pictures of starving children were broadcasted by international media and led to a wave of sympathy that accused the Nigerian government of genocide. As a result of the famine, Hentsch (1973:93) notes that "Biafra is born. Yesterday unknown, today a martyr". The famine became the "principle diplomatic resource of Biafra" (Destexhe 1993:64). From this perspective, the eradication of famine through a targeted and massive aid mission appeared to threaten the very existence of the 'Republic of Biafra'. On television, Ojukwu stated that "in the long term we have achieved quite a lot. No matter what one says, indeed, if the 14 million people, Biafrans, are killed, the notion of Biafra will persist until the end of time. That is an achievement".[21]

All in all, neither of the warring parties was willing to make humanitarian considerations a top priority. Their sets of interests converged in the refusal of a massive aid mission for the benefit of the vulnerable population in the enclave of Biafra. In addition, donors' policies on famine aid for Biafra and Nigeria were all but unanimous. Regardless of Cold War coalitions, Great Britain, the Soviet Union and other Eastern bloc countries supported the federal government's 'One-Nigeria-policy'. France and a number of African countries acted in favor of the Biafran cause. The US, the biggest donor of food aid, was internally split on the issue of aid to Biafra.[22] While the White House and Congress were more responsive to the public's call for massive humanitarian aid, the State Department put priority on the political stability in the region and was reluctant to support any activity that could result in political support for Biafra (see Thompson 1990:169-170). Thus, the US were not directly pushing for humanitarian access to famine areas and limited themselves to supporting mainly the ICRC. In the words of President Nixon, "the US policy will draw a sharp distinction between carrying out our moral obli-

---

[20] For a more detailed analysis of the Biafran leadership's policies see Hentsch (1973:55-59).

[21] *La Pitié Dangereuse*, a TV documentary by Rony Brauman and François Margolin, Arte, June 1996. Quoted in Terry 2000:67.

[22] For details see Thompson 1990.

gations to respond effectively to humanitarian needs and involving ourselves in the political affairs of others" (quoted in Thompson 1990:109).
Therefore, in contrast to their role in the Russian famine, the United
States were not willing to exert political pressure for the sake of humanitarian considerations.

Likewise, the countries that were supportive of the Biafran side did
not accord primary importance to humanitarian issues. France, being
the most important player on this side, provided military support to an
extent that, according to the CIA, enabled the Biafran forces to continue
fighting the war after the fall of Port Harcourt (see Thompson 1990:125).
Regarding its humanitarian engagement, the French government sent
the National Red Cross to Biafra. It did not, however, exert political
pressure on the Biafran leadership in favor of unhindered humanitarian
access to the famine-affected populations.

b) Dilemmas of Famine Aid in Biafra

Differing ways of behaving in a dilemma situation are illustrated by
the two main humanitarian actors in the Nigerian civil war: the ICRC
and Joint Church Aid (JCA), a consortium of international faith-based
NGOs. In many ways, the ICRC mission in this conflict was a new experience for the organization. It was the first time that the ICRC had been
engaged in a famine aid mission of that magnitude. Only since Biafra,
relief is one of the main fields of activity of the ICRC (see Destexhe
1993:65). The ICRC delegates tried to reach an agreement with the warring parties that guaranteed the effective provision of aid to the needy on
all sides. Notably, according to statements made by the Head Representative in Nigeria and its President, the ICRC seemed to assess the needs
as being of an equal size on both sides (see Thompson 1990:78). Generally, the ICRC preferred the establishment of a land corridor, or at least
the provisioning of food via air in a manner that respected its neutral,
humanitarian character. Thus, in order to avoid military supply planes to
intermingle with relief planes, the International Red Cross opposed an
airlift at night.

The ICRC tried to achieve its goals through negotiations. The organization's mandate and principles were perceived as not leaving room for
any other way, such as activities without governmental consent or a massive media campaign. The ICRC was praised by the Nobel Peace Prize
Committee in 1963 for its "complete neutrality", which means that gov-

ernments "have full confidence in its impartiality".[23] Neutrality in the
sense of secrecy is, as argued in earlier chapters, a self-imposed principle
of the ICRC that derives from the organization's specific mandate. The
consent of the warring parties is indispensable to visit prisoners of war
or transmit messages between family members separated by conflict. In
the Nigerian conflict, the ICRC was shaping its behavior largely in accordance with its concept of neutrality. Negotiations with the warring parties were lengthy, frustrating and rarely successful.[24] The federal as well
as the Biafran side were largely unwilling to make concessions, and the
Red Cross did not dispose of any decisive bargaining chip. At times, one
even had the impression that both warring parties were coordinating
their standpoints in order to decline ICRC's demands (see Hentsch
1973:58). The emphasis on negotiations out of respect for its organizational mandate meant that people in the Biafran enclave received no or
only very moderate aid for several months. The result was that international media heavily criticized the Red Cross for wasting time at the negotiation table while "food is rotting within 30 minutes' flight of starving
Biafrans".[25] This criticism, too, was a new experience for the ICRC since
the end of World War II.

Joint Church Aid adopted a different approach. The organization was
an *ad hoc* consortium of more than 40 catholic and protestant private
aid agencies. Well-established principles or traditional mandates played
no role for the simple reason that they were non-existent. According to
Destexhe (1993:65), JCA carried out its operations in a great enthusiastic
spirit, "but with an amateurism that was even greater". The churches
preferred action to negotiation and sympathy to neutrality. JCA argued
that vulnerability to famine in Biafra had to be understood in political
terms. In their view, the starving population of Biafra was the victim of a
genocidal policy of the federal government in Lagos. As a result, JCA was
prepared to deliberately take side in favor of the secessionists. The main
objective was the provision of massive aid to the enclave while keeping
distance from the federal government. In its explanation of famine,
JCA's analysis was therefore clearly based upon what we have called the

---

[23] Nobel lecture delivered on 11 December 1963. Found at www.nobel.se/peace/ laure-
ates/1963/red-cross-lecture.html (7 September 2002).
[24] For details see Hentsch (1973).
[25] *Evening Herald* (Dublin), 30 July 1968. Quoted in Hentsch (1973:110).

benefits paradigm and opted for an extrovert approach by refuting the principle of secrecy.

JCA ignored the federal authorities' claim for sovereignty and provided a total of 57,000 tons of food aid by air (Destexhe 1993:64). Following Biafra's request, the relief planes operated at night and did not stop on federal territory. Due to this *fait accompli,* the ICRC decided to give up its original demands and also took part in this airlift. The Red Cross' insistence on a land corridor became illusory since the airlift allowed the Biafran authorities to decline the ICRC demands.[26] The government in Lagos stressed that ICRC planes were operating at their own risks. Thus, JCA and ICRC accepted the Biafran conditions, "the former by conviction, the latter by necessity" (Hentsch 1973:169). ICRC contributed about 22,000 tons to the airlift that became the biggest operation of its kind since the Berlin blockade (Destexhe 1993:64).

c) Results and Conclusions

Compared to the Russian famine in the 1920s, Biafra was a more traumatic experience for international humanitarianism. As for the concrete humanitarian impact of this famine aid mission, the results were at best ambiguous. Regarding the ICRC, four times more aid has been delivered to the federal territory than to the Biafran enclave. A fact that, as noted above, was in striking contrast to the real needs (Destexhe 1993:62). The ICRC may have effectively addressed the needs on the federal side. Regarding the Biafran side, however, an estimation of the effects is "at a time more difficult and more painful" (Hentsch 1973:153).

Furthermore, both the ICRC and JCA were in no position to prevent their efforts being abused for the benefit of one side or the other. The federal government effectively prevented massive aid being provided to the Biafran side by keeping the ICRC at the negotiation table and without making concessions. As for the JCA, it provided aid to Biafra without setting any conditions on the secessionist leadership. Actually, the Biafran leadership did its best to intermingle military supply planes with relief planes. Pilots of both Red Cross and JCA planes later reported that

---

[26] See Hentsch (1973:168-169).

their cargo in fact had contained arms.[27] In short, humanitarian actors were partly unable and partly unwilling to avoid the accomplice role.

Aid agencies also played an ambiguous role in their relation with governmental donors. Public opinion pressed Western governments to become engaged in humanitarian action for the starving Biafran population. In a sense, in such a case just doing something may be more important than doing well. A representative of Catholic Relief Services (CRS) thus told the members of the US Senate committee on foreign relations that "because of governmental inaction, the religious-sponsored voluntary agencies became 'bootleggers of mercy' in the name of humanity" (quoted in Thompson 1990:78).

Most importantly, the Biafran experience led to the emergence of a new approach to dealing with the famine aid dilemma. In the tradition of JCA, neutrality as the respect for the sovereignty of states was rejected.[28] From this perspective, the Biafra experience has proven that "humanitarianism, contrasting with what the founders of the Red Cross had in mind, cannot be neutral" (Destexhe 1993:69). As a consequence, one of the main characteristics of this new generation of humanitarianism is the disrespect of sovereignty. Where universal humanitarian considerations reign supreme, no borders set by the sovereignty of nation states can be respected. Consequently, 'without borders' became the slogan of the movement, and Doctors Without Borders (MSF), founded in 1971 in France, became the prototype of this *sans-frontiérisme* or "rebellious humanitarianism" (Bouchet-Saulnier 2000).[29] The differences between both traditions of humanitarian action are illustrated in the awarding of the Nobel Peace Prize to those organizations that are the prototypes of the 'traditional' approach and the 'second generation' of humanitarianism: the International Red Cross in 1917, 1944 and 1963 and Doctors Without Borders (MSF) in 1999. In 1963, the Nobel Peace Prize Committee praised the Red Cross' "complete neutrality" and notes that "gov-

---

[27] Interview with Dieter Hannusch, member of the FAO/WFP missions to DPRK and former WFP official, Rome, 25 October 2001.

[28] See Destexhe (1993:62): "These churches are the unjustly unknown predecessors of Médecins Sans Frontières."

[29] It has to be added that some meanings of neutrality – namely the principle of not taking sides in a conflict – were not questioned by MSF. Thus, the MSF Charter says that "Médecins Sans Frontières observes neutrality and impartiality in the name of universal medical ethics and the right to humanitarian assistance and demands full and unhindered freedom in the exercise of its functions."

ernments, therefore, have full confidence in its impartiality".[30] In 1999, MSF was awarded the prize, one could say, for exactly the opposite, namely its practice "to form bodies of public opinion opposed to violations and abuses of power".[31]

It has to be noted that, in a sense, the creation of MSF was founded on a misleading assessment of the Biafra conflict. In 1969, the group of French doctors that worked with the French Red Cross in Biafra founded the 'International Committee Against the Genocide in Biafra'; this organization was one of the predecessors of MSF.[32] Actually, the sympathy with the Biafran cause and the conviction that the Lagos government was seeking to destroy the Biafran people, was present in the minds of the founding group of MSF, called "the Biafrans" (Siméant 2001:49). However, in retrospect, the former President of MSF France notes that

> at the very moment that one spoke of genocide, half of the Ibo population, i.e. seven million people, was living under Federal administration without any particular annoyances. And the very day when the Biafran army surrendered its arms, violence was brought to an end, and the officers were amnestied (Brauman 1996:22).

On the repeated reference to the Biafran 'genocide' as the founding myth of his organization, he continues: "it is perfectly understandable that one was wrong at that time. But that one continues to be wrong after 25 years, is rather sad" (Brauman 1996:23). Oxfam Great Britain argued in a similar way in the Biafran war as did JCA, and "predicted a humanitarian disaster which never occurred" (Fox 2001:281). Nicholas Stockton, former Head of Emergencies at Oxfam Great Britain refers to the agency's experience in Biafra: "The truth is we're very good at retrospective analysis but very bad at getting it right at the time or at predicting the future consequences of our actions" (quoted in Fox 2001:281).

Thus, the political engagement of a humanitarian actor in favor of the allegedly weak in Biafra was based on very shaky foundations concerning the crisis' political context. The fact that the extrovert approach needs to be based on solid political analysis – that possibly is not easy to achieve

---

[30] Nobel lecture delivered on 11 December 1963. Found at www.nobel.se/peace/ laureates/1963/red-cross-lecture.html (7 September 2002).

[31] Press release by the Norwegian Nobel Committee. Oslo, 15 October 1999.

[32] For the founding history of MSF see Siméant (2001:48-56).

at the time of an ongoing crisis - is also a lesson from the Biafran experience.

In a way, the Biafra famine led to the emergence of a new branch of humanitarianism opposite the ICRC and its concept of neutrality. For the ICRC, however, the Biafra mission gave no reason to question its principles. In fact, some authors argue that weaknesses and failures of the ICRC operation in the Nigerian conflict were due to compromises made on the principle of neutrality.[33] Furthermore, a number of authors recommend that the main lesson the ICRC should draw from the Biafran case is of technical rather than ethical nature, namely the improvement of its operational capacities in terms of relief aid (see Hentsch 1973:255-256, Goetz 2001:13).

III.3 Cambodia 1979-80: Competition and Dispute

From the beginning of the refugee crisis in 1979 until the repatriation mission led by the United Nations in 1992-93, a "total imbroglio" took place in the Thai-Cambodian border area (Destexhe 1993:108). Three kinds of aid missions were carried out in this period: famine relief in 1979-80, a long-term maintenance operation until 1991, and finally, a repatriation program as part of a multifaceted UN operation in 1992-93. This chapter will focus on the first phase, the famine aid to refugees along the Thai-Cambodian border in 1979-80, which was arguably "the greatest challenge to the international humanitarian system of the Cold War period" (Terry 2000:151).

The Vietnamese invasion of Cambodia in late 1978 caused a political stalemate in the region that lasted for 15 years. Vietnam replaced the Khmer rouge regime in Phnom Penh with a client government headed by Khmer rouge defector Heng Samrin. As Vietnamese troops marched westward across Cambodia, civilians and Khmer rouge troops fled before them to Thailand. The Khmer rouge, with the consent of the Thai government, gathered their forces in the border region in order to organize resistance to the new regime. On both sides of the border, the situation was reportedly dramatic. In summer 1979, the Cambodian government

---

[33] Delorenzi (1999:22-23) argues that the ICRC "was far from accustomed to the pressure of operating under the spotlight of the media and in competition with humanitarian associations that openly criticized its policy: certain aberrant policy decisions were taken as a direct consequence, for example its apparent policy bias towards the Biafran side which seriously undermined its relations with the Federal Government".

announced that 2.5 million people were threatened by famine. The political interests of the regional and global powers engaged in this crisis were complex. For humanitarianism, this complexity turned out to be fatal. With regard to the situation in Cambodia, Destexhe (1993:95) concludes that "the more profound a political disaster, the more necessary is humanitarian action, and the more ambiguous its results".[34]

a) Interests, Obligations and Dilemmas

The advance of Vietnamese troops towards the border of Thailand was perceived as a threat by the Thai government. Its main objective was to establish the *status ex ante,* i.e. the presence of an independent Cambodian state as a buffer between the two regional powers Thailand and Vietnam. According to a number of observers, the government in Bangkok therefore had an interest in supporting the military opposition to the new Cambodian regime installed by Vietnam. The biggest faction within this opposition were the Khmer rouge which were mainly supported by China. Thus, Thailand pursued an "open door policy" (Destexhe 1993:101) and not only tolerated the presence of the Khmer rouge on its territory but also provided military support. In order to prevent destabilizing effects within Thailand, the Khmer rouge were allowed to gather in the border region only. The Thai government thereby created a buffer between Thailand and the approaching Vietnamese forces. Altogether, the provision of aid to the Khmer rouge camps was politically opportune for the political leadership of Thailand. Humanitarian considerations that would have meant delivering primarily aid to the civilian population, however, were not necessarily in line with these political objectives.

As far as the humanitarian situation in Cambodia was concerned, the Phnom Penh authorities had an interest in alleviating suffering, since this would have earned it some legitimacy as a government. On the international scene, Vietnam and the new regime in Phnom Penh were not granted this legitimacy. In September 1979, the UN General Assembly decided that the UN seat of Cambodia continues to be held by the Khmer rouge.

The main political objective of Hanoi and Phnom Penh was the complete defeat of the strongest opposition force, the Khmer rouge. How-

---

[34] For the most comprehensive studies on the humanitarian and political crisis see Reynell (1989) and Shawcross (1984).

ever, any kind of support to the camps under the control of the Khmer rouge ran counter to this overall goal and this included humanitarian aid. In the words of Hun Sen, the Cambodian Foreign Minister, "our people would prefer to eat grass or to die than to share aid with Pol Pot" (quoted in Shawcross 1984:150).

On the donor side, the Eastern bloc provided some aid, China was engaged in military supply to the Khmer rouge, but the main funding for international humanitarian assistance came from Western countries. The largest single donor, funding one third of the border programs, was the United States (see Reynell 1989:57). Compared to the long time critical stance towards the Khmer rouge upheld by the US, its government's animosity to communist Vietnam prevailed. Thus, assistance to the Cambodian refugees was one goal of US policy; support to the Khmer resistance forces was another (see Terry 2000:184). However, the United States refrained from directly providing bilateral aid. According to a State Department official, "we wanted the ICRC and UNICEF to do the feeding because we did not want it to be a US effort" (quoted in Mason/Brown 1983:159).

The complexity of interests involved in this crisis resembles the situation in Biafra to the extent that the alleviation of human suffering on all sides did not coincide with the political interests of any of the political actors involved.

b) Famine Relief on Both Sides of the Border

Humanitarian needs existed to a great extent on both sides of the border. Thus, the principle of impartiality and proportionality obliged humanitarian actors to become active on both sides of the Thai-Cambodian border. But any support to the Khmer rouge controlled refugee camps on Thai territory was taken as an affront by the Cambodian government. This meant that the impartial delivery of aid to the needy on both sides ran counter to the political will of the Cambodian authorities. "The choice, then, was not between a political position and a neutral position but between two political positions: one active and the other by default" (Brauman 1998:181).

As a result, the famine aid efforts developed into two distinctive aid operations. The first addressed the needs of the refugee population living in territories along the border that were under the control of Khmer rouge and other opposition forces. The second was engaged in famine relief to the population inside Cambodia. Aid organizations had to decide which operation they were going to support. On both sides, however, their operational space was very limited.

As for the decision on which side to support, political preferences among some aid agencies played a certain role. Some agencies, such as Catholic Relief Services, advocated an anti-communist position and were thus more willing to provide aid to the camps in the border region. Others, such as Oxfam GB, were more sympathetic to the communist rulers in Phnom Penh and to famine relief to the Cambodian side (see Brauman 1998:179, Terry 2000: 190).

Two of the main humanitarian actors engaged in this crisis, ICRC and UNICEF, attempted to organize assistance on both sides of the conflict. The Cambodian government laid down three conditions: a detailed description of relief goods and dates of delivery, the distribution of food aid under the total control of Cambodian authorities and, finally, ICRC's and UNICEF's covenant not to deliver aid to the population under Khmer rouge control "under the cover of so-called 'aid to all parties'" (quoted in Shawcross 1984:147). This 'aid to all parties', however, reflects the principle of impartiality as a core obligation of humanitarian action. Therefore, ICRC and UNICEF regarded the proposed agreement as unacceptable and refused to sign.

Oxfam agreed. The British NGO accepted the conditions and agreed to lead an NGO consortium that was designed to carry out a relief program in Cambodia costing about GB£2 million a month. In addition, Oxfam was told to stay separate from the ICRC/UNICEF program in the border region and to refuse any cooperation. Oxfam also agreed to this condition and apologized for the fact that the first Oxfam shipment still might be carrying UNICEF supplies (see Shawcross 1984:150-151).[35]

In terms of working conditions, aid agencies faced a number of obstacles in both relief operations. In summer 1979, Cambodian authorities claimed that up to three million people were about to starve. Although

---

[35] See also Black (1992:226): "he [Brian Walker, director of Oxfam GB] agreed to the demand that Oxfam would give no aid to those under Khmer Rouge control. He was under great pressure, keen to 'break the logjam', confident that other NGOs would deliver aid at the border and that it was therefore unnecessary for Oxfam to do so. Nevertheless, this agreement to drop the humanitarian principle UNICEF and ICRC were insisting upon cut the ground from under their negotiation position. It was also in breach of Oxfam's own principles and its policy towards victims of conflict, a policy articulated only months before".

not able to conduct comprehensive assessment studies,[36] aid organizations accepted these figures and, along with international media, were using the term 'holocaust' in order to describe the situation inside Cambodia.[37] "The warning that there could be 'two million dead by Christmas' began to echo around the world like a curse" (Shawcross 1984:124). Some months later, however, Cambodian and Vietnamese officials denied the existence of a "so-called famine that the West is playing up" and declared that the food crisis had been relieved thanks to the generous and unconditional aid given by the socialist allies (Shawcross 1984:154). This polemics – questioning the very existence of a famine - left the aid organizations in a state of confusion.

Generally, the same goes for the distribution and monitoring of food aid. "No one knows anything", noted the ICRC delegate in Phnom Penh in 1980 (quoted in Shawcross 1984:367). The number of expatriate staff was kept to a minimum by Cambodian authorities; visas were issued in direct proportion to the budgets of the agencies (see Terry 2000:185). In sum, aid organizations working in Cambodia were not able to verify where exactly their aid was going. The situation was similar for the aid operation in the border region. Some agencies such as ICRC and UNICEF tried to specifically address the needs of women and children by distributing aid directly to the affected population. These attempts were undermined by WFP's policy, which accepted the Thai army as the distributor of food aid (see Destexhe 1993:106, Terry 2000:170). In addition, aid workers were hindered by both sides from directly communicating with the population they were trying to assist. With regard to relief work in Cambodia, Terry (2000:192, also see Heininger 1997:118-119) summarizes:

---

[36] See Shawcross 1984:124: "Every Westerner who was allowed to make a brief, strictly controlled visit to Phnom Penh in July and August 1979 was overwhelmed by the extent of the destruction, by Khmer Rouge brutality and by the country's needs. On the basis of what they all saw it would have been humanly impossible for them to question the government's claim that three million Cambodians had died under the Khmer Rouge and that famine now threatened to wipe out over half the four million survivors".

[37] See *The New York Times*, 6 October 1979. The article states that the suffering of the Cambodian population "justifies a word that should not be cheapened by overuse: holocaust" (quoted in Shawcross 1984:153).

Organisations usually professing support to 'grass roots organisations' and 'proximity to the victims' found themselves working exclusively with members of the government from their offices in hotels reserved for foreigners. Cambodians were forbidden to speak to the 'imperialist spies' and aid organisations allocated finance to construction projects with little human dimension.

Aid agencies dealt with these limitations to their operational space in differing ways. As was the case in the Nigerian civil war, working principles provided a basic guideline for the ICRC. Consequently, the ICRC was not prepared to provide aid 'at any cost'. It did not accept some of the working conditions as formulated by the Cambodian government. After months of negotiations with the Thai authorities and Vietnamese attacks on the refugee camps in the border region, the ICRC closed its food aid program. UNICEF decided to continue after the Thai authorities had agreed to a reduced program designed to support only women (see Terry 2000:176).

Oxfam's behavior, in a sense, resembles the strategy followed by JCA in Biafra. Faced with the choice between the respect of well-established principles of humanitarian action, such as neutrality and impartiality, on one side and the immediate delivery of aid on the other, JCA and Oxfam preferred the latter. The primary argument in support of this choice is the duty to relieve human suffering. In Cambodia as well as in Biafra, this decision that we have called the victim-centered approach was accompanied by a deliberate partiality, based on very doubtful analyses.[38] Shawcross (1984:424) comments on the parallels between Biafra and Cambodia:

> The nearest parallel to what happened in Cambodia in 1979-80 is Biafra in 1968-69. Then too holocaust and genocide were the principal refrains. Then too their constant invocation for propaganda purposes had vast emotional impact throughout the Western world (...). In Biafra, too, the memory of the holocaust and a determination to prevent it led to some suspension of critical judgment.

A further way of dealing with the dilemma of famine relief was introduced into humanitarianism in the Cambodian crisis: public advocacy. In 1980, MSF and two other NGOs (Action Internationale Contre la

---

[38] See Destexhe (1993:99): "In Biafra, the churches have chosen some of these principles in order to respond more quickly to the emergency. Oxfam followed this approach, but without knowing that the basic assumptions are wrong".

Faim, AICF, today: Action Contre la Faim, ACF and the International Refugee Committee) organized a 'march for the survival of Cambodia' along the Thai-Cambodian border, an event later named by former President of MSF France Rony Brauman "our first tug of war *("bras de fer")* with a government" (Brauman 1996:28). The organizers aimed to draw international attention to Cambodia and to help "open the eyes of the public to the true nature of the Phnom Penh regime" (Brauman 1998:180-181). It did not, however, contribute to an essential improvement of the situation. Terry (2000:190) comments on the campaign: "Although fairly successful in publicising the lack of access to the Cambodian population, the march added to the propaganda war of political powers and further polarised the aid community".

c) Results and Conclusions

In view of the lack of access and reliable data, the humanitarian effects of the aid operations in Thailand and Cambodia in 1979-80 are most difficult to measure. Shawcross' study, being the most in depth source in this respect, shows that the amount of food aid that aid workers considered to be distributed to the needy in Cambodia does not correspond to the amount of food reckoned necessary to avert famine.[39] However, there is no evidence that large numbers of people actually died of famine. Shawcross therefore concludes that "the threat of famine was exaggerated in 1979" (1984:370).

Concerning the refugee camps in the border region, most observers conclude that the provision of aid helped to consolidate the Khmer rouge's control over the civilian population. According to a UNICEF monitoring report, 30 percent of relief supply went directly to the Khmer rouge soldiers (cited in Mason and Brown 1983:140). Inside the camps, the distribution of food and medicine was used as an instrument of power and control (see Terry 2000:161). In sum, "humanitarian aid, os-

---

[39] For instance, according to Shawcross (1984:369) an FAO official "had recently traveled around ten provinces, and his figures had shown that 'in certain provinces distribution has been negligible, sometimes as little as 200 grams per person per month'. This was exactly what many villagers told me on my own trips around the countryside". With regard to another study cited by Shawcross, it is noted that "this would mean well under 5,000 tons a month – again nowhere near the 30,000 tons a month that the Joint Mission had reckoned necessary to stave off famine at the end of 1979" (Shawcross 1984:369).

tensibly given to people in need because they are members of a shared humanity, helped to revive and sustain a military force which showed the least regard for humanity" (Terry 2000:195).

Some aid organizations publicly admitted the risks of this aid operations, others did not. Some actors deliberately took a political stance, others tried to uphold the principle of impartiality. Some attempted to exert pressure on the political actors responsible for the restriction of the humanitarian space, others accepted their conditions. Again, humanitarianism was in no position and in parts not willing to push through the respect for its principles. Moreover, the Cambodian experience illustrates the variety of convictions and approaches among humanitarian actors that resulted in open dispute and further undermined their bargaining power. This polarization of humanitarianism came to a head a few years later in the Ethiopian famine.

III.4 Famine Aid and Population Transfer: Ethiopia 1984-85

In 1995, ten years after the famine relief mission to Ethiopia, representatives of some of the aid agencies which had been engaged in this aid mission met in Addis Ababa. The final statement of this meeting summarizes:

> It took ten years to reflect on the 1984-85 famine because issues are contentious. The discussion was thus heated at times, reflecting divergence of opinion between those wishing to explore theory and those wanting to focus on practice; those who see their actions as neutral and those who believe them to be inherently political. (...) Concerning some issues sharply diverging opinions and complimentary views were forwarded and remain. It was strongly felt that it is the least we can do, in honoring the victims of the 1984-85 disaster, to have frank and open debate about how and why they died.[40]

In fact, the Ethiopian famine of 1984-85 triggered an unprecedented amount of controversy among humanitarian actors. In particular, the debate opposed UN agencies and MSF and focused on the effects of aid

---

[40] *The Addis Ababa Statement on Famine in Ethiopia, "Learning from the Past to Prepare for the Future"*, 18 March 1995. Found at www.sas.upenn.edu/African_Studies/ Hornet/Ben_InterAF.html (3 June 2002).

on the population transfer programs undertaken by the Ethiopian government. For the first time, aid agencies were publicly criticizing each other for their behavior in a famine situation. In contrast to the Cambodian experience, not a deliberate political partiality of humanitarianism was at stake, but the allegation that a silent, naïve complicity of aid passively supported a government's inhumane policy.

The 1984-85 famine resulted from a variety of factors. In terms of food availability decline, the collectivization and restructuring of agriculture in the aftermath of the coming into power of Major Mengistu Haile Mariam in 1974 who installed a socialist-style political system was one important factor. Furthermore, the war between the Ethiopian government and forces in the north of the country seeking independence, namely Eritrea and Tigray, had devastating effects on the country's food production. Thus, a drought that affected the entire Sahel in 1983-84 had particularly negative effects on the Ethiopian harvest (see Brauman 1998:182-183).

The famine mainly affected the northern regions of the country and is believed to have killed between 500,000 and one million people (Black 1992:257). It brought about famine relief activities that were the largest until that time: US$1,2 billion were raised and allocated in 1985 alone (Destexhe 1993:114, Clay and Holcomb 1986:2).

a) Interests, Obligations and Dilemmas

Officially, drought and the failure of the West to provide aid in time were declared the causes of famine.[41] In order to move people from "traditional drought-prone areas" in the north to the southwest of the country, the Ethiopian government set up a population transfer program that aimed to 'resettle' 1.5 million people. The population transfer was supposed to be accomplished by the end of 1985. The 'resettlement' from

---

[41] Prior to fall 1984, the government did not publicly admit or comment on the existence of the ongoing famine. According to a number of authors, this policy was due to the tenth anniversary of the coming into power of Mengistu and the establishment of the Workers' Party of Ethiopia in September 1984 (see, for instance, Clay and Holcomb 1986:29, Brauman 1998:182). Without raising the attention of international media, however, the Ethiopian government already informed UN agencies and potential donor governments in March 1984 about the expected gravity of the famine and presented a request for 450,000 tons of food aid. Due partly to distrust and their own miscalculations, the donors' reply was very modest (see Black 1992:259).

north to south was not new to Ethiopian society and had been undertaken under preceding regimes. In 1984, Ethiopian authorities presented
the ongoing 'resettlement' program as the means to eradicate famine.
The program was introduced to international funding donors in this way
(see Clay and Holcomb 1986:26-31). Moreover,

> the initial announcement of the resettlement program as a cure for
> famine was accompanied by assurances that relocation would be
> voluntary and that families would be moved intact. Relief and
> Rehabilitation Commission (RRC) officials, in interviews with the
> press, reported that settlers were being sent to fertile, unoccupied
> regions and that each family would be given 10 hectares of land to
> farm as they chose (Clay and Holcomb 1986:33).

In 1985, testimonies by refugees who had fled from Ethiopia to Sudan
were recorded and were published the following year (Clay and Holcomb
1986). The study provides an insight into the circumstances of the 'resettlement' program and throws light on its underlying motives. The
interviewees unanimously reported that they were being forced to leave
their homes (1986:86). Some reported that, on the way to the southwest,
they were deliberately separated from their family members (1986:92).
Moreover, the official claim that the famine was the main motive for 'resettlement' appears questionable. Clay and Holcomb (1986:86-87) note
that people suspected of having a particularly large following for the Ti-
grean People's Liberation Front (TPLF) were transferred from relatively
productive areas that were close to Tigray. Furthermore, many of those
interviewed who were themselves forced to 'resettlement' reported that
large numbers of people died during the deportation, either in holding
camps or during transport.[42]

The study is based upon interviews with 277 people. No reliable data
is available that could draw a more comprehensive picture and could
allow one to crosscheck the figures given by Clay and Holcomb. How-

---

[42] See Clay and Holcomb (1986:89): "In November 1984, when the Mersa camp had
nearly 5,000 people, from 25 to 50 people died each day. By December, when the
camp's population had grown to between 20,000 and 30,000 people, those interviewed who were in the camp at the time reported that nearly 100 died each day. Most
people who passed through the camp at Mekele reported that about five out of every
1,000 died each day. Those interviewed had passed through Mekele from early November until the end of December (...). It is not clear from the reports whether the
captured individuals' malnourished states or the camp conditions (sleeping outside,
little food or water) contributed more to the deaths".

ever, in view of the recorded testimonies, the official declarations of the government concerning the population transfer have to be seen as an attempt to cover up the political nature of the program. With regard to the reports of those who had been 'resettled', the breaking of the people's resistance to the central government appears as the most plausible motive behind the population transfer efforts.

The government's declaration of intent caused an immediate reaction by the rebel movements of the north (TPLF and Oromo Liberation Front, OLF). In a joint statement, both groups denounced the 'resettlement' program as a politically motivated endeavor that aimed to break the support for their movements. In addition, the statement accused the central government of coercing people to take part in the population transfer program (Clay and Holcomb 1986:29).

Ethiopia's socialist allied countries followed the government's request to support the 'resettlement' activity. For this purpose, the Soviet Union delivered cargo aircrafts, trucks and other transportation devices to the government, which did not dispose of the logistics necessary to carry out the program (see Clay and Holcomb 1986:31).

As for the policy of Western donor countries, media and public opinion played a very important role. The public was mobilized in a manner that surpassed the reaction to the Biafran or Cambodian famines. In October 1984, British television carried a report that was subsequently shown by 425 TV stations all over the world. "Western audiences watched in glazed disbelief as children with ravaged faces and stick-like limbs died before their eyes" (Black 1992:257).[43] Newspapers and TV stations launched fund raising campaigns, the most important campaign being 'Band Aid' organized by the Irish pop singer Bob Geldof which raised GB£50 million in 1985 (Black 1992:261). Notably, Western media gave the impression that drought and underdevelopment were the primary causes of the famine. The war played a minor role in Western press coverage (see Clay and Holcomb 1986:4-5). All in all, domestic public opinion urged Western governments to provide large-scale humanitarian assistance to Ethiopia.

---

[43] The report (BBC, 23 October 1984) began with this often cited commentary: "Dawn, and as the sun breaks through the piercing chill of night on the plain outside Korem, it lights up a biblical famine, now, in the 20th century. This place, say workers here, is the closest thing to hell on earth" (quoted in Black 1992:257).

With regard to the 'resettlement' program, however, a number of Western governments took a skeptical stance. The United States and the European Economic Community (EEC) expressed their concern about the population transfer and decided not to fund projects in the 'resettlement' zones. However, these statements had no real effect since several countries, such as Italy and Canada, did finance projects in these areas (see Brauman 1998: 185, Jansson 1990:67, Clay and Holcomb 1986:34). One former WFP official who had worked in the Ethiopian famine thus concludes: "donors did not want to know the truth".[44]

As a result, the massive provision of international famine aid was deemed necessary by both, recipient government and the vast majority of donors.

b) Famine Relief and Population Transfers

NGOs and UN agencies had a specific mandate in Ethiopia. Due to international public opinion and an unprecedented flow of private funds, the Ethiopian famine was "an extraordinary source of legitimacy for NGOs. It was the moment when, more than at any time before, they appeared as veritable actors" (Brauman 1996:31). As for the UN, its specific position resulted from the fact that many of the donor governments had poor relations with the government of Ethiopia. A special UN office for the relief operation in Ethiopia was installed in Addis Ababa that was headed by a Special Representative of the UN Secretary General. This office reportedly had privileged access to the political leadership of Ethiopia (see Borton 1995:31).

Aid agencies active in famine relief established feeding centers to distribute food and provide medical assistance. This work was subject to a number of restrictions. Aid workers had no influence on the location of feeding centers and were not allowed to travel or to set up programs in the areas beyond the centers. The distribution of food was carried out by the aid organizations but the authorities determined who qualified for admission to the feeding centers. Aid agencies did not publicly complain about these working conditions (see Clay and Holcomb 1986:3). It was the 'resettlement' program that raised concern in some organizations

---

[44] Interview with Dieter Hannusch, member of the FAO/WFP missions to DPRK since 1996 and former WFP official, Rome, 25 October 2001.

and unleashed the controversy among the aid agencies active in Ethiopia.

Aid workers did not have comprehensive information concerning the 'resettlement' program at their disposal. In view of official declarations, aid agencies had differing opinions. Some considered the population transfer a useful means to fight famine, others had no opinion or criticized it privately. In any case, aid agencies considered the government's program none of their business (see Brauman 1998:185-186). During their presence and work in the feeding centers, however, aid workers witnessed the employment of force against people in the centers who were about to be transported to the southwest. As a result, aid workers started to question the official presentation of the program and also questioned the sense of their own doing. Some were convinced that their aid was being abused as a lure in order to gather people and force them to participate in the 'resettlement' program (see Destexhe 1993:114, Brauman 1998:187).

The UN office in Addis Ababa, under the leadership of Special Representative Kurt Jansson, opposed these views. After the end of the mission, Jansson explained his position in a book in which he heavily criticized "inexperienced NGO workers" for making these allegations (Jansson 1990:24). He notes that some NGOs

> tended to apply Western standards and were appalled at the conditions they saw. They were not used to seeing watchmen in the camps using sticks to control large crowds. But in Ethiopia practically every young man and young boy constantly carries a stick which serves many purposes (Jansson 1990:24).

The description of the 'resettlement' program as a brutal means of warfare against the north was incompatible with Jansson's understanding of the Ethiopian leadership and of Chairman Mengistu in particular. Jansson describes his impression of Mengistu, who was later accused of genocide, war crimes and crimes against humanity by the Ethiopian justice, as one of "intelligence, quiet dignity, reserve and great courtesy" (1990:29). In Jansson's view, Mengistu's willingness to cooperate with the UN reflects his "deep concern for the fate of his own people" (1990:31). When an NGO reported in April 1985 that people had been forced by the Ethiopian army to leave a camp in the northwest, Jansson, following Mengistu's request, issued a statement in which he presented the official version of the government.[45] On the 'resettlement' program, Jansson notes (1990:64):

> The resettlement of people from drought-prone and ecologically degraded areas in the northern regions to more fertile areas in the southwest of the country is considered by agricultural specialists as a necessary aspect of Ethiopia's economic and social development.

Jansson thus approves the program as such and merely criticizes that "in practice it worked badly" (1990:65). Notably, he argues in an entirely Malthusian way by claiming that "rapid population growth and primitive methods of cultivation continued to aggravate the situation to the point that food production could not even sustain the peasant population" (1990:64). Put briefly, Jansson's and thus the UN's approach to dealing with the "politically charged atmosphere in Ethiopia" was "based on trust and confidence" (Jansson 1990:76).

Most NGOs did not publicly comment on the population transfer program. One exception was MSF. In the camp where the aid agency was mainly active, MSF staff observed that food distributions were authorized only to those who agreed to being transferred to the south. According to MSF, blankets and part of the food supplies were confiscated from those who did not (Brauman 1998:184). MSF decided to publicly denounce these practices and demanded the conditioning of aid in order to prevent it being instrumentalized. Brauman (1998:188) summarizes the MSF view on the role NGOs in Ethiopia: "Although the NGOs were clearly not responsible for the resettlement policy, it is equally clear that their silence made them passive accomplices". Being the sole protestor, MSF was expelled from Ethiopia in December 1985. In mid-1986, after 600,000 people had been relocated, the government halted the 'resettlement' program. In MSF's view, this was due to its "noisy departure"

---

[45] See Jansson (1990:61): "Chairman Mengistu confirmed that the action at Ibenat had been taken by local officials and that neither he nor members of his government had authorised it. He stressed that he neither agreed with nor approved of it and that such actions would not be allowed to recur; appropriate measures would be taken against the local officials responsible (...). At the end of our meeting I said to Chairman Mengistu that, since the international uproar continued, it was essential for him to issue a statement confirming the position he had taken (...). He added that on the basis of our meeting he would prefer that I do it, which I did, in a statement to the news media the same day and it was widely published in the international press".

(Destexhe 1993:121) that led donor governments to suspend their funding.[46] However, the program resumed in November 1987.[47]

According to Destexhe (1993:120), the majority of those NGOs who preferred to remain silent privately shared MSF's criticism. However, a number of NGOs (Mercy Corps, Church World Services, Save the Children, World Vision) called MSF's argumentation in a joint statement "an affrontery to truth" and stated that aid agencies involved in the aid effort "have every right to be proud of what is widely recognized as the greatest humanitarian effort in recent memory" (quoted in Jansson 1990:77).[48]

It has to be noted that the majority of NGOs were reluctant to get involved in relief and rehabilitation work in the 'resettlement' areas. The first NGO that agreed to work in these areas was a new and small Austrian organization, funded and run by Karlheinz Böhm, a well-known actor. Likewise, Geldof was willing to finance aid projects in the southwest, arguing that the needs in this region were imminent and demanded assistance. Confronted with the accomplice reproach, Geldof replied that he would have tried to mitigate the suffering in Nazi concentration camps if he had had the power to do so (see Destexhe 1993:123). Thus, in Geldof's perspective, as long as people are in need one has the duty to act, and so no ethical dilemma exists.

c) Results and Conclusions

The balance of famine relief to Ethiopia in 1984-85 is ambivalent. Some authors claim that the relief operation was an unprecedented success that "kept alive around seven million" (Black 1992:257). Jansson cites sources including the US General Accounting Office that highlight the efficiency of the operation, claiming that diversion and corruption were as good as non-existent (1990:56-57). However, even though international aid might have reached the designated recipients, the question

---

[46] See *Ethiopie 1984 – Une catastrophe annoncée,* found at www.paris.msf.org, (19 December 2001).

[47] See Federal Research Division of the Library of Congress: *Ethiopia. A Country Study,* Washington D.C.: Library of Congress, 1991.

[48] Jansson (1990:77) comments on MSF's behavior: "The result of all this was that MSF is totally isolated from the rest of the large NGO community, and its credibility is seriously undermined. Given this fact, the longer-term effect of MSF's action will have only a nuisance value. But it demonstrated how easily irresponsible individuals can create a nuisance through the media which do not take the trouble to check the facts".

remains as to how far the most needy were among those who qualified for international assistance. In this respect, Duffield (1994:62-63) notes that over 90 percent of the aid supplies went to government territory where actually only 22 percent of the population at risk lived.[49]

In retrospect, famine aid in Ethiopia appeared to be an important instrument used by the government in order to carry through its 'resettlement' program that as such was part of the warfare against rebel movements in northern territories. Testimonies show that people unwilling to take part in this program were taken to holding camps when they went to feeding centers to get food (Clay and Holcomb 1986:85). Thus, in Ethiopia, the situation described in earlier chapters as the accomplice scenario became reality. As was the case in Cambodia and Biafra, humanitarian action largely failed to live up to its principles.

As noted earlier, whenever their principles are threatened by the political surroundings, humanitarian actors face three divergent sets of obligations that stem from the existence of human suffering, from the political environment and from an agency's mandate and principles. A number of actors were primarily inclined to the first obligation and opted for a victim-centered perspective that largely ignored political realities. In the Ethiopian famine, the famous saying "a hungry child knows no politics" was coined (see Duffield 1994:63). The victim-centered view helped to refute criticisms and to blame those who stopped their aid activities in Ethiopia of immoral behavior. For instance, the former President of MSF France reports that, when he was confronting the UN representative in Addis Ababa with MSF's observations of forced population movements, the UN official accused him of "spreading a future famine over Ethiopia. I was found guilty of the following deaths of children" (Brauman 1996:62).

At the same time, an aid agency made the choice to exert pressure on the recipient government that was held responsible for the famine aid

---

[49] "At the end of 1984, aid officials estimated that the Ethiopian government had access to only 22 per cent of at risk civilians. Despite this recognition, over 90 per cent of donated resources went to the government or NGOs working in government territory. Publicly, though, the major multilaterals were putting a different gloss on the issue of access. The UN and ICRC alleged in mid-1985 that the Relief and Rehabilitation Commission of the Ethiopian government could reach 80 per cent of the Tigrayan population, and 76 per cent of civilians in Eritrea. Throughout the period, main stream media coverage helped perpetuate the erroneous view that people in Front-controlled territories were being assisted through town based distributions in government held areas".

dilemma. For the first time, a humanitarian organization opted for the extrovert approach of dealing with moral conflicts and was prepared to stop its aid in order to bring about the change of a government's policy. In retrospect, neither the victim-centered nor the extrovert strategies overcame the dilemma. MSF tried to address the causes of the dilemma, namely the policy of the Ethiopian government. But unlike the ARA in Soviet Russia in the 1920s donors had no major political interest in pressuring the recipient government into accepting principles of International Humanitarian or Human Rights Law.

One striking feature of famine relief in Ethiopia is the apparent unwillingness of humanitarian actors to question the surrounding and, ultimately, the sense of their work. Famine aid was largely perceived as a technical, apolitical endeavor that did not require political analysis or ethical decision. In 1995, the Addis Ababa Statement on Famine in Ethiopia says:

> It was strongly felt by some that the technical and managerial aspects of famine response should not be allowed to obscure or indeed replace a frank analysis of the political dimension of famine disasters (...). While a humanitarian, technocratic approach, based on improved procedures and largely funded by foreign aid could facilitate the prevention of famine in Ethiopia, it is at the same time necessary to move beyond this approach to a strategy of empowering the people to prevent famine through political accountability of all actors to the peoples of Ethiopia in recognition of their fundamental political, economic and human rights.[50]

Conclusion

The famine relief missions presented above provide empirical evidence for a number of hypotheses described in earlier chapters. Generally, moral obligations deriving from humanitarian ethics can collide with the interests of political actors on recipient and donor side. It is this collision between humanitarian obligations and political considerations that lies at the heart of the dilemma of humanitarian action.

---

[50] *The Addis Ababa Statement on Famine in Ethiopia, "Learning from the Past to Prepare for the Future"*, 18 March 1995. Found at www.sas.upenn.edu/African_Studies/ Hornet/Ben_InterAF.html (3 June 2002).

The famines in Soviet Russia, Biafra, Cambodia and Ethiopia all illustrate that political factors play a major role in the genesis and management of famines. In all the studied cases, humanitarianism had to act in a politically charged environment. Therefore, famine relief is particularly prone to moral dilemmas since "the more profound a political disaster, the more necessary is humanitarian action, and the more ambiguous its results" (Destexhe 1993:95).

The discussion of the case studies focused on three issues: the relation of vulnerability and famine relief to politics, the behavior of aid agencies in moral dilemma situations and the effect of their behavior on the outcome of the relief mission. As for the political dimension of famine aid efforts, relief missions in Biafra, Cambodia and Ethiopia illustrate the risk of aid being abused for the political or military benefit of an authority in place. Whereby the aid was used as an accomplice in various ways: as a cover for military supply (Biafra), as a power instrument (distribution of aid items in refugee camps, Cambodia) and as a lure and source of legitimacy for human rights violations (population transfer, Ethiopia).

In Biafra, Cambodia and Ethiopia, core principles of humanitarian action (impartiality, proportionality) were not in line with the political or military interests of the recipient side. As for the donor governments, the incentive to provide aid largely pushed aside the consideration of principles. Put differently, in view of domestic public opinion – mobilized by media coverage of the human suffering – the delivery of aid was more important than the insistence on impartial and proportional distribution. One exception in this regard is the relief mission in Soviet Russia 1921-23. Here, the otherwise opposed objectives of recipient and donor governments converged in one decisive point: the effective relief of human suffering. This congruence of political interests and humanitarian obligations explains that US financed relief efforts effectively addressed the needs of the most vulnerable population groups.

Humanitarian actors adopted differing ethical approaches to famine relief missions. Thanks to its particular link to the US government, the ARA was able to exert pressure on the recipient authorities and was thus in a position to influence and enhance the operational space. In Cambodia and Ethiopia, a mainly extrovert approach also prevailed in the developing 'sans-frontiérisme' branch of humanitarianism, but led to rather ambivalent results. In both cases, aid agencies could not achieve respect for principles of humanitarian action on the part of political authorities. The witnessing and publicly denouncing of human rights violations was one component of the extrovert approach in these cases. The reasoning of MSF illustrates that the promotion of human rights is not being seen equally important than the provision of humanitarian aid. Instead, the publicly denouncing of human rights violations is a tool that serves humanitarian goals, namely the respect for principles of humanitarian action. The former President of MSF France points out that "when the humanitarian space is being limited by a politics of terror, the only arm at the disposal of aid workers is the liberty of speech" (Brauman 1995:103).[51]

Established principles and mandates played an important role in the behavior of the ICRC in Biafra and Cambodia (introvert approach). An action-focused strategy (victim-centered approach) prevailed for agencies such as Joint Churches Aid in Biafra and Oxfam in Cambodia. In some cases, the diversity of approaches led to controversy and open dispute among aid organizations.

To a considerable degree, the moral integrity of an aid mission depends on the congruence of political and humanitarian considerations. Humanitarian actors can hardly effect this politico-humanitarian congruence. In other words, the primary factor that leads to moral dilemmas is beyond the influence of humanitarian organizations. Humanitarian actors alone have no means to avoid or overcome moral dilemmas. As a consequence, the only objective for aid agencies that is both reasonable and feasible is the consistency between claim and action. That is, to take the political context into consideration and to acknowledge that some moral principles need to be violated for the sake of other obligations.

The major findings of the four case studies are presented in figure 3.

---

[51] At the same time, Brauman argues: "Having no other goal than to alleviate distress, driven by an imperial desire to act which is the very basis of their dynamism, humanitarian organizations are particularly prone to confound the means they mobilize and the ends they pursue" (Brauman 1995:101).

Fig. 3: Famine relief mission in Soviet Russia, Biafra, Cambodia, Ethiopia

	causes of dilemma	politico-humanitarian congruence	behavior of aid agencies	
			approach (hum. actor)	*outcome*
Soviet Russia *1921-23*	undemocratic nature of recipient regime	high	- extrovert (ARA)	dilemma was avoided
Biafra *1968-70*	instrumentalization of aid by warring parties	low	- introvert (ICRC) - victim-centered (JCA)	dilemma remained
Cambodia *1979-80*	instrumentalization of aid by warring parties	low	- introvert (ICRC, UNICEF) - victim-centered (Oxfam) - extrovert (MSF)	dilemma remained
Ethiopia *1984-85*	instrumentalization of aid by recipient government	low	- victim-centered (UN) - extrovert (MSF)	dilemma remained

What influences an aid agency's course of action in moral conflicts and dilemmas? And in how far does an aid agency's ethical decision have an impact on the consistency between claim and action? In order to show how today's humanitarianism deals with moral dilemmas, we will now turn to the analysis of famine relief work in North Korea.

Part B. FAMINE AID IN NORTH KOREA

In view of the case studies presented in the foregoing chapter the North Korean case resembles its historical predecessors in a number of aspects. As was the case in Soviet Russia, Biafra, Cambodia and Ethiopia, aid work in North Korea raises controversies and dispute among policy makers and among aid agencies themselves. Again, humanitarian actors face criticism and moral challenges that derive from their threefold obligation: the moral imperative to help, principles of action and the necessity to cooperate with the political environment in place. Similar to the Ethiopian case in 1984-85, the debate surrounding the moral integrity of aid has split the humanitarian actors into two groups: agencies that decide to work under the set conditions, and others that regard the working conditions and the effects of aid as ethically unacceptable.

It is often argued that the aid mission in North Korea is a historically unique case due to the country's political and ideological characteristics. The distinctive features of the aid operation in North Korea, as will be shown in this second part of our study, concern each of the three sets of obligations and constraints that aid agencies have to deal with. Most importantly, the North Korean aid mission is a particular case because the dilemma experienced by aid agencies in this country is particularly intense. This is due to the specific nature of the three sets of obligations that aid organizations are facing in the DPRK:

Firstly, the humanitarian imperative plays an important role due to the magnitude and duration of the crisis. In terms of malnutrition rates and mortality estimates, the North Korean famine is one of the most devastating of the 20th century. At the same time, however, it is difficult for aid agencies to get information concerning the humanitarian crisis in the DPRK. Thus, aid agencies carry out a famine aid operation of a massive size that is based upon rather meager information.

Secondly, as for the obligations that emanate from organizational mandate and principles, the North Korean crisis caught the international aid system at a moment of internal confusion about the humanitarian mandate and principles of action. This will be discussed at the end of this study.

Thirdly, operational constraints that derive from external political interests are particularly important in North Korea due to the political sensitivity of the famine crisis. As for this set of constraints, famine aid operations in the past have shown that two main variables determine the political dimension of a famine relief effort: first, the existence of strategic donor interests and second, the existence of the political will on the side of the recipient government to shape the aid effort according to its priorities. Importantly, in the past, these two variables hardly coincided. In Soviet Russia, strategic donor interests were imminent but essentially the Soviet government was prepared to accept basic humanitarian standards. In Biafra, Cambodia and Ethiopia, the authorities concerned were shaping the aid effort according to their goals. Donor interests, however, were influenced by domestic public opinion and only to a minor degree by strategic political considerations. In the North Korean case, by contrast, the international famine aid operation is a politically sensitive issue for both donor and recipient. The result is that under these conditions, the humanitarian agencies' freedom of action is limited by both recipient and donor side.

In the following text, we will analyze the causes and the scale of human suffering in North Korea as the first incentive for humanitarian action (chapter IV). We will then turn to the external political interests that determine the crisis management of the DPRK government as well as donor policies (chapter V). The implications of these sets of political interests for the work of aid agencies will be presented in chapter VI. The differing approaches of aid agencies in dealing with working restrictions and moral dilemmas in North Korea as well as the general lessons to draw from these differing approaches will be discussed at the end of the study (chapters VII and VIII).

Chapter IV.

The North Korean Famine: Causes and Scale

As noted in earlier chapters, famines have to be analyzed in the context of vulnerability of people to food scarcity. In view of the North Korean famine we will have to distinguish between factors that led to a decline in food availability on one side and those factors that define vulnerability to food scarcity on the other. The causes of the North Korean famine are controversial to the extent that differing weight is accorded to ecological and political factors respectively. We will refer to the famine paradigms that impact on the behavior of an aid agency in a dilemma situation and discuss the extent to which these paradigms apply to the North Korean famine.

IV.1 Industrial Collapse and Food Availability Decline

In the case of North Korea a collapse of domestic food production plays an important role. This food availability decline has to be seen in the context of the overall economic situation of the DPRK. For a multitude of factors, the country's economy entered into a vicious circle in the early 1990s. A decline of agricultural output is one consequence of this.

a) The Yearning for Autarky: Reason for Success – and Crisis

At the time the famine hit the population, North Korea was a highly industrialized country. Only about 30 percent of the population was employed in agriculture.[1] According to official figures from 1993, about 61 percent of the population lived in urban areas.[2] In this respect, the North

---

[1] FAO/WFP: *Special Report. Crop and Food Supply Assessment Mission to the Democratic People's Republic of Korea*, 8 November 1999. The Report notes: "The official estimate of population as of end August 1999 stood at 22.554 million people. Of these, approximately 6.6 million people were classified as agricultural workers who receive annual food supplies at harvest and are not provided PDS rations". See also Noland (2000:76).

[2] DPRK Central Bureau of Statistics (1993 population census), data available at www.korea-np.co.jp/pk (6 December 2002). This figure is widely in line with outside estimations. So, according to Williams, von Hippel and Hayes (2000:4), 60 percent of

Korean famine fundamentally differs from the famines in Soviet Russia, Biafra, Cambodia, Ethiopia and from other even more devastating famines such as in the Ukraine (1932-33) and China (1958-61), where about 80 percent of the population lived in rural areas. Forced collectivization and regime consolidation occurred almost 50 years ago. Thus, these factors – in contrast to the Ukrainian or Chinese famine - cannot be blamed for the current food crisis in North Korea. As Foster-Carter (1997:44) points out: "The current crisis looks more like the death throes of a communist system than its forcible early consolidation".

In a way, the DPRK was Asia's first economic miracle after the Second World War, beside Japan. In terms of GNP per capita, the North Korean economy performed better until 1973 than the South Korean economy (Young 1993:61). Concerning industrialization, mechanization of agriculture, rural electrification, public health system or education, the country served as a model for developing countries. It was also providing development aid in a number of socialist countries in Africa and Southeast Asia. In Laos, for instance, North Korean experts worked to bring forward the mechanization of rice cultivation. North Korea was able to export tuberculosis medicine as a result of its successful struggle against the disease at home. Paradoxically, the policy of autarky as one component of Juche ideology and the high degree of industrialization are both the secret of North Korea's success and the reason for its decline. Eberstadt (1997:188) comments that "the economic pressures and problems confronting the DPRK's socialist system today appear to have no precise analogy in recent historical experience".

In various sectors including mechanical engineering and heavy industry, North Korea was quite successful in achieving self-sufficiency, its overall economic goal. In terms of energy supply, however, this target was particularly difficult to reach. Electricity generation is primarily based on coal, of which the DPRK has substantial reserves, and hydropower. The transport sector, however, heavily relies on oil that had to be 100 percent imported. In 1990, North Korea imported about 2.5 million tons of crude oil from the Soviet Union, China and Iran (Williams, von Hippel and Hayes 2000:4).

---

the population lived in urban areas in 1990. The 1990 average urbanization rate on the Asian continent is less than 30 percent (World Resource Institute 1990:271).

Both sectors, coal mining and transport, determine the country's energy supply capacity since coal needs to be transported to power stations. The industry at the backbone of the country's economy and the largest consumer of energy thus directly depended on the country's coal mining and transport infrastructure. In addition, most of the coal mines, thermal power stations and hydroelectric plants were built with substantial technical assistance from the Soviet Union during the 1950s to 1980s. In 1990, the energy infrastructure was already "at retirement age" (Williams, von Hippel and Hayes 2000:5). The North Korean energy sector depended on Soviet assistance in terms of expertise and spare parts for its maintenance.

Agriculture played a key role in the economic development of North Korea. The short-term increase of agricultural production was high on the political agenda from the inception of the DPRK in 1948. North Korean officials often point out that major food-producing regions were located in the south of the peninsula while agricultural conditions in the colder and more mountainous north (80 percent of its surface is mountainous) are unfavorable. Most studies on food production in the DPRK note that the ratio of cropland to population is rather low (0,11 hectares per capita). However, it has to be noted that this ratio is comparable to food exporting countries such as Israel (0,10), Vietnam (0,10) or the UK (0,12). In addition, North Korea's ratio is still considerably higher than those of Japan (0,04) and South Korea (0,05; World Resource Institute 1990:281).

According to some reports, the national production of grain doubled between 1961 and 1988 and was sufficient to cover domestic needs in the late 1980s. Other sources, however, claim that North Korea has never reached self-sufficiency in food even at the best of times (for an overview see Smith and Huang 2000:201). In any case, since the principle of autarky did not allow the agriculture to rely on foreign inputs, the DPRK's agricultural output directly depended on domestic industrial performance. Large parts of the cultivated areas are irrigated, mostly through electric pumps.[3] North Korea produced fertilizers and pesticides

---

[3] FAO/WFP: *Special Report. Crop and Food Supply Assessment Mission to the Democratic People's Republic of Korea.* 28 October 2002, p.11. It has to be noted that the available data on irrigation vary greatly. According to the World Resource Institute (1990:281) 48 percent and according to the European Commission (EC 2001:10) 70 percent of the cropland is being irrigated.

domestically but needed to import the raw materials necessary for the production of some items.[4]

In short, the policy of autarky reached its objective in a number of economic sectors. These successes, however, were achieved at the expense of a closed and thus highly sensitive economy. In particular, the lack of trade and interaction with foreign countries created "the curious economic structure of North Korea that bound agriculture extremely close to industry and the energy regime" (Woo-Cumings 2002:24). In addition, the lack of external trade cut the DPRK economy off from hard currency, a resource that became crucial in the 1990s.

b) The Consequences of Geo-Political Changes

Some observers note that, as early as the mid 1980s, the North Korean economy "had reached the limits of classical socialist 'extensive' growth, and had entered into stagnation or even decline" (Eberstadt 1997:152). In any case, with the changes in the former socialist world and the Soviet Union in particular, the DPRK's economy suffered a heavy blow.

A satellite picture from July 1999 that shows the Asian continent by night has become a popular starting point for presentations on the North Korean crisis. On this picture, North Korea is wrapped in almost complete darkness so that South Korea virtually appears as an island.[5] This picture illustrates one of the key problems North Korea has been struggling with for more than a decade: the lack of energy.[6]

The dissolution of the Soviet Union had a devastating impact on the DPRK's energy infrastructure. First and foremost, the breakdown of the socialist block hit the North Korean transport system at its sore spot: the dependence on imported oil. The Soviet Union was the primary source of oil, mainly crude, that was delivered on a concessionary basis. As a con-

---

[4] See Smith and Huang (2000:204): "High yielding varieties require sufficient amounts of fertilizers, and North Korean agriculture failed to receive crucial support in the form of sustained progress in chemical fertilization and farm mechanization. For an economy geared for self-sufficiency, North Korea has never developed domestic sources of potassium and has thus remained dependent on the availability of foreign exchange for its imports".

[5] The picture is available at: antwrp.gsfc.nasa.gov/apod/ap990728.html (26 November 2002).

[6] For greater detail see Williams, von Hippel and Hayes (2000) and Von Hippel, Savage and Hayes (2002).

sequence of political change and economic distress, the Soviet Union and Russia stopped this policy and demanded payment at prevailing market rates and in hard currency. North Korea, due to a lack of foreign currency, was not able to meet these conditions. As a result, in 1993, crude oil imports from Russia were about one-tenth what they were in 1990 (Von Hippel, Savage and Hayes 2002:5).[7]

North Korea did not try to replace Soviet oil imports by intensifying trade with China. In the early 1990s, China demanded hard currency in exchange for goods. The DPRK decided to conserve its own resources and thus further limited external trade. Consequently, Chinese fuel exports dropped by over a quarter between 1990 and 1994 (see Eberstadt 1995:673). Still, however, even in view of the modest volume of Chinese imports, China became the main source of oil and other goods.[8] It has to be noted that in view of the US economic embargo, North Korea's options to seek new sources of fuel were very limited.

In addition, the dissolution of the Soviet Union ultimately had an impact on the modernization and maintenance of the North Korean energy infrastructure. The provision of spare parts and the transfer of knowledge necessary to maintain the Soviet type energy infrastructure was no longer an act of socialist solidarity.

The vast drop in fuel imports and its effect on the transport infrastructure, as well as the inability to maintain the existing energy production, affected the country's coal industry. One significant indicator for the actual output of the coal industry is the coal export to China, which had declined from 1990 to 1993 at 90 percent.[9] Once coal production and fuel supply had declined, the entire North Korean industry and, thus, economy entered into a vicious circle. Although no complete and reliable data from inside the DPRK are available, the Nautilus Institute concludes that "we have reason to believe that this economic decline has been both a result and a cause of substantial changes in energy demand and supply in North Korea over the last decade" (Von Hippel, Savage and Hayes 2002:4).

---

[7] See also Eberstadt, Rubin and Tretjakova (1995).
[8] Flake (1995:15) notes that "in 1993 North Korea received 72 percent of food imports, 75 percent of oil imports, and 88 percent of its coking coal imports from China".
[9] See von Hippel, Savage and Hayes (2002:5).

c) The Impact of Ecological Factors

Decades of highly intensive agriculture that relied on a maximum exploitation of soil, on bringing marginal lands into production, as well as widespread deforestation (for export and for heating purposes) rendered the soil vulnerable to erosion and floods. The UN appeal summarizes in 1998: "Efforts to increase the area under cultivation result in the degradation of hillside slopes, further aggravated by deforestation by exporting timber to earn foreign exchange. The environmental degradation has led to an increase in the incidence of and severity of floods" (UNOCHA 1998:8).

In 1995 and subsequent years, the general economic malaise was exacerbated by natural catastrophes. Of these, the floods of 1995 and 1996 had the most devastating effects. They not only destroyed crops and cultivated land but also severely damaged coalmines and hydropower stations (see Williams, von Hippel and Hayes 2000:5).[10]

In addition, in 1997, North Korea "seems to have been at the center of a global ecological disaster" (Woo-Cumings 2002:28). Severe drought - related to the El Niño phenomenon – hit the country in 1997, followed by a tidal wave. These disasters particularly affected agriculture and hydroelectric production. They were followed in subsequent years by droughts, floods and storms. A FAO/WFP mission report states that "only 1998 and to some extent 1999 were relatively hazard-free".[11]

It has become redundant to stress that ecological factors exacerbated food scarcity but did not trigger it. Noland (2000:275) points out that "North Korea was already experiencing a famine prior to the floods that commenced in July 1995. (...) while natural disasters may have exacerbated the food availability problem, the famine is not a product of bad weather".[12] It is telling to note that, in 1998, a South Korean NGO reports

---

[10] Noland (2000:267) notes that 15 percent of arable land was destroyed in the 1995-96 floods, with the impact being more devastating on high quality land (28 percent) than on medium and low quality land (13 percent).

[11] FAO/WFP: *Special Report. Crop and Food Supply Assessment Mission to the Democratic People's Republic of Korea*, 27 July 2001, p.3.

[12] See also Smith and Huang (2000), Natsios (1999, 2002). Differing views highlighting the relevance of ecological factors are upheld by Aaltola (1999) and Woo-Cumings (2002).

that most of their 770 North Korean interviewees (55 percent) recall that food distribution had ceased in their home regions prior to 1995.[13]

d) The Result: A Country in Permanent Crisis

All three factors – macroeconomic shocks, the decay of the energy infrastructure and natural disasters – led to the economic decline of North Korea. This collapse of a highly industrialized economy - given the fact that it occurred in a surrounding of factual peace - is without precedent. The overall industrial output in the year 2000, following von Hippel, Savage and Hayes (2002:93), amounted to about 18 percent of the 1990 level, varying by subsector between 11 and 30 percent.

Public expenditure is difficult to assess in detail due to the unknown share devoted to the military and military-related purposes. Although no precise data in this respect is available, most observers agree that the DPRK "is the most militarized economy on earth" and "appears to devote a higher share of national income to the military than any other country in the world" (Noland 2000:72). There is a general consensus that the economic crisis has led to some reduction in military expenditure in absolute terms, although the military's share of the economy has probably risen.[14] Importantly, according to official North Korean figures, public revenues halved between 1994 and 1998.[15]

---

[13] Korean Buddhist Sharing Movement: *The Food Crisis in North Korea (witnessed by 1,694 food refugees)*. Posted on www.reliefweb.int on 31 December 1998. The report notes that the interviewees' claims concerning the end of public rationing differs according to their geographical origin. Based upon these statements, the NGO concludes that the provinces in the east and northeast of the country had to face a decline in food availability earlier than other regions.

[14] For estimates of the military's share of output see Noland (2000:71-73), and the references therein. It is important to note, however, that it is impossible to clearly distinguish between civil and military sectors due to the militarization of North Korean society. See Bennett (1999:2): "The army is inevitably a prioritised sector of the population, yet it has also been a key component in the production and distribution of food to civilians and in providing labour for reconstruction projects. Those who argue for a strict division of army and civilians in the distribution of food misunderstand the political and socioeconomic nature of North Korea as a country on permanent military alert where hundreds of thousands of civilians are under temporary conscription".

[15] From about 41.6 billion Won in 1994 to about 19.8 billion Won in 1998 (sources: Korean Central News Agency and DPRK National Yearbook, found at www.korea-np.co.jp/pk, 26 November 2002).

The country's economic collapse led to an unprecedented decline in food production. As one result of the industrial collapse, fertilizer use in 1998 was about 18 percent of what it was in 1989.[16] Some authors claim that the national food production has already been in a fragile state due to over-intensive cultivation methods and soil degradation.[17] Most sources note that a considerable food gap emerged at the beginning of the 1990s. In 1991, the government launched a "let's eat only two meals a day" campaign (Noland, Robinson and Wang 1999:4). In the same year, the national grain production was hardly sufficient to cover the requirements for food, feed and seed. From 1992 onward, these basic requirements could not be met through domestic production (see figure 4). Reportedly, North Korea was engaged in the early 1990s in negotiations to obtain food with the governments of Thailand, Japan and South Korea (Noland, Robinson and Wang 1999:4,9 and Woo-Cumings 2002:21).

Since the beginning of the international food aid operation, the primary source in terms of food conditions in the DPRK are the FAO/WFP crop assessments. They are based on satellite pictures, government figures and site visits. The reliability of these estimations is somewhat limited to the extent that some data is not accessible for international organizations, such as information on market and barter mechanisms, or production figures on non-staple food (vegetables, fruits, fish and livestock). The most important factor that, according to one member of the FAO/WFP missions, is essential for the overall assessment and that remains inaccessible for FAO/WFP, are the yields of privately cultivated land. Since this factor is not included in the calculation, the findings of

---

[16] FAO/WFP, *Special Report*, 2002, p.10, see note 3 in this chapter.

[17] See, for instance, Noland (2000:171-172): "Given unpromising objective conditions in the agricultural sector (a high ration of population to arable land, hilly terrain, northerly latitude, and short growing seasons), the achievement of the production goals required the maximization of yields through heavy application of chemical fertilizers and agricultural chemicals, and reliance on electrically powered irrigation systems. Continuous cropping led to soil depletion and the overuse of ammonium sulfate, as nitrogen fertilizer contributed to acidification of the soil and eventually a reduction in yields. As yields declined, hillsides were denuded to bring more and more marginal land into production. This contributed to soil erosion, river silting, and, ultimately, catastrophic flooding. Isolation from the outside world has meant that the genetic diversity of North Korean seeds have declined, making plants more vulnerable to disease".

the assessment mission, as this mission member concludes, are of limited value.[18] However, according to the chief of FAO's information sys-

Fig. 4: Food Availability Decline in North Korea (1988-2003) (in millions of metric tons)[19]

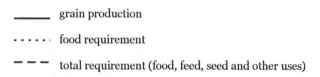

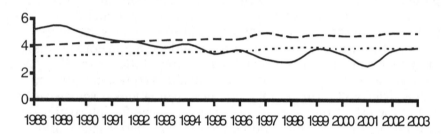

---

[18] Interview with Dieter Hannusch, member of the FAO/WFP missions to DPRK since 1996, Rome, 25 October 2001. For a critical review of the FAO/WFP assessment missions to DPRK see Bennett 1999:7-8.

[19] Grain production includes milled rice, maize, wheat, barley and other minor crops such as sorghum and millets. Output for 2003 is FAO/WFP estimate. Food requirement data for 1988 to 1996 is calculated on the same basis as FAO/WFP figures since 1997 (consumption requirement of 100 kg/caput of rice and 67 kg/caput of maize per annum providing 1600 Kcal or 75 percent of the daily calorie requirement of 2130 Kcal/day/person). Calculations for 1988 to 1996 are based upon the population data of the US Bureau of the Census, International Data Base (www.census.gov/ipc/www/ idbprint.html, 9 December 2002). Total requirement includes feed use, seed requirements, industrial use and estimated post harvest losses. Total demand data for 1988 to 1996 is calculated on the basis of FAO/WFP data for 1997-2003. Sources: FAO/WFP Crop and Food Supply Assessment Mission to the Democratic People's Republic Korea (various issues), Rural Development Administration (Kwon and Kim 1999:49, Smith 1997).

tem, Abdur Rashid, figures that are provided by the DPRK government proved quite accurate whenever FAO/WFP had the possibility to cross-check them. In his view, the government regards the assessment missions as useful in order to get foreign assistance and is thus willing to cooperate.[20]

Although data on demands and output in absolute terms varies, the consensus is that North Korea was and still is unable to meet the food demands of its population by means of domestic production and import capacities. According to the FAO/WFP assessment missions to the DPRK, commercial imports of food between 1996 and 2003 are estimated to be in the range of 100,000 and 500,000 tons. In the same period of time, domestic grain production only covered between 55 and 80 percent of the total demands, including the requirements for human consumption, feed and seed use.

In sum, the decline of the North Korean industry preceded and caused the food availability decline. The industrial collapse, in turn, is the result of economic, political and ecological factors. However, as has been noted in earlier chapters, this alone is neither a necessary nor a sufficient condition to famine. Accordingly, Andrew Natsios, now head of USAID, comments on food supply assessments (2001:113): "FAO/WFP crop assessments conducted in North Korea (...) focused on the production, not distribution, of grain (...). Although this approach may be useful in determining agricultural production under ordinary circumstances, it is not useful in a famine". In how far food scarcity leads to famine is a matter of people's vulnerability to a decline in food availability.

IV.2 Entitlement Failure and Totalitarianism

As noted earlier, the entitlement failure paradigm argues that famines do not result from supply failure alone. A failure of demand is a crucial, sometimes even the only factor that leads to starvation and famine (see chapter II.1). When food is distributed equally among all the members of a society, food availability decline alone would be a sufficient condition for famine. But "there is no such society" (Sen 1982:451). Instead, the amount of food that a person or a group of persons can command differs within a society to the extent that it is governed by the set of means at

---

[20] Interview with Abdur Rashid, Chief GIEWS (Global Information Early Warning System)/FAO, Rome, 22 October 2001.

the disposal of this person or group. We call the lack of these means (economic resources, political rights etc.) vulnerability. The factors that render people vulnerable to food availability decline are closely related to the political, social and economic context of a society.

a) The Public Distribution System

In North Korea, the individual means to command food are extremely limited. Food is not purchased, it is distributed by the state through a public distribution system (PDS). With the exception of the farming population, people receive their staple food ration from the PDS. The state buys the food from the farmers who are allowed to keep a part of the harvest. The state resells it at highly subsidized prices to the population. In PDS centers, which are primarily located in public buildings, people can buy their ration provided that they received a form at their work place.[21] Perishable food such as fruits and vegetables can be bought in public shops at prices determined by the state. The North Korean population is therefore not 'entitled' to command food freely and individually. An individual or a group does not dispose of the means to effectively demand food outside state controlled channels. Thus, entitlement failure is intrinsic to North Korean society and results from the omnipotent role of the state.

When the population depends on the public distribution of food, access to the PDS determines the vulnerability of population groups in times of crisis and food scarcity. In other words, the disposal of means to command food outside the PDS can be vital in times when the PDS collapses. In this regard, one factor is particularly important: access to food production. Here again, the high degree of industrialization exacerbates the humanitarian situation since less than one third of the population works in the agricultural sector. More than 60 percent, or 15.5 million people, entirely depended on the PDS (UNOCHA 2002:13). Therefore, it

---

[21] Due to the economic and financial changes undertaken in summer 2002, the future of the PDS is unclear. In August 2002, the Humanitarian and Development Working Group comprising of aid organizations active in DPRK, reported that "the Government has indicated that eventually, after a period of transition, the PDS may be abandoned". In a paper from October 2002, by contrast, it is noted that "the PDS will remain in place for the foreseeable future" (Humanitarian and Development Working Group, *Economic Changes in the Democratic People's Republic of Korea*, 6 August 2002 and 28 October 2002).

is widely assumed that urban-based workers and their families are facing high levels of vulnerability, as they do not dispose of coping mechanisms available to rural dwellers. FAO/WFP estimates that the average urban family has to spend 75 to 80 percent of its income on food, compared to 20-35 percent of state farmers and much less for cooperative farmers.[22]

b) Regional Disparities

With regard to regional differences in North Korea, most observers note that the mountainous and industrial areas, particularly in the northeastern parts of the country, are most severely hit by food scarcity. The UN appeal for 2003 (UNOCHA 2002:12), for instance, says:

> North–eastern DPRK, which has been hardest hit by the economic decline, exacerbated by adverse climatic conditions, has an increased degree of vulnerability from a food security perspective. The region accounts for over one-fifth of the country's population. Once industrial strongholds, the provinces of Ryanggang, North Hamgyong and South Hamgyong bore the brunt of the loss of the Soviet export markets over a decade ago, forcing their large populations into a heavy but precarious dependence on the very limited marginal land available in this mountainous region. On a per capita basis, cereal production in the north-east – much of it on very steep slopes – is 30 percent below the already inadequate national average. Poor transport infrastructure aggravates the region's food supply situation in many ways, not least by reinforcing its isolation.

Although the Northeast has some advantages such as the proximity to China and a high productivity on the available farmlands (see Natsios 1999:7), it is most unlikely that these factors are sufficient to compensate for the effects of the economic collapse.

Notably, the responsibility to cope with the scarcity of food and other items has gradually been transferred from the central to the county authorities.[23] Counties reportedly developed trade links with each other, so that they were able to receive food in exchange for other resources such as fuel or coal. Aid agencies report that considerable differences exist between counties even within one province including the north-eastern areas. Nevertheless, most of the counties that produce food sur-

---

[22] FAO/WFP *Special Report. Crop and Food Supply Assessment Mission to the Democratic People's Republic of Korea.* 28 October 2002, p.18.
[23] For details see Natsios 2001:110-111.

pluses are located in the west and southwest. Therefore, and in view of the country's massive transportation problems, one has to assume that a relatively high number of counties in the northeast of the country were particularly ill prepared to cope with the declining food availability.

IV.3 The Benefits Paradigm: Food and Political Loyalty

Since the beginning of international aid efforts in North Korea, the PDS has been the center of controversy among analysts and aid workers. Essentially, this discussion surrounds what has been described as the benefits paradigm, namely the role of political power and powerlessness with regard to the causes and effects of famines.

a) The Classification Theory and Its Implications

For some observers, North Korea refutes Sen's hypothesis of a non-existent society where all resources are shared equally. The PDS mechanism is regarded as a guarantee for equitable distribution among all members of North Korean society. In 1997, FAO and WFP, for instance, claimed that "widespread starvation has been largely avoided through the public (food) distribution system (PDS), which has at least provided the barest minimum for survival".[24] A WFP report further notes that "food was reasonably equitably distributed throughout the population through institutional structures such as the public distribution system".[25] Likewise, the non-governmental aid organization World Vision describes the PDS as "a guarantee for an equitable distribution of scarce resources".[26] In this view, the North Korean description that PDS rations vary only according to occupation and age, can be accepted.[27]

For others, the PDS is exactly the opposite of an equitable distribution mechanism. François Jean (1999:22,23), former research director at MSF France, argues that the PDS is "a means of social control". He notes

---

[24] FAO/WFP: *Crop and Food Supply Assessment Mission to Democratic People's Republic of Korea*. Special Alert No. 275. 3 June 1997.

[25] WFP: *Emergency Operation DPR of Korea No. 5959. "Emergency Assistance to Vulnerable Groups"*. 31 December 1997.

[26] World Vision Germany: "Nordkorea: Winter verschärft Hungersnot" [North Korea: Winter Aggravates Famine], Press release, 25 February 1998.

[27] On the estimated rations according to occupation and age see for instance KINU 1996:58.

that the rations "are profoundly inequitable and strictly codified". Jean refers to a caste-like social system in North Korea that defines the individual's social rank and also determines his daily food ration. Natsios brings forward the same argument in his study on the PDS (2001:93). Both authors base their argument upon one source, namely "Human Rights in the Democratic People's Republic of Korea" by Kagan, Oh and Weissbrodt (1988). The authors note that North Korea's society is divided into categories of political function and loyalty. The rank within this complex system may be decisive for many aspects of one's life including "one's treatment under the legal system, one's allocation of rations, one's ability to receive permission to travel, and a multitude of other factors affecting one's livelihood" (Kagan, Oh and Weissbrodt 1988:39).

Reportedly, Kim Il-Sung presented a classification system at the 5th party congress in 1970, dividing the society into three classes and 51 sub-categories. The most detailed presentation in this respect can be found in official South Korean publications. With reference to the Ministry of National Unification in Seoul, the Korean Institute for National Unification (KINU) notes that

> the entire North Korean population is classified into nucleus, unstable and hostile classes. The nucleus class, comprising about thirty percent of the population, is the ruling class that spearheads the North Korean system. (...) The unstable class is the basic stratum of North Korea, comprising those ordinary workers, technicians, farmers, office workers, teachers and their families who do not belong to the nucleus class and who are not party members. They represent about forty-five percent of the population. (...) The hostile class accounts for about twenty-seven percent of the population. They are families of previous landowners and capitalists, public officials under the Japanese rule, religiously active persons and those who collaborated with the advancing South Korean forces during the Korean War. (KINU 1997:57-58).[28]

The US State Department also refers to this classification system and notes that "virtually all the members of the core class live in Pyongyang

---

[28] Similar passages can be found in various issues of the *White Paper on Human Rights in North Korea*, published by KINU. Regarding the classification system they primarily refer to the Ministry of Unification (1995): *An Overview of North Korea*. Seoul: Ministry of Unification Press, p.275.

or other urban areas, where services and amenities are concentrated".[29] Kagan, Oh and Weissbrodt (1988: 34) say further that the design of the pin with Kim Jong-Il's or Kim Il-Sung's image on it, which each person is required to wear, indicates the rank.

The classification theory has major implications on the way the food distribution system and, ultimately, the North Korean famine is interpreted. MSF bases its view on the PDS and the famine upon this categorization theory. In a hearing in the US House of Representatives, an MSF delegate claimed that "the three class levels, which are core, wavering and hostile, continue to be used to prioritize entitlement to items distributed to the PDS".[30] Accordingly, Kagan, Oh and Weissbrodt report that food ration levels are determined by a combination of age, occupation and rank (1997:189-199).[31] Other authors challenge this view. Bennett (1999:9), for instance, does not mention political criteria and notes that the food rationing "depended on a person's age and the number of workpoints earned".

A number of authors base their vulnerability analyses on the assumption that a classification of political loyalty directly affects food rationing. Jean argues that certain groups did not receive food distributions, "notably those who were socially 'stigmatized'" (1999:24). On the other hand, "even in neglected regions, the privileged categories continued to receive some food" (Jean 1999:25). Natsios explicitly compares the size of the classes of political loyalty to rates of malnutrition. He concludes:

> What is most instructive about the malnutrition rates, though, is that they are proximate in size to the three basic classes of political loyalty (...). The similarity of these numbers gives pause. If the theory of rationing according to political classification is correct, the malnutrition statistics should approximate the political classification proportions, and they do (Natsios 2001:210).

Existing literature offers two explanations. First, it is argued that food scarcity has deliberately been used by the regime to starve disloyal population groups. Brunel (1998), for instance, mentions this 'triage'-

---

[29] US Department of State/Office of International Information Programs: "State Department Official Deplores Conditions in North Korea", 29 April 2002.

[30] Federal News Service: "Hearing of the East Asia and the Pacific Subcommittee of the House International Relations Committee. North Korea: Humanitarian and Human Rights Concerns", 2 May 2002.

[31] See also Lautze (1997:9).

hypothesis. Secondly, famine mortality is seen as effect of unequal distribution of political power in the context of the classification system. In this perspective, famine mortality is not derived directly from political intention. Instead, "the favored classes may simply have had more political power to command food because of their status within the political system" (Natsios 2001:210-211). However, the political leadership accepts high death tolls among particular population groups.

b) Challenging the Classification Theory

It goes without saying that no independent and complete insight into North Korean society is available that would allow one to definitely prove or disprove the existence of such a system and then to assess its factual effect. Nevertheless, in our view, the definition of famine vulnerability by means of the alleged classification system appears to be very doubtful. For a number of reasons, a direct linkage between political loyalty and access to food has to be questioned.

Firstly, the classification argument tends to be simplistic. As noted above, a number of factors define a person or a group's ability to command food. Social status is one of these factors. It is the nature of a totalitarian society that social status and economic resources are accorded to political criteria including loyalty to the party and political leadership. Therefore, those who are loyal to the political leadership are more likely to have a higher professional, economic and social status than other population groups such as non-party members or even prisoners. For instance, it appears more plausible that people in higher political functions are better dressed (and wear more sophisticated Kim Il-Sung or Kim Jong-Il pins) because their social and economic position – and not their rank in an institutionalized class system - allows them to.

The classification hypothesis suggests that the regime's political will directly decides on food rationing and, ultimately, life or death. In other words, when political loyalty directly defines one's access to food, famine mortality appears as deliberate, targeted destruction. By contrast, when loyalty to the political leadership indirectly affects one's livelihood, the 'triage' hypothesis appears misleading. Ranking people according to their alleged political loyalty would not only be an inhuman act in itself, but, in times of famine, would accuse the regime of systematic mass murder. It should be assumed that political loyalty affects one's access to education, choice of profession and social status.[32] It is important to note, however, that there is no evidence that famine mortality in North Korea is an act of deliberate political will.

Secondly, the geographic spread of vulnerability to famine does not coincide with the political loyalty argument. As mentioned earlier, it is widely assumed that people in the northeast of the country suffered most from famine (also see following chapter). Traditionally, however, the northeast, the country's industrial backbone, has been a privileged region, both economically and politically. According to Hazel Smith from the United States Institute for Peace, the party of North Hamgyong province was and continues to be a powerful group within the total Korean Workers' Party (KWP).[33] Thus, in terms of political benefit it is all but evident why eastern or southern provinces should be treated in a better way than the northeast.

Thirdly and most importantly, the classification hypothesis is based upon very few sources that, in addition, cannot be cross-checked. Testimonies made by former North Korean citizens in South Korea provide the primary basis for reports on the rationing of food according to political loyalty. Essentially, three sources refer to these testimonies: a report prepared for the Minnesota Lawyers International Human Rights Committee and Asia Watch in 1988 (Kagan, Oh and Weissbrodt), a 1995 publication from the South Korean Ministry of Unification,[34] and the White Paper on Human Rights in North Korea, published annually by the Korean Institute for National Unification in Seoul (KINU). Most authors who describe the classification system and its effect on food rationing ultimately refer to at least one of these publications.[35] Concerning their own report, Kagan, Oh and Weissbrodt point out the possible lack of scientific reliability:

> The Republic of Korea (South Korea) has also engaged in a systematic pattern of issuing misinformation and inaccurate

---

[32] Reportedly, family background also plays a role in the definition of social status. See KINU: *White Paper on Human Rights in North Korea*, (various issues), and Kim Mi-Young: "Social Status and Family Background Can Be Crucial", *Chosun Ilbo* (Digital English Edition), 24 June 2002.

[33] Interview, Washington D.C., 29 November 2001.

[34] See note 28 in this chapter.

[35] See, for instance, Chun (1997), Gustavson and Lee-Rudolph (1997), Jean (1999), Natsios (2001).

information about the DPRK, often providing inaccurate data to outsiders and then quoting their reports as if they were independent. As a result, any material which derives directly or indirectly from South Korean sources must be checked and rechecked against independent data (...). It would have been best primarily to have interviewed persons whose first place of residence outside the DPRK was not South Korea, as such persons might provide somewhat more reliable information. Unfortunately, we had only limited sources in this regard, as most of the ex-residents of North Korea whom we interviewed came first to live in the South (1988:5,8).

To date, no independent source has delivered data that could prove the testimonies referred to in the aforementioned publications. Available reports from refugees and defectors interviewed in China and South Korea in more recent years suggest that food rations are calculated according to age and profession. These reports affirm that people in higher professional and social positions such as officers, party cadres or government officials are better off. They do not, however, claim that they have been ranked in a system of political loyalty that, in turn, defines their access to food. In sum, the hypothesis that a ranking system of political loyalty determines people's access to food exclusively emanates from South Korean sources.

In conclusion, the DPRK is no exception to Sen's hypothesis that the individual means to command food depends on the economic, social and political context of the given society. In a totalitarian state like North Korea political factors, in particular political loyalty to the leadership, play a very important role concerning the individual's social position and economic income. The assumption that people's political loyalty is assessed in a classification system that directly determines the individual food ration and that, consequently, political loyalty in times of food scarcity directly decides over life or death, is not convincing. Asked about the categorization system, a North Korean refugee asserts that there is such a system, which places military and party officials at the top. According to his testimony, however, these categories have no impact on the rationing of food.[36] In sum, there is a striking discrepancy between the monstrosity of the allegations on one side, and the meagerness of the available information on the other.

---

[36] Interview, Seoul, 3 November 2000.

IV.4 The Scale of the Famine

a) Malnutrition

The development and magnitude of the North Korean famine are still widely unknown. To date, the government has allowed international organizations to conduct two surveys in order to assess the nutritional status of children. Both surveys were not able to gather information on famine mortality.

In 1998, 18 nutritionists from UNICEF, WFP and ECHO in collaboration with the DPRK government, measured the height and weight of more than 1,500 children from six months to seven years of age. The report indicated that 62 percent of the children suffered from chronic malnutrition (height-for-age), 16 percent were acutely malnourished (weight-for-height). In a joint press release, the agencies underlined that "this puts North Korea among the top 10 countries with the highest malnutrition rates in the world".[37] According to an FAO official, these reports to the world public caused a lot of discomfort in the North Korean government.[38] In any case, until fall 2002, the government did not allow international agencies to conduct any similar nutritional survey.

The 1998 survey faced a number of restrictions. First, the nutritionists did not have access to all counties that received food aid at that time.[39] Second, no institutions were included, only households. Third, the households could be randomly selected, but there was no possibility to check if the selected households were the ones actually visited. In addition, the survey did not measure regional differences of child malnutrition. However, the 1998 assessment study was the main reference until a second assessment was carried out in 2002.

Broadly, the main findings of the 1998 study are consistent with observations made by international aid agencies in the field. No humanitarian organization working in the country doubted that large population groups, children in particular, were malnourished. Consistent with the

---

[37] WFP/UNICEF/ECHO: *Nutritional Survey Confirms Serious Malnutrition in North Korea*, joint press release, 18 November 1998.

[38] Interview with Abdur Rashid, Chief GIEWS (Global Information Early Warning System)/FAO, Rome, 22 October 2001.

[39] 172 of a total of 212 counties received food assistance, 130 were accessible for the nutrition survey team.

1998 assessment, aid agencies noted a significantly higher presence of chronic malnutrition. An MSF report, for instance, summarizes:

> In this country we met with a nutritional problem we usually do not see: a chronic malnutrition is wide spread, probably the result of food shortages during several years, and is more marked in the big towns. The usual standard height of 110 cm for the five year old is in many places the height of a ten year old.[40]

Most aid workers who had an overview over the humanitarian situation in different provinces indicate that the conditions in the mountainous, industrial and – as a result of Japanese colonial policy and industrialization - densely populated urban centers in the northeast of the country was worse than in other parts of North Korea. On the situation in North Hamgyong province, David Morton, UN Humanitarian Coordinator from 1998-2002 reports: "It is very logical that they suffered. But the Koreans didn't tell us, we had to find out by ourselves. Traditionally, in humanitarian missions, people in urban areas are better off than those in rural areas. In DPRK it's vice versa".[41]

A survey that the DPRK government conducted in 2000 without foreign participation, was not accepted by aid agencies as a scientific and reliable reference. In 2002, the government conducted a further survey in cooperation with UNICEF and WFP. Unlike 1998, the report on the 2002 nutrition assessment, which repeatedly underlines the consistency with the results from the 2000 survey, was worded and issued by the DPRK Central Bureau of Statistics.[42] Scientific support was provided by health institutions from Thailand and the UK who describe the survey a "credible and accurate assessment".[43] The 2002 study is the largest nutrition assessment that has ever been undertaken in the DPRK. 6,000 children under seven years of age in randomly selected households were weighed and measured. The assessment includes data on regional differences in terms of the nutritional status of children and their mothers.

---

[40] MSF: *Report of the Programme of MSF in DPR Korea. July 1997 – September 1998*, p.12.

[41] Interview, Rome, 4 February 2002.

[42] DPRK Central Bureau of Statistics: *Report on the DPRK Nutrition Assessment 2002*. Pyongyang, 20 November 2002.

[43] UNICEF/WFP: *Child Nutrition Survey Shows Improvements. UN Agencies Concerned About Holding Onto Gains*, joint press release, 20 February 2003.

The report finds considerable improvement since 1998. However, rates of 9 percent for acute malnutrition and 42 percent for chronic malnutrition, as indicated by the study, still are, according to WHO criteria, "high" and "very high".[44] Only fourteen countries in the world have a higher rate of chronic malnutrition.[45]

Furthermore, the report shows considerable regional differences in terms of child malnutrition rates (figure 5). In Pyongyang and the western city of Nampo, malnutrition rates are lower than in the rest of the country, especially than in Ryanggang or North and South Hamgyong. Although the geographic spread of famine vulnerability needs further specification, the 2002 survey broadly proves observations made by aid workers in the country.

Fig. 5: Child Malnutrition (2002 survey)[46]

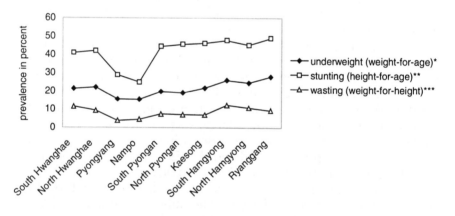

* underweight is an indicator for general nutritional status
** stunting is an indicator for chronic malnutrition
*** wasting is an indicator for acute malnutrition

---

[44] UNICEF/WFP: *Child Nutrition Survey Shows Improvements. UN Agencies Concerned About Holding Onto Gains,* joint press release, 20 February 2003.

[45] UNICEF (2003): *The State of the World's Children 2003,* Geneva: UNICEF, pp.88-91.

[46] UNICEF/WFP DPR Korea: *Nutrition Assessment 2002 DPR Korea.* Pyongyang: February 2003. Survey does not include Chagang and Kangwon province.

The findings of the 2002 survey are consistent with reports from aid agencies working in North Korea. The overall impression is that the nutritional status of children has improved compared to previous years, but still raises concern. Caritas, for instance, reports that 40 percent of children under five years of age appeared to be malnourished.[47] In sum, although no independent nutritional survey has been conducted to date, there is enough evidence of widespread malnutrition that – in view of massive chronic malnutrition rates – must have hit large population groups several years before the first nutritional survey was conducted in 1998. The prevalence of chronic child malnutrition in the 1998 and 2002 surveys supports the description of the North Korean crisis as a "slow-motion famine" (Noland 2000). Not least, this is a further argument against the attribution of the famine causes to the natural disasters in 1994/95.

b) Mortality

A number of authors argue that the time between the government's aid appeal in 1995 and the beginning of the international aid efforts in 1997 must have been the harshest period (see Natsios 2001). For three reasons, such an assessment appears plausible. Firstly, the very fact that the government asked the international community for assistance, and thus risked to losing face, suggests that the situation in 1995 must have been particularly difficult. Secondly, there is no evidence that North Korea was able to bridge the time gap until the arrival of international food aid through other channels (such as stocks, commercial or concessional imports). Thirdly, domestic grain production further declined, compared to the time prior to 1995. It fell to a historic low in 1995 and hardly recovered in 1996 (see fig. 4).

Due to the lack of complete data, famine mortality in North Korea is still very difficult to assess. Conjectures on famine deaths range widely from about 200,000 to 3.5 million. Government figures and extrapolations based upon official figures thereby tend to be at the lower end, aid agencies' estimations at the upper end of the scale.[48] In order to get a

---

[47] *Chosun Ilbo* (English digital edition), 2 July 2002.

[48] See, for instance, Jean-Fabrice Piétri, Asia Desk Officer of Action Contre la Faim (ACF): "An estimated 3,5 million North Koreans may have died from starvation and

more precise picture of famine mortality in North Korea we will briefly discuss the existing data that primarily derives from three sources: the DPRK government, aid agencies working in the country and North Korean refugees.

Unexpectedly, in March 1999, the DPRK government released death rate figures for 1995 and 1998. Based on these statistics, excess death rates caused by the famine would be about 230,000 (Goodkind and West 2001:225-227). This figure is the lowest estimate of famine mortality in North Korea. But according to the majority of observers it does not reflect the real magnitude of the famine (see, for instance, Goodkind and West 2001:227).

The second sources of data are aid agencies that were or still are engaged in North Korea. Their estimates, however, vary greatly. Notably, aid workers' assessments that are based on longer-term experience inside the country differ in regard to even the most basic information. In view of the situation in 1997, the country director of German Agro Action (GAA) reported that the entire population was hit by a famine.[49] Likewise, Caritas International described the situation in 1997 as "slow, wide spread starvation that virtually hits every person and most regions equally"[50] (Caritas 1997:13). A medical doctor from MSF, by contrast, noted in early 1998 that a food crisis could only be observed in few areas. According to his report, the situation did not allow one to speak of a famine. In his view, it was primarily the state of the country's public health system that needed foreign assistance.[51] Most aid agencies refrain from issuing own mortality estimates.

The third source of mortality data are a number of surveys based upon interviews with North Korean refugees and commuters,[52] primarily

---

related illnesses between 1995 and 1998, and more than 8m – over a third of the population – are in need of food aid" (Piétri 2002:13).

[49] GAA (1997): *Annual Report 1997*. Bonn: GAA, p.13.

[50] Caritas Germany: *Annual Report*, 1997, p.13.

[51] See *Messages. Journal Interne des Médecins Sans Frontières*, No. 97, March 1998, p.6.

[52] Good Friends reports (1999:2-3) that most North Koreans (74,6 percent) who were interviewed in the border region (Yanbian prefecture) stay in China for less than three months and voluntarily return to their families and homes. Likewise, Robinson et al. (1999:293) note: "Migrations into China can be characterised typically as short-term movements by a single member of a household whose other members remained in North Korea". It has to be noted that in areas more distant from the border, the dura-

conducted in the Chinese border area.[53] Good Friends/Korean Buddhist Sharing Movement[54] and the Johns Hopkins School of Hygiene and Public Health (Robinson et al. 1999) gathered information to determine famine mortality in North Korea. The Johns Hopkins study is based on interviews that were conducted in summer 1998. Good Friends permanently follows the situation in the region and subsequently conducts famine mortality surveys. One of these surveys was conducted between September 1997 and September 1998 and thus covers the same period as the John Hopkins study. 1,694 people were interviewed by Good Friends, 440 by the John Hopkins study.

Both studies focused on basic demographic information about households and families. The respondents of both studies were primarily working in the industrial sector and originated from North Hamgyong province. Both studies gathered information about a comparable period of time (36 months beginning in January and August 1995, respectively). In terms of mortality rates, the results vary greatly. Good Friends conclude that 28,7 percent of the respondents' family members have died. Robinson et al. report that 12 percent of the migrants' household members have died.[55] The death rates concluded by Robinson et al. were already exceptionally high. The study notes that a 3-year average rate of 42,8 per 1000 was nearly eight times more than the 5,5 per 1000 derived from the 1993 official figures. Both studies conclude that the mortality rate increased from 1995 to 1997/98 and that the very young and very old show the highest absolute mortality rates. Robinson et al. specify that the increases in death rates among children are the highest in relative terms (1999:294). In short, the findings of these studies seem to prove that at least the province of North Hamgyong faced excess death rates, at

---

tion of stay is longer (Good Friends 1999:3). Anyhow, the term "refugees" is misleading when applied to all North Koreans who illegally cross the border.

[53] Good Friends focused on the immediate border area (Yanbian and Changbai prefectures) while the John Hopkins study was conducted in five border and three interior counties of Yanbian prefecture.

[54] *The Food Crisis in North Korea (witnessed by 1,694 food refugees).* Posted on www.reliefweb.int on 31 December 1998. Since May 1999, the Korean Buddhist Sharing Movement (KBSM) is renamed Good Friends, Center for Peace, Human Rights and Refugees.

[55] The Johns Hopkins study states that no more than one member of a family travelling together was interviewed. A similar limitation is not to be found in the Good Friends study.

least between 1995 and 1997. It should be added that other surveys that focused on the living situation of North Korean refugees and commuters in China gathered information that also suggest increased and exceptionally high mortality rates.[56]

In regard to the situation in the entire country the mortality studies draw very differing conclusions. Good Friends extrapolated from the data gained from the respondents to the whole of North Korea. As a result, excess deaths caused by the famine were estimated at about 3,5 million.[57] Good Friends claims that people from western and southern provinces in North Korea have affirmed its estimates.[58] The Johns Hopkins study, by contrast, stressed: "We do not argue that our findings are generalisable to all migrant households or to their non-migrant families, let alone to an entire province or country" (Robinson et al. 1999:294).

A minority view is upheld by Natsios, who argues that the northeastern provinces are better off than the rest of the country. He assumes that "extrapolating the Johns Hopkins death rates to the country as a whole understates rather than exaggerates the famine's severity" (Natsios 2001:215). Therefore, based upon the findings of Robinson et al. and not including Pyongyang residents and people in the military, he estimates that about 2,5 million people have died in "the great North Korean famine" (Natsios 2001).

As noted above, we assume that because of their dependence on industrial production and a functioning food transport and distribution system, the northeastern provinces are particularly ill prepared to deal with food scarcity and economic collapse. Proximity to China and access to industrial equipment that could be bartered were valuable resources to cope with food scarcity in some counties. In view of the overall economic disadvantages of the northeast, however, it is doubtful that these

---

[56] The South Korean NGO Commission to Help North Korean Refugees (CNKR) conducted interviews in China in late 1999. Of 2,044 respondents, 1,462 (71,5 percent) reported that at least one immediate family member has died of starvation (Chang 1999:13).

[57] The average mortality rate in the interviewees' families was 28,7 percent. It was assumed that 9 million people out of a total of 22 million were not hit by the famine due to political position or direct access to food production. KBSM thus applied the mortality rate to a total of 13 million people and concluded that "at least 3,5 million people have died during the last 3 years (Aug 95 - Aug 98)." See note 54 in this chapter.

[58] Interview with Erica Kang, International Coordinator/Good Friends, 9 November 2000.

resources were sufficient to compensate the 'entitlement failure' of this densely populated, industrial and primarily urban region. Consequently, the extrapolation of data gathered from North Korean refugees and commuters most likely leads to inaccurate estimates. It has to be added, though, that refugees or commuters are by definition an unrepresentative group since those willing to take the risk of crossing the border are likely to be those most severely affected by the famine.

The most recent attempt to measure famine-related mortality in North Korea has been undertaken by Goodkind and West (2001). They conclude that, from 1995 to 2000, between 600,000 and one million people died due to the famine. For two reasons, this assessment appears to be too low. First, the authors assume that the famine peaked in 1997 and 1998 and was initiated by the flooding in the summer of 1995 (Goodkind and West 2001:227,229). No excess death rates were presumed to exist prior to 1995 and later than 1999. As noted above, there is some evidence that the humanitarian situation was worse before the arrival of international assistance and that, consequently, the peak of the famine was rather in 1995 to 1997. Moreover, the PDS reduced its rations prior to 1995.[59] The assumption that no famine-related deaths occurred prior to 1995 is thus too optimistic. Secondly, the estimate is based on China's famine experience during the Great Leap Forward. The authors argue that "the contextual circumstances of the Chinese and the North Korean famines were similar, with each resulting from the interplay of natural calamities and overzealous attempts to transform social institutions in line with Marxist ideals" (Goodkind and West 2001:234). As noted above, the North Korean famine is a particular case to the extent that it occurred four decades after the transformation efforts (collectivization etc.) that, in other communist countries such as China, have led to food crises and famines. It therefore appears a doubtful scientific method to use the Chinese mortality data from 1958 to 1961 in order to measure the demographic impact of a famine that occurred almost forty years later under very different circumstances.

In sum, it still is impossible to give precise figures on famine mortality in North Korea. The extrapolation from data gained from northeastern provinces leads to estimates that are too high, while Goodkind and

---

[59] A North Korean refugee who lived in Pyongyang city reports that food distributions have decreased since 1992. Interview, Seoul, 3 November 2000.

West's lower-bound figure of 600,000 famine-related deaths seems to be too low. If one takes the average of all estimates, famine mortality will be in the range of one to two million. This means that five to ten percent of the North Korean population has died due to the famine.

Conclusion

The North Korean famine is the result of multiple causes. The conception of food availability decline can be applied to the North Korean case in as far as it helps to explain the emergence of food scarcity in times of economic slump. Due to the country's dependence on energy input on a concessionary basis from socialist allies and because of extremely close links between industrial output and highly mechanized agriculture, the country's economy entered into a vicious circle in the aftermath of the collapse of the socialist block. Ecological factors further exacerbated the general economic malaise. Consequently, North Korea's highly industrialized economy made a "Great Leap Backward" (Woo-Cumings 2002:21) that ultimately led to a massive decline in domestic food production.

The absence of individual means to command food outside state controlled mechanisms defines vulnerability to this decline in food availability. Entitlement failure is intrinsic to the North Korean form of totalitarianism to the extent that large parts of the population traditionally depend on the public distribution system (PDS). As a consequence, dependence on public food distribution became the major criterion for people's vulnerability and lack of coping mechanisms.

In terms of the interpretation of the North Korean famine, the benefits paradigm is at the center of the controversy among observers and aid agencies. A direct linkage between political loyalty and starvation, which is made by a number of authors, appears to be simplistic and factually doubtful. Moreover, the fact that the allegations ultimately emanate from sources that have been gathered and published by South Korean public institutions, casts doubts on their scientific reliability. In any case, it appears questionable to base the analysis of the North Korean famine on these allegations.

That said, it needs to be stressed that, as in any society, social position determines one's means and resources to command food in times of crisis. In the totalitarian context of North Korea, social position cannot be separated from political aspects. Contrary to the Ukrainian famine in the

1930s, however, there is no evidence that the North Korean regime deliberately used the food availability decline to starve critical or disloyal population groups. Vulnerability to food scarcity in North Korea is largely defined by dependence on the state in terms of food supply. This dependence may vary according to socio-economic position and geographical location. In addition, as in any society, physical factors also determine a person's means to command food. Infants and children, elderly people and pregnant women are also defined as vulnerable population groups in North Korea. In theory, any aid intervention that seeks to reduce vulnerability to famine would have to target these population groups that are facing socio-economic, geographical and physical disadvantages. As we will see, the debate on the North Korean aid operation focuses on the question of how far aid agencies can effectively address these vulnerabilities. In any case, the answer of one North Korean refugee who left the country in late 1998 and who was asked about the fate of those who entirely depended on the public distribution system, sounds credible: "They died".[60]

At the end of the day, the North Korean famine is linked to the lack of individual economic and political means to command food, to the collapse of an economy that traditionally sought to achieve self-sufficiency and to a number of additional factors including natural disaster. All of these factors are beyond the scope of humanitarian agencies. Effectively addressing the 'causes' of the North Korean famine would mean fundamentally breaking with a number of economic and political traditions and, for international donors, providing massive financial, technical and structural inputs. As the following chapter will show, both changes are most unlikely to happen. Aid organizations, in the eighth consecutive year, continue to alleviate suffering in an endless cycle of humanitarian needs, without seeing any light at the end of the tunnel. Asked about the UN's exit strategy, the former UN Humanitarian Coordinator in the DPRK answers: "we know what the strategy is but we don't get there".[61]

---

[60] Interview with a refugee originating from Hamhung City/South Hamgyong province who left North Korea in late 1998. Seoul, 25 November 2000.

[61] Interview with David Morton, Rome, 4 February 2002.

Chapter V.

The Political Environment of Aid

We will now focus on the source of constraints that impacts on an aid agency's behavior and that ultimately causes moral dilemmas: the political environment of aid. Humanitarian action is linked by two "dependency relationships" (Eberwein 2001:14), to the donor (financial resources) and to the recipient side (access, staff safety). The analysis of famine aid missions in the past has illustrated that humanitarian organizations are most likely to face moral dilemmas whenever political interests on recipient and/or donor side are at stake which do not correspond with, or even run counter to humanitarian principles.

For a number of factors, the North Korean famine takes place in politically precarious surroundings.[1] Internally, the humanitarian crisis potentially calls into question economic and social policies as implemented in the DPRK for five decades and therefore poses a potential threat to the political system in place. Furthermore, North Korea's difficulties and its dependence on foreign aid have to be seen in the context of security concerns on the part of major donor countries, some of which are still in a formal state of war with the DPRK. We will now discuss the political interests at stake on the recipient side. The main question thereby is to assess in how far these interests correspond to or contradict the principles of humanitarian action, namely the impartiality and proportionality of aid.

V.1 The Recipient Side: Famine, Aid and Juche

The maneuverability of aid agencies and the respect for their principles of action largely depends on the political characteristics of the country in which they work. In the specific North Korean context, three factors are particularly relevant: the notion of sovereignty, the govern-

---

[1] In our analysis of political interests of the DPRK government and of donor governments, we refer to terms that are differently defined by theorists of international relations ('sovereignty', 'security', 'interest' etc.). A theoretical discussion of these notions goes beyond the scope of this study. We thus refer to the terms the way they are used by the actors themselves.

ment's crisis management and the North Korean understanding of non-governmental actors.

a) The North Korean Understanding of Sovereignty

It has been argued in earlier chapters that it is a core task of any state to guarantee the sufficient supply of food for its population. Failure in this respect puts the legitimacy of any government and political system at risk. In a famine aid mission, foreign organizations step in, carry out this task and are therefore, by the very nature of their doing, placed in a latent conflict with what ultimately defines a state: its sovereignty. Brauman's famous imaginary example of an Iraqi humanitarian organization that fights malnutrition and diseases in the city of New York illustrates this tension between sovereignty and humanitarianism (Brauman 1995:8). The political system of North Korea has a very particular understanding of sovereignty that further exacerbates the latent tension between sovereignty concerns and humanitarian action.

Western media often describe the DPRK regime as 'communist' or 'Stalinist'. The DPRK government and media, however, stress the unique and independent character of their political system and ideological basis. The preamble of the North Korean constitution, for instance, states: "The Democratic People's Republic of Korea is a socialist fatherland of Juche which embodies the idea of and guidance by the great leader Comrade Kim-Il Sung." Neither Marx nor Lenin is mentioned in the constitution. The term 'communist' appears only one time in Article 43, which describes the goal of public education, namely the creation of a "people of a new communist type".

The North Korean ideological and political system is best characterized by the term it itself uses: Juche. The term was first used by Kim Il-Sung in 1955 and might best be translated as 'subject' (see Chung 1996:9, Maretzki 1991:68). It is closely related with the term 'dschadschusong' that is often (and inaccurately) translated as independence. In Juche terminology, dschadschusong means something like collective self-determination and is "an attribute of man to live and develop as a social being" (Kim Jong-Il 1974). Thus, on the one hand, the yearning for self-determination is described as a fundamental characteristic of man. On the other hand, it is understood that man as a social being longs for this self-determination only in the context of a group, not as an individual. The history of man is seen as "the history of the struggle of the masses for dschadschusong" (Kim Jong-Il 1982). Juche ideology further expresses this intention to liberate a group without, in a sense, liberating its members. In the words of Kim Jong-Il (1986) Juche "seeks to defend and implement dschadschusong, which is the life and soul of a man as a social being". In a celebrated essay from 1982, Kim Jong-Il lays down the characteristics of Juche ideology:

> As has been clarified by Comrade Kim Il Sung, the masses are the subject of history and the driving force of social development (...). The masses need a wise leadership to be able to deal with their position and role as the subject of history. Although the masses create history, they can become effective as the subject of history only under a wise leadership.

Evidently, Juche is all but a philosophy of liberation and serves one main purpose: the legitimization of power. The image of a strong people led by a wise leader is one aspect of Juche ideology. At the same time, Juche is "the antithesis to the traditional submissiveness of Korea to her great neighbors" (Chung 1996:45). In his essay, Kim Jong-Il (1982) argues:

> A nation with strong national pride and high revolutionary dignity is invincible, otherwise it is powerless. For the people of a small country that has been oppressed for a long time, it is all the more necessary to be guided by great national pride and high revolutionary dignity (...). The entire people must be proud of the wise and courageous Korean nation, particularly of the dignity of a people that carries out the revolution under the leadership of Comrade Kim Il Sung

According to Helga Picht (1994, cited in Chung 1996:61), from the late 1950s to the 1970s Juche was merely seen as a political idea that was propagated in order to enhance national conscience and erase the old image of Korea as a tributary country. This points to Korea's traditional predicament as a 'shrimp between whales' as being the historical background of North Korea's rigid understanding of national independence and sovereignty.

Juche ideology combines the ideal of absolute leadership and national pride with the notion of sovereignty. The main principle of Juche is to retain one's independent and sovereign position. Kim Il-Sung coined the slogan: "Juche in ideology, sovereignty in politics, autarky in economy and self-defense to protect the country" (see Kim Jong-Il 1982). Kim Jong-Il (1982) argues:

> In politics, dschadschusong requires independently making and carrying out decisions, based upon an independent ideology (...). The one who allows pressure and interference on part of the other, or who acts according to the other's commands, cannot respect one's own principles, and, ultimately, revolution and reconstruction are lost (...). In foreign relations, the dschadschusong of a party and a state becomes evident (...). Sovereignty is the holy right of all revolutionary parties, countries and nations.

In sum, the radical understanding of national sovereignty in the DPRK exacerbates the general tension between sovereignty and humanitarian action, a tension that lies in the very nature of humanitarian aid. Collectivism, leader principle and sovereignty have most rigorously been pursued in the DPRK. In terms of this ideological rigidity, North Korea has outpaced its socialist allies by far. The last East German Ambassador to the DPRK notes that North Korea is no copy of Stalinism, but "its highest perfection" (Maretzki 1991:7).[2] Due to the North Korean understanding of Juche and sovereignty, as will be shown in later chapters, the DPRK authorities consider a number of aspects that concern aid agencies and their work to be related to national sovereignty. On the role of Juche in regard to the international aid operation, Snyder (2003:3) concludes:

> Humanitarian aid constituted a direct threat to the myth of juche upon which the North Korean ideology was built and threatened to undermine the central role of the state. Thus, for the North Korean

---

[2] The same goes for the personality cult that surrounds Kim Il-Sung and Kim Jong-Il. Descriptions of father and son as divine beings are without equivalent, even compared to the People's Republic of China under Mao. See Noland (2000:62): "This is no ordinary neo-Confucian state, however, and the cult of personality surrounding the Kims is extreme even by the disheartening standards of the 20th century. (...) the hagiographic mythology surrounding the birth of present-leader Kim Jong-il appears to draw upon Christian imagery. According to the legend, a swallow appeared to an elderly man on the slopes of sacred Mt. Paekdu, heralding the imminent birth of a great general. This was accompanied by three guiding stars leading the faithful to the log cabin where the infant Kim lay. Propaganda has been explicit in its religious content: Kim Jong-il is described as 'a contemporary God', 'superior to Christ in love, superior to Buddha in benevolence, superior to Confucius in virtue, and superior to Mohammed in justice', and, ultimately, 'the savior of mankind'".

leadership, humanitarian assistance and the physical presence of outsiders in Pyongyang and elsewhere were intensely political.

b) Juche Ideology and Crisis Management

Concerning its crisis management, the DPRK government theoretically had a number of options to deal with the famine and its causes. Using the terms of Noland, Robinson and Wang (1999), the government could put priority on an increase of domestic food production (production-oriented strategy), it could attempt to bridge the food gap for the longest period of time possible through international aid (aid-oriented strategy), it could try to strengthen external trade to get access to sufficient imports of food (trade-oriented strategy) and, finally, the government could fundamentally change its economic policy (reform-oriented strategy). As for the country's mid-term perspective, Noland, Robinson and Wang (1999:22) conclude:

> Because of North Korea's lack of comparative advantage in the production of grains, the production-oriented strategy fails to attain the country's minimum human needs target. (...) the North Korean regime may prefer a mixed strategy in which attempts to boost domestic food production are supplemented by the acquisition of external assistance. Since domestic production alone is unlikely to meet even minimum human needs, such a strategy appears quite limiting. Escape from the famine will almost surely require at least some liberalization of trade policies.

Therefore, most observers argue that, in view of the causes of the North Korean crisis, any fundamental improvement of the overall economic - and thus humanitarian - situation requires a significant recovery of the country's industry. "In the end, North Korea has to export manufactured goods", states Marcus Noland from the Institute for International Economics.[3] Humanitarian aid cannot achieve such a change for the better that requires far-reaching political and economic reform. Noland concludes (2000:348):

> The real issue is not whether reform would be beneficial – it would, though the technical difficulties of reforming the North Korean economy should not be minimized. The real issue is whether reform would be compatible with the continued existence of the Kim Jong-il

---

[3] Interview, Washington D.C., 27 November 2001.

regime and, if not, what the world should expect. The key questions relate to the intentions of the regime. How much internal transformation can it tolerate?

In view of Juche ideology, the government's tolerance and space of action is quite limited. For the DPRK government, the very act of asking for foreign assistance already bears more risks than only the danger of 'losing face'. A public admittance that the country depends on international charity to feed its people would deprive the political leadership of its ideological power basis. In its communication with the international community, blaming nature offered the most convenient and face saving course of action. Reportedly, parts of the political leadership already planned to launch an appeal in 1994, but other members successfully opposed. The floods in 1995 then offered a face-saving opportunity to launch the appeal.

In the first appeal of August 1995, for instance, the government only referred to the floods of the summer of that year as the causes of the crisis. However, the very fact that such a decision was taken suggests that the humanitarian situation in summer 1995 must have been desperate. The government requested "food and medicine, assistance for rehabilitation of dwellings, schools, hospitals, roads and railways, telecommunications facilities, factories and other public buildings".[4] It gave no hint of the magnitude and real nature of the crisis. In any case, the international community including the UN World Food Programme was taken by surprise.[5]

In a Juche perspective, the options listed above by the Institute for International Economics appear quite academic. To reconsider collectivism and central planning is incompatible with the most fundamental Juche principles. The same goes for the trade-oriented strategy for it implies to acknowledging that the country cannot produce sufficient amounts of food by itself and has to rely on foreign imports. That is, the government would have to give up the economic principle that derives from Juche: autonomy. Kim Jong-Il (1982) notes:

---

[4] UN Department of Humanitarian Affairs (1995): *DPR Korea – Floods Situation Report No. 2.* DHA-Geneva 95/0392. 28 August 1995.
[5] Interview with Jens Schulthes, WFP Regional Director Asia Pacific 1992-1997, Rome, 24 October 2001.

> Concerning the reconstruction of the economy (...) one has to trust one's own power and has to rely on it. A people that trusts in itself and that fights tirelessly is able to overcome any difficulty whatsoever. By contrast, a people that has no trust in itself and that only looks at others is incapable to solve a single problem.

The very fact of receiving aid and depending on it undermines the Juche principle of autonomy and self-reliance. In the words of the former UN humanitarian coordinator in the DPRK, "the North Koreans think that importing food means to be vulnerable to the outside, no matter who the outsider is".[6] Furthermore, it does not matter whether food is received from the outside as commercial imports or in the form of humanitarian aid. If Juche is to be upheld, the reception of aid can only be justified as a necessary and temporary evil. To the North Korean public, the state propaganda explains that "wishing or asking for 'aid' and 'cooperation' from the imperialists leads to national subordination and ruin".[7]

Summing up, neither aid, nor trade, nor reform offer cures that are in line with Juche, which, in turn provides the ideological legitimization for the political system and its leadership. To forsake Juche means to deprive the political system of its legitimization. In addition, the dynastic character of the North Korean regime entails that any major ideological change could appear as treason committed by the son against the father's heritage. Noland compares the crisis management in earlier famines in Asian communist countries to North Korea today and concludes (2000:282):

> The point is that reformers in both China and Vietnam were relatively free to construct tortured rationalizations about how market-oriented reforms were what Marx, Mao, or Ho really had in mind. The ideological terrain faced by the current North Korean regime is very different.

In view of Juche ideology, the increase of domestic food production is the only way to deal with the crisis without undermining the country's ideological and political status quo. Moreover, it is perfectly in line with the ideological tradition that prioritizes strengthening own means over

---

[6] Interview with David Morton, UN Humanitarian Coordinator 1998-2002, Rome, 4 February 2002.
[7] *Rodong Shinmun*, 22 July 2001.

assistance from the outside world. In concrete terms, this means that inputs to increase food production such as technical equipment, spare parts, fuel, fertilizers, pesticides etc. are, at least in the long run, more attractive than the delivery of food.

It can be assumed that political stability is a key interest of the DPRK government in dealing with the famine. In this regard, the lack of information within North Korea about the outside world is of particular importance. The North Korean population has, to a great extent, no possibility to compare the living conditions in the DPRK with conditions in other countries. With the possible exception of the political elite, the population has no access to foreign print media, neither radio or TV.[8] Even if people in some regions in North Korea may theoretically be able to receive radio or TV broadcasts from China or South Korea, their domestically produced technical devices lack the necessary means to receive anything other than the DPRK state channels (see, among others, Maretzki 1991:115-116). Although in recent years modern Japanese TVs were brought into the DPRK from China, and although radio receivers can be secretly modified so that foreign broadcasting stations can be received,[9] the number of those with access to information from outside North Korea is still marginal.

Thus, the North Korean population lacks even the most basic information about the outside world. The drastic gap between the reality of life in the DPRK and living conditions in China or other countries, not to speak of South Korea, are widely unknown. Direct and uncontrolled communication between foreigners and North Korean citizens would most probably destroy a number of images and illusions upheld by the official propaganda and would therefore, ultimately, pose a serious threat to the political status quo.

---

[8] Information on the elite's access to international media is rather inconsistent. Kagan, Oh, and Weissbrodt (1988:35) report on one side that "members of the elite are permitted (...) to possess radios that can receive foreign radio broadcasts". On the other side the same report (1988:154) says that "despite the punishments for listening to or talking about unauthorized broadcasts, two friends of Kim Jung Il from 1978 to 1986 reported that some members of the elite have transistor radios and secretly tune in for-eign broadcasts".

[9] A North Korean refugee from South Hamgyong province reported that he was able, after having modified a radio receiver, to tune in to South Korean radio broadcasts. He had signed off his radio, telling the authorities that it was out of order. Interview, Seoul, 25 November 2000.

If we assume that the DPRK government is not prepared to question Juche ideology and to risk its own survival, it will have to pursue two main interests in dealing with famine and famine aid: first, the medium to long term goal is to receive the inputs necessary to increase domestic food production to a sufficient level. Second, the international aid effort has to be shaped in a manner that prevents direct and unhindered communication between North Korean citizens and foreigners. In concrete terms, it is much more in line with Juche ideology to enhance one's own capacities to produce goods (electricity, industrial output, medicine, food) than it is to seek short-term humanitarian benefits through foreign organizations distributing food and offering medical treatment. In view of ideological and political considerations, the delivery of fuel and spare parts for the farming sector, for instance, is much more attractive than a therapeutic feeding program that would allow foreign doctors to treat (and communicate with) Korean patients. As a consequence, the humanitarian priority to address immediate needs – that is, to prevent people from starvation through food and medical assistance – is hardly in line with the political and ideological interests of those in power and responsibility in the DPRK.

c) The View on Humanitarian Organizations

Aid agencies are not necessarily perceived by beneficiaries or local authorities as neutral, impartial organizations exclusively seeking to re-lieve suffering. A recent study on humanitarian action in Central Asia, for instance, concludes that local people "viewed humanitarian activity in a religious context, and suspected that humanitarian action can have missionary goals or serve as a cover for spying activities". The study further notes that aid agencies do not pay sufficient attention to their problematic public image and "do not put enough effort into countering these misconceptions".[10]

As far as the perception of humanitarian actors is concerned, the situation in the DPRK is similar. Not only that the very fact of depending on foreign assistance contradicts the North Korean understanding of national sovereignty and other Juche principles. Furthermore, large

---

[10] Centre for Humanitarian Dialogue: "Humanitarian Engagement With Armed Groups. The Central Asian Islamic Opposition Movements". *Case Study*, Vol.1, No.1, p.44.

parts of this assistance are provided by organizations whose self-perception totally differs from the view of North Korean authorities.

North Korea is a totalitarian state that by definition leaves no space for civil society or any sort of private organization. The very notion of a *non*-governmental organization therefore raises both skepticism and suspicion. Since NGOs have their headquarters in a specific – mostly Western - country, primarily employ citizens of that country as expatriate workers and, in their vast majority, are at least in parts funded by the government of that state, it is not surprising that North Korean authorities see NGOs as representatives of their home country. Consequently, the motives of expatriates for their presence in the DPRK that NGOs describe as non-political and non-financial are hardly credible to North Korean officials. Erich Weingartner, former Head of the Food Aid Liaison Unit (FALU) of WFP in North Korea, summarizes the situation as follows (2001:22, 21):

> NGOs generally consider themselves to be 'the good guys' (...) DPRK counterparts view this glorified self-perception not as naive, but as hypocritical (...) part of my job description as head of FALU was to explain NGOs to the DPRK and the DPRK to NGOs (...). My North Korean counterparts wanted to understand how NGOs are funded, and how that funding determines their policies. They found it difficult to understand how NGOs could obtain government funding, and yet make decisions independent of their paymasters. They also could not comprehend how some of the largest NGOs could possibly obtain their funding through the generosity of large numbers of individuals from their home countries contributing money freely out of their own pocket.

North Korean authorities were more accustomed to the nature of inter-governmental bodies such as UN agencies or governmental actors like the Swiss Agency for Development and Cooperation (SDC), an institution within the Swiss Foreign Ministry. In the words of a UNOCHA official, formerly working in the DPRK, "for North Korea, UN is a known quantity, NGOs are an unknown quantity".[11] Nevertheless, North Korea was all but at ease with UN organizations. Natsios argues (2001:166):

> If any other nation in the world appealed to the United Nations for food aid after a failed harvest, it would not seem peculiar, but for

---

[11] Interview with Oliver Lacey-Hall, former Humanitarian Affairs Coordinator DPRK/ UNOCHA, Geneva, 19 October 2001.

North Korea it was. It was a UN coalition led by the United States that had fought North Korea's attempted absorption of South Korea in 1950. North Koreans saw the United Nations as a thinly disguised instrument of US power pointed at them. Although they had joined the multinational organization in 1991, they did so only because the South Koreans had become a member: much of the state bureaucracy remained deeply suspicious of the United Nations.

To sum up, in the DPRK, humanitarian actors raise suspicion by definition. The self-perception of NGOs necessarily had to clash with the reality of a totalitarian society. Not to mention the fact that terms that aid agencies consider essential for their work such as 'monitoring' or 'evaluation' were unheard of in the DPRK before the arrival of humanitarian organizations in the country. All these factors came on top of a political environment of aid that – in a humanitarian perspective – is hostile to its fundamental principles.

V.2 The Donor Side: Aid as Stick and Carrot

As noted earlier, the policy of donor governments had a major impact on humanitarian action in famines in the past. Whenever principles of humanitarian aid conflicted with the political setting in a famine-stricken country, donor governments played a crucial role for the emergence of and the dealing with dilemmas that the aid agencies had to face. In Biafra, Cambodia and Ethiopia, as argued above, donors' interests hardly coincided with aid agencies' pressure for their principles of action, such as impartiality and proportionality. As a result, the outcome of these relief operations remained ambiguous.

In the past, the role of ethical and humanitarian considerations in the drafting of donor policies has been contentious. As has been noted with regard to US famine aid to Russia in the 1920s, some authors argue that "moral obligation", "humanitarian responsibility" and "Christian duty" (McElroy 1992:86) shaped US policy. Others assert that donor policy is exclusively determined by *Realpolitik*, being independent from any ethical consideration. In view of the theoretical debate surrounding decision-making in foreign policy, however, it has to be noted that not even the most rigorous advocates of the realist school of thought argue in favor of a complete separation of the political and ethical spheres. Ethical considerations and political interests are not by definition mutually exclusive. Thus, the definition of donor policy is, first and foremost, a matter of prioritization.

In addition, historical evidence from famine relief missions in the past suggests that the correspondence of political interests with humanitarian considerations has a greater impact on aid work on the ground than humanitarian intentions alone. As has been argued in case of the famine aid in Soviet Russia, for instance, a coalition of political strategic interests and humanitarian priorities positively influenced the efficacy of aid in that case. The main question in regard to the role of donors in the relief effort for North Korea is therefore: What interests do donor governments pursue, and in how far do these interests overlap with principles of humanitarian action in the DPRK?

a) The Main Donors

Since 1995, a large number of countries have provided food aid to North Korea through both bilateral and multilateral channels. The largest single donor of bilateral aid is China. The Chinese government did not notify the UN or international media of all contributions that it made, so that the exact amount of the Chinese contribution can only be estimated. China is also the only major donor that maintains friendly relations with the DPRK and that thus has a specific obligation to provide aid to its neighbor. A USAID official therefore remarks: "the best argument that I have heard against the US providing aid to North Korea is that all we are doing is buying out the Chinese. If we send 500,000 tons, they have to send 500,000 less".[12]

In consideration of the position of the North Korean government, some aid contributions were officially declared as 'foreign trade' or not mentioned at all. "Do good but do not speak about it", was the answer of Chinese officials to a Western visitor who asked about the amount of Chinese aid to the DPRK.[13] China traditionally does not allow the export of food. But since 1990, in view of the worsening situation in North Korea, China began to send food to its neighbor.[14] According to various

---

[12] Interview with Leonard Rogers, Deputy Assistant Administrator, Bureau for Humanitarian Response/USAID, Washington D.C., 30 November 2001.

[13] Interview with Gerhard Michels, Representative of the Hanns-Seidel-Stiftung in South Korea, Seoul, 5 October 2000.

[14] Oral presentation of a former Chinese customs officer and teacher at a party school at the seminar "Development in Northeast Asia and Economic Cooperation", Yanji and Changchun/People's Republic of China, 27 August to 2 September 1999. Notes by Gerhard Michels, Hanns-Seidel-Stiftung/Republic of Korea.

sources, the amount of food that China has annually provided to North Korea in the form of food aid, as concessional imports, or in exchange for commodities such as wood and seafood, is estimated to be in the range of half to one million metric tons.[15] This would make China the prime donor of food to North Korea.

The largest single donor of multilateral food aid is the US government. Between 1995 and 2002, the US contributed more than 1.8 million metric tons of food aid with a value of about US$600 millions.[16] The US government does not provide bilateral aid and watches over the 'catechism' according to which it provides food aid to the WFP, not to North Korea.[17] The decision to contribute to the UN efforts on a large scale was taken by the Clinton administration after years of internal debate and skepticism over reports of a famine situation in North Korea.[18] Obstacles to the provision of food aid were of a political, not legal nature. The sanction regime in place in the mid-1990s, which has been eased ever since, contained a 'not-withstanding clause' that explicitly excluded humanitarian assistance from the US embargo.[19] In addition, Public Law 480 defines the eligibility of countries to food aid without mentioning any political condition. A State Department official explains: "There has never been a bilateral contribution to North Korea, although this is legally possible. It's a matter of politics".[20] In 2002, US contributions were

---

[15] See Noland (2000:187) and the references therein.

[16] For further details on US contributions see the various issues of the UN Consolidated Appeal, Natsios 2001:151, Noland 2000:186-187.

[17] Interview with Jeffrey A. Beller, Chief of the Economic Division/Office of Korean Affairs at the US Department of State, Washington D.C., 28 November 2001.

[18] On the reports of a State Department delegation that had visited North Korea, Natsios notes (2001:142): "The US Central Intelligence Agency (CIA), the Defense Intelligence Agency (DIA), and the Pentagon dismissed these reports as a cynical attempt by North Korea to obtain humanitarian aid. According to these agencies, the State Department had been 'taken for a ride by the North Koreans'". For the debate within the US government and the reluctance to refer to the crisis in North Korea as a famine see Natsios 2001:141-164.

[19] Interview with Jeffrey A. Beller, Chief of the Economic Division/Office of Korean Affairs at the US Department of State, Washington D.C., 28 November 2001.

[20] Jeffrey A. Beller, Chief of the Economic Division/Office of Korean Affairs at the US Department of State, Interview, Washington D.C., 28 November 2001.

about 62 percent of the UN allocated food aid (i.e. 34 percent of the total humanitarian assistance to DPRK).[21]

Other major donors of multilateral food aid are South Korea, the European Union (European Commission and member states) and Japan. South Korean aid to the North began under the Kim Young-Sam government and was increased further under President Kim Dae-Jung. In 2002, South Korean contributions represented about 8 percent of UN food aid. Since large amounts of food and non-food items were provided bilaterally, South Korea's contributions made up almost 35 percent of the total volume of humanitarian assistance.

In 2002, the European Commission (EC) and EU member states provided 2.5 percent and 13 percent respectively of the total humanitarian assistance to the DPRK. Although these figures are rather modest in comparison to US or South Korean contributions, the EC plays a very important role concerning NGO work on the ground because most NGOs that are currently resident in the DPRK are EC-funded. In addition, both European donor agencies that are in charge of humanitarian assistance to North Korea – the Food Security Unit and the Humanitarian Aid Office (ECHO) – have permanent delegates in Pyongyang. The fact that residency status has only been granted to European agencies is most likely to be due to a 'comparative advantage' in relation to US, South Korean and Japanese organizations. In the words of an EC official, "our big advantage is that the EU is seen as neutral, unlike the United States, South Korea and Japan".[22]

Japan has given considerable amounts of food in the past. In 2001, for instance, almost 50 percent of food aid provided to the UN came from Japan. In 2002 and 2003, the Japanese government – for reasons to be discussed later - almost entirely stopped its aid program and did not contribute to UN appeals.

The political relevance of food aid for North Korea is evident when it comes to decision-making processes within the donors. The US government and the European Commission serve as illustration. As for the US government, the Inter-Agency Food Aid Committee plays an important

---

[21] Total humanitarian assistance includes non-food sectors and contributions outside the UN Consolidated Appeal process (bilateral, via Red Cross etc.). Figures do not include carry over. Source: UNOCHA 2002: annex X.

[22] Maria Castillo Fernandez, Korea Desk Officer, RELEX/EC, interview, Brussels, 16 October 2001.

role. The Committee comprises of representatives from the State Department, the National Security Council (NSC), the US Department of Agriculture (USDA) and the US Agency for International Development (USAID). It goes without saying that the mandates of the member organizations of the Inter-Agency Food Aid Committee clearly differ. Only USAID has the organizational mandate to consider living standards, economic and social development in the recipient country. USDA, by contrast, that is the primary source of food aid to North Korea since 1999, has no humanitarian mandate. In most cases, the amount and timing of food aid shipments is decided inside USAID. In the case of food aid for North Korea, however, amount and timing are defined in consultation with State Department and NSC.[23]

On the European side too, institutions with an organizational emergency interest do not shape aid policy towards North Korea independently. As for the European Commission, three institutions deal with the matter.[24] Firstly, the EuropeAid Co-operation Office, which is the development aid branch of the Commission. Part of it is the Food Security Unit that deals with food aid issues. This body organizes the EC food aid to North Korea via WFP, NGOs as well as bilateral contributions. Secondly, the Humanitarian Aid Office (ECHO), which is in charge of emergency relief programs, funds non-food activities in DPRK (health, water and sanitation). With regard to the DPRK, it works exclusively via NGOs. Thirdly, the External Relations Directorate General (*relations extérieures*, RELEX) is the Commission's primary foreign policy institution. While EuropeAid and ECHO have a development and humanitarian agenda – comparable to USAID's - RELEX is the Commission's foreign affairs office and is in charge of the European Union's political, bilateral relations.[25] In terms of humanitarian aid to North Korea, the hierarchy is clear. As a RELEX official put it with regard to humanitarian aid to

---

[23] Interviews with Leonard Rogers, Deputy Assistant Administrator, Bureau for Humanitarian Response/USAID, Washington D.C., 30 November 2001 and with Jeffrey A. Beller, Chief of the Economic Division/Office of Korean Affairs at the US Department of State, Washington D.C., 28 November 2001.

[24] Under its President Romano Prodi, the Commission has undertaken a restructuring of the services dealing with external relations that also concerned development and humanitarian aid. We only refer to the current system that has been shaped since the Prodi Commission came into office in September 1999.

[25] With the exception of Africa, the Caribbean, the Pacific, and EU-applicant countries.

North Korea: "RELEX does not consult others in political issues, but others consult RELEX".[26]

b) The Strategic Role of Aid

In contrast to Biafra, Cambodia or Ethiopia, North Korea does not stand on the edge of world politics. The country occupies a prominent place on the diplomatic agenda in regard to regional and international security issues. In addition, the DPRK's bilateral relations with a number of donor countries – the US and South Korea in the first place – is marked by distrust and hostility. In a way, the general setting in regard to the relation between recipient and donor is comparable to the famine situation in Soviet Russia in the early 1920s. "Diplomacy", as Natsios (2001:145) notes, "is after all an attempt to affect the behavior of another country by the use of incentives and disincentives". As in the Russian case, famine and famine relief cannot be seen as being outside or above this political sphere. In particular, the international aid effort plays a role in relation to four strategic, long-term policy goals that are pursued to a differing degree by donor governments. These four goals are: regime change, soft-landing, reform inducement and information.

Regime change

Regime change in North Korea and the end of the world's harshest totalitarian state is an attractive long-term vision for foreign policy makers in the West, Japan and South Korea. The DPRK, from its inception onwards, has been perceived by South Korea, Japan and the West as a threat to national and international security. Regime change and democratization in DPRK would open new opportunities, from a security perspective, but also in regard to human rights or reconciliation concerns. As has been the case with Soviet Russia in the 1920s, North Korea is in the economically desperate situation that the West, South Korea and Japan have long waited for. From this perspective, famine as the extreme form of socio-economic crisis is the final and most evident proof of the failure of North Korea's ideological and political system. Natsios (1999:9), for instance, argues:

---

[26] Interview with Maria Castillo Fernandez, Korea Desk Officer, RELEX/EC, Brussels, 16 October 2001.

> The food aid program is visible evidence of the failure of juche, the governing state ideology; it has undermined state propaganda about the outside capitalist world; and it has accelerated the privatization of the economy (...). Thus, the food program is undermining state ideology rather than propping the system up.

It is often argued that the power basis of this system is the isolation of the North Korean people, that is, its ignorance of the outside world and its deprivation of the possibility to compare. The assumption is that the regime will collapse once the population can compare their daily food ration, their living standards and their freedom to the reality in other countries. Essentially, it is argued that the North Korean people will most likely draw the same conclusions as did the East Germans when they watched West German TV.

The soft-landing concept

The second policy goal, the soft-landing concept, also focuses on regime change as a long-term policy goal. It was coined under the Clinton administration in the context of the 1994 Agreed Framework between the DPRK and the US (see Natsios 2001:127). Although regime collapse might be an appealing scenario in the long run, an immediate breakdown of the Kim Jong-Il government scared policy makers in neighboring countries and the West. It is argued that an immediate breakdown, caused by social unrest and violent hunger riots, contains uncontrollable risks. In view of the North Korean military power, scenarios such as a desperate leadership in Pyongyang having nothing to lose were regarded as an imminent threat to regional and international security. The sudden falling apart of the North Korean state therefore had to be avoided. Jean comments on the motives behind donor engagement (1999:16-17):

> The principle reason of this engagement is the fear of implosion. Although hoping that the end of this totalitarian system comes closer, everyone fears its sudden falling apart. The fear of instability, refugee movements, of political uncertainty and its strategic implications, as well as of reunification and its economic consequences, determines all reflection.

Instead of a sudden breakdown, the soft-landing policy aims at a gradual and controllable power erosion of the DPRK regime. Stanley Roth, assistant Secretary of State for East Asian and Pacific affairs in the

Clinton administration, makes clear: "a soft landing for North Korea is in our national interest".[27]

Reform inducement

As for the third policy goal, reform inducement, national security concerns play a role in a more long-term perspective. In the first place, reform inducement seeks to promote change in various fields inside DPRK and in regard to the country's relations to foreign countries. The EU Council, for instance, says:

> The European Union (...) is prepared, for its part, to consider any initiative which might assist the opening up of North Korea, thus contributing to the stability of the region. (...) emphasising that the character of the Union's relations with the Democratic People's Republic of Korea would go hand in hand with developments in that country's attitude in various fields, the Union has made and will continue to make its contributions to the process of dialogue and rapprochement between the two Koreas.[28]

Encouraging internal reform, thus promoting the 'opening up' of the DPRK are important policy goals of donor governments, particularly of EU countries. In the words of an ECHO official who commented on European famine relief efforts, "ECHO's projects are peanuts, but our objective is to open their minds. North Koreans are still not at all levels aware of the structural causes of the famine, many still think it's a temporary problem that can be addressed by temporary foreign aid".[29] Importantly, however, EU member states have differing attitudes concerning the efficacy of humanitarian assistance as a means to induce reform in DPRK. Italy, Sweden and Germany are traditionally more in favor of the reform inducement policy than France or Portugal.[30] Some observers argue that the height of EU contributions to the famine aid program in

---

[27] Peggy Hu: "State, defense officials discuss US policy toward North Korea". Article on a forum on North Korea that was held in Washington D.C., 19 September 1997. Found at usinfo. state.gov/regional/ea/easec/koreafrm.htm (4 April 2003).

[28] General Affairs and External Relations Council: "Korean Peninsula – European Lines of Action Towards North Korea". 2308th Council meeting, press release (13430/00), Brussels, 20 November 2000.

[29] Javier Menendez Bonilla, Desk Officer, ECHO, interview, Brussels, 17 October 2001.

[30] Interview with Maria Castillo Fernandez, Korea Desk Officer, RELEX/EC, Brussels, 16 October 2001.

1997, that exceeded the amount of US contributions at that time, illustrate the EU's initiative to encourage the DPRK to implement economic and political reform.[31]

Information

The fourth policy goal that is at stake is information. In the often-quoted words of the former US Ambassador to South Korea, Donald P. Gregg, North Korea is "the longest running intelligence failure in US history".[32] The isolation of the DPRK not only hindered information from the outside to enter the country, it also effectively cut the outside world from information on North Korea. This cut concerned almost all areas of reality in the country. Since the 1960s, the DPRK was more and more reluctant to issue data on its economic performance. Basic figures such as GNP, trade balance or food production had, by and large, to be estimated from the outside. One result was that the actual military capacity of the DPRK and the conditions within the armed forces at times of economic crisis could only be guessed. The opening up of the country for humanitarian aid was therefore of great interest for the intelligence of those countries for whom the DPRK was the unknown enemy. In this regard, Snyder (2003: 2-3) argues:

> Although the overriding interest of humanitarian aid workers from UN organizations and from non-governmental organizations was to help North Koreans facing starvation and to forestall an even greater humanitarian disaster, their entry into North Korea constituted an unprecedented opportunity for outsiders to experience directly the real situation of a country that had heretofore severely limited foreign access to North Korea.

c) Aid as a Tactical Bargaining Chip

In addition to long-term, strategic interests, food aid to North Korea has a part to play in regard to tactical short- and mid-term goals. Food

---

[31] Interview with Leonard Rogers, Deputy Assistant Administrator, Bureau for Humanitarian Response/USAID, Washington D.C., 30 November 2001.

[32] Mitchell B. Reiss (2001): "Avoiding déjà vu all over again: lessons from US-DPRK engagement". In: *North Korea's engagement – perspectives, outlook, and implications. Conference report.* 23 February 2001. Found at www.cia.gov/nic/pubs/conference _reports/nk_conference.html (4 April 2003).

aid has been used by all major donor countries to increase their leverage in talks with the DPRK government in a number of areas. The specific policy goal differs according to the interest at stake within the respective donor government. It is important to note that all sides, donors and recipient country, use food aid as a bargaining chip. In some cases, donors offered or withheld food shipments in order to get North Korean concessions. On other occasions, the DPRK demanded food aid as a prerequisite for participation in talks.[33] It is telling to note that the DPRK uses diplomatic means in order to obtain food aid even from China. Natsios (2001:139) reports that North Korea, as a reaction to Chinese announcements that food provisions would be stopped, entered into negotiations with Taiwan for regular airline flights between Pyongyang and Taipei. As a result, China made substantial food aid commitments, and North Korea finally broke off the negotiations with Taiwan. Thus, it is fair to say that recipient as well as donor countries are well aware of the role of food aid as a bargaining chip. Since the US, South Korea and Japan were primarily engaged in bilateral negotiations with the DPRK, we will now focus on these three donor governments and their tactical interests in regard to North Korea.

DPRK-US relations

As for the US, the use of food shipments as a bargaining chip in diplomatic struggles with the DPRK has raised some controversy. In 1995/96, State Department officials including the then US Special Envoy to North Korea, Charles Kartman, made clear at several meetings with US NGOs that the government was using humanitarian assistance for political goals. In particular, US demands concerning North Korea's adherence to the Agreed Framework and its participation in four-party talks with the US, South Korea and China have been accompanied by the provision or withdrawal of food aid.[34] These statements provoked harsh protests on the part of US NGOs and thus "galvanized an unlikely coalition of organizations and people" (Natsios 2001:149). Newspaper articles were written and TV spots produced that asked the public: "Did you

---

[33] According to Snyder (1999:79) North Korea demanded food aid in 1996 and 1997 as a prerequisite for participation in a preparatory meeting for the four-party talks.

[34] Interview with James K. Bishop, Director Humanitarian Response, Interaction, Washington D.C., 28 November 2001. See also Natsios (2001:149-151) and Noland (2000:186).

know that the US government is responsible for the death of North Korean people?"[35] The US government decided to provide food aid on a much larger scale in 1997. However, it would be daring to attribute this decision to NGO lobbying and to a shift within the US government from political to humanitarian considerations.[36] In any case, the timing of US food shipments in following years suggests that food was given as a *quid pro quo* for North Korea's agreement to participate in negotiations (missile proliferation talks, four-party talks, negotiations over suspected nuclear sites).[37] Interestingly, in a report on US support for a consortium of American NGOs, the US General Accounting Office (GAO) implicitly distinguishes between the political motives on donor and recipient side on the one hand, and the NGO consortium's humanitarian motivation on the other hand:

> According to US officials, the food aid was provided for humanitarian purposes, reflected the modest progress that had been made in the relationship with North Korea, and could serve as a basis for possibly expanding the relationship with North Korea. North Korean officials were described by US officials as having seen the project as a way to obtain needed food, as something received for allowing the United States to inspect the Kumchang-ni facility, and as a step toward normalizing relations with the United States. The [NGO] Consortium saw the project as an opportunity to provide needed food aid to unemployed factory and agricultural workers through food-for-work programs and initiate a small pilot

---

[35] Interview with James K. Bishop, Director Humanitarian Response, Interaction, Washington D.C., 28 November 2001.

[36] See Natsios (2001:155): "It remains unclear why the administration was willing to pledge this additional food aid. Part of the decision may be attributed to the campaign waged by the NGO coalition and Congressman Hall's efforts to end the famine. The White House claimed that the WFP appeal in late June was the tacit explanation for the administration's decision. But perhaps more important may have been North Korea's assertion in the negotiations over the four-party talks that its participation was contingent on a further pledge of food aid. This element in the United States' decision cannot be ignored, given Pyongyang's previous success in getting its demands met. Perhaps the NGO campaign provided the Clinton administration with a convenient defense to hard-line opposition in Washington. Whatever the reasons for the decision, however, more food aid was on the way".

[37] For details see Noland 2000:188.

agricultural project that could help improve North Korea's food security.[38]

DPRK-ROK relations

Tactical calculations and expected political benefits of food contributions to North Korea heavily influenced the South Korean government's decisions to provide food aid to the North. From the moment North Korea asked foreign countries for assistance, the food aid issue played a prominent role in inter-Korean political relations. Noland (2000:184) reports on the situation in 1995:

> As the situation worsened, North Korea turned to Japan, its former colonial master, presumably because Japan had substantial reserve grain stocks. Plus, it would be less humiliating to accept assistance from Japan (which could be portrayed as a kind of reparations) than from rival South Korea (...). A positive response by Japan was opposed by the Kim Young-sam administration in South Korea, whose Deputy Prime Minister Rha Woong-bae warned Japan of 'soured relations' if Japan were to provide aid in the absence of South Korean participation.

In the following years, South Korean governments regularly used food aid as a bargaining chip in negotiations with the North. Food is given to get the DPRK at the negotiation table or withheld as a punishment for activities that the South sees as a provocation. For instance, in the aftermath of a naval battle between South Korean and North Korean ships in July 2002, the Seoul government decided to withhold rice aid that had been previously arranged. In addition, the agriculture ministry announced that rice, that had been set aside as food aid to the DPRK, could be donated to other countries or used as cattle feed.[39] A few weeks later, the South Korean government said it might provide 300,000 metric tons of rice on the condition that the North agrees to participate in an inter-Korean ministerial meeting.[40]

---

[38] GAO: *Foreign Assistance. US Bilateral Food Assistance to North Korea Had Mixed Results.* Report to the Chairman and Ranking Minority Member, Committee on International Relations, House of Representatives. Report Number: GAO/NSIAD-00-175). Washington D.C.: June 2000, p.5.

[39] *Joongang Ilbo*, 3 July 2002.

[40] *Joongang Ilbo*, 30 July 2002.

DPRK-Japan relations

Japanese food aid to North Korea has to be seen in the context of a number of unsettled issues that have weighed upon relations between the two countries since decades. In the words of a Japanese diplomat who commented on the DPRK aid program, "every grain of rice in Japan is politicized".[41] The bilateral issues include the fate of a number of Japanese citizens kidnapped by North Korean in the 1970s and 1980s as well as the presence of the hijackers of a Japanese airliner in 1970 in North Korea. In 2002, the Japanese government, previously the second largest donor of food aid to the DPRK, stopped its contributions. According to a number of observers, the Japanese government saw itself in a comfortable negotiating position as a result of general donor fatigue and the review of North Korea related policies in the US. Since no other country was willing or able to replace Japanese aid provisions, the situation offered "a historic opportunity for breakthroughs on a range of diplomatic problems".[42] In any case, the North Korean government agreed to hold a summit in Pyongyang in September 2002 and to give information on the abduction cases. The North Korean side admitted the kidnapping cases and allowed the kidnapped persons to visit their families in Japan. Negotiations went on but reached a stalemate shortly after the summit. In 2003, Japan still did not participate in the international aid program for the DPRK.

d) Aid and Domestic Public Opinion – The Hungry Child and Politics

As argued earlier, domestic public opinion plays an important role in the shaping of donor policies. Media coverage of humanitarian crises ultimately exerts pressure on donor governments to 'do something'. This is also true in regard to the North Korean famine. At the same time, however, public sentiment is in parts critical to 'aiding the enemy', particularly in the DPRK's neighboring countries. Thus, donor governments find themselves in a difficult position concerning domestic public opinion, though to a differing degree. The challenge is to show that a government cares "about the suffering of the North Korean people" (George

---

[41] *Washington Post*, 5 December 2002.
[42] *New York Times*, 17 May 2002.

W. Bush)[43] while at the same time displaying a hard stance vis-à-vis the North Korean regime.

Public opinion in the US

The US government, in particular, has to face divided public opinion and maneuvers between various points of view. On the one hand, US NGOs strongly lobbied in favor of generous famine aid to North Korea with no political strings attached. They argue that it is a US tradition to generously provide humanitarian aid to suffering populations regardless of the political and ideological affiliation of the country in crisis. The use of food aid for political goals, as announced by US government officials to NGO representatives, was therefore regarded a shift away from traditional US policy. James Bishop from the NGO consortium Interaction argues: "We were surprised. Didn't President Reagan say 'A hungry child knows no politics'? Plus, the three biggest food aid missions in Africa were for Marxist countries: Ethiopia, Angola and Mozambique".[44] On the other hand, the fact that the US government was providing food aid on a large scale to a hostile state caused some negative public sentiment that was also expressed in the US Congress. Some Congress members remained skeptical about governmental food aid to North Korea and were highly susceptive to any report that cast doubt on effective and well-targeted aid distribution. For instance, in 1997, a Congressman argued that the US government should stop its contributions to the UN food aid for the DPRK and leave aid activities for that country to NGOs.[45]

An appropriate means of avoiding public debates on US food aid contributions for North Korea is the description of the food aid as a purely humanitarian endeavor. Thus, whenever this 'catechism' is not respected, the credibility of the alleged purely humanitarian grounds is damaged, both in the US and on the international stage. In 1999, at the request of US Congress, the US General Accounting Office (GAO) reported on the issue of US food aid to North Korea. In the first draft of this report, GAO states that "US national security concerns, including concern about North Korea's development of nuclear weapons and the

---

[43] Ron Fournier: "Bush says food, energy aid possible if North Korea disarms", *Associated Press*, Washington D.C., 14 January 2003.

[44] Interview with James K. Bishop, Director Humanitarian Response/Interaction, Washington D.C., 28 November 2001.

[45] See Natsios 2001:155.

maintenance of peace on the Korean peninsula, are also part of the underlying rationale for these donations".[46] State Department and USAID objected to this assertion and argued that "our worldwide motivation for the provision of food aid is to meet identified humanitarian needs". USAID noted that, even though "any 'diplomatic dividend' to the food aid program has always been welcomed – the rationale for food aid is entirely humanitarian".[47] GAO changed the original formulation but still mentioned foreign policy goals in its presentation of food aid motives.[48] Furthermore, in 2002, a GAO representative in a testimony on US food aid programs worldwide argued before the US Senate that, in regard to the DPRK, foreign policy interests prevail even over humanitarian considerations:

> Certain programs also have foreign policy goals. In one case, the United States continued to provide emergency food aid to North Korea for humanitarian purposes even though the North Korean government prevented the World Food Program (WFP) from effectively monitoring whether the food aid reached the intended recipients. In that situation, the United States weighed foreign policy considerations against the assurance that food aid was achieving its humanitarian purposes.[49]

In addition, US governments are placed in a somewhat awkward position whenever the DPRK publicly denounces the role of food aid as a

---

[46] Quoted in the comments of the US Department of State to the draft report as attached as Appendix I to the final report (GAO: *Foreign Assistance. North Korea Restricts Food Aid Monitoring*. Report to the Chairman, Committee on International Relations, House of Representatives. Report Number: GAO/NSIAD-00-35). Washington D.C.: October 1999, p.24).

[47] GAO 1999:25,28, note 46 in this chapter.

[48] The final version asserts: "According to the Department of State and the World Food Program, food aid is being provided for humanitarian purposes and is intended to be distributed primarily to children, women, and the elderly at schools, hospitals, and other institutions. The Department of State also believes that food donations may improve the climate of the bilateral relationship with North Korea on a host of issues, including concerns about North Korea's development of nuclear weapons and the maintenance of peace on the Korean peninsula". GAO 1999:3, note 46 in this chapter.

[49] Testimony of Loren Yager, Director International Affairs and Trade/GAO before the Subcommittee on Oversight of Governmental Management, Restructuring and the District of Columbia, Committee on Governmental Affairs, US Senate, 4 June 2002. Reproduced in GAO: *Food Aid. Experience of US Programs Suggests Opportunities for Improvement*. Report Number: GAO-02-801T. Washington D.C.: 4 June 2002, p.3.

bargaining chip; although, as mentioned above, it itself demands food in exchange for concessions. In spring 1999, for instance, the US wanted North Korea to allow US inspections of an underground construction site. The North Korean government accepted and, as a *quid pro quo*, received 600,000 tons of food from the US in April 1999. In the following month, the DPRK government publicly accused the US of linking aid to politics. As a result, a bad light was shed on the US, not on the DPRK. In an article from May 1999 *Agence France Press* (AFP) reports:

> Famine-stricken North Korea (...) said aid coming from the United States was linked to talks between the two countries. The comment was made after US experts were in North Korea to inspect an underground site, suspected to be used for nuclear purposes. The United States denied food aid was linked to the inspections but after Pyongyang agreed to allow US inspections of the facility, Washington pledged 200,000 tonnes of food aid. This week the United States announced an additional 400,000 tonnes.[50]

Furthermore, the US government has to calm those who argue that food aid to the DPRK may prop up the regime. The Bush administration, like its predecessor under Clinton, publicly stresses that US efforts seek to ensure that the food reaches the intended recipients and is not being diverted to the military or party apparatus. In a hearing on North Korea at the US House of Representatives, Henry J. Hyde, Chairman of the Committee on International Relations, mentions the twofold motive that US donor policy has to deal with:

> I agree with President Reagan that 'a hungry child knows no politics', and am proud that our food assistance has saved the lives of millions of vulnerable Koreans. On the other hand, the admonition to 'love your enemies' does not, in my view, include putting rice in the bellies of a hostile North Korean army which threatens our friends in South Korea and the thirty-seven thousand American troops who stand with them.[51]

---

[50] "North Korea says food aid from US linked to on-going discussions". *Agence France Press*, Seoul, 21 May 1999.
[51] Opening statement for the "Hearing of the East Asia and the Pacific Subcommittee of the House International Relations Committee. North Korea: Humanitarian and Human Rights Concerns". Federal News Service, 2 May 2002.

Public opinion in South Korea

Essentially, the twofold point of view – humanitarian obligation to help, but no aid to an enemy regime – is also to be found in other main donor countries. The respective weight of both arguments, however, differs largely depending on the specific country context. In South Korea, a strict separation between humanitarian and political issues finds relatively few supporters. One reason is the relatively small number of humanitarian NGOs which – due to a lack of private funding tradition – have fewer resources and political impact than Western aid agencies.

In South Korea, arguments in favor of and against food aid to the North both refer to political interests. Aiding the DPRK is described as a national duty, an act of patriotism and national reconciliation rather than an apolitical act. In addition, South Korean aid agencies are relatively young. With few exceptions, South Korean private aid organizations are one-country NGOs that provide aid to the DPRK and to no other country. Thus, inter-Korean relations dominate the debate surrounding food aid rather than general considerations of a non-political tradition of humanitarian aid. The controversial issue is whether the ROK government is attaching sufficient political strings to its aid provisions or whether it should be more demanding. The main opposition party, the conservative Grand National Party (GNP) reproached the Kim Dae-Jung administration for being too soft. In October 2001, for instance, after the government's announcement of additional food aid to the North, the GNP did not object but called for more benefits from North Korea in terms of the extension of family exchange and the installation of a ROK liaison office.[52]

Consequently, people's satisfaction with the overall state of inter-Korean relations influences public opinion concerning the food aid issue. The general support for a policy of reconciliation therefore has a positive impact on people's view on food aid. A 2002 survey found that 73 percent of ROK citizens back the government's policy of reconciliation, and that a similar number (66.1 percent) believes that the level of humanitarian aid to the DPRK should be maintained or raised.[53] Likewise, military tension and escalation lead to a more critical sentiment among the ROK public on aid activities for North Korea. For instance, when the

---

[52] *Joongang Ilbo*, 9 October 2001.
[53] *Joongang Ilbo*, 17 June 2002.

North announced the reactivation of its nuclear program in December 2002, the marine transportation union refused to load a food aid provision onto a cargo ship, and received popular support for this refusal. The inter-Korean summit in June 2000, however, had a negative impact on South Korean aid agencies and their fundraising activities. Aid to North Korea was primarily regarded a governmental task by the public that the ROK government was prepared to fulfil. Oh Jae-Shik, President of World Vision Korea, explains:

> The South Korean NGOs have been involved in DPRK assistance since 1996 but with the June 15ᵗʰ Declaration of 2000, the South Korean government (...) pushed herself hard to cover as many areas as possible without leaving much room for NGOs. Influenced by such atmosphere, the public became reluctant in supporting and donating to the NGOs (...). As a result, the moral and substantial burden to be borne by the government increased, while fundraising by NGOs decreased.[54]

In addition, the TV picture of Pyongyang citizens made the South Korean public believe that the situation in the North was "not too bad".[55] In sum, the organization of food aid according to principles of humanitarian action is hardly demanded by any lobby group in South Korea. Therefore, in terms of domestic public opinion, the ROK government has no reason to push for the respect of these principles.

Public opinion in Japan

In Japan, public opinion on food aid for North Korea is also heavily influenced by bilateral relations. As is the case in South Korea, no NGO coalition or other civil lobby group refers to humanitarian traditions that may suggest separating aid from political interests. Due to the unsettled and highly emotional issues mentioned above, public sentiment toward North Korea is more negative than it is in South Korea. The North Korean-Japanese summit in September 2002 all but improved this public sentiment. The main result of the summit was a public outcry in Japan in the aftermath of the North's public admittance and revelation of details

---

[54] Presentation at the Third International NGO Conference on Humanitarian Assistance to North Korea: Cooperative Efforts Beyond Food Aid, Seoul, 17 to 20 June 2001, p.3.

[55] Interview with Hong Song Young, Manager Planning Department/Korean Sharing Movement, Seoul, 10 November 2000.

concerning the kidnapping cases. Japan is the only country within the group of main donors where the withholding of food finds major support with the public. So, in May 2002, the Japanese Chief Cabinet Secretary indicated that the government would not resume food aid to North Korea due to the negative public sentiment toward North Korea.[56] It is telling to note that in December 2002 the shipment of a modest 45 tons of food by a private organization with links to the government was treated as a scandal and forced the head of the organization to resign.[57]

Public opinion in European countries

As for European countries, both arguments – the humanitarian duty to provide assistance and the intention not to prop up an oppressive regime – can be found in public discourse. Bilateral political relations and security issues play a less important role in public in European countries. At the same time, private aid organizations have a much greater influence than they have in Japan or South Korea. Thus, European governments are more susceptible to providing aid in order to calm public pressure to 'do something'. One example is the delivery of beef from Germany to the DPRK in fall 2001 which, primarily, was the result of the lobbying efforts of Cap Anamur and its high-profile former head, Rupert Neudeck. The delivery of beef - that was wrongly assumed to be infected by a cattle disease but could not be sold on the European market – was heavily criticized by nutritionists and other aid agencies. However, in a meeting in which a number of these critics participated in January 2002, the former Minister of State within the German Foreign Office, Ludger Volmer, explained that the government at that time, in view of public pressure, simply had no choice.

Implications for Humanitarian Action in the DPRK

Aid agencies face conflicting obligations in the DPRK. Firstly, the magnitude of the humanitarian crisis appeals to the moral imperative to relieve human suffering. Secondly, the political interests of both recipient and donor governments are, by and large, not in line with humani-

---

[56] *Joongang Ilbo*, 9 May 2002.
[57] *Washington Post*, 5 December 2002.

tarian concerns and principles. To the extent that donor policy is determined by national security concerns, humanitarian agencies will have to struggle by themselves to make the principles of their work respected in the DPRK. A politico-humanitarian coalition based on the model of the aid operation in Soviet Russia in the 1920s therefore remains an illusion. Consequently, moral dilemmas of aid as a result of the non-respect for principles of humanitarian action appear to be inescapable in North Korea.

For both sides, recipient and donors, famine and famine aid are linked to a number of political interests, strategic concepts and tactical calculations.

The dependence on foreign assistance in itself undermines Juche ideology and thus the legitimization of political power in North Korea. In order to minimize these risks, the DPRK leadership has a strong interest in keeping the freedom of action of aid agencies to a minimum and in shaping the famine aid effort according to its own priorities. This has major implications for humanitarian organizations working in North Korea. Above all, aid agencies in North Korea are dealing with an operational space that is, in the words of an Action Contre la Faim (ACF) Officer, "reduced to zero"[58]. In addition, due to the ideological background of DPRK politics, attempts to reestablish the country's own food production capacity are of utmost importance. As a result, food production inputs are the most welcome kind of foreign assistance, while short-term nutritional relief appears to be less attractive. Generally, aid activities that go in hand with direct communication between locals and foreigners and with a large presence of foreign expatriate staff in the country pose a risk to the traditional ideological principles of the DPRK.

As for donor interests, strategic security concerns, as well as tactical considerations concerning North Korea's negotiating behavior heavily influence famine aid policies. In terms of the policy of the US – as the main donor of multilateral aid – Noland remarks that the funding of famine aid "has been determined by traditional national security concerns, by 'big politics', namely the Agreed Framework and missile talks".[59] Regime change, soft-landing concept, reform inducement and the search for information on the reality in the DPRK define the strategic

---

[58] Interview with Jean-Fabrice Piétri, Desk Officer/ACF, Paris, 20 July 1999.
[59] Interview with Marcus Noland, Institute for International Economics, Washington D.C., 27 November 2001.

interests at stake in regard to famine aid for North Korea. These sets of strategic interests and concepts have a number of implications for humanitarian action in the country.

First, from a *regime change* perspective, famine aid has the function of a poisoned carrot, of "caressing the enemy to death".[60] Scott Snyder (2003:2) notes:

> The voluntary admission of international humanitarian aid workers into North Korea (...) marked the beginning of the end of North Korea's hermetic isolation and the dawn of a new challenge of the survival of North Korea's political system. Previously, there was virtually no 'external window' or on-the-ground foreign presence in North Korea beyond a few diplomats in their isolated diplomatic enclave at the center of Pyongyang.

A food aid program that is carried out by international and Western aid workers and, most importantly, that is visible to the local population may potentially undermine the ideological and political basis of the North Korean state. The regime change concept therefore has one major implication for humanitarian work in DPRK: aid fulfils its function first and foremost through the visible act of giving. The visibility of foreign aid is most important, while the humanitarian impact and the effect on the needs of the population is, from a regime change perspective, secondary.

Secondly, famine aid plays a very important role in regard to the *soft-landing* concept. Humanitarian aid helps to meet the immediate humanitarian needs, it prevents people from starvation. Therefore, food aid prevents the collapse of the North Korean regime that, from a soft-landing perspective, needs to be averted. Implications for humanitarian action in the DPRK are twofold. At first, this strategic consideration ultimately influences the set of activities that aid agencies can carry out in the DPRK, because donors are more willing to fund emergency activities than longer-term projects. Controlling the process of power erosion means keeping the DPRK dependent on foreign assistance without resolving the economic crisis. Development aid or technical assistance that could help to improve the economic performance of the DPRK in a sustainable manner undermines the soft-landing concept. What a former UN official finds deplorable concerning the effect of food aid, makes

---

[60] François Jean in: *Die Weltwoche,* 12 November 1998.

sense in a soft-landing perspective: "Food aid causes dependencies, solves none of the underlying causes of the deficit, and uses up resources that might be better spent on the rehabilitation of industry and international trade" (Weingartner 2001:26). The US is the most rigorous advocate of an 'only-food' approach. To date, the US government has left the legal obstacles to development aid for North Korea untouched and has not funded any longer-term aid activities that would shift the focus from relief to development. Although UN agencies appealed for donor contributions to various sectors, the US generously, but exclusively, funds the food aid sector.

In addition, principles of humanitarian action play no role from a soft-landing perspective. First and foremost, the famine aid operation needs to effectively stabilize the North Korean society. In a sense, this objective suggests supporting those population groups whose disloyalty would effectively undermine the regime's basis of power. These groups, however, are not necessarily those in greatest humanitarian need. With regard to food aid donations from North Korea's neighboring countries, WFP Regional Director John Powell comments that "those countries would not only want to see the bulk of the population of DPRK fed, I should imagine have a hungry Army on their borders. So I can understand why some people might want to give undirected food assistance".[61]

Thirdly, the *reform inducement* strategy uses aid as a gesture of good will and as evidence that reform efforts will be awarded. The proportional affording of aid is no integral part of the reform inducement approach. It pushes for dialogue, exchange and increased contact between the DPRK and democratic countries. In that regard, aid agencies play an important role that needs to be strengthened. From 1997/98 on, the EC reduced their UN contributions and augmented the funding of NGOs. In particular, the EC announced that it was prepared to fund NGO projects only under the condition that these aid agencies were permanently resident in the DPRK. As a result, for the first time in the history of the DPRK, NGOs opened offices in North Korea run by international aid workers living in Pyongyang. The use of aid as a 'door-opener' to open minds and, ultimately, to induce reform, therefore opened new perspectives for humanitarian action in the DPRK. And at least in theory, a per-

---

[61] Federal News Service: "Hearing of the East Asia and the Pacific Subcommittee of the House International Relations Committee. North Korea: Humanitarian and Human Rights Concerns", 2 May 2002.

manent presence on the ground promised to facilitate the distribution of aid according to needs and people's vulnerability.

Fourthly, donors see the famine aid operation as an opportunity to gather *information* on the DPRK. Freedom of movement for international organizations, direct communication with local people and in-depth information on the humanitarian situation are related to necessities of humanitarian action. In a way, these demands are also in line with intelligence interests. However, from an intelligence perspective, the content of aid activities and the humanitarian effect they engender are of no major interest.

In addition to strategic considerations, famine aid – food aid in particular – plays an important role in donor policies as a means of increasing a government's leverage in talks with the DPRK. The use of food aid as a bargaining chip in negotiations has guaranteed the steady flow of funds and food to the UN led food aid operation. However, as a bargaining chip, food aid does not primarily aim to improve people's nutrition or health status. First and foremost, the important effect of food aid is the reaction of the North Korean side to the provision or withholding of aid. In some cases, even the mere announcement of providing certain amounts of food may suffice to get the intended concessions. What happens in the country, once the food is handed over to WFP or North Korean authorities, is of no major importance. Thus, aid agencies benefit from the role of aid as a bargaining chip only in respect to the amount of food aid. But, essentially, humanitarian principles and the diplomatic intention to influence North Korean negotiating behavior have nothing in common. Moreover, the use of food aid to influence North Korea negotiating behavior ultimately jeopardizes the credibility of humanitarian agencies working in the DPRK. The presentation of aid as exclusively serving humanitarian purposes in combination with efforts to increase the operational space of aid agencies must sound quite unconvincing to North Korean authorities. Natsios (2001:162) remarks that "the North Koreans recognized that the food aid was an inducement to talk, not an effort to end the famine, so they intended to use it as they wished". Summing up, bilateral contributions that are attached to political but not to humanitarian strings, weaken efforts that aim to promote the respect for principles of humanitarian action.

Beside foreign policy interests, donors' North Korean famine aid policy takes domestic politics and public opinion into consideration. As for South Korean and Japanese agencies, these factors have a rather negative impact on their work in North Korea, primarily in terms of funding. Domestic politics is a particularly important factor in the US. Due to the political sensitivity of the North Korean famine aid operation, the US Congress closely observes the practices of food distribution in the DPRK. It can be argued that the congressional insistence on accountability and proportionality is "motivated not by humanitarian zeal but by the desire to ensure that none of the food went to the military" (Natsios 2001:162). However, the desire not to support the military also emanates from the humanitarian principle of reaching people in need and not people in power. In a way, the policy of the US Congress, in this regard, is in line with principles of humanitarian action.

One result of the various political implications of famine aid to North Korea is the delay of the aid program. It took two years after the North Korean appeal for international assistance, before international donors began to fund famine aid on a large scale.[62] The implications of the external political interests on the working conditions of aid agencies in the DPRK will be discussed in detail in the following chapter.

---

[62] In view of the controversy in the US, Natsios (2001:162-163) notes: "The clash of these geostrategic interests with the humanitarian imperative to stop the famine caused the worst paralysis I have witnessed in any major relief effort since the close of the Cold War".

Chapter VI.

Humanitarian Space in North Korea

It has been argued that dilemmas of humanitarian action derive from the tension between moral obligations on the one hand and real constraints stemming from the political environment of aid on the other. Both donor and recipient sides determine the operational space of aid and the respect for the principles of humanitarian action. The maneuverability of aid agencies and the respect for the principles of their work is called 'humanitarian space'. This concept translates the principle of proportionality into operational imperatives of humanitarian action. Brauman (1996:43) describes the humanitarian space as a "symbolic space" where three freedoms are respected: freedom of dialogue, freedom of movement and needs assessment and freedom of verification of aid distribution.[1]

In North Korea, the translation of the principles of impartiality and proportionality into action faces a number of obstacles that are related to the restricted humanitarian space in the DPRK. It will be shown that these principles play a differing role according to the specific aid activity being carried out. This is in parts due to the priorities of the North Korean authorities, which prefer some sets of projects to others. In addition, the specific activism of an aid agency is linked to specific conditions in terms of freedom and principles of action. Put differently, some activities might be more compatible to the working environment in the DPRK than others. We will therefore discuss the humanitarian space and the role of proportionality with regard to specific sectors of aid. The discussion thereby focuses on the most important segments of the international famine relief effort: food aid, nutrition and public health and food security/agriculture.

---

[1] Likewise, Van Brabant (1998:22) notes that the understanding of 'humanitarian space' "implies aid personnel have full freedom of movement and of interaction with civilians, and can make their own independent assessment of needs on which the provision of relief will be based". Von Pilar (1999:6) adds that the freedom of access in a humanitarian space not only concerns the assessment of needs but also "independent and impartial distribution of aid according to the level of need" and "independent impact monitoring".

At first, we will present one basic characteristic of the North Korean aid mission, which concerns the role of DPRK authorities with regard to the organization of aid activities.

VI.1 The Role of North Korean Authorities

Aid agencies in all sectors of aid carry out their programs in close co-operation with North Korean authorities, namely the Flood Damage Rehabilitation Committee (FDRC)[2] and the Asia Pacific Peace Committee (APPC). The FDRC is in charge of contacts to UN agencies and aid organizations based in the West and Japan, while the APPC is the primary interlocutor for South Korean organizations.[3] Both institutions belong to the DPRK Ministry of Foreign Affairs.

The primary player for the organization of the international food aid program is the FDRC. The FDRC was established in 1995 at the request of international donors who preferred one central authority to be their interlocutor. According to the country's administrative structure, the FDRC is part of the county and provincial administration. FDRC officials deal with all kinds of requests from international aid agencies, such as the location and shape of aid projects as well as daily project work (monitoring visits etc.). Notably, with the FDRC, the DPRK government did not establish an entirely new administrative body. Instead, officials of county and provincial administration took over the responsibility of dealing with international humanitarian organizations. The Deputy Chairman of a county administration is thus at the same time the county's FDRC Chairman.

Due to the omnipresence of the FDRC, it is problematic for aid agencies to enter into direct dialogue with line ministries (Food, Public Health, Agriculture etc.) or other institutions that might be relevant in the area of food aid. Furthermore, the hierarchical and centralized structure of the FDRC renders it difficult for humanitarian organizations

---

2 'Flood Damage Rehabilitation Committee' is the most frequently used term. Other translations are 'Flood Damage Rehabilitation Commission' or 'Flood Damage Preparedness Committee'. The original term 'keun mul pihae daetchaek uiweonhoe' literally means 'commission/committee for measures against flood damages'.

3 One exception is the Quaker organization AFSC whose counterpart is an organization of the Korean Worker's Party – the Korean Committee for Solidarity with the World's Peoples. Interview with Karin Lee and John Feffer, East Asia Quaker International Affairs Representatives/AFSC, Seoul, 24 October 2000.

to achieve concessions on the part of local authorities. According to aid agencies' reports, the local FDRC level has very limited decision-making power. All written agreements, for instance, that define project design and basic working conditions are negotiated with the central authorities. However, to the extent that the responsibility for feeding the population has been transferred to county authorities,[4] county officials appear to be particularly interested in receiving food assistance. Mercy Corps, for instance, reports that in negotiations on food-for-work programs county officials appeared to be more concerned about the food situation than central FDRC delegates.[5]

Communication with authorities is a particularly difficult issue in North Korea for three reasons. First, two separate parties are responsible for negotiation and for decision-taking respectively. As a result, NGOs have had the frustrating experience where the seeming nodding in agreement of FDRC representatives at the negotiation table turns out to be meaningless at the following meeting. Second, aid agencies report that there is a lack of horizontal communication between distinct authorities. Therefore, it needs time and is often up to the aid agency itself to transmit a decision from one authority to another. Third, unlike aid missions in other countries, the high decision-taking level is beyond the reach of aid agencies. In addition, the military most likely takes a number of decisions concerning the freedom of action of aid organizations (access, communication devices etc.). However, as the former UNOCHA coordinator in DPRK asserts, "you never get in touch with the military".[6]

VI.2 Food Aid

In terms of their operational focus, food aid, nutrition and food security are distinct areas of humanitarian action. Food aid comprises the provision and distribution of food. According to the SPHERE Handbook (chapter "Food Aid")[7] "the purpose of food aid is to:

---

[4] See Natsios 2001:110.

[5] Interview with Nancy Lindborg, Executive Vice President/MCI, Washington D.C., 29 November 2001.

[6] Interview with Oliver Lacey-Hall, former UNOCHA Humanitarian Affairs Officer DPRK, Geneva, 19 October 2001.

[7] The Handbook is available at www.sphereproject.org.

Sustain life by ensuring adequate availability and access to food by people affected by disaster.

Provide sufficient food resources to eliminate the need for survival strategies which may result in long-term negative consequences to human dignity, household viability, livelihood security and the environment.

Provide a short-term income transfer or substitution to people to allow household resources to be invested for recovery."

The provision of food therefore aims at the short-term consolidation of a society that is hit by a food crisis or famine. It thereby focuses on particular population groups or geographical locations: "Recipients of food aid are selected on the basis of food need and/or vulnerability to food insecurity" (SPHERE Handbook, chapter "Food Aid", Section 3).

Food aid seeks to support those people whose health status is threatened by the lack of (access to) food. Nutrition, by contrast, primarily provides assistance to population groups whose nutritional status is already affected by the lack of food. Differing sets of activities emanate from these differing operational objectives. The provision of food is an effective means to ensure the food supply for people who are still in a normal health and nutritional state. Malnutrition programs address the needs of those whose nutrition status requires more than just the provision of food. The SPHERE Handbook asserts: "Programmes aiming to correct malnutrition may consider appropriate feeding, medical treatment and/or supportive care" (chapter "Nutrition"). In short, food aid seeks to *sustain* life, nutrition aims to *save* life. It goes without saying that, in practice, famine relief consists of a combination of both.

While food aid and nutrition pursue the short-term improvement of the humanitarian situation, food security projects aim to provide longer-term and sustainable assistance. The main focus is on enhancing a population's capacity to produce food. Food security operations therefore primarily include activities such as the delivery of agricultural inputs (seeds, fertilizers, pesticides, fuel etc.), the rehabilitation of existing production capacities (greenhouses, bakeries, food factories etc.) or the transfer of farming know-how.

a) The Food Aid Program

In terms of funding and staff resources, the delivery and distribution of food is the largest component of the international aid effort in the DPRK. The food aid program is primarily carried out by WFP and, to a minor degree, by NGOs.

WFP activities

WFP, which is the lead UN agency in North Korea and main player in terms of food aid to DPRK, delivered about 3.1 million tons of food between October 1995 and December 2002. In 2003, WFP aimed to reach about 6.4 million people (UNOCHA 2002:24). Food aid funds make up about 87 percent of the total sum that has been requested by the UN inter-agency appeal for 2003 (UNOCHA 2002:52-58). In terms of WFP's requested funds, the provision of food is by and large the most important component (99,2 percent). Up to 2001, donor governments covered more than an extraordinary 85 percent of the UN food aid appeals. From 1996 to 1998 donors contributed even more food to the food aid operations than WFP previously had requested. Between April 1997 and March 1998, for instance, WFP received more than 480,000 tons of food aid, which was 146 percent measured against the appeal.[8] The WFP Country Director in March 2002 states that "the DPRK is the only place in the world where since six years every project is funded".[9] Notably, food aid resources cannot be shifted to non-food sectors since donors primarily give food (surpluses) and are reluctant to give money.[10] From a food aid perspective, this is an advantage. As the former WFP Regional Director for Asia and the Pacific remarks (Schulthes 2000:272): "Among the comparative advantages of food aid is the fact that, after all, it can be done with food, and not cash".

---

[8] WFP Emergency Operation No. 5710.02. For an overview of WFP Emergency Operations between October 1995 and June 1999 see WFP Executive Board: *Protracted Relief and Recovery Operation – DPR Korea 6157.00*. Document No. WFP/EB.3/99/7-B/6, Rome, 19-22 October 1999, p.8.

[9] Oral statement in a meeting with GAA staff, Pyongyang, 8 March 2002. Author's notes.

[10] A UNOCHA official asserts: "for food aid, donors give their surpluses. But funding of non-food items is a problem. OCHA tries to push them to give money so that the UN decides what to do with it". Interview with Susan DeSouza, Desk Officer/UNOCHA, Geneva, 18 October 2001.

However, while donors delivered more than 95 percent of the requested food aid in 2001, less than 50 percent of WFP appeals were funded in the following year.[11] This was due to the lack of Japanese contributions and considerable reductions in the food aid program by the US and European countries.

WFP operations began in 1995 on a modest scale. Food aid worth US$9 million was sent to regions that were most severely hit by the floods. In subsequent years, WFP expanded its program to all accessible counties. In 1998, all children under seven years of age as well as hospital patients were designated as target groups for WFP food assistance. In 1999, WFP integrated schoolchildren and elderly people into the aid program. In addition, food-for-work projects became a WFP activity. The bulk of food is delivered to institutions, "as it focuses on most vulnerable and it is the easiest to track and monitor".[12] The primary task of WFP staff in the DPRK is monitoring. The transport, storage and documentation of food as well as the management of warehouses is done by North Korean authorities.

NGO activities

Beside UN agencies, NGOs were providing food aid from the beginning of the international aid effort to the DPRK. In most cases, NGOs approached North Korean authorities and proposed possible aid activities. Also, a number of organizations have been contacted by North Korean officials. Mercy Corps International, for instance, reports that it received a phone call from the North Korean mission to the UN in 1995.[13]

---

[11] UNOCHA DPRK notes in late 2002: "During November, almost 3 million nursery, kindergarten, primary and secondary school children, as well as pregnant and nursing women – all on the west coast – did not receive WFP food assistance as had been planned. Owing to a lack of confirmed shipments, distributions will not likely continue at planned levels until February, at the earliest. Without immediate, additional contributions, WFP will be unable to reach nearly 3.2 million vulnerable people with cereal distributions from early in the New Year. Local Food Production stocks of Dried Skimmed Milk and cereals are running out in all seven biscuit factories". UNOCHA: *DPR Korea. Situation Bulletin.* November 2002, No. 09/02, p.1.

[12] Judy Cheng-Hopkins, WFP Director for Asia and CIS Region, in: *Conference Proceedings. International NGO Conference on Humanitarian Assistance to the DPR Korea. Past, Present, and Future.* Beijing, 3-5 May 1999, p.19.

[13] Interview with Nancy Lindborg, Executive Vice President/Mercy Corps International, Washington D.C., 29 November 2001.

A number of non-resident NGOs supports the WFP food aid mission. Since 1997, a UN body – the Food Aid Liaison Unit (FALU) – has coordinated the programs of these aid agencies. Current and former FALU members are primarily faith-based agencies, such as Action Churches Together (ACT), Adventist Development and Relief Agency (ADRA), Canadian Foodgrains Bank (CFGB), Caritas International, Food for the Hungry, Mercy Corps International or World Vision International. The food aid mainly targets children. Notably, Caritas and CFGB primarily focus on the east coast. The food aid is distributed and monitored by WFP and FALU officials. In addition, the FALU member organizations regularly send monitoring delegations to the DPRK. Caritas and CFGB have made the largest contributions to the FALU mechanism since its establishment in 1997 (about US$18 million worth of food each).

As for NGOs not working with FALU, the delivery of food was the most important component of their activity in the beginning of aid programs in 1995-1997. For a number of European aid organizations, food aid was a 'door-opener' for a future engagement in the DPRK and preceded the opening of an office in Pyongyang. Children's Aid Direct (CAD), Campus für Christus (CfC) and the Swiss Disaster Relief Unit[14], for instance, delivered food aid in 1995 and 1996 before gaining residency status in 1997. US-based NGOs formed a consortium (Private Voluntary Organization Consortium, PVOC) in 1997 that, in conjunction with UN agencies, monitored five rounds of food aid distribution until 2001, every round amounting to about 100,000 tons of food. The PVOC received funds from the US Department of Agriculture and USAID that totaled approximately US$60 million.[15] Since the withdrawal of CARE in April 2000, the PVOC is made up of eight agencies.[16]

Resident NGO food aid projects were primarily located in the west of the country (mainly South and North Hwanghae, South and North Pyongan). Exceptions were the IFRC which also focused on Chagang province in the north, and the PVOC that delivered 20 to 40 percent of

---

[14] In May 1999, the Swiss Disaster Relief Unit handed over its office in Pyongyang to the Swiss Agency for Development and Cooperation (SDC).

[15] For an overview on PVOC activities see Flake 2003:29-31.

[16] ADRA, Amigos Internacionales, the Carter Center, Catholic Relief Services, Church World Services, Korean-American Sharing Movement, Latter Day Saint Charities, Mercy Corps International.

its assistance to the northeast.[17] Resident NGOs target their food aid on children in institutions and, to a lesser extent, school children and elderly people.

In 1998-99, European and American aid organizations shifted their approach from food aid to other sectors, mainly to food security, agriculture, health and water and sanitation programs. One reason was the growing magnitude of the WFP program in DPRK. In the opinion of most NGOs, food supply was more and more being taken care of by donor governments and WFP so that other sectors appeared to be more appropriate for NGO activities.[18]

The delivery of food was and still is an important component of South Korean and Japanese NGOs' aid activities. Under the Kim Young-Sam administration South Korean NGOs were only allowed to send commodities to the DPRK via the Korean National Red Cross. The Kim Dae-Jung government changed this policy and enabled 13 NGOs to deliver aid directly. In contrast to their European and US counterparts who primarily sent cereals, South Korean and Japanese NGOs deliver a large variety of food (including fruits, eggs, bread). The Korean Sharing Movement, for instance, initiated and managed the transport of oranges donated by farmers from Cheju Island, or eggs donated by the farmer union. In most cases, the food was sent to the North without designating specific target groups or regions. Notably, South Korean aid agencies also used informal channels to send food aid to the DPRK. In 1995 and 1996, the Join Together Society (JTS) and Good Neighbors Korea provided food aid outside official Red Cross channels via China. From October 1995 to October 1996, Good Neighbors Korea in collaboration with a Chinese-Korean organization sent 20,000 pieces of bread per week, produced in the Chinese city of Dandong, to children in elementary schools

---

[17] Interview with Nancy Lindborg, Executive Vice President/MCI, Washington D.C:, 29 November 2001.

[18] As an example, Kenneth Quinones from Mercy Corps International notes: "the governments in Seoul, Washington, Tokyo, and the European Union are better equipped to assemble the large amounts of food aid still critical to the health of North Korea's most needy population. It seems we NGOs, with our significantly smaller resources, would do well to concentrate our energies on areas other than food aid". Presentation at the Third International NGO Conference on Humanitarian Assistance to North Korea: Cooperative Efforts Beyond Food Aid, Seoul, 17 to 20 June 2001, p.5.

in the North Korean border town of Shinuiju.[19] JTS, prior to 1997, sent trucks loaded with food aid to specific areas in North Hamgyong province more than 30 times. These activities were also carried out in cooperation with the Korean minority in the Chinese border region.[20]

Since the inter-Korean summit in June 2000, in particular, South Korean NGOs have regarded the provision of food aid a primarily governmental task.[21] In view of increased governmental food contributions, the majority of South Korean NGOs refocused on other sectors, mainly food security projects.

b) The Food Aid Operation and the Principle of Proportionality

Working conditions for aid agencies active in the food aid sector have raised controversies from the inception of the aid mission on. It is important to note that the following analysis of working conditions in regard to principles of humanitarian action only concerns the multilateral food aid effort carried out by WFP, FALU and NGOs. Bilateral donations primarily from China and South Korea are 'government-to-government' provisions that are not attached to any condition such as the distribution to specific geographical areas or population groups. This includes the donations of South Korean NGOs via the South Korean Red Cross that did not contain any agreement on distribution or monitoring issues.[22]

The most restricted understanding of a humanitarian space implies that "aid personnel have full freedom of movement and of interaction with civilians, and can make their own independent assessment of needs" (Van Brabant 1998:22). Therefore, in theory, an impartial famine aid mission that affords food in proportion to needs has to be carried out in three steps: firstly, it has to independently identify those population groups in greatest needs. Secondly, it has to distribute the food directly to these target groups and, finally, it should be placed in a position to

---

[19] Interview with Lee Yoon-Sang, Director Planning Division/Good Neighbors, Seoul, 14 July 2000.
[20] Interview with Lee Ji-Hyun, General Secretary/JTS, and Park Ji-Hyun, Desk Officer International Affairs/JTS, Seoul, 6 November 2000.
[21] Interview with Lee Yoon-Sang, Director Planning Division/Good Neighbors Korea, Seoul, 14 July 2000.
[22] Interview with Park Chan-Uk, Head of Division (Bureau for Separated Families)/Korean National Red Cross, Seoul, 26 October 2000.

monitor the end-use and the effect of the food aid. In North Korea, such ideal conditions do not exist.

Identification of vulnerable population groups

Access to and communication with ordinary North Korean citizens is hindered in various ways. The working and living conditions of international staff as well as people's fear of coming into contact with foreigners do not allow aid workers to start a conversation with people in the street. Even North Koreans who work for international organizations take care not to become too familiar with their Western colleagues. It is a particularly frustrating experience for international aid personnel in North Korea that, unlike other countries, they have no possibility of getting an insight into the life of ordinary people in their host country through their local counterparts. Experiences that aid workers often describe as valuable sources of relaxation and motivation in other countries – having a drink with local people after work, being introduced to a colleague's friends and family, or being invited to his home – can hardly be made in North Korea.

To sum up, expatriates in the DPRK, including those who permanently live in Pyongyang, have no means of interacting with ordinary North Korean citizens. A UNICEF official who had worked in Uganda, Afghanistan and Zaire thus comments on the DPRK: "this is the most difficult location - not because of physical safety, but because of a sense of not knowing what is going on" (quoted in Natsios 2001:41).

Due to the lack of interaction and information, aid agencies do not have the means to independently identify those population groups which have no or only very limited access to public food distribution. The FAO/WFP crop assessment studies contain data on regional differences in food supply. In addition, WFP possesses information on the daily ration distributed by the PDS. But aid agencies can hardly assess the individual means to demand food or the geographic and social differences in terms of access to the PDS or farmer markets. No aid worker has ever been allowed to visit such a market.

It is important to note that aid agencies that implement food aid programs define the vulnerability of population groups according to physical criteria, namely age and gender. Children, pregnant and nursing women, hospital patients and elderly people are designated as primary beneficiaries of food aid programs. The specific North Korean context that limits the means of identifying and addressing vulnerability may play a role in this regard. In addition, as will be argued in later chapters, such a definition of famine vulnerability is linked to the ethical framework of food aid agencies and, in particular, their understanding of famine.

The distribution of food

As for the implementation of food aid projects, aid agencies are in no position to distribute the food directly to the targeted beneficiaries. In famines in other countries, such as in Ethiopia, Cambodia or Biafra, those who were at risk of starvation left their homes and gathered in camps accessible for foreign aid. The situation in the DPRK is very different. Although large numbers of North Koreans reportedly left their homes in order to seek food, they did not gather in camps, and many of them did not seek assistance in North Korea but in China. In other famines in the past, such as in Soviet Russia in the 1920s, international aid agencies set up public soup kitchens where people in search for food could eat. In the Russian famine aid mission, the American Relief Administration (ARA) insisted that "food must be consumed by the beneficiary at the feeding point. (...) it was the only method by which the designated beneficiary could be assured of receiving the full value of the ration" (Fisher 1927:102-103). In North Korea, Action Contre la Faim (ACF) wanted to establish street kitchens in Chongjin city in North Hamgyong province. The FDRC did not agree on the modalities of such a program and declined the proposal.

The only possible way to direct food aid to specific population groups in the DPRK is to send food to institutions such as nurseries, kindergartens, orphanages, schools, clinics and hospitals. The food is not transported and distributed by aid agencies but by the public distribution system (PDS). There have been further attempts to distribute food outside PDS channels. The IFRC supplied a daily ration of food to specific population groups (children, disabled, elderly people) that was aimed as a supplement to the food ration received through the PDS. However, monitoring activities revealed that the beneficiaries of Red Cross rations were excluded from the PDS supply. The IFRC concluded that there is no value in establishing a food distribution system separate from the PDS and closed the food aid program in 1998.[23]

The possibility of geographical targeting is further reduced due to the fact that international staff does not have access to all counties. Although the number of accessible counties has increased in the course of the food aid mission, 43 out of 206 counties (about 15 percent of the population) remained inaccessible for international organizations in 2002.[24] Since WFP introduced a policy of 'no access-no food' in May 1998 – arguing that an accountable food aid distribution is otherwise impossible – it has excluded inaccessible counties from international food aid assistance.

Humanitarian organizations are free to decide which population group benefits from food assistance (children in nurseries, hospital patients etc.). The FDRC then designates the institutions that are included in the food aid program. Some aid agencies report that food aid projects cover all institutions of a specific population group in a designated area. Other agencies, such as Children's Aid Direct for instance, report that not all institutions benefit from the program. In these cases, according to North Korean counterparts, the remaining institutions are covered by other sources.[25]

Thus, an agency's means to target food aid are very limited. A CESVI project coordinator summarizes: "Even if CESVI can theoretically decide the target groups, the restrictions in the access to counties, institutions and families, and the limited data available make [it] difficult to reach this objective".[26] Under these circumstances, two methods of balancing geographic and social differences remain. First, aid agencies can designate population groups as target groups of food aid only in specific provinces. Caritas, for instance, delivers food aid primarily to areas along the east coast.[27] WFP targets food aid to the northeast of the country by

---

[23] Interview with Aurélia Balpe, Officer Asia and Pacific Department/IFRC, Geneva, 19 October 2001.

[24] Testimony of John Powell, Regional Director Asia/WFP at the "Hearing of the East Asia and the Pacific Subcommittee of the House International Relations Committee. North Korea: Humanitarian and Human Rights Concerns", Federal News Service, 2 May 2002.

[25] Interview with Wube Woldemariam, Regional Program Manager Asia/Children's Aid Direct, Reading/UK, 12 September 2001.

[26] Monti Feliciano, former Project Coordinator DPRK/CESVI, E-mail to author, 1 August 1999.

[27] For a summary on Caritas food aid projects see Smith 2001b:28.

adding categories of target groups such as secondary school children and elderly people. In addition, in fall 2002, when the WFP mission in the DPRK faced a critical resource gap in the cereals pipeline for the first time since 1995, WFP began to exclude beneficiaries from food distribution on the west coast in order to continue distributions in the northeast.[28] In view of the various food aid programs since 1995, however, it has to be noted that the geographical targeting was, by and large, not a priority of the international food aid effort. Although international donors have provided food aid since 1995, the first shipment reached North Hamgyong province in July 1997. In addition, in 1997 and 1998 only 18 percent of WFP and bilateral food aid was delivered to ports along the east coast, even though about one third of the North Korean population lives in the eastern provinces (see Natsios 2001:107-108). WFP did not try to include geographical targeting mechanisms prior to 2001. When WFP finally proposed expanding the food aid program in the northeast only, the UN agency was surprised to find that the North Korean authorities accepted their proposal.[29] The only aid agency that asserts to have delivered food aid in direct cooperation with local officials without any contact to authorities in Pyongyang is the South Korean organization JTS.[30]

As mentioned above, concerning the project location of resident NGOs during the first years of their presence in the DPRK, most activities focused on the west and southwest of the country. In negotiations with international aid agencies, the FDRC made it clear that it preferred these regions as NGO project areas. Most organizations argue that they had planned to carry out aid programs in the northeast in the long term and, in 1997/98, were satisfied to have a foot in the door. Therefore, they followed the FDRC's request concerning the location of their projects.

Besides geographical targeting, aid agencies and international donors can influence the distribution of food by the choice of the commodity they provide. The fact that WFP distributions are composed of com-

---

[28] See OCHA 2002:21.

[29] WFP proposed to add secondary school children, elderly people, and food-for-work programs for adults to the food aid portfolio designated for the northeast. Interview with David Morton, UN Humanitarian Coordinator DPRK 1998-2002, Rome, 4 February 2002, and oral statement made by Richard Corsino, WFP Country Director, in a meeting with GAA staff, Pyongyang, 8 March 2002. Author's notes.

[30] Interview with Lee Ji-Hyun, General Secretary/JTS, and Park Ji-Hyun, Desk Officer International Affairs/JTS, Seoul, 6 November 2000.

modities other than rice is often mentioned as an obstacle to the diversion of international food aid. For example, in a hearing before the US House of Representatives, John Powell, Regional Director of WFP, argues:

> On the issue of the alleged diversion of WFP food assistance to the military, let me be direct. The Army takes what it wants from the national harvest, up front in full. It takes it in the form of food Koreans prefer: Korean rice. The food that WFP provides is overwhelmingly maize or wheat or Japanese brown rice, commodities not preferred by those in power. They do not need to take WFP food, nor have we seen any evidence that they do.[31]

Some aid organizations also delivered non-storable food in order to be certain that the commodities cannot be stored and transported to other than the designated areas.[32]

Monitoring the effect of aid

Besides the freedom to assess and the freedom to effectively target needs, transparency and independent impact monitoring is the third component of a humanitarian space. It derives from the principles of impartiality and proportionality that aid agencies should be in a position to measure the impact of their assistance. With regard to the famine aid effort in North Korea, issues such as the monitoring of food aid and the evaluation of its effects have caused the most intense debates.

Since the inception of the food aid program in 1995, a number of changes have taken place that have actually enhanced aid agencies' monitoring capacities in the DPRK began its operation with only three expatriates (of which one was a full-time employee). In 2002, WFP staff comprised of some 50 international team members.[33] Furthermore, in

---

[31] "Hearing of the East Asia and the Pacific Subcommittee of the House International Relations Committee. North Korea: Humanitarian and Human Rights Concerns", Federal News Service, 2 May 2002.

[32] In 1995 and 1996, Good Neighbors Korea for this reason delivered non-storable bread that contained egg to primary schools in the border city of Shinuiju (Interview with Lee Yoon-Sang, Director Planning Division/Good Neighbors Korea, Seoul, 14 July 2000.)

[33] Testimony of John Powell, Regional Director Asia/WFP, at the "Hearing of the East Asia and the Pacific Subcommittee of the House International Relations Committee. North Korea: Humanitarian and Human Rights Concerns", Federal News Service, 2 May 2002.

addition to its Pyongyang office, WFP was able to open sub offices in five cities.[34] In view of bad travel conditions, a permanent presence in these cities in the far north and east makes it much easier to monitor food aid distributions in remote areas. Additionally, as noted above, the number of counties that are accessible to international monitoring activities has increased since the beginning of the food aid program. As a result, the frequency of monitoring visits has considerably increased during the course of food aid activities in the DPRK. WFP asserts that, in 2002, it conducted more than 300 monitoring visits per month.[35]

What is controversial, however, is not the frequency of monitoring visits but their actual validity. The SPHERE project, as one of the most widely agreed frameworks of humanitarian action, states that a key indicator of monitoring and evaluation activities is that "end-user monitoring through household-level visits and interviews ensure people can provide feedback on the effectiveness of the food aid intervention" (SPHERE Handbook, chapter "Food Aid"). According to the 2002 UN Consolidated Appeal for the DPRK, the monitoring of the end-use of food aid should include, *inter alia*, "unscheduled visits within accessible counties, permission for Korean speakers to work in DPR Korea" and "direct access to households/beneficiaries" (UNOCHA 2001:130). However, all aid agencies working in North Korea have to notify the FDRC several days to one week in advance of which counties or institutions they wish to visit. The monitoring itinerary then depends on FDRC's approval.

No aid agency that is permanently working in DPRK has random access to institutions or households. Some agencies report that on very rare occasions, North Korean authorities have allowed unscheduled visits. In general, however, aid agencies are in no position to monitor the end-use of food aid. The food track system put in place by WFP and North Korean authorities tracks the transportation of food aid from the seaport to county warehouses. Monitoring visits are conducted in recipient institutions where monitors check the records, food stocks and facilities. WFP is not allowed to conduct unrestricted spot checks along the

---

[34] These cities are Shinuiju/North Pyongan province, Wonsan/Kangwon province, Hamhung/South Hamgyong province, Chongjin/North Hamgyong province, and Hyesan/Ryanggang province.

[35] Interview with David Morton, UN Resident Coordinator/WFP Representative 1998-2002, Rome, 4 February 2002.

transportation route or storage sites.[36] Thus, WFP monitors are able to control whether a certain amount of food aid effectively reaches the target institution, but the tracking system does not cover the final distribution of food to individual recipients.

In addition, monitoring visits are conducted in a very formal way. Particularly well-dressed institution staff and inmates, speeches and children's performances illustrate the official character of these visits. WFP or NGO visitors are therefore treated as high-level visitors rather than as people who are interested in the concerns of ordinary people and institution inmates. Furthermore, FDRC officials are always present at monitoring visits. In addition, aid agencies that are permanently present in DPRK are not allowed to employ Korean-speaking staff. Thus far, the member organizations of the PVOC were the only agencies that employed Korean speaking monitors, albeit without notifying the DPRK authorities in advance.[37]

Aid agencies that seek to measure the impact of food aid distributions depend on observations and assumptions rather than on hard data. The UN inter-agency appeal for 1999 (UNOCHA 1998:3) stresses:

> Monitors were not permitted to conduct unscheduled, unsupervised visits. The lack of access – that was not pre-determined – to conduct assessments, monitoring and impact analysis, combined with the lack of adequate data results in conclusions that were based more on observation and inference than statistical information.

Summary: humanitarian space in the food aid sector

Working conditions in the food aid sector do not allow humanitarian organizations to independently identify the most vulnerable population groups and to independently target the international food assistance to these groups. North Korean authorities determine that food aid is channeled through the public distribution system and primarily reaches people in institutions, not households. North Korean authorities decide which institutions benefit from international food aid and which do not.

---

[36] For details, see GAO: *Foreign Assistance. North Korea Restricts Food Aid Monitoring.* Report to the Chairman, Committee on International Relations, House of Representatives. Report Number: GAO/NSIAD-00-35. Washington D.C.: October 1999, p.11-13.

[37] Although this caused some problems, the staff was finally allowed to stay in the DPRK (interview with James K. Bishop, Director Humanitarian Response/InterAction, Washington D.C., 28 November 2001).

After the FDRC approves the monitoring sites, aid agencies can control whether the food reaches the designated institutions. They cannot, however, monitor the final distribution to individual recipients. It is telling to note that, to a certain extent, working conditions differ according to the specific project context. Reportedly, the German Corporation for Technical Cooperation (GTZ), for instance, that monitored the distribution of beef donated by the German government in winter 2001/02, had relatively good working conditions. According to the WFP country director, this was due to three reasons: beef is a highly desired commodity, GTZ was present only for a short period of time and, finally, the GTZ had sent senior staff (unlike NGOs) which –given the North Korean cultural context- is an asset.[38]

At the end of the day, the food aid program in the DPRK is not an international aid effort that is carried out independently by international humanitarian organizations. Essentially, the operation aims to assist the DPRK in its efforts to manage the crisis. The 1999 US General Accounting Office report therefore concludes:

> WFP (...) describes its operations in North Korea as essentially a North Korean government program, in which WFP's role is to help North Korean authorities implement the program by providing advice, establishing internal control systems, monitoring to see if systems work, and training government officials in food management.[39]

c) Proportional Aid or Diversion? The Debate on the Effects of Food Aid.

The effects of the food aid mission in the DPRK are highly controversial. Between aid agencies, within donor governments and within the UN system, the food aid program is seen by some as a success, and by others as a failure. Does the food aid, according to the core principle of humanitarian action, reach the recipients in proportion to their needs? Three differing answers are given to that question. First, it is argued that

---

[38] Oral statement made by Richard Corsino, WFP Country Director, in a meeting with GAA staff, Pyongyang, 8 March 2002. Author's notes.

[39] GAO: *Foreign Assistance. North Korea Restricts Food Aid Monitoring.* Report to the Chairman, Committee on International Relations, House of Representatives. Report Number: GAO/NSIAD-00-35. Washington D.C.: October 1999, p.11.

the food aid reaches those in need and has thereby effectively saved lives *(success hypothesis)*. According to the second position, the food aid does not reach those it is intended to reach. Instead, large amounts of food are being diverted to the military and the political elite *(diversion hypothesis)*. The third view asserts that the food aid is effectively distributed to the designated groups. However, it is argued that the most vulnerable are not part of these target groups *(manipulation hypothesis)*.

The success hypothesis

The success hypothesis is primarily upheld by UN agencies. For instance, on the WFP mission in the DPRK, the agency's former Executive Director Catherine Bertini comments that "this is a success story. Without these massive amounts of aid, we would be reading dire reports of millions of people every year dying of starvation".[40] This assertion relies on two aspects. The first is the evidence that the humanitarian situation is presently better than it was at the beginning of the food aid efforts. It is the general observation of aid agencies that the nutritional status of the North Korean population has improved over the last years. In addition, as noted above, the two nutritional surveys that were conducted in 1998 and 2002 showed a considerable reduction in children's malnutrition. In view of the findings of the 2002 survey, Kenzo Oshima, UN Under Secretary-General for Humanitarian Affairs, points out: "The results are very encouraging and our assistance is clearly reaching the people intended with positive effect".[41] The second argument supporting the positive effects of food aid is that international monitors from WFP and NGOs have found no evidence of a systematic diversion of aid. International staff have documented no single case of diversion to the military or political elite. Losses that appeared in the documentation system were due to transportation problems or, more often, due to communication problems in the handling of the documentation and waybill system. UN agencies and NGOs unanimously report that food aid effectively reaches the designated institutions and that losses are clearly lower than in food aid missions in other countries. NGOs that provide food aid through the FALU mechanism also assert that international food aid effectively im-

---

40 *Washington Post*, 24 August 2001.
41 Quoted in WFP/UNICEF: *Child Nutrition Survey Shows Improvements. UN Agencies Concerned About Holding Onto Gains*. Joint press release. Pyongyang, Geneva: 20 February 2003.

proves the humanitarian situation in North Korea. After a visit to the DPRK in October 2002, a delegate from Canadian Foodgrains Bank (CFGB), for instance, notes: "While we observed noticeable stunting in children, they do appear healthier and not as malnourished as on previous visits. This is due to the food aid provided over the last several years".[42] Likewise, a Caritas program review concludes: "Starvation has been prevented" (Smith 2001b:27).

Donor governments support the view that international food aid has averted a famine and saved lives. For instance, US State Department and USAID criticized GAO's assessment of restrictive monitoring conditions in the DPRK as an "unbalanced view" and pointed at the positive effects of food aid. USAID argues:

> the GAO asserts that there is insufficient evidence to demonstrate that the proper amount of food is reaching the intended beneficiaries. To the contrary, there is substantial evidence that food is reaching intended beneficiaries. This comes from WFP's monitoring system, and from the observations of many independent observers who report that the nutritional status of children is much improved since 1997, when hunger was greatest, and prior to the arrival of most US food aid.[43]

However, as noted earlier, WFP's monitoring system does not provide information on the final distribution of food aid to individual recipients. It is therefore more than daring to say that "substantial evidence that food is reaching intended beneficiaries (...) comes from WFP's monitoring system". WFP officials themselves stress the fact that their monitoring reports do not cover the end-use of food. It can only be assumed that

---

[42] CFGB: *Canadian Food Aid Delegation Returns from North Korea*. News Release. Winnipeg, Canada.: 25 October 2002.

[43] Comments from USAID as attached in Appendix I to GAO: *Foreign Assistance. North Korea Restricts Food Aid Monitoring*. Report to the Chairman, Committee on International Relations, House of Representatives. Report Number: GAO/NSIAD-00-35. Washington D.C.: October 1999, (p.29). Likewise, the State Department comments: "the GAO report presents an unbalanced view of WFP's ability to monitor food aid which relies on the presentation of mostly negative examples to draw the conclusion that, since every aspect of aid distribution cannot be randomly monitored, US policy is being contravened. We believe there is ample evidence to conclude that US humanitarian assistance to North Korea, which is channeled through WFP, is reaching those for whom it is intended". Comments from the Department of State as attached in Appendix I to the same report, p.25.

the food that reaches the institutions is distributed to the intended individual recipients. Again, this assumption relies on the observed improvement of people's health but not on a monitoring system that meets international standards. UN officials working in the DPRK are therefore cautious in their statements. Former WFP Representative in DPRK, David Morton, asserts:

> Our observation is that the institutions are getting the food. Nurseries and kindergartens physically get the food. Primary schools don't have kitchens, so a parent of the primary school child gets the ration at the PDS station and you can't monitor the end-use. But the general nutrition status has improved, the health of children in schools has improved. So, we believe that children get the food.[44]

Likewise, the former Humanitarian Affairs Coordinator from UNOCHA in North Korea concludes: "I think that international food aid has saved lives. I think".[45]

The diversion hypothesis

The diversion hypothesis rejects WFP's position. It asserts that the food aid is systematically diverted and primarily supports the DPRK's political elite and the military. A special report to the UN Commission on Human Rights on the right to food, issued in February 2001, says:

> a terrible famine was ravaging the Democratic People's Republic of Korea in the early 1990s: WFP and several NGOs made a massive effort there, especially after 1995, but it gradually became clear that most of the international aid was being diverted by the army, the secret services and the Government.[46]

The report mentions only one source as the basis for this statement: a press dossier issued by the French NGO Action Contre la Faim (ACF) in the aftermath of the agency's withdrawal from the DPRK in spring

---

[44] Interview, Rome, 4 February 2002.

[45] Interview with Oliver Lacey-Hall, Geneva, 19 October 2001.

[46] UN Economic and Social Council/Commission of Human Rights: *Economic, Social, and Cultural Rights. The Right to Food*. Report by the Special Rapporteur on the Right to Food, Mr. Jean Ziegler, Submitted in Accordance With Commission on Human Rights Resolution 2000/10. Document Number E/CN.4/2001/53, 7 February 2001, p.11.

2000.[47] In this dossier, however, ACF does not speak of diversion. The NGO criticizes that food aid only reaches public structures. And, based on its own experience in the DPRK, ACF concludes that "the most vulnerable populations are not inside the public structures whereto the Korean authorities direct humanitarian assistance".[48] ACF does not claim that only those in power have access to these public structures, nor does it assert that international food aid is diverted from these institutions to "the army, the secret services and the Government", as the UN Special Rapporteur has noted. Thus, it is not surprising that the WFP Executive Director in a letter of protest to the Special Rapporteur, states that "the phrase 'most of the international aid has been diverted' is unsubstantiated, not referenced and is not based on first-hand observation of our food aid programme".[49]

Besides the controversial UN report, the diversion hypothesis relies on North Korean refugees' reports. A number of testimonies from North Korean citizens interviewed in China and South Korea contradicts the statements by UN agencies, NGOs and donor institutions on the positive impact of international food aid. A survey conducted by a South Korean NGO in late 1999 notes that more than 90 percent of the interviewees (1402 out of 1544) say that they did not receive international food aid (Chang 1999:13-14). It has to be noted that the large majority of the interviewees were male adults and therefore not a target group of the WFP program (Chang 1999:5-6). The population groups that aid agencies define as vulnerable (children under five, pregnant and nursing women, hospital patients) hardly cross the border. Thus, only a relatively small number of those people who international aid agencies aim to support could have been interviewed. MSF, that after its withdrawal from the

---

[47] *Agence France Press* ("World Food Programme Official Denies Report on North Korean Aid", Geneva, 6 June 2001) notes that the author of the report, Jean Ziegler, "defended his findings that significant amounts of aid were being diverted by the DPRK army and government, asserting that they had been backed up by information from non-governmental organizations such as Action Against Hunger." The reference added to the statement on food aid to DPRK in the report is: "Journal d'ACF, No. 7, Paris: March 2000" (reference no. 17, p.27), see note 46 in this chapter.

[48] ACF: *Dossier de Presse. Action contre la Faim Décide de Se Retirer de Corée du Nord*, Paris, March 2000, p.9. This text is identical with the text referred to in Ziegler's report.

[49] Quoted in *Agence France Press*: "World Food Programme Official Denies Report on North Korean Aid", Geneva, 6 June 2001.

DPRK is present in the border region, interviewed two pregnant women in February 2002 who originate from counties where food aid is distributed and, in addition, where WFP is present with sub-offices (Hyesan county in Ryanggang province and Chongjin city in North Hamgyong province). Both women reported that they had not received any food from the PDS. Furthermore, they said that pregnant women in general were not entitled to any sort of public food assistance.[50]

North Korean citizens interviewed in China and South Korea further report that bags carrying the logo of a donor country or organization appear on markets.[51] However, there is no comprehensive information on the question of whether donations are diverted and sold on the market or whether the bags are reused after the food has reached the intended recipients.

In addition, some refugee reports assert that UN and NGO monitors have actually been deceived by North Korean authorities. One refugee interviewed by MSF said that the authorities gathered malnourished children in order to hide them from UN officials. Another refugee, also interviewed by MSF, asserted that authorities dug out streets in Musan/North Hamgyong province in order to exaggerate the damage that was caused by floods.[52] On a food aid monitoring visit, a former officer of the North Korean People's Army reports:

> My superior gave the order to take two trucks loaded with cereals from our barracks to the PDS distribution center in the dong [urban district]-administration. He told me that a foreign organization wanted to take pictures of the food distribution. I carried out the order with my subordinates. Some food was distributed to civilians, and the foreigners took pictures of that. After that, we brought the food back to our barracks. No more than four bags were distributed.[53]

---

50 MSF: *Témoignages de Réfugiés Nord-Coréens en Chine*, 10 June 2002. Found at www.paris.msf.org (17 June 2002).

51 MSF interviews, note 50 in this chapter, and interviews by author with two North Korean refugees from South Pyongan and South Hamgyong province who left North Korea in 1998 and 1999. Interviews were conducted in Seoul, 25 November 2000.

52 MSF interviews, note 50 in this chapter.

53 Interview by author, Seoul, 3 November 2000. The interviewee had left the DPRK in April 1997. His unit was stationed in Pyongyang area.

In sum, anecdotal evidence suggests that something "has gone wrong with aid relief effort".[54] The targeting of population groups may not be as efficient as it is described by aid agencies. However, there are very few sources that report on the diversion of aid. Since the monitoring reports of all aid agencies engaged in the DPRK provide no evidence of massive and systematic diversion of international food aid, it appears that the reports on diversion describe the exception rather than the rule.

The manipulation hypothesis

Thirdly, the manipulation hypothesis asserts that food aid is not being diverted but does not reach those in greatest need. The food aid operation is regarded a failure because it has failed to save the lives of those who were most severely affected by hunger and starvation. Essentially, it is argued that the most vulnerable people do not benefit from the food aid program because they are situated outside public distribution channels. This view is mainly upheld by medical relief agencies that withdrew from the DPRK. Christophe Reltien (2000:163) from Action Contre la Faim concludes:

> One of the major constraints is that all humanitarian aid must be channeled through Korea's state distribution system. The regime thus controls the aid and provides aid only to those people whom it wishes to help. These people are not necessarily the same ones that the humanitarian organizations would like to benefit (...). Access to the most vulnerable sectors of the population is a major objective, but one of the reasons for their vulnerability is precisely their exclusion from the system under which humanitarian aid is distributed.

Unlike the diversion reproach, this view asserts that food aid in North Korea is being manipulated in a rather subtle way. Importantly, none of the agencies that pulled out from DPRK has experienced any diversion of aid. On the contrary, these organizations agree with WFP and all other agencies still working in the DPRK that the PDS effectively distributes the international food aid to the designated institutions and beneficiaries. "Losses are minimal, and diversion has never been

---

[54] Testimony of Jasper Becker, former Beijing Bureau Chief/South China Morning Post, at the "Hearing of the East Asia and the Pacific Subcommittee of the House International Relations Committee. North Korea: Humanitarian and Human Rights Concerns", Federal News Service, 2 May 2002.

proved", states an MDM Officer.[55] The main argument is to say that the most vulnerable population groups have no access to the institutions that benefit from international food aid. Pierre Salignon from MSF France summarizes: "the aid is not diverted but it does not achieve its objective".[56]

This view does not deny a general improvement of people's health status. However, positive changes are not seen as the outcome of a successful international food aid mission. Jean-Hervé Bradol, President of MSF France, argues:

> In all mechanisms of famine, the situation actually improves once the famine victims are dead (...). To say that an improvement takes place when all vulnerable populations have been sacrificed (...) and that this is a success of aid, is a perverted reasoning.[57]

It is important to note that, according to MSF and ACF, the exclusion of certain population groups from food aid distribution has political reasons and directly relies on the alleged classification system (see chapter IV.3). For instance, an MSF representative asserted in a hearing before the US House of Representatives:

> As to the Public Distribution System, I should explain to you in North Korean society the three class levels, which are core, wavering and hostile, continue to be used to prioritize entitlement to items distributed to the PDS (...). Since '98, MSF has denounced the fact that any assistance which was channeled through the PDS was discriminatory by nature.[58]

Thus, MSF and ACF[59] interpret their in-country observations according to the 'triage' argument. The manipulation hypothesis relies on

---

[55] Interview with Nathalie Bréchet, Desk Officer/MDM, Paris, 21 July 1999.

[56] Interview with Pierre Salignon, Desk Officer/MSF, Paris, 22 July 1999.

[57] Interview broadcast by the French radio station RMC Info, 24 August 2001.

[58] Sophie Delaunay, North Korea Project Representative/MSF at the "Hearing of the East Asia and the Pacific Subcommittee of the House International Relations Committee. North Korea: Humanitarian and Human Rights Concerns", Federal News Service, 2 May 2002.

[59] Sylvie Brunel, Strategic Consultant of ACF argues (1998:135): "Since a certain number of provinces remains inaccessible, aid organizations suspect the government of pursuing a strategy of 'triage', that is, using a real famine to attract relief, while at the same time deliberately depriving the hard hit regions, considered as 'secondary' to external aid. The suspected objective is to concentrate the relief on the neuralgic points of the regime, namely the west of the country, the capital, Pyongyang, the port of supply,

in-country observations and in parts on a political analysis that, as argued earlier, is based on rather shaky grounds. One major difference between the *success* and the *manipulation hypotheses* is therefore a differing interpretation of the North Korean famine and its political implications.

VI.3 Nutritional and Health Programs

One important part of the international aid effort for North Korea aims to improve the population's nutritional and health state. Nutrition programs thereby provide enriched food and offer therapeutic assistance. These programs were part of the international famine relief effort from 1995. Most agencies that decided to leave the DPRK were active in the nutrition sector. As will be shown below, this program activity is related to specific principles of action and to specific ethical frameworks, ideals and traditions.

a) Program activities

International aid organizations carry out a variety of programs in the public health sector. These activities include, first and foremost, nutrition and the delivery of drugs, medicine and medical equipment, but also vaccination and immunization programs, the rehabilitation of medical facilities (operating theaters etc.), and health promotion and public awareness campaigns. In addition, water and sanitation programs became a more important area of activity that we present as part of the public health related efforts.

UNICEF's nutrition programs

UNICEF and NGOs with a medical mandate (MDM, MSF, ACF) have carried out or continue to carry out nutrition projects in the DPRK. Following the DPRK government's appeal for international assistance, UNICEF established a resident presence in 1995. Until 1999, UNICEF primarily provided high-energy milk and other enriched food to children under five years of age, delivered assistance to pregnant and nursing

---

Nampo. About a third of the national territory remains inaccessible. Did not the North Korean dictator Kim Jong-Il in late April 1996 declare that he would prefer to let 70 percent of the population of his country die, so that he can reconstruct the country on a new basis with the remaining 30 percent?"

women and supplied basic drugs and medicines. UNICEF observed that the DPRK public health system did not lack skilled medical staff but medicine and technical equipment. On the performance of the country's public health system in the past, the former UNICEF Country Representative comments that "there is some vanity and pride, and there is reason to".[60] In recent years, however, medicine and equipment became scarce so that "hospitals in rural areas are almost totally dependent on traditional medicine".[61] From 1999, UNICEF expanded its activities and provided broader support to the country's public health system (immunization and vaccination, vitamin A campaigns, safe motherhood program, water and sanitation). However, poor funding has limited UNICEF's capacity to carry out programs in the DPRK. In 1999, for instance, when WFP actually received more funds than it had appealed for, only about 24 percent (US$4.8 million) of UNICEF's requested funds were met.

Nutrition programs of NGOs

In addition to UNICEF, a number of European NGOs implemented nutrition programs in North Korea. The FDRC invited NGOs to design and implement programs of a considerable size, both in regard to budget, number of beneficiaries and distributed goods. However, the North Korean side was very restrictive concerning the number of expatriate staff. ACF, for instance, reports that the number of expatriate staff was the most controversial point in the negotiations with the FDRC. In addition, as experienced in other aid sectors, medical relief agencies report that it was not possible to integrate local staff into the project activities to the degree as in missions in other countries. The ACF Desk Officer therefore asserts: "North Korea is the only mission of ACF without local staff".[62]

---

[60] Oral statement made by Dilawar Ali Khan at the Third International NGO Conference on Humanitarian Assistance to North Korea: Cooperative Efforts Beyond Food Aid. Seoul, 19 June 2001. Author's notes.

[61] Dilawar Ali Khan, former UNICEF Country Representative: *Improving the Quality of Basic Social Services for the Most Vulnerable Children and Women*. Presentation at the Third International NGO Conference on Humanitarian Assistance to North Korea: Cooperative Efforts Beyond Food Aid. Seoul, 17 to 20 June 2001, p.6.

[62] Interview with Jean-Fabrice Piétri, Desk Officer/ACF, Paris, 20 July 1999.

MSF was the first European NGO that started to work in the DPRK. In the aftermath of the 1995 floods an MSF expatriate team provided drugs and gave training to medical staff on the use of drugs and medicine. From July 1997 to September 1998, the Belgian, the Dutch and the French section of MSF carried out nutritional programs that included the distribution of medicine, the setting up of therapeutic feeding centers and the training of local medical staff. MSF projects were located in the South Pyongan, Kangwon and North Hwanghae provinces. In early 1998, MSF was able to expand its program to North Hamgyong province in the northeast. In terms of the number of expatriate staff, MSF was the biggest NGO with 13 international staff. 64 feeding centers were established in the pediatric wards of county and provincial hospitals that aimed at the nutritional rehabilitation of children suffering from moderate or severe malnutrition. MSF provided high-energy milk and held training sessions on the preparation and use of the milk. In addition, the program aimed to give training to doctors about the diagnosis and treatment of malnutrition. After the end of its program, MSF failed to reach an agreement with the FDRC on a further engagement, and decided to leave the country in September 1998 (details will be discussed in chapter VII). In total, MSF's budget for activities in the DPRK amounted to about US$9.3 million, of which 70 percent were ECHO funds.

MDM carried out a similar program in the eastern province of South Hamgyong. At the beginning, MDM was also present in Nampo city in the west, but decided to focus on the east. Between October 1997 and July 1998, the French section of MDM established therapeutic feeding centers in hospitals and children's institutions, supported health structures with the donation of medicine and training of medical staff. MDM also set up a surgical-support program in the Hamhung provincial hospital (rehabilitation of an operating theater). In addition, high-energy milk provided by UNICEF was distributed to children's institutions. The total cost of the program was about ECU2.7 million (about US$3 million). ECHO was the main donor. MDM personnel consisted of four permanent expatriate staff. Attempts to renegotiate MDM's operational space failed in summer 1998. After only ten months of presence in the DPRK, the NGO decided to withdraw from North Korea.

In regard to the size of medical and nutritional programs, MDM and MSF accepted the wishes of the North Korean side. As a consequence, these agencies supported a relatively large number of institutions with a relatively small number of staff. MDM intended to renegotiate its terms of intervention and aimed to reduce the scale of its "enormous" program.[63] The FDRC declined this proposal. Likewise, MSF regretted the terms of the memorandum of understanding with the FDRC. An MSF report that was written after the organization's withdrawal concludes that "MSF has placed itself in a situation where it was impossible to get out: negotiation on a volume of intervention that was much too big (FF50 million), contractual presence in too many institutions".[64]

ACF is the third NGO that carried out nutritional projects in DPRK between January 1998 and March 2000. ACF set up a nutritional program designed to support nurseries in the province of North Hamgyong. This program also included activities in pediatric hospitals and the training of staff in nurseries and kindergartens on the detection and treatment of malnutrition. Unlike MDM and MSF, ACF was also active in the food security sector and provided agricultural support to cooperative farms in North Hamgyong and South Pyongan province. However, it was the nutritional program that caused the most internal debate and finally led to ACF's withdrawal from the DPRK in March 2000.

Public health related programs

Most NGOs that are active in the DPRK support the public health system by donating medicine and basic drugs, but do not implement nutrition programs. One example is the International Federation of Red Cross and Red Crescent Societies (IFRC) that supports health and care programs in four provinces. In terms of NGO programs in the public health sector, IFRC's program is the largest activity. Since 1995, the Federation has supported health institutions in the DPRK, at first with food, later with medicines, medical equipment and other items. The program was further expanded to include community-based first aid, winterization activities, health promotion training at community level, and water and sanitation projects.

The rehabilitation of health institutions is a further field of aid activities in North Korea. The German NGO Cap Anamur, for instance, provided various material support to 15 hospitals in the South Hwanghae, South Pyongan and North Hamgyong provinces. Cap Anamur - whose

---

[63] Interview with Nathalie Bréchet, Desk Officer/MDM, Paris, 21 July 1999.
[64] MSF: *MSF et les Famines. Le cas de la Corée du Nord,* December 1998 (internal report, in author's files).

former Chairman stresses that "our work in North Korea is the most difficult we have ever had to face"[65] - failed to obtain an agreement with the
FDRC on an improvement of working conditions and therefore decided
to pull out in September 2002. Eugene Bell is another example of a
highly specialized NGO that provides assistance to North Korea's health
system. The Seoul-based organization supports health institutions in the
DPRK that treat tuberculosis through the donation of tuberculosis medicine packages (Direct Observed Treatment System, DOTS), mobile x-ray
units and other equipment. Eugene Bell receives funding from US and
South Korean citizens, the South Korean government as well as from
other NGOs.

Aid agencies observed that one major health risk in the DPRK are
water-borne diseases. The lack of chlorine treatment and safe water,
combined with the nutritional status of the population, was regarded an
extreme risk to people's health. Since 1999, UNICEF and IFRC have implemented a variety of programs that aim at the improvement of water
quality (drilling wells, rehabilitation of water pumps and treatment stations, training courses etc.). In addition, the DPRK government contacted the British section of Oxfam and asked for aid projects in the wa-
ter/sanitation sector,[66] which is traditionally a very strong area for Oxfam. In 1998/99, Oxfam GB delivered chlorine and introduced modern
water treatment technology in the western provinces of the DPRK. In
following years, due to ECHO's financial engagement in the wa-
ter/sanitation sector, resident European NGOs such as CAD, CESVI and
GAA also began to implement programs in this sector.

A particularly controversial activity in the public health sector is the
material support of pharmaceutical factories in North Korea. Since late
1997, ACT has delivered raw materials to a pharmaceutical factory in
Pyongyang. UNICEF and WHO support ACT's project. Diakonie Germany, the cooperating agency within the ACT network, regards this project as an important step towards a more sustainable assistance. A Diakonie report states that "this is an effective kind of aid that strengthens

---

[65] Rupert Neudeck: "The New Crisis is that Boundaries Between NGOs and Governments
Are Blurred". Interview by *Humanitarian Affairs Review*, 16 April 2000, found at
www.reliefweb.int (3 May 2002).
[66] Interview with James Darcy, former Regional Director Asia/Oxfam GB, Oxford/UK, 11
September 2001.

the infrastructure".[67] In 1998, the FDRC had proposed the same type of support for the same factory to MSF, which declined the offer. In MSF's view, what the North Korean population needed most was immediate medical aid and no structural assistance.[68]

b) The Targeting of Nutritional and Public Health Efforts

It is the nature of nutritional programs that they seek to target those individuals most severely affected by malnutrition. The provision of high-energy food and therapeutic feeding has to focus on malnourished people. Unlike the food aid operation that defines vulnerability according to age and gender, nutritional programs include additional physical criteria based on medical considerations. The therapeutic feeding centers that were set up by MSF, for instance, targeted children whose weight-for-height proportions were less than 80 percent of the international standard.

Needs assessment

The assessment of the nutritional and health state of the population is particularly difficult in the DPRK. As noted above, conducting nutritional surveys is a sensitive issue in North Korea. Notably, the first withdrawal from the DPRK occurred in January 1996 when MSF, after the Memorandum of Understanding with the FDRC expired, could not obtain an agreement with the authorities regarding a nutritional survey.[69] To date, no NGO has been allowed to conduct nutrition assessment studies in the DPRK. Most NGO nutritional programs were designed before international governmental agencies obtained the agreement to conduct the first nutrition survey in fall 1998.

In the absence of their own data, medical relief agencies tried to design their activities according to general observations and the information available. Importantly, as in all sectors of humanitarian action in the DPRK, aid agencies in the nutrition and public health sector have to deal primarily with the FDRC. In other countries, these agencies are more

---

[67] Diakonie Emergency Aid: *Nord-Korea – Geduld und Hoffnung im Land der Morgenstille.* [North Korea – Patience and Hope in the Land of Morning Calm]. Press release, Stuttgart/Germany: 21 February 2002.

[68] Interview with Pierre Salignon, Desk Officer/MSF, Paris, 22 July 1999.

[69] *Report of the Programme of MSF in DPR Korea July 1997 - September 1998* (internal MSF report, in author's files).

used to cooperating with the Ministry of Public Health. It is often argued, that the organization of programs with a medical component would be easier if aid agencies could cooperate directly with the Ministry of Public Health instead of the FDRC.[70] As for geographical targeting of nutrition and health programs, the IFRC asserts: "Access to providing aid to different geographical areas seems to be guided by political bodies not connected with the Ministry of Public Health, and not, therefore, by professional epidemiological assessment".[71]

The targeting of needs

As for the targeting of nutritional programs, aid agencies rigorously intended to set up their programs in the east and northeast of the country. This, however, was all but easy to obtain in negotiations with the FDRC. North Korean officials, particularly in the early years of NGO activity, preferred the west and southwest as the main location of NGO projects, including nutritional and health programs. In the end, the location of nutrition programs was the result of a compromise. NGOs were allowed to establish aid programs along the east coast, but had to agree to direct some of their activities to the west. MDM, for instance, reports that the FDRC only agreed to the establishment of projects in the eastern province of South Hamgyong after MDM had accepted the FDRC's request to carry out one part of the program in the western city of Nampo.[72] Likewise, MSF began its activities in the southern provinces of South Pyongan, North Hwanghae and Kangwon. After seven months, MSF was able to expand its operation to the northeastern province of North Hamgyong. ACF, which arrived in North Korea after MSF and MDM, was the only aid organization that was able to exclusively focus on the northeast. According to ACF, negotiations on program details were extremely lengthy (three months), but the geographic location of projects was no major obstacle.[73]

---

[70] MSF, for instance, notes: "MSF is a medical organisation, and in the countries we work it is the Ministry of Public Health who is our counterpart in the activities we implement. Here however it was the FDRC, and it is not easy to explain the details of the programme to non medical people". MSF: *Report of the Programme of MSF in DPR Korea July 1997 – September 1998*, (internal report, in author's files).

[71] IFRC: *Annual Report 2002. DPR Korea. Appeal No. 1.38/2002.* 8 May 2003, p.5.

[72] Interview with Nathalie Bréchet, Desk Officer/MDM, Paris, 21 July 1999.

[73] Interview with Jean-Fabrice Piétri, Desk Officer/ACF, Paris, 20 July 1999.

Likewise, with regard to medical supply programs North Korean authorities seemed to set other geographic priorities than aid organizations. Cap Anamur, for instance, aimed to distribute four tons of medicine to South Hwanghae province in May 1998, as had been agreed with the FDRC. After its arrival in North Korea, however, the authorities intended to give the items to the university hospital of Pyongyang. Cap Anamur had to announce stopping all activities in the DPRK until the North Korean side gave in.[74] As for the location of IFRC's health program, the FDRC preferred the activities to take place in the west and south of the country while the national Red Cross society was appointed to take care of the rest of the DPRK. The IFRC thus asserts that it cannot assess the situation in the northeast:

> The FDRC assigned four of the 13 provinces/municipalities as operational areas for the health and care programmes supported by the International Federation. It is not possible to assess how this influences the capacity of the Red Cross Society of the DPRK (...) in the remaining parts of the country. (...) The nutrition survey confirms that the malnutrition rate may be about three times as high in the eastern and northern provinces than in the west and south where the large-scale programmes of the Federation are implemented.[75]

Unlike the distribution of food aid, enriched food was only channeled through the PDS at the beginning of nutritional activities. Since late 1997, aid agencies have had the permission to regard enriched food as a medical item and transport it to the institutions. Nevertheless, aid agencies working in the nutrition and medical sector select their beneficiaries in basically the same way as the organizations that provide food aid. Thus, nutritional projects focus on public institutions (hospitals, pediatric clinics, kindergartens, nurseries, orphanages etc.). As for the selection of target institutions, aid agencies in the nutrition sector are in the same position as they are in the food aid sector. General restrictions of movement and of access to counties apply to all kinds of foreign assistance.

Some nutritional programs intended to reach all children's institutions in the accessible counties of a given province. Due to the restricted

---

[74] Cap Anamur: *Kamsanida! Vielen Dank!*, project information found at www.cap-anamur.org/projekte/korea/ nordkorea.html (2 October 2001).
[75] IFRC: *Annual Report 2002. DPR Korea. Appeal No. 1.38/2002.* 8 May 2003, p.1.

access to information, the aid organizations were not always able to determine whether, in fact, all institutions in the project area benefit from nutritional assistance or medical supply. Depending on the operational focus of a nutrition or public health program, and due to the hierarchical structure of the country's public health system (one provincial hospital per province, one county hospital per county etc.), some agencies can assess whether a project effectively covers all institutions in a project area. In terms of the provision of material supply to clinics and hospitals, as carried out by the IFRC or Eugene Bell, for example, it is easy to determine whether all institutions are listed in the information given by the FDRC. However, once an agency seeks to reach groups of people in numerous institutions (malnourished children in nurseries and kindergartens, for instance), this certainty does not exist. The ACF Head of Mission notes that "no comprehensive list of the nurseries and kindergartens was provided by the authorities".[76] Likewise, MSF doubts the completeness and reliability of the lists of institutions provided by DPRK authorities:

> A lot of data exist but authorities are reluctant to share this information with foreigners, even a simple list of all health facilities seems to be difficult, we don't obtain a complete one. To obtain the data we have to insist a lot, some we never get. On the other hand we have our doubts about the quality of the figures given: sometimes we have the impression that they do not correspond with the reality and that figures are given just to please us.[77]

Impact monitoring

In terms of impact monitoring, nutrition programs face the same restrictions as projects in other aid sectors. Random monitoring visits are not possible. The agreements with the FDRC contain clauses on monitoring activities that explicitly require international staff to notify the authorities prior to monitoring visits. The Memorandum of Under-

---

[76] Michel Anglade, Head of Mission DPRK/ACF, in: *Conference Proceedings. International NGO Conference on Humanitarian Assistance to the DPR Korea. Past, Present, and Future.* Beijing, 3-5 May 1999, p.50.

[77] MSF: *Report of the Programme of MSF in DPR Korea July 1997 – September 1998,* (internal report, in author's files).

standing between the FDRC and MDM of September 1997, for instance, stipulates:

> Every endowed structure will be visited at least one time between each consignment (...). MDM expatriate staff can travel freely, even when climatic conditions are bad, and perform their duties in the areas of the described program, these travels will be based on a week-to-week planning to be provided to the authorities.[78]

The monitoring of nutritional programs primarily consisted of the inspection of the institutions' warehouses. Neither in nutritional nor in other medical programs are aid agencies able to systematically monitor the end-use of donated commodities. Concerning UNICEF's support for vaccination campaigns, for instance, the former UNICEF Country Representative asserts: "I have never succeeded in visiting a vaccination spot".[79]

Consequently, neither in terms of nutritional activities, which are carried out by local medical staff, nor in regard to monitoring, are expatriate staff required to have medical skills. Humanitarian organizations in the nutrition and medical sector do not themselves implement the medical work. It is therefore not surprising when the UNICEF Country Representative asserts that "our human resources are mostly geared for logistics".[80] With very few exceptions, international staff is not allowed to treat patients or to directly check the nutritional status of institution inmates.[81] Medical agencies therefore questioned the sense of the presence of foreign medical staff in the DPRK. Cap Anamur, for instance, asserts:

> In 1998, we were about to throw in the towel. It appeared pointless to employ a medical doctor (...) who was rarely able to visit one of

---

[78] "Memorandum of Understanding Between the Flood Damage Rehabilitation Committee and Médecins Du Monde", Pyongyang, 26 September 1997.

[79] Interview with Dilawar Ali Khan, former UNICEF Country Representative, Seoul, 19 June 2001.

[80] Oral statement made by Richard Bridle, UNICEF Country Representative DPRK, at the Third International NGO Conference on Humanitarian Assistance to North Korea: Cooperative Efforts Beyond Food Aid. Seoul, 19 June 2001. Author's notes.

[81] Cap Anamur reports that one of its medical doctors was allowed to carry out a surgical operation. The organization stresses that "normally, this is an absolute taboo for foreigners". Cap Anamur: *Nord Korea. Kohleversorgung für fünf Krankenhäuser in der Provinz Süd-Hwanghae*, [North Korea. Supply of Coal for Five Hospitals in South Hwanghae Province], Cap Anamur newsletter, 17 December 1998, p.1.

the hospitals, and, in addition, who was not allowed to work as a medical doctor there.[82]

Hindering access to medical information at monitoring visits further limits the capacity of aid agencies to supervise the impact of nutritional programs. Monitors are only able to communicate with institution staff and patients through a translator. As noted above, no Korean-speaking international is allowed to work permanently in the DPRK. An MDM nutritionist summarizes that "we only saw the Koreans through the windows of our car".[83] The NGO therefore concludes: "We have no direct access and do not have the means to evaluate the effects of our program".[84]

Medical aid organizations that implement nutrition programs more often report monitors being deceived than non-medical agencies. ACF asserts that "monitoring visits are pre-arranged by the authorities" and that "we mainly saw what the authorities wanted to show us".[85] MSF observed that admission books were arranged for the MSF visit. Children were "invented on paper", or incredible weight gain was noted. Furthermore, MSF saw mothers arriving or leaving who brought children from outside the institution, evidently just for the purpose of the monitoring visit.[86]

In addition, aid agencies that worked in the nutrition sector report that access to patients' medical files was sometimes denied. On its own experience, MSF reports:

> In an attempt to know more about the morbidity and prescription habits we asked to study a sample of patient files which are kept at the level of the section doctors, but access to these files was refused. Even in some feeding centres, located in paediatric wards of hospitals where all children have besides a nutritional file also a medical file, the MSF doctor was not allowed to consult this medical file during the visits in the feeding centre. In other provinces some of

---

[82] Cap Anamur: *Kamsanida! Vielen Dank!*, project information found at www.cap-anamur.org/projekte/korea/nordkorea.html (2 October 2001).

[83] Pierre Capitaine, Nutritionist/MDM, quoted in *Libération*, 11 July 1998.

[84] Interview with Nathalie Bréchet, Desk Officer/MDM, Paris, 21 July 1999.

[85] Michel Anglade, Head of Mission DPRK/ACF, in: *Conference Proceedings. International NGO Conference on Humanitarian Assistance to the DPR Korea. Past, Present, and Future.* Beijing, 3-5 May 1999, p.50.

[86] MSF: *Kangwon Province – Final Nutritionnal Report. February 98 – August 98.* (Internal report, in author's files).

these files could be consulted, but not all of them, there seemed to be patients that they preferred not to show us for one reason or another.[87]

Notably, these reports contrast with the assertions made by non-resident NGOs who provide medical supplies without carrying out nutritional programs. According to reports from Diakonie Germany, for instance, authorities and local institution staff were not reluctant to show patients' medical files. At monitoring visits in children's hospitals, the Diakonie delegation was even able to take pictures of patients' medical files that were later published in Germany.[88] Likewise, the Korean-speaking delegations from Eugene Bell that monitor the distribution and use of tuberculosis medicine can directly communicate with institutions inmates and inquire about their health status. In most cases patients appear to talk freely. However, as is also reported by most other agencies, answers given by patients sometimes seem to be memorized. Stephen Linton from Eugene Bell points out, that, for the most part, patients are ordinary people from the countryside, and that "it is easy to get access to them".[89] It is important to note that the non-resident organizations such as Diakonie, Eugene Bell or Caritas, that do not share the criticisms expressed by MSF or ACF, do not intend to directly treat patients and to implement the medical work themselves.

Summary: humanitarian space in the nutrition and public health sector

The humanitarian space in the DPRK does not allow medical relief agencies to independently assess nutritional needs, expatriate staff to carry out medical work or the evaluation of the impact of nutritional programs on the beneficiaries. The targeting of those people who are most severely hit by malnutrition is therefore, first and foremost, the task of the FDRC and other North Korean authorities. In June 2001, Richard Bridle, UNICEF's Country Representative in the DPRK, listed

---

[87] MSF: *Report of the Programme of MSF in DPR Korea July 1997 – September 1998.* (Internal report, in author's files).

[88] Diakonie Emergency Aid: *Nord-Korea. Die Hilfe greift.* [North Korea. The Aid Takes Effect]. Report by Hannelore Hensle on a trip to DPRK from 18 - 25 April 1998, p.8.

[89] Interview with Stephen Linton, Chairman of Eugene Bell Foundation, Seoul, 15 November 2000.

the main restrictions that limit the capacity of his organization to address the nutritional needs of vulnerable population groups:

Restricted movement and limited access to focused population and geographic areas

Indirect access to counterparts

Limited feedback from government agencies and beneficiary institutions on the end-use of supplies

Delays in the delivery of supplies from the central and provincial warehouses to the targeted institutions and communities

Inadequate focus on skills development – training remains a low priority

Lack of disaggregated data on the situation of children and women.[90]

In addition, NGOs that carried out nutritional programs between 1997 and 2000 report that the relationship with North Korean authorities, local staff and institution personnel was particularly problematic. In the words of an MDM Officer, the relationship with North Korean counterparts was primarily a "relation of control".[91] In this regard, organizations that primarily focus on the provision of medical supply assert that their relations with the North Korean side are much more cooperative. Caritas, for example, reports that the DPRK counterparts express their "appreciation and gratitude" for the agency's efforts (see Smith 2001a:38-39).

In conclusion, although working conditions are more or less the same for any kind of activity, the willingness on the North Korean side to make compromises in one way or another depends on the specific type of aid that is provided. In this regard, the implementation of therapeutic feeding programs is a particularly frustrating area of work. After having worked in the DPRK, an MSF nutritionist concludes:

I have never seen a real sign of respect from the authorities for our work as [a] medical organization, neither the positive desire to know

---

[90] *UNICEF Response to the Humanitarian Crisis in DPR Korea.* Presentation at the Third International NGO Conference on Humanitarian Assistance to North Korea: Co-operative Efforts Beyond Food Aid. Seoul, 17 to 20 June 2001, p.6-7.
[91] Interview with Nathalie Bréchet, Desk Officer/MDM, Paris, 21 July 1999.

and understand us (...). If we want to do something serious, our work must be accepted, not our money, and our program must be supported (not tolerated) by the authorities.[92]

Likewise, training courses and public awareness campaigns (disaster preparedness, health problems) often meet the resistance of North Korean counterparts.[93] Concerning the priorities of North Korean authorities in this regard, Stephen Linton from Eugene Bell argues:

Because of pride in what they have achieved on their own, political tensions with the outside world, and severe shortages of medical supplies, programs designed to deliver medical knowledge instead of medical goods are far less welcome.[94]

As for the water and sanitation sector, impact monitoring was the most controversial point. It is not possible to assess the quality of water using international standards, such as the standards included in the SPHERE project, in the DPRK. These standards would require direct contact with consumers – household visits, direct contact with technical staff in water treatment plants and unhindered access to hospitals in order to check for the presence of water-borne diseases.[95] Oxfam did not expect these conditions to be met in North Korea. But the North Korean view was that Oxfam's task was merely to deliver chlorine to designated

---

[92] See note 86 in this chapter.

[93] See, for instance, IFRC: *Annual Report 2002. DPR Korea. Appeal No. 1.38/2002*. 8 May 2003, p.4: "Public awareness campaigns and information dissemination is considered to be a sensitive issue and was discouraged to date".

[94] Paper presented at the Third International NGO Conference on Humanitarian Assistance to North Korea: Cooperative Efforts Beyond Food Aid. Seoul, 17 to 20 June 2001, p.3.

[95] As key indicators for the initial assessment of water quality, the SPHERE project mentions, *inter alia:* "An immediate initial assessment that follows internationally accepted procedures is carried out by appropriately experienced personnel. The assessment is conducted in cooperation with a multi-sectoral team (water and sanitation, nutrition, food, shelter and health), local authorities, women and men from the affected population and humanitarian agencies intending to respond to the situation. The information is gathered and presented in a way that allows for transparent and consistent decision making. Data are disaggregated by sex and by age, where feasible. The information gathered identifies needs and health risks related to water supply and sanitation for different gender, social and age groups, and provides baseline data for monitoring and evaluation" (SPHERE Handbook, chapter "Water and Sanitation", Section 1).

sites.[96] Therefore, Oxfam could visit chlorine stocks, but the testing of water was a more difficult issue. Oxfam was able to test the amount of chlorine in the water, but it was not allowed to gather data concerning the spread of water-borne diseases. Since Oxfam aimed to effectively improve the state of consumers health, the NGO argued that it needed to know the spread of water-borne diseases in order to determine whether the program was achieving its goal or not. North Korean authorities argued that water availability affects the country's industrial and agricultural development. In addition, it was argued that North Korean experts had the intellectual capacity to conduct assessment studies themselves and they merely lacked the equipment.

Although the Memorandum of Understanding from July 1999 grants the freedom to assess the quality of water within its operational areas, Oxfam was not able to conduct comprehensive surveys in practice. It therefore deemed it impossible to measure the program's impact, and decided not to continue the program beyond December 1999.

All other agencies which are active in the water and sanitation sector continue to implement projects. Working conditions are still comparable to those experienced by Oxfam. But unlike Oxfam, most agencies are prepared to provide technical and material supply and do not intend to measure the impact of their work in regard to the health status of individual consumers. Working restrictions concerning impact monitoring do not therefore present a dilemma for most organizations engaged in the water/sanitation sector.

Humanitarian activities in the water/sanitation, public health and nutrition sector illustrate that some aid organization are more prepared to accept the priorities set by the North Korean side than others. It therefore appears that the emergence of a dilemma in humanitarian action also depends on the organizational background. It remains to be seen in how far mandate, activity and political environment influence an aid agency's ethical course of action.

c) The Effects of Nutritional and Health Programs

Most of the doubts and criticisms concerning the entire aid operation in North Korea emanate from the experiences of humanitarian agencies

---

[96] Interview with James Darcy, former Regional Director Asia/Oxfam GB, Oxford/UK, 11 September 2001.

in nutritional programs. The work of aid agencies in this sector provides some evidence that supports the manipulation hypothesis according to which the most vulnerable population groups are out of the reach of aid agencies in the DPRK. At the same time, however, a number of agencies that carry out nutrition and public health related programs draw differing conclusions from their field experience and argue that their programs as well as the overall aid operation are a humanitarian success.

As for the delivery of donated commodities to institutions, medical relief agencies – like organizations in the food aid sector - unanimously assert that the donations effectively reach the targeted institutions. No single case of diversion of enriched food or medical supply has been reported by aid organizations working in the DPRK. Furthermore, in as far as aid agencies were able to check the use of donated enriched food, international staff by and large asserts that the local medical personnel used the commodities correctly. No agency that is or was active in the nutrition sector in the DPRK doubts the positive effect on the beneficiaries. On the feeding program, an MSF report concludes: "Many children were treated in the centres and certainly benefited from it".[97] The controversial question is how far malnourished people have access to the institutions where feeding centers have been set up and where supplies are distributed.

The number of beneficiaries

One observation of aid agencies in the nutrition sector is that relatively few institution inmates were present at monitoring visits compared to the general capacity of the respective institution and in view of registered children or patients. ACF asserts that in average only 45 percent of the children registered in nurseries and kindergartens were actually present at monitoring visits.[98] Likewise, MSF reports that the number of children treated in the feeding program was very low, and "at no moment (...) exceeded one percent of the under five population (estimated at ten percent of the general population), which is normally the

---

[97] See note 77 in this chapter.
[98] Michel Anglade, Head of Mission DPRK/ACF, in: *Conference Proceedings. International NGO Conference on Humanitarian Assistance to the DPR Korea. Past, Present, and Future.* Beijing, 3-5 May 1999, p.50.

target group for this kind of feeding programme".[99] In regard to its feeding program, MSF therefore concluded: "Time showed that it was not a good solution and that our efficiency was very poor compared to the input".[100]

Several aid agencies made very similar experiences in terms of the number of children in visited institutions. But their interpretation of the findings differs. The ACF Head of Mission reports that, when asked about the low number of admissions, the institution staff asserted that mothers prefer their children to stay at home because of bad conditions in institutions (no heating etc.), long distances and lack of transport facilities. In addition, it was said that mothers needed to stay with their children when they were under five years of age. This is not always possible, particularly when a mother has other children at home.[101] However, the ACF official suspected other reasons than the ones mentioned by institution staff such as social deprivation or limited access to public structures.[102] Caritas, by contrast, argues that the lack of equipment and medical supply makes people stay at home, rather than political exclusion from medical care. On a visit to the Sepo county hospital in Kangwon province in March 1999, a Caritas official notes:

> It is very cold, and only few rooms are heated. In one room, 20 ill, apathetic and emaciated children are present, mostly between eight and thirteen years old. I ask about the infants. 'They do not come any more to the hospital, many are too weak. We hardly have medicines, and no food', says the doctor. The same situation in the day-nursery. 200 children could be admitted, but only 76 are registered, and only a group of 21 is present. 'Parents do not bring their children any more. Once we have food, their number immediately increases', reports the director while she is showing us the empty larder.[103]

---

[99] MSF: *Report of the Programme of MSF in DPR Korea July 1997 – September 1998*, (internal report, in author's files).

[100] See note 86 in this chapter.

[101] See note 98 in this chapter.

[102] See, for instance, Michel Anglade, note 98 in this chapter, p.50: "What about the 55 percent absent? Are they too weak to attend because of health/nutritional problems? Parents with social problems? Children excluded from the official system? Street children? A lot of questions to which we didn't get any answers".

[103] Caritas International: *Der tödliche Hunger kehrt zurück*. [Mortal Hunger Is Returning], Trip Report by Kathi Zellweger/Caritas Hong Kong, March 1999. Found at www.caritas-international.de/hm02/aktuell2.htm (1 July 1999).

The nutritional state of beneficiaries

As well as low attendance rates, the actual nutritional state of the children present caused medical relief agencies to doubt the sense of their doing. According to a number of reports, beneficiaries of feeding programs were in a much better nutritional state than available information on the humanitarian situation in the project area had suggested. ACF's feeding program supported about 1,300 nurseries and 1,000 kindergartens in the northeastern province of North Hamgyong where some 155,000 children from six months to six years of age were registered. According to general observations and in view of the findings of the 1998 nutrition survey, the nutritional situation in this region was worse than in the rest of the country. Consequently, it was assumed that malnutrition rates among the targeted children were higher than the 62 percent for chronic and 16 percent for severe malnutrition in the national average (see chapter IV.4). However, in 450 monitoring visits conducted between May and December 1998, ACF found only 29 malnourished children in the nurseries and kindergartens. In all the institutions visited by ACF staff, less than one percent of the children present were severely malnourished.[104] MDM and MSF also assert that, in total, the majority of the children present in visited institutions were not malnourished. MSF reports that only two or three severely malnourished children were present at each monitoring visit in Kangwon province.[105] In some hospitals the number of children suffering from chronic and acute malnutrition was higher.[106]

Moreover, the manipulation hypothesis relies on aid agencies' reports suggesting that institutions and North Korean authorities do not seem to specifically direct the international aid to the most vulnerable groups or individuals. Their primary objective seems to be to ensure that public health institutions continue to function and are able to offer medical

---

[104] Michel Anglade, Head of Mission DPRK/ACF, note 98 in this chapter, p.50; interview with Jean-Fabrice Piétri, Desk Officer/ACF, Paris, 20 July 1999. See also Piétri 2002:14.

[105] See note 86 in this chapter.

[106] Concerning the province of Kangwon, the MSF report notes that severely malnourished children were more numerous in the county hospitals of Wonsan and Chonnae; see note 86 in this chapter.

service to the common population. Therefore, the received supplies are afforded according to people's access to health structures, and not according to needs. This is not necessarily the same, as some observations made by international staff in the DPRK suggest. The first example of this are observations made by UNICEF and MSF staff in the pediatric hospital of Pyongsong county, which is the referral center for all pediatric services in South Pyongan province. MSF set up a nutritional center at this hospital that also served as the location for training courses on malnutrition offered by UNICEF and MSF for local pediatricians. Severely malnourished children were present in the hospital during the first training course in July 1997, but they were not seen again at a regular monitoring visit two days later, nor were they present at subsequent visits in the following months. These children were kept in a separate building and showed physical characteristics that MSF had not seen in other institutions. Compared to children in other feeding centers in the same province, these children were older (average 8.8 years), and in a worse nutritional, hygienic and general state of health.[107] The presence of scabies and lice was seen as a sign that the children had lived in crowded places. Cases of frostbite further suggested that some of the children had

---

[107] MSF-DPRK: *Identification of an at Risk Group. Socially Deprived Children,* 23 July 1999 (internal report, in author's files). The report notes on the characteristics of the children present at visits in this building: "(1) General condition: Upon their arrival the poor hygiene of their body and clothes is not found in the general Korean population. Their clothes are dirty and in poor state. (2) Nutritional status: The majority of the malnourished children are severe cases (often kwashiorkor) which is in contrast to the observations in other centres where we see mainly moderate cases of marasmus (...). The mortality is higher than in other centres: 3 % in the city hospital centre, 3.8 % in the provincial centre and 0.3 % in the other centres. This is probably due to the serious condition they present at admission. Some cases of deficiencies have been diagnosed: many have anaemia, some cases of pellagra and in one case of scurvy. (3) Skin diseases: Almost all children have scabies often complicated by bacterial infection on the hands resulting in inflammatory edema. Many have abscesses or scars from healed abscesses, mainly on the scalp. The ears are very often infected, marked by a moist inflammation of the ear lobe. Lice is very common and was present in all children during the month of February. Many children admitted [having] their heads shaved (...). (4) Psychological status: Some children are very absent minded: fixed look, absence of emotional reactions, even after nutritional recuperation. (5) Other problems: Some cases of frost bite on the feet with amputation of toes have been seen. Certain children are suspected tuberculosis cases. The prevalence of diarrhoea is important during the whole year, also respiratory tract infections are often noticed but with a seasonal pattern".

lived on the street before they came to the Pyongsong hospital. On the children's origin, MSF therefore makes the following assumptions:

> Their general state shows that they have lived under extremely precarious conditions: some of them most surely in the street, the existence of this problem has recently been admitted by the authorities. Others probably come from children's institutions that we cannot visit. Because in institutions that we had access to, the kids did not show the same characteristics.[108]

Likewise, an ACF report suggests that children who are in a particularly bad state, live in institutions that do not benefit from nutritional assistance. On a visit to two orphanages[109] in Chongjin/North Hamgyong province, that was conducted in July 1999, ACF reports:

> Out of a total of 380 children (...) more than 20 percent were malnourished, most of them showed symptoms of an extremely severe malnutrition. (...) Here, malnutrition that did not exist in nurseries and kindergartens was evident. The most severe cases were children under one year of age. The majority urgently needed to be fed through nasogastric tube, and to be rehydrated. Otherwise they were most likely to die within the following days. (...) No treatment against malnutrition was applied. The institution staff confirmed that these children are not to be referred to a clinic or hospital. (...) Action Contre la Faim proposed to set up a therapeutic nutrition unit in the Chongjin orphanage (...). In October 1999, this intervention was refused by the Korean authorities, without giving a real explanation.[110]

The interpretation of monitoring reports

The reports from MSF and ACF illustrate the basic problematic of nutrition aid in North Korea. Nutritional and medical aid effectively reaches health facilities and institution inmates. The main focus is on the support of the country's public health structure and not on targeted assistance to most vulnerable populations. Efforts are directed at enhanc-

---

[108] From the final report on the MSF mission in DPRK. Extracts reprinted in *Messages. Journal Interne des Médecins Sans Frontières*, no. 101, November 1998, p.2.
[109] The ACF report adds that the term 'orphanage' for these institutions is misleading, because not only orphans are admitted.
[110] ACF: *Dossier de Presse. Action contre la Faim Décide de Se Retirer de Corée du Nord*, Paris, March 2000.

ing the public health system's capacity to treat the ordinary population. Again, the challenge is to sustain life rather than to save life. Therefore, aid agencies that implement nutritional programs have, by and large, no access to those most severely affected by malnutrition and, consequently, judge that their programs did not obtain the intended effects. On the work in the northeastern province of North Hamgyong, the ACF Head of Mission concludes:

> We believed that two worlds/realities may coexist at the present time in North Hamgyong. The reality of people starving to death, as it is described by Korean refugees interviewed in China, [and] the reality of the apparent and official world to which humanitarian workers have access.

Agencies that primarily seek to enhance the capacity of the North Korean public health system and do not aim to treat those who are about to starve, have a more positive perception of the impact of their projects. The IFRC, for instance, concludes on its health and care program in the DPRK:

> It is difficult to quantify the impact of most of these initiatives, as the data from the Ministry of Public Health (MoPH) is insufficient and lags in time behind the onset of the more intensive support from the Federation to analyze cause and effect. However, subjective reports from the MoPH and the local health authorities do provide indications that the decline was significantly slowed in 2001 and 2002, partially due to the assistance from the Federation.[111]

Likewise, Eugene Bell does not doubt the positive effect of its tuberculosis program in the DPRK. The monitoring visits have shown that the donations (medicine and technical equipment) have effectively reached the designated institutions and thereby improved their capacity to diagnose and treat tuberculosis.

In sum, aid agencies interpret the effects of their nutrition and public health related efforts in differing ways. Some see their activities as a success, while others argue that their humanitarian objectives could not be achieved in the DPRK. It thereby seems to play a role whether a humanitarian organization seeks to enhance the capacity of institutions, or whether it aims to provide direct and immediate assistance to individuals. These differences between aid agencies will become more evident

---

[111] IFRC: *Annual Report 2002. DPR Korea. Appeal No. 1.38/2002.* 8 May 2003, p.4-5.

with regard to the approaches adopted by aid organizations to dealing with dilemma situations (which will be discussed in greater detail in chapter VII).

VI.4 Food Security and Agriculture

Most NGOs that had provided food aid and medical supply at the beginning of their engagement in North Korea refocused on food security programs and agricultural rehabilitation in subsequent years. This sector thus became the main area of activity of NGOs in the DPRK. WFP, FAO and other UN agencies also implement programs that seek to enhance the country's capacity to produce food.

a) Program activities

UN and NGO programs

A number of programs aims to enhance local capacities to produce food outside the agricultural sector. These projects focus on the production of noodles or enriched biscuits. World Vision was the first international aid agency that set up noodle factories in the southwest of the country in 1997. World Vision has now established 40 factories of this kind across the country. Other NGOs and WFP have also undertaken efforts in this field of activity. Beneficiaries of these programs are primarily children in institutions, and pregnant and nursing women. The rehabilitation and material support of bakeries also became an important component of food security activities. Between 2000 and 2003, GAA locally produced high-energy biscuits that aimed to improve the nutritional state of about 240,000 school children in South Hwanghae province. The project was handed over to WFP, and GAA began to implement a similar school feeding program in North Pyongan province (rehabilitation of five bakeries for the distribution of fortified biscuits to 223 primary schools). JTS is the only organization that is active in the special economic zone of Rajin Sobong where it supports a grain factory producing nutrition powder.

As for agricultural programs, international organizations provide inputs such as fertilizers, seeds, herbicides, technical support (rehabilitation of greenhouses, provision of tools, spare parts etc.) or assistance in animal breeding. Agricultural recovery programs are carried out by European, US and South Korean aid agencies, and are the largest component of NGO efforts in the food security sector. North Korean authorities welcomed the provision of seeds and fertilizers which, like the delivery of food and medicine, was part of aid activities from the beginning of the international aid program. Swiss Disaster Relief, for instance, already provided seeds and fertilizers in 1995. In terms of budget size (more than EUR2.8 million in 2001) and number of resident expatriate staff, the largest effort in this area is currently undertaken by GAA, which is also the largest resident NGO in the DPRK. Most NGOs in this activity sector are heavily dependent on public funds. GAA as well as other European NGOs that are or were active in agricultural recovery such as ACF, CESVI, Children's Aid Direct, Concern Worldwide, PMU Interlife and Triangle received or receive funds primarily from the European Commission and from European governments. Due to financial constraints, Children's Aid Direct had to close its program in North Korea in June 2002.[112] One exception in the food security sector is the Swiss NGO Campus für Christus, which is exclusively privately funded. Beside private donations, US NGOs − with the exception of American Friends Service Committee (AFSC) - receive the bulk of their funds from the US government (USAID, USDA).[113]

Project portfolios pursue a variety of objectives such as diversification of crops, production of vegetables in greenhouses, environmental rehabilitation or animal breeding. Most NGOs focus their assistance on particular cooperative farms. This "adoption" (Flake 2003:33) means that the selected farms receive various sorts of agricultural support. Commodities delivered include seeds, fertilizers, plastic sheeting, farming equipment and apple seedlings.[114] One exception is the South Korean

---

[112] For details see Miranda Weingartner: *Children's Aid Direct Closes DPRK Office.* Canada-DPR Korea E-Clipping Service, CanKor No. 86, 6 June 2002.

[113] The Quaker organization AFSC gets financial support from other US NGOs and from the Swedish International Development Agency (SIDA). Historically, AFSC has not received any US government aid. The Canadian Foodgrains Bank receives funds from the Canadian government.

[114] Between July 1999 and May 2000, the US NGO consortium − PVOC − that had residency status in North Korea and oversaw the distribution of US food donations, was also engaged in a food security program seeking to plant 1,000 tons of potato seed. This program ended in a "PVOC waterloo" (Flake 2003:30) and the withdrawal of two core member organizations, CARE and Catholic Relief Services (CRS). CARE publicly argued that working conditions did not allow for a longer-term and more sustainable engagement. However, a number of observers assert that the main reason for the end of PVOC's potato project were internal problems (management, staffing, disputes

International Corn Foundation that provides one commodity - corn seeds - to about 1,500 cooperatives. The organization's Chairman has a vast experience in corn production in African countries, and is seeking to repeat this success in North Korea.[115]

Cooperation with North Korean authorities

North Korean authorities seem to particularly appreciate programs that aim to improve local food production capacities, especially in terms of new initiatives to breed animals. In the past, the DPRK government, and even Chairman Kim Jong-Il himself, propagated the breeding of particular animals as being a very promising endeavor to improve the food situation in the country. Campus für Christus (CfC), for instance, signed a contract with the FDRC in 1997 for a goat breeding and milking project. This contract was based on a decree by Kim Jong-Il, which said that efforts should be undertaken to breed and milk goats particularly in mountainous regions. CfC concentrated on goat breeding and installed milk-processing units in Pyongyang, North Hwanghae and South Hamgyong province. CfC received a mark of distinction from Kim Jong-Il for its work (see UNOCHA 2002:138-139).

The willingness of the North Korean authorities to accept aid agencies' proposals to introduce North Koreans into modern farming methods, both in the DPRK and abroad, further illustrates the importance accorded to agricultural recovery. Training courses in North Korea and also in China, Europe and the US are part of a number of programs. In spring 2000, Mercy Corps International hosted a visit by the management of a collective farm to farms in Oregon. AFSC sponsors study-tours each year for North Korean agronomists to visit farms and agricultural research institutes in the US and China. As part of an agricultural rehabilitation program, GAA organized training courses in China and Ger-

---

among members organizations). The US General Accounting Office concludes that the PVOC did not adequately monitor the potato project although the FDRC had agreed to the monitoring modalities (see GAO: *Foreign Assistance. US Bilateral Food Assistance to North Korea Had Mixed Results.* Report to the Chairman and Ranking Minority Member, Committee on International Relations, House of Representatives. Report Number: GAO/NSIAD-00-175). Washington D.C.: June 2000, pp.23-24. See also Flake 2003:29-31, and Thomas McCarthy: *CARE's Withdrawal from North Korea.* Nautilus Policy Forum Online (No. 00-03A), 26 April 2000, www.nautilus.org.).

[115] Interview with Cathy Choi and Kim Jongwon, Planning Department/ICF, Seoul, 23 October 2000.

many on sustainable vegetable and potato production for North Korean agronomists. Concern invited staff from tree nurseries they are supporting and from the Ministry for Land Management to a study tour to China in 2002. Caritas sponsors a training program for North Korean fish farmers who are send each year to a small family enterprise in Switzerland. CfC organized training courses for 60 North Korean citizens from 1997 to 2000, also in Switzerland. More information exchange and study tour programs have taken place in the area of food security and agriculture than in other aid sectors. It is important to note that donors appreciate efforts to send North Korean citizens abroad for training purposes. For example, a German government official makes it clear that "of course, at the back of our mind, we hope that a stay in Germany may influence their views".[116]

In some cases, however, the FDRC's priorities concerning food security programs do not correspond with aid agencies' understanding of the purpose of their action. One example of this are the so called double cropping programs that aim to plant an additional crop on maize and rice fields that allows for a second harvest. North Korean counterparts invite aid agencies to support these programs, but a number of organizations providing material assistance to double cropping activities actually doubt their beneficial effect. It is argued that a possible short-term production increase is achieved at the expense of further soil degradation. Thus, in view of agricultural conditions in North Korea, some observers argue that double cropping is all but a sustainable farming method. In spite of these doubts, double cropping programs became a major focus of international aid agencies, primarily because they were "the door through which we could go".[117]

Furthermore, the DPRK government is undertaking large size construction and agricultural rehabilitation programs such as embankment or irrigation projects. NGOs are skeptical of these projects. It is argued that they present the traditional, centrally organized way of dealing with unfavorable farming conditions that seeks to gain short-term benefits without taking environmental or sustainability aspects into consideration. The DPRK government receives financial support from some inter-

---

[116] Interview with Helmut Siedler, Head of East Asia Department/German Federal Ministry for Development and Economic Cooperation, Berlin, 24 April 2002.

[117] Interview with Nancy Lindborg, Executive Vice President/Mercy Corps International, Washington D.C., 29 November 2001.

national donors for this kind of projects, but not from UN or non-governmental agencies. For example, the OPEC Fund for International Development signed a US$10.2 million loan with the DPRK in 2002 to support the rehabilitation of an extensive irrigation system in North Pyongan province.[118]

Donor policies and the shift towards development

In addition to the priorities set by North Korean authorities, aid agencies that are engaged in food security and agricultural recovery also have to deal with restrictions that emanate from donor interests. This sector of activity appears to be particularly sensitive from the perspective of some main donors since it focuses on rehabilitation rather than on emergency relief. Longer term structural and technical support, however, are politically more sensitive than the provision of food or medicine that can be presented as a humanitarian gesture. UN agencies, and UNDP in particular, seek to refocus the aid operation from emergency to development-oriented interventions in order to address the underlying structural causes of the crisis. In 1997, UNDP, with the support of the DPRK government, began to develop a program to provide a more sustainable input to the country's food production capacity. This Agricultural Recovery and Environmental Protection (AREP) plan aims to rehabilitate and modernize agricultural food production, to enhance appropriate land use and crop diversification, and to strengthen rural institutions (credits to households and farms, training programs for cooperative farms etc.). Between 1998 and 2002, UNDP organized three round-table meetings on AREP that brought together UN agencies, NGOs, donor governments and the DPRK government. In the words of a UNDP official, the AREP process aims to

> foster a more sustained and far-reaching policy-level effort that involves especially the main partners that have so far declined assisting with longer-term issues for political as well as security reasons. In other words, it will require a specific long-term mandate by the international community. This new mandate would be for the

---

[118] OPEC Fund for International Development: *OPEC Fund Extends US$10.2 million loan to Korea DPR in support of irrigation improvement project*. Press release. Vienna, 29 October 2002. The program *inter alia* includes the construction and improvement of canals, the excavation of tunnels, and a compensation scheme for buildings and land affected by the project.

UN to go ahead as a system with the type of assistance that will phase out the humanitarian program within a given timeframe in favor of sustainable recovery.[119]

To date, donors have been reluctant to give such a "new mandate". An official from the German Ministry for Development and Economic Cooperation, for instance, points out that official development aid for North Korea is impossible for political reasons:

> We see the needs but we do not want to support the regime. In addition, without the willingness to reform, any development aid is in vain. China, for example, has great deficits from a political perspective, but there is an enormous willingness to reform.[120]

As a result, for aid agencies seeking to move towards development aid in the DPRK, funding was, and is continually a major problem. Between 2000 and 2003, donor governments covered only 3.8 to 22.1 percent of UNDP's and FAO's appeals. In addition, donors' support for the AREP program has been very modest.

To sum up, on one side, North Korean counterparts welcome programs that seek to strengthen local food production capacities. On the other side, donors are reluctant to fund activities that might present a shift from emergency relief to development aid. Consequently, aid agencies in the food security sector maneuver between the priorities of their North Korean counterparts, funding constraints, and the own intention to provide some sustainable impact. In the words of an IFRC official, "after six years we're still providing basic items. What we need in DPRK is something we have no name for. It's neither relief nor development."[121]

b) The Role of Proportionality in Food Security and Agricultural Programs

The primary focus of food security and agricultural recovery programs is on the needs of cooperative farms and food factories. In con-

---

[119] Kirsten Jorgensen, Deputy Resident Representative DPRK/UNDP. Presentation at the First International NGO Conference on Humanitarian Assistance to the DPR Korea. Beijing, 3-5 May 1999, p.16.

[120] Interview with Helmut Siedler, Head of East Asia Department/German Federal Ministry for Development and Economic Cooperation, Berlin, 24 April 2002.

[121] Interview with Aurélia Balpe, Officer Asia and Pacific Department/IFRC, Geneva, 19 October 2001.

trast to food aid and nutritional assistance, the improvement of people's nutritional state is rather the indirect result than the primary objective of this set of activities. Food security programs that support bakeries or food factories define population groups that are supposed to receive the goods produced. In these cases, aid agencies monitor the distribution of the goods to institutions such as primary schools or orphanages. Agricultural recovery programs that, as has been mentioned, are the main activity in this sector, also define population groups that will benefit from a higher agricultural output. To monitor the distribution or sales of agricultural goods in a specific geographic area, however, is not part of this type of project. In addition, some products that aid agencies seek to promote are directly sold to the population. Vegetables, for instance, are not sold to the state or distributed to specific institutions. These projects therefore also seek to generate income for farmers and their families. In general, program objectives are measured in terms of increased production, and not in regard to the health status of consumers. Concern, for instance, describes the objective of its agricultural project in South Pyongan province as follows:

> Our objective is to increase food production by 20 percent and provide an adequate supply of appropriate planting material for future years. Beneficiaries are 900,000 inhabitants (rural and urban) of the six target counties.[122]

Needs assessment and the location of projects

In terms of needs assessment, aid agencies often have a different understanding than their North Korean counterparts. The FDRC is the main interlocutor for aid agencies also in this sector of activity. Direct contact to the Ministry of Agriculture or the Academy of Agricultural Sciences is only allowed to a very limited degree, and remains a postulate of aid agencies. Working conditions are virtually the same in this sector as they are in the food aid and public health sector. GAA, for instance, asserts that on monitoring visits, GAA program managers are generally not allowed to visit the projects that are not managed by themselves but by colleagues. It is telling to note that the bulk of projects in this sector

---

[122] InterAction: *InterAction Member Activity Report North Korea. A Guide to Humanitarian and Development Efforts of InterAction Member Agencies in North Korea.* Washington D.C.: InterAction, September 2002, p.19.

are located in the agricultural heartland of the DPRK along the west coast. In addition, Kangwon province in the southeast is another project area where cooperative farms received or continue to receive support from the PVOC, CFGB and CESVI. Programs that provide agricultural assistance in the north and east of the country, where farming conditions are particularly difficult, are less numerous. They include Caritas, CfC, CAD (until June 2002) as well as an IFAD project in the northern province of Ryanggang. In sum, as for the location of project sites, the FDRC appears to select potential project areas according to the criterion of production capacity. It proposes relatively big cooperatives that produce under relatively good conditions, while aid agencies with an agricultural mandate such as GAA prefer to support smaller and more disadvantaged farms.

Aid agencies that implement agricultural programs assert that they believed that the humanitarian situation in northeastern parts of the DPRK was particularly difficult. However, they accepted the request from the FDRC to work in other regions for two reasons. First, organizations with an agricultural mandate were prepared to adopt a longer-term perspective of their engagement in North Korea. In 1996/97, the main goal was to get a foot in the door. Agencies regarded the geographical expansion of programs to northern and eastern regions as an objective that should be achieved step by step. In the long run, this approach was quite successful. CAD and GAA, for instance, were allowed in the third and fourth year to expand their programs to South Hamgyong and North Pyongan province respectively. Secondly, aid agencies were convinced that the farms or food factories in the proposed project areas were in fact in need of foreign assistance. The state of cooperative farms or bakeries as well as the overall humanitarian situation in counties in southern or western provinces was perceived as troubling and therefore appropriate for the establishment of food security and agricultural recovery programs. In view of initial project sites in South Pyongan province, one CAD Officer, for instance, asserts that "needs were there as anywhere in North Korea".[123] In addition, to the extent that food security and agricultural rehabilitation programs became more important, NGOs argued

---

[123] Interview with Wube Woldemariam, Regional Program Manager Asia/CAD, Reading/UK, 12 September 2001.

that it made sense to establish these programs in the agricultural core regions along the west coast.

The targeting and monitoring of aid

Aid agencies face difficulties whenever they attempt to provide assistance according to other criteria than production capacities. According to experiences with famines in other countries, people develop alternative ways to purchase or produce food. It is the policy of aid agencies in the agricultural sector to specifically support these coping mechanisms that become essential for people's livelihood and access to food. In North Korea as well, people developed means to produce food for their own consumption or to sell it on markets. The farming population thus began to cultivate private plots in addition to their work on cooperative land. Reportedly, people are particularly motivated to cultivate this private land. According to a number of observers, the yields from private plots cover a considerable portion of people's food needs.[124] In addition, people in urban areas use their balconies to grow vegetables or to breed rabbits and chicken. Public health and social institutions also began to grow their own food. The manager of a hotel in Huichon county/Chagang province proudly presented a greenhouse and a pigsty to a GAA delegation, which the hotel staff had constructed on their own initiative. He explained that the produced food was not only enough to feed the hotel staff and guests, but that families in the neighborhood also benefited from it. The DPRK authorities tolerate and sometimes promote the development of these alternative ways to produce food.[125] However, aid agencies hardly ever obtain the agreement to support these coping mechanisms. GAA, for instance, aimed to deliver tools and seeds to families on cooperative farms in order to support their work on private plots and thereby help to improve their livelihood. The FDRC suggested that the families should have the choice of using the kits themselves or of handing them over to the cooperative. GAA, fearing that people would almost certainly not be able to keep the material for themselves, insisted

---

[124] Dieter Hannusch, Member of FAO/WFP Food and Supply Missions to the DPRK since 1996, estimates that privately produced food covers up to 30 percent of the overall food needs. Interview, Rome, 25 October 2001. See also Natsios 2001:116.

[125] *Korea Herald*, 23 August 2002, reports that the size of individual farming plots has been expanded from 30-50 pyeong (99-165 square meters) to 400 pyeong (1,320 square meters).

on monitoring modalities that included direct contact to these families in order to ensure that they kept and actually used the provided items. During the course of the negotiations, FDRC officials openly expressed their general dislike of food production outside cooperatives by saying that they wished people to go back to collective work. The FDRC finally rejected the proposal, and GAA did not deliver any kits.

Conclusion

The political dimension of the North Korean famine impacts on various aspects of the international aid effort in the DPRK. The famine relief operation is a politically delicate undertaking for both, recipient government and donor institutions. Consequently, donor governments and North Korean authorities strongly influence humanitarian projects in North Korea. The politically charged environment of aid has a three-fold impact on humanitarian work in DPRK: first, on the maneuverability of aid agencies; second, on the effects of their efforts; and third, on the ethical integrity of humanitarian organizations.

The operational space of aid agencies working in North Korea is very limited. North Korean authorities place a number of working restrictions on aid agencies and their work. As a result, humanitarian organizations are in no position to independently conduct assessment studies, to independently define target institutions and individual recipients, or to measure the impact of their projects on the nutritional or health status of individual beneficiaries. What we have described as the ambiguity of aid (the incapability of aid agencies to determine the political environment of their work) becomes evident in view of the restricted humanitarian space in the DPRK.

With regard to both the lack of information and the magnitude of the international aid effort, the UN inter-agency appeal in 1998 concludes (UNOCHA 1998:4) that "the data available are far less than that normally required in justifying a humanitarian operation of the present magnitude." In his study on humanitarian action, Tony Vaux (2001:180-181) argues that the challenge for aid managers

> lies in finding local people, even from among the victims of disaster, who have the greatest understanding and sympathy, and in building that short sturdy bridge to those in need rather than sending our own space-mission directly to those we do not understand.

In view of the lack of information on the humanitarian situation in North Korea, one could argue, that the famine relief mission in that country resembles what Vaux describes as a 'space-mission'. At the same time, North Korean authorities invite aid agencies to implement projects of a considerable size and budget. Also, in some cases, NGOs were only able to send exploratory missions to the DPRK after having provided a first donation of aid.[126]

Furthermore, donor institutions heavily influence the design of programs, primarily through the decision to fund some activities and not others. Thus, due to the restricted operational space in the field on the one hand, and the considerable donor influence on program details on the other, humanitarian organizations in North Korea focus on activities where recipient and donor interests intersect. These activities are primarily food aid, food security and short-term agricultural recovery programs. Other sectors find less support from recipient and/or donor side, such as nutrition programs or longer-term, development-oriented programs. In a sense, aid agencies that are financially dependent on US, South Korean or European government funds appear to be implementation agencies rather than organizations with their own independent humanitarian agenda. Furthermore, although NGOs generally describe the beneficiaries as the most important of their stakeholders, most agencies acknowledge that, in the DPRK, they have the least influence on project design and implementation. A former project coordinator in North Korea remarks: "if you fulfilled the requests of your donor, you would be expulsed from North Korea. If you reported objectively on the conditions of your work, you would get no money any more. You have to speak double-tongued".[127]

The humanitarian effects of the international aid operation are highly controversial. International organizations cannot monitor the end-use of the provided items. However, there is sufficient evidence to say that no massive and systematic diversion of aid has occurred in the DPRK. The first source of information are monitoring reports that unanimously report that the commodities (food, medicine, agricultural inputs etc.) effectively reach the designated institutions. An IFRC official argues that it would take the North Korean authorities an enormous effort to transport

---

126 Interview with Nathalie Bréchet, Desk Officer/MDM France, Paris, 21 July 1999.
127 Interview with Hubertus Rüffer, former Head of Mission DPRK/GAA, Berlin, 17 July 1999.

food to every institution just for the monitoring visits.[128] Although some cases of such deception of international monitors are reported, the systematic diversion of aid is most unlikely. The majority view is expressed by an FAO official who asserts that "once the goods reach the port of entry, the distribution is very efficient. Compared to other countries, the North Korean government is highly efficient."[129]

Furthermore, the restrictions regarding monitoring activities within target institutions do not necessarily aim to deceive aid agencies. GAA, for instance, reports that its staff is not allowed to visit all the classrooms of primary schools that benefit from its food assistance. When one monitor ignored the restriction and entered into the 'forbidden' classroom, he found that the children – their nutritional state, their clothing, etc. - looked exactly the same as they did in the rooms he was allowed to visit. In addition, even in the absence of a comprehensive monitoring system, the effective distribution of items to intended beneficiaries is in some cases visible. For instance, children were evidently wearing the winter clothes, that were donated by ECHO and distributed by European NGOs during the last winters. At the end of the day, monitoring restrictions in North Korea seem to be a matter of principle, and no hint for systematic diversion to politically loyal groups.

The efficacy of the international aid program can hardly be questioned. The main criticism focuses on whether the most vulnerable population effectively benefited from the program, and, accordingly, whether it is fair to say that the international effort has saved lives. In other words, the main question is to determine in how far aid is being afforded to needs and thus, in how far the principle of proportionality is respected in the DPRK. It has been argued that the international aid operation primarily focuses on populations living in stable social structures. The bulk of aid focuses on institutions, such as children's institutions, public health facilities, cooperative farms or food factories. The international aid thereby reaches the average North Korean population, that is, those population segments whose life is being affected, but not destroyed, by famine or food scarcity.

---

[128] Interview with Aurélia Balpe, Officer Asia and Pacific Department/IFRC, Geneva, 19 October 2001.

[129] Interview with Guy Sneyers, Country Project Officer/FAO, Rome, 23 October 2001.

The assertion of some NGOs, that these population groups receive foreign aid because "the regime has chosen to privilege them",[130] is misleading. The privileged most likely do not need foreign assistance. In addition, there is no evidence that people's political loyalty directly determines whether one benefits from foreign assistance or not. Humanitarian organizations observe considerable differences in terms of people's needs. Aid agencies report that children of party officials attend relatively well-equipped kindergartens in the city centers. More remote children's institutions are poorly equipped and admit children who appear to be less well fed and clothed.[131] The simplest explanation would be to say that these differences are due to a political loyalty classification system and the rank of the children's parents therein. However, it appears more plausible to say that political loyalty and geographical, economic and social criteria are intertwined and determine together people's quality of life.

All in all, the official crisis management aims to strengthen the country's own capacities to deal with the famine and its consequences. Foreign assistance is directed to areas and institutions with the highest potential and capacity to improve the situation. Therefore, the international aid effort has successfully contributed and continues to contribute to the stabilization of the North Korean society.

The North Korean case illustrates that proportionality and its operational implications in terms of needs assessment, targeting and impact monitoring differ in importance depending on an agency's portfolio and ethical framework. This explains why some humanitarian organizations working in the DPRK see their aid efforts as, by and large, successful. Others, who focus on proportional and life saving aid interventions, consider themselves to be caught in a dilemma due to the working restrictions in place in North Korea. From this perspective, the international aid effort is being manipulated by both recipient and donors.

It has been shown that humanitarian agencies have a differing perception of the purpose of their action in North Korea and come to differing conclusions regarding the effects of their efforts. It is therefore not

---

[130] ACF: *Dossier de Presse. Action contre la Faim Décide de Se Retirer de Corée du Nord,* Paris, March 2000.

[131] See, for instance, CESVI: *Winter Relief for Children in Nurseries and Kindergartens in Three Counties of Kangwon Province, DPRK. Monitoring Visits Findings.* 7 February 2002. Found at www.reliefweb.int (20 May 2003).

surprising that aid agencies adopted differing approaches in dealing with the restricted humanitarian space in the DPRK. These differing strategies will be discussed in the following chapter.

Chapter VII.

Dealing with Moral Dilemmas in North Korea

Both recipient and donor are restricting the humanitarian space in North Korea. Humanitarian organizations have only very limited means to independently design, implement and evaluate their interventions. Thus, the ambiguity of aid is evident. This ambiguity translates into concrete dilemma situations that aid agencies face in the DPRK. Depending on the specific ethical framework of a humanitarian organization, the intensity of such a dilemma differs. Likewise, aid organizations adopt differing approaches to deal with these dilemma situations. Coming up, we will present the approaches adopted by humanitarian organizations, and analyze how agencies justify their course of action.

VII.1 Victim-Centered, Introvert and Extrovert Approaches in North Korea

As has been argued in earlier chapters, aid agencies' courses of action are determined by three sets of factors: the agency's own agenda and principles, the political environment of their action and the suffering of people. Whenever the humanitarian space is restricted, aid organizations shape their action along these factors. That is, humanitarian actors might focus on the needs and well being of the individual recipient of aid *(victim-centered approach)*, they might accord priority to principles of action and 'good practice' *(introvert approach)*, or, finally, they primarily aim to change the politically motivated restrictions of their work *(extrovert approach)*. It will be seen that different decisions rely on differing priorities, rather than on an exclusive focus on one of the approaches. Thus, introvert, extrovert and victim-centered justifications of action provide tool boxes that can also be complementary.

a) The Victim-Centered Approach

The magnitude of humanitarian needs in North Korea and the empathy for individuals suffering from lack of food and medical assistance influences the course of action and the decision-making process of all aid agencies that have worked or are still working in the DPRK. As in all humanitarian crises where international aid organizations are involved, the individual famine victim and recipient of aid plays a particularly important role when it comes to fundraising campaigns and donor appeals. A starving child in the logo of CESVI's 'SOS Korea' campaign, children's faces on the front pages of UN Consolidated Appeals or of the Caritas' Five Years Review are examples of this common practice in aid agencies' public relations activities. The focus on the individual recipient of aid is sometimes more than a public relations tool but also influences an agency's strategy in the field.

On the effects of aid, the victim-centered argumentation notes that an aid agency's work in the DPRK makes a positive difference. Allegations that the aid does not reach the most vulnerable are countered by saying that the aid effectively reaches the targeted beneficiaries and that these beneficiaries are in need. A report from Diakonie Germany, for instance, notes that the aid "gets there where it is needed".[1] Likewise, the WFP Regional Director argues that "like in any WFP operation anywhere in the world, we do not know where each and every bag of food is going, but we do have a reasonable degree of assurance that the food provided through WFP gets to those who need it".[2] A distinction between 'need' and 'greatest need' is, by and large, not made. From this perspective, the most important question is to know whether the beneficiary is in need or not. Whether there are other people who are still more needy, plays no major role.

The focus on the individual beneficiary allows highlighting the human gesture that lies in the act of giving and that provides the link between the one who gives and the one who takes. A Caritas official, for example, asserts that "hundreds of North Korean children are just like my own children, and whenever they remember me, I go back there with a mother's heart".[3] In this view, humanitarian aid is, first and foremost, an act of solidarity that seeks to stress the equality of men and the common humanity: "Caritas works to alleviate poverty, hunger and suffering and instead of highlighting differences and problems, tries to bridge the

---

[1] Diakonie Emergency Aid: *Nord-Korea. Die Hilfe greift.* [North Korea. The Aid Takes Effect]. Report by Hannelore Hensle on a trip to DPRK from 18 to 25 April 1998, p.1.

[2] Testimony of John Powell, Regional Director Asia/WFP at the "Hearing of the East Asia and the Pacific Subcommittee of the House International Relations Committee. North Korea: Humanitarian and Human Rights Concerns", Federal News Service, 2 May 2002.

[3] Chosun Ilbo (English digital edition): *DPR Korea. Tremendous Famine to Come Before this October.* Interview with Kathi Zellweger/Caritas Hong-Kong, 2 July 2002.

ideological gap through emphasizing a common humanity."[4] Here, it is most important to show that North Koreans, in the words of a Diakonie official, are "people like you and me".[5]

The victim-centered view is skeptical of all factors that negatively impact on this relationship between helper and helped. One of these factors is the debate on working conditions and the adherence to a certain set of principles. In this regard, the victim-centered perspective highlights progress that has been achieved in certain respects and avoids drawing a negative or critical picture of the overall working conditions in the DPRK. In addition, consensus statements and codes of conduct are endorsed, but the focus on the helper-helped relationship does not allow an agency to take the lead in this debate or to argue in favor of a rigorous and comprehensive set of principles of action. In some cases, aid organizations tend to be skeptical or even disinterested when it comes to the establishment of standards of action. The US based United Methodist Committee for Relief Work, for instance, remarks that "we do not have a policy, or a standard that we've established to measure situations against. Our giving to the DPRK is pushed mainly by donors (as is most of our giving)."[6]

Likewise, political analyses of people's vulnerability to famine, or the gathering or evaluation of North Korean refugees interviews are incompatible with a victim-centered approach. When asked about the relationship between human rights work and humanitarian assistance in the DPRK, one NGO delegate replied: "A starving child needs food and no human rights advocacy".[7]

To the extent that the act of giving as an act of human solidarity reigns supreme, the humanitarian imperative prevails over principle debates or vulnerability analyses. Thus, the withdrawal out of respect for principles of humanitarian action cannot be an option. The decision to withdraw from North Korea is seen by some as an incomprehensible act

---

[4] Caritas Hong-Kong: *1999 Emergency Appeal Democratic People's Republic of Korea, SOA 01/99.* Hong Kong: 23 December 1998, p.8.

[5] See note 1 in this chapter, p.5.

[6] Quoted in Smith 2001b: paragraph 8.10.

[7] Oral statement made at the Third International NGO Conference on Humanitarian Assistance to North Korea: Cooperative Efforts Beyond Food Aid, Seoul, 19 June 2001. Author's notes.

of dogmatism. In response to MSF and ACF, a former NGO delegate and UN official argues:

> When MSF and ACF abandoned their work in North Korea with much fanfare, they put themselves on a higher moral plane than the organizations which chose to remain. Their decisions to leave were interpreted as the result of purely ethical considerations. They could not compromise humanitarian principles. Is it always unethical to compromise principles? (...) How can we demand compromises from governments when we are not ready to sacrifice our own purity for the sake of others? Will the hungry children of the DPRK thank us for abandoning them in order to safeguard our humanitarian principles?[8]

In addition, the withdrawal of a number of humanitarian organizations is interpreted primarily as an act of politically motivated protest against the North Korean regime, and not as the result of humanitarian considerations. Therefore, it is often argued that those aid agencies that pulled out from the DPRK gave up their humanitarian mandate in favor of political engagement. As a result, withdrawal and extrovert behavior are described as immoral. In the words of the former Head of the UN mission in the DPRK, "we cannot condemn a Korean child to death, just because that child was born in North Korea".[9] Likewise, an interview of *Libération* (22 August 2001) with Catherine Bertini, former WFP Executive Director, illustrates this reasoning:

> Your position is thus to say that, whatever they do, as long as one can feed the children, one is morally right?
>
> I simply say that the idea of letting these children die of hunger because we do not like that government, is an immoral idea.

Summing up, the victim-centered view allows aid agencies to deny a dilemma situation. No moral obligation or principle is regarded as equally important – and thus a potential rival – to the humanitarian im-

---

[8] Erich Weingartner: "Appropriateness vs. Inevitability". In: *Conference Proceedings. The Second International NGO Conference on Humanitarian Assistance to DPRK*, Tokyo, 30 June to 2 July 2000, p.89.

[9] Quoted in World Vision International: *North Korea Trip Report* by Dean Hirsch, President of World Vision International, 29 May 1999, p.4.

perative. Therefore, in comparison to the introvert and extrovert approaches, this perspective effectively avoids moral dilemmas.

b) The Introvert Approach

The majority of aid agencies seek to overcome the restrictions in place in North Korea with a longer-term perspective. The primary means to minimize doubts and questions about the sense of one's own actions is seen in the agreement on a common approach and a common set of principles of action.

The starting point of such an approach is the conviction that the aid effort in North Korea obtains positive results. UN agencies and the majority of NGOs argue that there is sufficient evidence that their aid efforts make a difference. In a press interview, the former WFP Executive Director sums up this point of view:

> I would never say that our system of verification works the way we wish it to work, this is not the case. But to say that, for that reason, the aid is being diverted, is wrong.
>
> Why do you accept the conditions of the North Korean government?
>
> If you do not accept them, you cannot feed the children. But this is our mission.[10]

Seen in this way, working restrictions hinder monitoring activities or might undermine a more efficient aid effort. However, aid organizations do not ultimately question the sense of their actions. Consequently, a large number of aid agencies do not see themselves as being caught in a dilemma. In addition, humanitarian organizations highlight cultural factors that are responsible for working restrictions in North Korea. Therefore, it is argued that a longer-term dialogue is the primary means to expand the humanitarian space. An IFRC report argues:

> The culture enhancing open discussions and open communication is very different in the DPRK, particularly so if compared with the transparency and the accountability demanded by the Federation itself and by donors. The overcoming of these cultural differences demands patience and a willingness to achieve mutual understan-

---

[10] *Libération*, 22 August 2001.

ding among all the partners involved in the humanitarian operations in the DPRK.[11]

Therefore, as a Caritas official argues, "aid agencies have a role to play not only by providing charity, but by creating an atmosphere for dialogue, for mutual understanding, for developing common strategies, methods, initiatives and concrete action".[12] It is important to note that this dialogue does not include any pressure or lobbying action on political aspects. The term 'advocacy' is primarily defined as the action that aims to raise awareness for the humanitarian crisis in North Korea in order to ensure appropriate funding. The UN Consolidated Inter-Agency Appeal (CAP) for the DPRK contains the following description of 'advocacy':

> The CAP Country Team sees advocacy (...) as a critical tool in situating the humanitarian response in relation to the wider political and economic context. (...) Advocacy will highlight the humanitarian implications of political action, as well as highlighting the consequences of inaction for the populations. Building on the success of combined advocacy efforts by WFP, UNICEF and OCHA in response to critical funding shortfalls this year, the Emergency Relief Coordinator and OCHA will be asked to play a robust role in the UN Secretariat in this regard.[13]

A number of NGOs have a similar understanding of advocacy. The US NGO consortium Interaction, as noted above, lobbied to get the US government engaged in the international aid effort for the DPRK. Likewise, Caritas International asserts that "the economic embargo of the DPRK is hindering recovery in the economic sector. Lobbying to lift these sanctions is desirable".[14] Thus, a considerable number of aid agencies actually try to influence donor policies but does not publicly comment on the North Korean government and its political priorities, nor do they try to exert any pressure via international media. The best means to influence the DPRK government is seen in effectively providing humanitarian aid. A CESVI official argues:

---

[11] IFRC: *DPR Korea, Appeal No. 1.38/2002, Annual Report.* Geneva: 8 May 2003, p.11.

[12] See note 4 in this chapter.

[13] *Humanitarian and Development Working Group Key Identified Lessons.* In: OCHA 2002: 132 (Annex V.).

[14] Caritas Hong-Kong: *Visit to the Democratic People's Republic of Korea (DPRK), 18-25 May 1999.* Hong Kong: 25 June 1999, p.6.

Our opinion is that despite the difficulties of monitoring project activities it is a moral imperative to do our best in order to reach the target groups and to provide aid. Also in terms of government openness and collaboration with the outside world, we believe we can do more by staying and working with them than by leaving the country.[15]

On a number of occasions, aid agencies insisted on minimum working conditions and objected to implementing specific aid activities due to working restrictions or uncertain project impact. In 1998, for instance, WFP initiated a program that aimed to support general hospitals. WFP monitors doubted that the aid was effectively reaching the targeted patients, and, after warning the authorities several times, the program was stopped.[16] Oxfam and the IFRC, after internal evaluations, decided not to continue their food aid programs due to restrictive monitoring conditions. Importantly, however, these decisions were taken without publicly criticizing the DPRK government.

As argued in earlier chapters, the focus on principles and standards of action is one important component of the introvert approach. In North Korea, all aid organizations that were providing assistance to the DPRK in November 1998 signed a 'Statement of Humanitarian Principles'. The Statement lists nine 'principles', of which three describe the operationalization of proportionality (needs assessment, impact verification, access).[17] The remaining 'principles' define longer-term project objectives (local capacity building, beneficiary participation) and staffing issues (adequate number of expatriate staff, health and safety needs). In addition, aid agencies agreed to distribute assistance only to accessible areas. In Consensus Statements in November 1998, December 1999 and March 2001 aid agencies referred to these operating principles and asserted that "we remain committed to these objectives".[18] Since October 2001, UNOCHA has established a benchmarking system that describes objec-

---

[15] Elisa Giunchi, Desk Officer/CESVI, E-mail to author, 29 July 1999.

[16] Interview with David Morton, UN Resident Coordinator 1998-2002, Rome, 4 February 2002. See also Catherine Bertini in *Libération*, 22 August 2001.

[17] "(1) Knowledge about the overall humanitarian situation in the country according to assessed needs; (2) Assurance that humanitarian assistance reaches sectors of the population in greatest need; (3) Access for assessment, monitoring and evaluation". Statement of Humanitarian Principles, 25 November 1998.

[18] Consensus Statement of All UN Agencies, NGOs and Donor Agencies Operating in the DPRK. December 1999.

tives and achieved progress in greater detail (see UNOCHA 2001:129-130).

Importantly, these statements from humanitarian organizations primarily address the aid agencies themselves. The DPRK government is not explicitly requested or urged to change specific policies regarding its crisis management or the handling of the international aid effort. Instead, the endorsing agencies stress that "all organisations providing humanitarian assistance to the DPRK are urged to similarly support these principles",[19] and that "only with adherence to these operating principles will we be able to work toward helping those in greatest need".[20] Principles are thus seen as objectives, and the agreement on them is already regarded a success. A former UNOCHA official argues:

> The utility of the Humanitarian Principles is obvious and vital. I don't think anyone would dispute their validity. However, their effectiveness remains to be seen. Principles 2 ['assurance that humanitarian assistance reaches sectors of the population in greatest need'], 3 ['access for assessment, monitoring and evaluation'] and 8 ['adequate capacity in terms of international staff'] may be compromised from time to time, but that is to be expected in a highly fluid situation. (...) they were drawn up (...) with the consent of the government, which in itself is a major step forward. (...) The important point is that the Principles provide a framework within which humanitarian actors are able to work. However, we are not in a position to 'enforce' these principles.[21]

It is important to note that aid agencies working in the DPRK issued the Statement of Humanitarian Principles as well as the subsequent Consensus Statements as a reaction to critical reports that questioned the sense of humanitarian aid in North Korea. The first statements, issued in November 1998, were the reaction to MSF's withdrawal and public allegations that international aid was not reaching the people in greatest need. The December 1999 statement explicitly refers to Oxfam's decision to withdraw from the DPRK that was taken in the same month. The latest Consensus Statement from March 2001 starts by saying that agencies working in North Korea "are aware of recent allegations re-

---

[19] Statement of Humanitarian Principles, 25 November 1998.
[20] See note 18 in this chapter.
[21] Shahwar Pataudi, former Humanitarian Affairs Coordinator DPRK/UNOCHA, E-mail to author, 18 August 1999.

garding humanitarian programming in the country". Here, the critical UN report by Jean Ziegler from February 2001 forced the aid organizations carrying out aid programs in the DPRK to react. In sum, the agreement on a common set of principles appears to be a means to defend and to justify the presence in the DPRK. Aid agencies refrained from commenting on the alleged manipulation of aid and the reported political motives behind the affording of aid. Instead it was argued that aid effectively reaches people in need, and that progress in terms of working conditions in North Korea needs time.

The majority of aid agencies perceive adherence to agreed upon principles as a means to achieve steady improvement. From this perspective, withdrawal is no option. Moreover, working under difficult conditions is regarded as a necessary task in North Korea that is more demanding than withdrawal. David Morton, the former UN Humanitarian Coordinator in the DPRK, summarizes:

> We do not have the luxury of choice that allows us to say 'we will not operate because minimum conditions are not reached' – we have to remain engaged and persevere, and work towards achieving those conditions. The minimum conditions will certainly not be achieved if we all simply pull out.[22]

Thus, according to the majority opinion, the focus on principles and minimum working conditions does not mean that the non-respect of these conditions has major consequences for the continuation of the program. By contrast, adhering to principles is seen as the duty to carry on. The CESVI program coordinator points out: "CESVI has decided to continue our help to DPRK not because we ignore the difficulties that MSF and MDM met, but because we are struggling day after day to overcome them".[23] In the words of the President of World Vision Korea, the adherence to standards and codes of conduct is a matter of "self-discipline". NGOs should be wary of their "own ethical pride".[24]

A group of NGOs has a different understanding of working standards and minimum conditions. Oxfam argues that principles and codes of

---

[22] Quoted in Smith 2001b: paragraph 9.

[23] Monti Feliciano, former Project Coordinator DPRK/CESVI, E-mail to author, 1 August 1999.

[24] Oh Jae-Shik, presentation at the Third International NGO Conference on Humanitarian Assistance to North Korea: Cooperative Efforts Beyond Food Aid, Seoul, 17 to 20 June 2001, p.7.

conduct not only define objectives and ideals, but also determine the line between what is ethically acceptable and what is not. When asked about Oxfam's reasons to withdraw, an Oxfam official referred to the Red Cross/NGOs Code of Conduct and listed the principles that were not being respected in North Korea. Likewise, MDM, which pulled out of the DPRK in July 1998, argues that minimum working conditions were not met. Jacky Mamou, the President of MDM, explains:

> To put an end to a mission means to abandon populations that undoubtedly are in great need. But the working conditions in North Korea are actually not acceptable in the view of a humanitarian ethics. The framework of intervention needs to be renegotiated so that the aid effectively reaches the population.[25]

Both organizations argue that their working conditions did not allow them to measure the impact of their efforts. An MDM official therefore concludes: "In other missions our operational space is also limited. But at least we can be certain that our activities are not in vain. In North Korea, we did not have this certainty."[26] Neither MDM nor Oxfam publicly criticized the North Korean authorities or aid agencies that preferred to continue their work in the DPRK. An Oxfam official points out: "Unlike MSF, we agreed not to take a high profile by criticizing the North Korean authorities. We only had an internal discussion with UNICEF, which was not fruitful".[27] Moreover, MDM stresses that, by pulling out of North Korea, it aimed to improve the working conditions for the humanitarian organizations remaining in the DPRK. It can be argued that MDM also adopted elements of the extrovert approach (forcing a government to expand the humanitarian space by stopping its aid activity). But it is important to note that MDM did not try to convince other aid agencies to take the same decision and to pull out of North Korea.[28]

Cap Anamur, which pulled out of the DPRK in September 2002, took a similar stance in not commenting on the DPRK government's political priorities or other agencies' behavior in the country. The primary argument was that the restrictive working conditions hindered the efficient provision of aid. The former Chairman of Cap Anamur argues: "What we

---

[25] Quoted in *Libération*, 11 July 1998.
[26] Interview with Nathalie Bréchet, Desk Officer/MDM France, Paris, 21 July 1999.
[27] Interview with James Darcy, former Regional Director Asia/Oxfam Great Britain, Oxford/UK, 11 September 2001.
[28] Interview with Nathalie Bréchet, Desk Officer/MDM France, Paris, 21 July 1999.

have achieved in the DPRK in the last five years, we would have easily achieved within twelve months under normal conditions."²⁹ Thus, unlike MDM and Oxfam, Cap Anamur argues that working conditions are unacceptable from an economic point of view rather than for ethical reasons.

To sum up, the majority of aid agencies working in the DPRK seek to expand their operational space through a steady and longer-term presence and interaction with North Korean authorities. Statements on common operational principles are an important tool to publicly define these longer-term objectives. Only a few agencies are prepared to stop their intervention due to the continuing non-respect of what they define as minimum conditions.

c) The Extrovert Approach

As argued earlier, alongside the moral obligation to relieve human suffering and an agency's own principles and mandate, the political environment presents the third set of obligations or constraints that affects an organization's course of action. It is this political environment of aid that the extrovert approach seeks to influence.

In the DPRK, a number of medical relief NGOs ultimately opted for such an approach. This decision relies on the conviction that the international aid effort, food aid and nutritional relief programs in particular, do not reach the people in greatest need. Unlike Oxfam, MDM or Cap Anamur, these organizations base their decision on a broader political analysis. MSF and ACF, as noted earlier, claim that access to food and international aid depends directly on the political loyalty of the people. Both organizations argue that the exclusion of particular population groups is a deliberate and politically motivated act of the DPRK authorities. Philippe Biberson, then President of MSF France summarizes the MSF position: "in August 1998, MSF withdraws its teams from North Korea after having gained the conviction that the international aid (...) did not save those people that the regime has condemned to die of hunger."³⁰ Likewise, ACF, in its report on "The Geopolitics of Hunger" presents the DPRK as a country where hunger is being used as a weapon.

---

²⁹ *Frankfurter Allgemeine Zeitung*, 27 September 2002.
³⁰ In: *Messages. Journal Interne des Médecins Sans Frontières*, No. 103, April/May 1999, p.1.

As a consequence, it is argued that international aid agencies ultimately support the system of political oppression. In addition, both organizations conclude that such support is precisely what donor governments and their 'soft-landing' policies seek to achieve.[31] In view of MSF and ACF, international aid is thus becoming both an accomplice of the North Korean regime and an instrument of donor interests.

Statements made by officials from both NGOs, before and after the respective decision to pull out of North Korea, illustrate that they were being caught in a dilemma situation. On the one side the magnitude of the crisis and the existence of great humanitarian needs was not denied. It goes without saying that both NGOs, as humanitarian organizations, were taking the moral obligation to relieve human suffering into consideration. As noted above, both NGOs describe their withdrawal as a very painful decision. In March 1999, an ACF representative, who was confronted with MSF's allegations of manipulated aid efforts, still justified the ongoing ACF program in the DPRK by saying that "we continue because we are at the children's side".[32] Like other agencies who decided to stop their programs in North Korea, MSF's and ACF's decisions were not taken without internal controversy and lasting doubts.[33] On the other side, the very limited number of malnourished children benefiting from the agencies' feeding programs seemed to underscore the assumption that the DPRK government intentionally excludes particular population groups from foreign assistance. In other words, MSF and ACF had to deal with two conflicting obligations: the principle of relieving human suffering and the principle of proportionality. In the view of these organizations, both principles turned out be mutually exclusive in North Korea. It is important to stress that neither MSF nor ACF referred to ethical ideals outside the humanitarian agenda. The promotion of democracy or human rights might be incompatible with a continued presence in the DPRK. In theory, it could be argued that humanitarian aid ultimately helps to prop up a dictatorial regime. However, these consid-

---

[31] See Brunel 1998:137-138 and Jean 1999: 16-18.

[32] Statement by Sylvie Brunel, former Strategic Counselor and President of ACF, broadcast by the French TV station *France 3*, 3 March 1999.

[33] See for instance Philippe Biberson, former President/MSF France, note 30 in this chapter: "Our decisions concerning North Korea and Sudan have prompted differing reactions, also within our movement. They (...) have had very limited impact on the respective situation and on the rest of the 'aid system'".

erations did not play the pivotal role in the decision-making process of these NGOs. Public statements as well as internal reports make it clear that the dilemma was seen, first and foremost, within the humanitarian ethical framework: the perceived impossibility of affording greatest aid to greatest need.

The lobbying activities that accompanied the withdrawal of MSF in September 1998 aimed to pressure the DPRK government into allowing the proportional affording of aid. At first, like Oxfam, Care or Cap Ana-mur, MSF asserted that working conditions in North Korea did not allow for a continued presence in the country. In a press release from September 1998, Eric Gomaere, the Director General of MSF International points out:

> It is not easy as doctors to pull out when so many people have died and when the health and lives of so many people are still in danger. But in the end, humanitarian assistance can only help those who need it when it is impartial and accountable. This is not the case in North Korea.[34]

Unlike the aforementioned NGOs, however, MSF publicly criticizes the North Korean authorities. Furthermore, MSF raises a number of highly sensitive issues that no aid agency working in the DPRK had publicly mentioned before. The press release from September 1998 says:

> In addition to the medical problems, there are worrying reports about widespread famine in North Korea. Refugees interviewed by MSF in April and August and who recently arrived in China from North Korea, speak of widespread famine, of relatives, friends, and neighbors dying of long term and recent lack of food. They also describe discriminatory food distribution systems according to social position and to party loyalty and speak of large numbers of homeless children roaming the countryside looking for food.[35]

MSF publicly urges the DPRK government to change its handling of the famine crisis and to reconsider its priorities. The Director General of MSF argues:

---

[34] MSF International: *MSF Calls on Donors to Review Their Policy in DPRK. Urgent Needs in North Korea But MSF Forced to Pull Out.* Press Release. Hong Kong/New York, 30 September 1998.
[35] See note 34 in this chapter.

It is clear that the priority in North Korea is now more to preserve the self-sufficient ideology than to provide effective and accountable assistance to those who need it most (...). Now it is time for the North Korean government to take [responsibility] for the health of its people and to allow direct humanitarian assistance.[36]

In March 2000, ACF decided to withdraw and issued equally critical statements on the DPRK government. ACF refers to the experience in Chongjin city/North Hamgyong province where the agency was not allowed to treat severely malnourished children and argues that this denial of access by North Korean authorities is "criminal".[37]

In addition, both organizations publicly criticized donor governments for using the aid operation as a foreign policy tool. ACF thereby reproaches donor governments for labeling their aid as 'humanitarian' although their contributions "conform much more to a political and diplomatic logic than to the real intention to assist the most vulnerable". ACF concludes that it "cannot sanction a policy that, under a humanitarian cover, sacrifices the North Korean population".[38]

Furthermore, by claiming that working conditions in the DPRK were incompatible with universal humanitarian standards, MSF and ACF also challenged the remaining aid organizations in North Korea to reconsider their engagement. It was argued that a "common approach by relief organizations and donors (...) is needed" and that "without adherence to basic humanitarian principles and proper access to the population, many people of North Korea will continue to suffer".[39] In its annual report from 2001, ACF criticizes aid agencies working in the DPRK and notes that they practice a head-in-the-sand "ostrich politics".[40] It is further

---

[36] See note 34 in this chapter.

[37] "According to the North Korean authorities, the malnourished children were 'taken care of by provincial authorities' (...) and the 'province will improve the conditions of these children by their own means, and does not need foreign aid'. This refusal of the Korean authority is criminal since Action contre la Faim could have saved these children if it had had access. Our volunteers suspect that these severely malnourished children (...) are condemned to a slow death." ACF: *Dossier de Presse. Action contre la Faim Décide de Se Retirer de Corée du Nord,* Paris, March 2000, p.10.

[38] See note 37 in this chapter, p.14.

[39] MSF: *Privation and Injustice in North Korea.* Press Release. 21 April 2000.

[40] See Reltien (2001:167): "One can only admire the United Nations agencies that claim that they are certain that the hundreds of thousands of tons of aid distributed in North Korea reach those sectors of the population most in need. Admirable but doubtful".

argued that UN agencies and US NGOs take a particularly soft stance in regard to principles of action and deliver aid "without any conditions attached" (Reltien 2001:166). This "humanitarian dumping"[41] is described as ultimately undermining the efforts of NGOs such as ACF, MSF and other European NGOs who are seen as being more concerned about principles of humanitarian action.[42]

Following its withdrawal, MSF continues to be present in the Korean-Chinese border area, gathers information from North Korean refugees and commuters, and continues to issue critical statements on the ongoing international aid effort. In particular, MSF criticizes the aid agencies working in the DPRK for their stance towards principles of action and codes of conduct. These criticisms reached a peak in early 2003, when an MSF official issued a statement saying that agreements on minimum working conditions are being misused in North Korea by the aid agencies themselves. Essentially, the Director of Research of the MSF Foundation, Fiona Terry, argues that statements on common principles, instead of promoting more ethical behavior, are used by aid agencies to conceal "their inability to act responsibly" and serve as "an impediment to reflection". The adherence to codes of conduct ultimately means to "defy the purpose for which they were conceived". The refusal to work in the DPRK is thus seen as more responsible and more ethical:

> With all the attention paid in recent years to increasing the accountability of aid organisations, it should logically have been the humanitarian agencies that refused to continue operating in a country that does not allow them even to assess who is the most vulnerable, let alone direct food towards them.[43]

---

[41] See note 37 in this chapter, p.13.

[42] See Reltien (2001:166): "During 1998, the organizations working in Korea were split into two groups, one from the European Union that insisted on strict respect for the humanitarian principles of aid distribution and another, from the United States, that favored 'no conditionality', or aid without any conditions attached".

[43] AlertNet: *N. Korea Aid Shows Limits of Codes of Conduct*. By Fiona Terry. 3 January 2003. Found at www.reliefweb.int (28 January 2003).

VII.2 The Ethical Framework of Humanitarian Actors in North Korea

It has been shown that, in practice, humanitarian organizations opt for differing approaches in dealing with the ethical challenge of famine relief. Furthermore, some actors do not perceive themselves as being in a dilemma in North Korea, while others see themselves caught between conflicting moral obligations. The differences in analyses and courses of action lead to controversy and open dispute between aid agencies, as they mutually reproach one another for acting irresponsibly and immorally.

These approaches and courses of action illustrate evident differences between the humanitarian actors. It would be misleading to argue that an aid agency's behavior in ethically difficult situations is the spontaneous outcome of an ad-hoc analysis. Instead, as will be shown in this chapter, an organization's course of action in North Korea is closely related to the organization's perception of itself and its attitude towards a number of fundamental aspects of humanitarian action. Put differently, an agency's choice of introvert, extrovert or victim-centered approaches expresses the respective organizational philosophy. Thus, the differences between the ethical frameworks of humanitarian actors lie at the heart of disputes and differing courses of action in the North Korean famine relief mission. We will therefore further elaborate on the correlation between course of action and ethical framework, and thereby seek to illustrate the most essential differences between humanitarian actors.

There are numerous attempts to categorize humanitarian organizations. Weiss and Gordenker refer to the organizational structure and financial resources as the main distinctive features of aid agencies (1996:20-21). They distinguish between government-organized nongovernmental organizations (GONGOs), quasi-nongovernmental organizations (QUANGOs) and donor-organized nongovernmental organizations (DONGOs). Brauman categorizes aid organizations according to their stance towards political actors (1995:107). He distinguishes between organizations that highlight their independence from politics on the one side (*conception libertaire*), and those that stress the complementing of NGOs and states (*conception légitimiste*). Nicholas Leader introduces a typology that considers an agency's set of activity and some aspects of organizational culture and philosophy (2000:42). He identifies "preventative, community-based, partner-oriented, faith-based, developmental, food delivery agencies" at one end of an idealized spectrum, and "emergency, objective/scientific, operational, curative, secular, 'health' agencies" at the other.

The differing courses of action adopted by humanitarian actors in North Korea show that all these characteristics play an important role. Yet the focus on the ethical framework of humanitarian organizations may help to draw a more comprehensive and detailed picture. We will present four components of the ethical framework of an aid organization that principally influence the agency's view on the humanitarian imperative and the principle of impartiality: the organization's mandate, the relevance of proportionality, the view of famine and vulnerability and the perception of politics.

a) Portfolio and Mandate

Aid agencies specialize in differing areas of activity and implement aid programs according to their specific capabilities. As presented above, aid organizations in North Korea focus on food aid, medical assistance, agricultural programs or water and sanitation activities. Each of these activities has two implications. Firstly, very broadly, one can place humanitarian actors on a spectrum with emergency relief at one end and long-term development at the other. Some organizations are more prepared to implement longer-term, structural and sustainable programs than others who focus on immediate life saving activities. Secondly, the area of activity is closely related to the ideals and values that an agency sees as its guiding principles. Here, the narrow and more traditional understanding of humanitarian action as the immediate relief of suffering lies at one end of the spectrum. Others have a broader agenda and perceive their actions as a contribution to peace and conciliation. In North Korea, humanitarian actors' portfolio and mandate are split into two groups: medical relief agencies focusing on the immediate alleviation of suffering on the one side, and rehabilitation and development-oriented organizations with a broader understanding of the humanitarian mandate on the other side.

Most agencies active in the DPRK have both a broad portfolio and a broader understanding of their mandate. All European NGOs currently working in North Korea carry out emergency, rehabilitation and development programs in a number of countries. Concern Worldwide's self-description serves as an example: "Concern Worldwide is a nondenominational voluntary organization dedicated to the relief, assistance and advancement of the poorest of the poor".[44] US NGOs providing assistance to the DPRK also carry out relief, rehabilitation and development programs. Some agencies, such as Mercy Corps International, for instance, focus more on development activities than on emergency relief.

Likewise, UN organizations cannot be classified as exclusive relief or development agencies. In addition, the mandate of UN agencies differs from NGO mandates in that it accords priority to the coordination with and support of governments. The mission statement of WFP, for instance, that describes itself as "the world's largest humanitarian agency", refers to the support of governments and their food aid efforts as one of WFP's core tasks: "WFP will provide services: advice, good offices, logistic support and information; and support to countries in establishing and managing their own food assistance programmes".[45] In a way, direct interaction with the individual recipients of food aid is not an integral part of WFP's mandate. In the words of the former WFP Regional Director in charge of the DPRK mission, "WFP has never been a distributing organization. The main focus has always been on cooperation with host governments".[46] Not surprisingly, NGOs criticize WFP and other UN agencies for not sufficiently insisting on standards of action and for not pushing as hard as they could in North Korea. A former GAA food aid monitor, for instance, comments on WFP's policy: "the lax WFP monitoring makes it difficult for NGOs to push through higher standards. We often heard from the North Koreans that WFP is softer concerning monitoring standards."[47] In this regard, a UNOCHA official remarks that "how much you push is a matter of how much you can afford, it depends on your role. WFP has no other choice, it has to consider North Korea's and donors' interests".[48]

---

[44] InterAction: *InterAction Member Activity Report North Korea. A Guide to Humanitarian and Development Efforts of InterAction Member Agencies in North Korea.* Washington D.C., September 2002, p.19.

[45] www.wfp.org (12 June 2003).

[46] Interview with Jens Schulthes, WFP Regional Director Asia and Pacific 1992-1997, Rome, 24 October 2001.

[47] Interview with Peter Van't Westende, former Monitor and Logistician/GAA, Bonn, 15 October 2001.

[48] Interview with Oliver Lacey-Hall, former Humanitarian Affairs Coordinator DPRK/UNOCHA, Geneva, 19 October 2001.

In terms of WFP's operational capacities, the main focus is on logistics. In a presentation of WFP's emergency work, the agency notes: "The secret to WFP's success in responding to emergencies lies in its ability to move food aid fast and efficiently, often at a day's notice".[49] Accordingly, with regard to WFP's North Korea program, the former WFP Regional Director points out: "With the exception of the food-for-oil program in Iraq, the focus has always been on the cooperation with governments. Therefore, as in other countries, WFP has fulfilled its mandate as an advocate for North Korea".[50]

In contrast, those agencies, that decided to withdraw from North Korea highlight the importance of direct interaction with the beneficiaries of aid. The founder of Cap Anamur, for instance, remarks: "If we lose first-hand contact with the reality of people's lives, we also to a certain extent lose our mandate".[51] It lies in the nature of WFP as a UN agency and intergovernmental organization that it works more closely with the recipient government. Impartiality and proportionality are not an integral part of WFP's mission.

Proportionality is an important principle of action in the view of classical medical emergency aid. Although agencies such as MSF or MDM have expanded their area of activity since their inception towards longer-term rehabilitation and capacity building projects, medical relief activities remain the primary focus in emergency situations such as famines.[52] Non-relief projects are thus implemented in countries where either no emergency situation can be detected (for example, China or Peru) or where this kind of project goes along with emergency relief (South Sudan). In the DPRK, medical relief agencies were convinced that they

---

[49] See note 45 in this chapter.

[50] Interview with Jens Schulthes, Regional Director Asia and the Pacific 1992-1997/WFP, Rome, 24 October 2001. See also Schulthes (2000:257): "During recent years, the WFP has developed into an exceptionally effective organisation precisely for what the donors need most: the logistical servicing of their large, bilateral food relief programmes, from the initial stage of procurement through international and national transport up to the delivery to the distribution authority".

[51] Rupert Neudeck: "The New Crisis is that Boundaries Between NGOs and Governments Are Blurred". Interview by *Humanitarian Affairs Review*, 16 April 2000, found at www.reliefweb.int (3 May 2002).

[52] The French section of MSF, for instance, spends a considerable portion of its finance (about 38 percent) on mid- and long-term missions. See MSF: *Rapport financier. Comptes 2000*. Paris: MSF, 2001.

were dealing with an emergency situation, and therefore aimed to accord priority to their primary activity field.

Humanitarian actors that carry out activities beyond classical humanitarian action also adhere to a set of values and ideals that goes beyond the traditional humanitarian ethical framework. An important group in this regard are faith-based organizations. Mercy Corps International, for instance, sees "peace and social justice" as its main values.[53] With regard to its North Korea projects, the agency points out: "Mercy Corps is committed to peaceful change on the Korean peninsula".[54] It is telling to note that Mercy Corps received funds from the US Institute for Peace for one project in the DPRK.

Faith-based agencies, more than secular organizations, present their aid to the North Korean population as an act of solidarity that expresses and promotes common humanity. The Quaker organization AFSC, for example, describes its work as "based on the belief in the worth of every person, and faith in the power of love to overcome violence and injustice".[55] Church World Services (CWS), the ministry of Protestant, Orthodox and Anglican denominations in the US, sees its activity as the coming together "with the ecumenical family worldwide to witness and share Christ's love with all people". The health kits that CWS has also delivered to the DPRK are labeled "Gifts of the Heart".[56]

The perception of humanitarian aid as the gesture of a common humanity entails that aid agencies see their work as a contribution to dialogue between the DPRK and the international community. For instance, a Caritas report notes: "To build up trust and understanding is, in an isolated country like North Korea, a slow and time-consuming process, but it is a worthwhile investment in the process of reconciliation and peace."[57]

South Korean NGOs, in particular, present their work as a contribution to peace and reconciliation between North and South Korea. The bulk of South Korean NGOs that provide aid to North Korea were founded in the mid 1990s in order to exclusively deliver assistance to

---

[53] Interview with Nancy Lindborg, Executive Vice President/Mercy Corps International, Washington D.C., 29 November 2001.
[54] See note 44 in this chapter, p.28.
[55] See note 44 in this chapter, p.8.
[56] See note 44 in this chapter, p.17.
[57] See note 4 in this chapter, p.8.

North Korea. These organizations are hardly influenced by the tradition of universal humanitarianism, and see their mandate as closely related to the specific situation on the Korean peninsula. The Korean Sharing Movement states that it "aims toward dissolving the antagonism and conflict among Koreans (...) and to build love and trust to open up a new chapter for the unification of Korea".[58] Likewise, Good Friends is "committed to active implementation of peace and human rights" and to "promoting reconciliation of North and South Korea".[59] The International Corn Foundation names three aspects in its mission statement: "Food self-sufficiency for the Korean peninsula, reconciliation between the two Koreas, the belief in 'Loving our brethren in the North as ourselves'".[60]

Likewise, World Vision International argues that the specific political context on the Korean peninsula requires a specific engagement for dialogue and peace. World Vision Korea plays a key role in regard to the North Korea program, both in terms of funding and strategic influence.[61] World Vision Germany, by contrast, is reluctant to contribute to this program due to a critical view on monitoring and evaluation conditions.[62] On the North Korean program and the specific mandate of the South Korean section, the DPRK Country Director of World Vision International notes:

> Reconciliation will be a major focus of the work – between south and north Korea and between the people of the DPRK and the rest of the world. For this reason, World Vision Korea continues to play a key role in the DPRK program (...). This is a sensitive and unique role being played by World Vision in this part of the world.[63]

Reconciliation and the promotion of peace are also important motives for the North Korean aid efforts of Japanese NGOs. For instance, the

---

[58] Mission statement found at www.ksm.or.kr (11 November 2000).

[59] Good Friends/Center for Peace, "Human Rights and Refugees: They Should Be Recognized as Refugees Under International Law". Leaflet.

[60] ICF: "The Hope of the 21st Century Flourishes in the Corn Fields". Leaflet.

[61] Interview with Chang Won-Suk, Assistant Manager/World Vision Korea, Seoul, 19 July 2000.

[62] Letter to author from Iris Manner, Public Relations Officer/World Vision Germany, Friedrichsdorf/Germany, 14 July 1999.

[63] Edward Reed, DPRK Country Director/World Vision International: *Continuing Needs and World Vision's Continuing Response to North Korea. News Vision Asia Pacific: North Korea.* 20 October 1998.

President of the largest Japanese private aid agency – the Japanese International Volunteer Center (JVC) – asserts that the aid to the DPRK expresses "our hope for living together, reconciliation and peaceful stability in this region". He refers to JVC's experience in Cambodia, Laos and Vietnam, where NGOs are seen as having played a significant role in peace processes.[64]

Most European NGOs that are engaged in North Korea are secular organizations and adhere to a set of values that highlight poverty reduction and international solidarity. Three of the most active NGOs in North Korea – GAA, CESVI, Concern – are members of the NGO network 'Alliance 2015' that proclaims "the eradication of poverty" as its primary objective. Furthermore, the mission statement notes that "social justice and equity are fundamental to the creation of just and democratic societies".[65] Likewise, Triangle Génération Humanitaire sees itself as an "international solidarity organization" that "fights for social integration [and] against poverty".[66] Thus, like South Korean, Japanese and US NGOs engaged in North Korea, the European NGOs that continue to be present in the country adhere to a mandate that includes longer-term, societal and economic change.

Agencies that decided to withdraw from North Korea, in particular those who opted for an extrovert approach in dealing with working restrictions, have a much narrower understanding of humanitarian action. Poverty reduction, or the promotion of reconciliation and peace play no major role in regard to the general organizational mandate of these agencies, or in relation to aid programs in the DPRK. The Charter of MSF, for instance, primarily refers to traditional principles of humanitarian action:

> Médecins Sans Frontières offers assistance to populations in distress, to victims of natural or man-made disasters and to victims of armed conflict, without discrimination and irrespective of race, religion, creed or political affiliation. Médecins Sans Frontières

---

[64] Kumaoka Michiya: "Exploring New Roles and Strategies for NGOs". Presentation at the Third International NGO Conference on Humanitarian Assistance to DPR Korea. Cooperative Efforts Beyond Food Aid. Seoul, 17 to 20 June 2001.

[65] See www.allliance2015.org.

[66] Triangle Génération Humanitaire: "Organisation de Solidarité Internationale". Leaflet.

observes neutrality and impartiality in the name of universal medical ethics and the right to humanitarian assistance.[67]

Other organizations that can broadly be described as being part of the 'sans-frontiérisme' branch of humanitarianism also accord priority to the saving of human lives and the alleviation of human suffering. Longer-term and more structural effects of aid are, to differing degrees, included in the agenda. ACF, for instance, in addition to emergency aid and nutritional feeding programs is experienced in providing longer-term food security benefits. However, in the case of ACF, a broader portfolio does not go in hand with the adherence to a more development-oriented mandate that refers to ideals such as peace or democracy. Instead, the agency refers to the saving of human lives as the primary objective of humanitarian action: "Our mission is to save lives by combating hunger, disease, and the crises threatening the lives of helpless men, women, and children."[68]

The political analyses that have been undertaken by this group of actors primarily focus on the issue of people's access to foreign assistance and the lack of transparency in aid efforts. Humanitarian action is not seen as an act that should bridge ideological and political differences. Instead, these differences are publicly addressed whenever they appear to be an obstacle to the immediate saving of human lives or the alleviation of suffering.

Likewise, human rights themselves are not part of the mandate of these humanitarian agencies, although some organizations highlight the importance of human rights-related work in aid missions. MSF, in particular, stresses that "it is part of MSF's work to address any violations of basic human rights encountered by field teams". In contrast to human rights groups, however, the issuing of information and the mobilization of international media in cases of human rights violations does ultimately aim to expand the humanitarian space. That is, this set of activities "guarantees equal access to its [i.e. MSF's] humanitarian assistance."[69] In other words, human rights do not provide an ethical framework equally important as humanitarian considerations. Denouncing

---

[67] See www.msf.org.

[68] See www.aah-usa.org

[69] Presentation of MSF found at www.msf.org (19 June 2003).

human rights violations is a means to an end, namely the effective alleviation of human suffering.

Summing up, there are evidently considerable differences in terms of the portfolio and mandate of humanitarian organizations active in North Korea. A broader set of activities that go along with a development-oriented mandate, including poverty reduction and the promotion of dialogue and peace, seems to positively influence an agency's willingness to make compromises in terms of working restrictions. On the other hand, the traditional understanding of humanitarian action does not include peace or social welfare as an integral part of an organizational mandate. This classical understanding of humanitarianism was most likely to conflict with the working conditions in the DPRK.

b) The View of Proportionality

It has been argued in earlier chapters that, in terms of the moral integrity of aid, the principle of proportionality is the sore spot of humanitarian action. Famine aid missions in the past have shown that the moral integrity of aid agencies is at risk whenever they do not have the freedom to afford their aid according to the needs of the affected population. In this regard, the North Korean case illustrates that aid agencies have differing views on impartiality and the principle of proportionality. Accordingly, the susceptibility of humanitarian organizations to moral ambiguities and dilemma situations differs.

As presented above, some aid activities are more welcome by the North Korean authorities than others. Food security and agricultural recovery projects, for instance, appear to be more compatible with the interests of North Korean counterparts than nutritional feeding programs. Humanitarian actors themselves argue that the strategy of dealing with working restrictions depends on the specific set of aid activities. For example, when asked about the different courses of action of MSF (withdrawal) and ACF (continuation of the program) in 1999, the ACF Desk Officer explained that ACF focuses more on food security while the medical component is not the program's priority.[70]

In addition to the compatibility of aid portfolios with the preferences of the North Korean authorities, aid activities by their very nature accord differing importance to the principles of impartiality and proportional-

---

[70] Interview with Jean-Fabrice Piétri, Desk Officer/ACF, Paris, 20 July 1999.

ity. As mentioned above, agricultural, food security or water and sanitation programs indirectly seek to improve the health status of target groups. The focus is on providing assistance that ultimately leads to beneficial effects for vulnerable population groups. Project designs and logical frameworks usually mention a certain number of individuals as 'target groups' of the program. Aid agencies engaged in these sectors of activity establish indicators in their plans of operation that allow them to assess the program's impact in terms of production output (biscuits, crops, etc.) and effective distribution to institutions. The monitoring and evaluation of school feeding programs, for instance, does not include any medical assessment of the health or nutritional status of school children in the targeted institutions. Indicators of success refer to the effective delivery of raw materials and production of a certain amount of goods. The directing of aid towards those population groups that are most seriously affected by food scarcity and malnutrition is certainly intended, but it is not the integral part of an agency's activity in the food security, agricultural or water and sanitation sector. In other words, aid agencies in some sectors choose indicators of needs that allow them to ignore working restrictions that other agencies perceive as the most hindering obstacles to a successful aid mission.

With regard to the implementation and evaluation of programs, medical relief projects, and nutritional feeding programs in particular, follow differing standards of action. Although therapeutic feeding programs also provide assistance and support to institutions, the primary focus is on the nutritional status of malnourished individuals. For a medical doctor or a nutritionist, the health status of people is the most important indicator for the design (location, size, etc.), monitoring and evaluation of an aid project. Since it is the very nature of a therapeutic feeding program to address the needs of the most seriously malnourished population groups, such a program necessarily pays great attention to the impartiality and proportionality of aid. Accordingly, agencies that carry out medical nutrition programs cannot ignore the doubts concerning the proportional distribution of aid.

As for food aid, agencies have a differing perception of their specific mandate that is related to their own history and traditional focus of intervention. Oxfam's or the IFRC's reasoning in regard to the targeting and monitoring of food aid in North Korea illustrate that a traditional humanitarian agenda in the sense of direct contact and assistance to people in need is seen as an integral part of the agencies' mandate. As argued earlier, WFP, as an intergovernmental organization, seeks to support a government's effort to deal with food scarcity. Consequently, its mandate allows WFP to be more flexible in terms of assessment and targeting of vulnerability and to achieve gradual progress in these areas in close cooperation with the DPRK government.

c) The View on Famine and Vulnerability

As noted earlier, a number of theories and paradigms can be distinguished that give differing answers regarding the causes of famine. Explanation models describe famine as the outcome of production shortfalls *(food availability decline)*, as the result of people's lack of means to command food *(entitlement failure)*, as an instrument of political oppression and exploitation *(benefits paradigm)* or, finally, as a product of undemocratic rule *(democracy paradigm)*. The perception of the causes of famine determines the understanding of people's vulnerability to famine. Food availability decline theories suggest that all members of a population are equally hit by food scarcity. The entitlement failure paradigm, by contrast, argues that an unequal distribution of resources and/or political power necessarily leads to a differing degree of vulnerability among the members of a society. Accordingly, the understanding of famine causes and the view of people's vulnerability determine the shape of a famine relief effort and the attempt to put an end to famine and starvation. Depending on the analytical focus, fighting famine means increasing the amount of available food, improving the (economic) means of a population to command food, addressing the distribution of political power in a society, or pushing for the democratization of political rule. It has also been noted that, in the academic discourse, most authors stress the importance of economic, social and political factors in the emergence and relief of famines. Famines are thus primarily described as distribution rather than as production crises.[71]

The North Korean famine aid effort shows that humanitarian actors have different views on the underlying causes of the famine and therefore have a differing perception of people's vulnerability to famine. Most aid organizations engaged in North Korea describe the famine as the result of a multitude of factors including economic decline and natural disasters. Importantly, the majority of humanitarian organizations ad-

---

[71] For details, see chapters II.1 and II.2.

here to food availability decline conceptions by arguing that domestic food production shortfall and countrywide food scarcity caused starvation and famine in the DPRK. The WFP Regional Director, for instance, summarizes: "It is simply they do not produce enough to feed themselves and they cannot find a way to buy it".[72] Aid agencies, by and large, do not refer to entitlement failure theories, be it in an economic or political view, when it comes to the explanation of the causes of famine in North Korea. Famine is primarily seen as a production crisis, not as a crisis of distribution or people's access to food. In this respect, academic discourse on one side, and the practice of humanitarian aid in North Korea on the other side, clearly differ.

In the tradition of food availability decline theories, a number of aid organizations does not define vulnerability in economic, social or political terms. Aid agencies that conduct food aid operations in the DPRK base their programs primarily on a physical definition of vulnerability. Famine vulnerability is primarily defined along two criteria: age and gender. The UN Consolidated Appeal for 2003, for instance, notes (UNOCHA 2002:12):

> Using global assessments, and internal assessments, such as rudimentary household food economy analyses, the most vulnerable groups in DPRK are identified as: all children under five years of age, pregnant and lactating women, orphaned children, school aged children, the elderly, people with special needs such as the physically handicapped, mentally ill and those suffering from chronic diseases.[73]

The role of political factors with regard to famine vulnerability is controversial among humanitarian organizations in North Korea. Public statements on the role of the DPRK government range from an uncritical

---

[72] Testimony of John Powell, Regional Director Asia/WFP at the "Hearing of the East Asia and the Pacific Subcommittee of the House International Relations Committee. North Korea: Humanitarian and Human Rights Concerns", Federal News Service, 2 May 2002.

[73] Likewise, the WFP's Regional Director before the US House of Representatives asserts: "What we are concerned about is to provide food to the most vulnerable in that country. The most vulnerable in that country are pregnant women, nursing mothers and small children up to the age of 16, secondary school kids. The other extraordinarily vulnerable group are the elderly". Testimony at the "Hearing of the East Asia and the Pacific Subcommittee of the House International Relations Committee. North Korea: Humanitarian and Human Rights Concerns", Federal News Service, 2 May 2002.

or even positive description of Juche ideology to criticisms blaming the government's political and ideological priorities for the magnitude of the human suffering. At an international NGO meeting, an official from World Vision International, for instance, states that "in spite of the supreme effort made by DPRK farmers under the Juche system, the DPRK territory may not be ecologically capable of food self-sufficiency".[74] A Diakonie field visit report, by contrast, refers to a "stubborn adherence to the ideological past that hardly allows for the development of own productive and creative forces".[75] Likewise, a Cap Anamur press release notes that, beside natural disasters, the North Korean "communism of privation" is also to blame for the ongoing misery.[76] The vast majority of aid agencies, however, rejects the benefits paradigm and the 'triage' theory. Most organizations argue that famine and starvation in the DPRK is no deliberate act of political will. Before the US House of Representatives, the WFP Regional Director refers to the shortfalls in domestic food production and food imports, and concludes: "I don't think there should be, in a sense, a misunderstanding of a policy of starvation".[77]

As has been shown with regard to the Ethiopian and Cambodian famines, organizations that belong to the 'sans-frontiérisme' branch of humanitarianism are more inclined to follow the benefits paradigm and the role of political oppression in famines. It is telling to note that ACF's annual report is called 'The Geopolitics of Hunger. Hunger and Power'; the literal translation of the original French version would be 'The Geopolitics of Hunger. When Hunger is a Weapon'. In famine relief missions in the past, MSF has paid particular attention to the role of the political interests of those in power. The same goes for the definition of vulnerability in the North Korean famine. An MSF delegate, appearing before

---

74 Edward Reed, Country Director DPRK/World Vision International, *Conference Proceedings. International NGO Conference on Humanitarian Assistance to the DPR Korea. Past, Present, and Future.* Beijing, 3-5 May 1999.

75 Diakonie Emergency Aid: *Nord-Korea – Geduld und Hoffnung im Land der Morgenstille.* [North Korea – Patience and Hope in the Land of Morning Calm]. Press release, Stuttgart/Germany: 21 February 2002.

76 Cap Anamur: *Schattendasein im Licht der Fussballweltmeisterschaft [Overshadowed by the Soccer World Cup]*, Cologne/Germany, 5 June 2002.

77 Testimony of John Powell, Regional Director Asia/WFP at the "Hearing of the East Asia and the Pacific Subcommittee of the House International Relations Committee. North Korea: Humanitarian and Human Rights Concerns", Federal News Service, 2 May 2002.

the US House of Representatives, stresses the political dimension of vulnerability to famine in the DPRK and criticizes aid agencies for their physical definition of famine vulnerability. She asserts:

> As for the Public Distribution System, I should explain to you in North Korean society the three class levels, which are core, wavering and hostile, continue to be used to prioritize entitlement to items distributed through the PDS. Everyone in North Korea, with the exception of cooperative farmers, depends on the PDS for the basic food rations they require for survival. Therefore, vulnerability and need have more to do with political and social standing than age and gender, the criteria used by aid organizations to define beneficiaries.[78]

ACF also criticizes the majority of aid agencies engaged in North Korea for their definition of vulnerability. In ACF's view, this definition is misleading and excludes people in greatest need from international assistance:

> The agencies should try to impose the inclusion of real criteria of vulnerability in regard to the distribution of aid in North Korea, particularly social criteria that would ultimately allow reaching those populations that are suffering from hunger. Essentially, the food aid targets institutions. Not a single criterion of social or economic vulnerability is taken into consideration when it comes to the distribution of aid.[79]

It is important to note that the debate on vulnerability is dominated by Western aid agencies. South Korean NGOs hardly participate in that discussion. An official from World Vision Korea explains: "Western and Korean views on vulnerability are very different. From a Korean perspective, all people in North Korea are vulnerable".[80] Likewise, the President of Good Neighbors Korea argues that one should not pay too much attention to needs assessment and vulnerability analyses: "it is

---

[78] Sophie Delaunay, Regional Coordinator for North Korea/MSF, testimony at the "Hearing of the East Asia and the Pacific Subcommittee of the House International Relations Committee. North Korea: Humanitarian and Human Rights Concerns", Federal News Service, 2 May 2002.

[79] ACF: *Dossier de Presse. Action contre la Faim Décide de Se Retirer de Corée du Nord*, Paris, March 2000, p.14.

[80] Interview with Chang Won-Suk, Assistant Manager/World Vision Korea, Seoul, 19 July 2000.

their needs, not ours".[81] In short, aid agencies not only adhere to differing definitions of vulnerability, but also accord a differing importance to the targeting of aid and the concept of vulnerability itself. This helps to explain why some agencies are caught in a moral dilemma in the DPRK, and others are not.

d) The Stance Towards Politics

The perception of the general role of humanitarian aid in regard to political actors as well as the understanding of an agency's specific position vis-à-vis politics illustrates the most fundamental differences between humanitarian organizations. In this regard, the North Korean famine aid effort is revealing.

The North Korean case suggests that the debate among aid agencies on the general relationship between humanitarianism and politics is much more controversial than between academic observers. Since the beginning of academic reflection on humanitarian action, the debate has focused on the relationship between humanitarianism and politics. Further academic discussion regarding this connection has become redundant: "Saying that humanitarian action is political is like saying orange is a colour, true, but not very illuminating" (Leader 2000:15). This statement may express academic consensus, it does not, however, describe a common position of the humanitarian actors themselves. There has been much confusion over the relationship between humanitarianism and politics that Leader (2000:56) explains as follows:

> Humanitarianism is a form of politics, but a form of politics heavily circumscribed by ethical rules, principally humanity and impartiality; it is adherence to these rules that mark[s] humanitarian politics apart from other forms of politics. The confusion over the humanitarian/political divide comes from the fact that humanitarianism is a form of politics in which it is useful to assert that one is non-political.

The North Korean case helps to assess aid agencies' different perceptions of the humanitarian/political divide. Leader (2000:20-21) distinguishes between three conceptualizations of neutrality. The concept of "neutrality elevated" describes the traditional principle of not taking sides in order to ensure the impartial affording of aid. The second model

---

[81] Interview with Yi Il-Ha, President/Good Neighbors Korea, Seoul, 14 July 2000.

– "neutrality abandoned" – argues that humanitarian agencies have to articulate, and contribute to, political objectives. The third conception sees humanitarian action as being part of a wider, peace-related strategy ("Third-way humanitarianism").

An agency's conceptualization of neutrality emanates from its perception of politics and the understanding of its own role in relation to political actors. Put differently, an agency's stance towards politics influences the understanding of neutrality, and not *vice versa*. The concepts of "neutrality elevated" and of "neutrality abandoned" thus describe effects rather than causes. As a consequence, these conceptions cannot explain the differing approaches of aid agencies in dealing with moral ambiguities and dilemmas. For instance, according to Leader's descriptions, aid agencies that opt for an introvert approach and those who adhere to an extrovert strategy would both belong to the category of "neutrality elevated".

The North Korean case suggests that, broadly, aid agencies perceive their relationship to politics in four differing ways. First, politics is seen as a sphere distinct from aid *(apolitical approach)*. Second, politics is regarded as the surrounding of aid *(neutral approach)*. Third, politics appears to be an ally of aid *(cooperative approach)*, which corresponds to the concept that Leader describes as the "Third-way humanitarianism". And fourth, politics is perceived as the opponent of aid *(rebellious approach)*. These conceptions determine the understanding of neutrality and ultimately determine an organization's behavior in cases of moral dilemmas.

The apolitical approach

Based on the apolitical understanding of humanitarianism, a number of aid agencies does not publicly refer to the general setting of political priorities by the DPRK government, or specifically, their way of dealing with the humanitarian crisis. Instead, aid officials argue that political statements or engagement are not part of their mandate. Concerning the famine relief effort in North Korea, James Morris, WFP Executive Director, asserts: "Our only objective is to feed the hungry. We're not interested in the political details of the country".[82] Political and humanitarian

---

[82] Associated Press: *At Food Summit, N Korea Objects to Conditionality of Aid*. Rome, 12 June 2002.

agendas are regarded as two distinct spheres. This apolitical view asserts that influence on political affairs is beyond the scope of aid agencies. The Swiss NGO Campus für Christus, for instance, argues:

> Our aid deals with people, not with politics. As an organization we are much too small to achieve much change here. We engage ourselves where we have our strong points. And we wish that those who have influence in the political arena engage themselves with good conscience where they have their strong points.[83]

The neutral approach

Secondly, following the conception of neutral humanitarianism, some organizations argue that the humanitarian mandate in itself is non-political, but that the carrying out of that mandate is closely inter-twined with politics. This view is illustrated by Jean Pictet's often quoted description of the International Committee of the Red Cross (ICRC) that "like a swimmer, is in politics up to its neck. Also like the swimmer, who advances in the water but who drowns if he swallows it, the ICRC must reckon with politics without becoming part of it."[84] Not becoming part of politics essentially means not taking sides in political dispute and re-maining equally distant from all parties and political actors involved. This is the classical understanding of neutrality as a principle of hu-manitarian action.[85]

The majority of European NGOs adheres to the classical conception of a neutral stance towards politics. Most agencies accept and heavily depend on public funding, and a particularly critical stance towards politics is not part of the tradition of the bulk of European aid agencies. Some agencies are particularly close to their respective home govern-

---

[83] Campus für Christus: *Hilfe für Hungernde – oder Stützung der 'Achse des Bösen'? [Aid for the Starving – or Support for the 'Axis of Evil'?]*, North Korea project infor-mation. Zurich, 20 January 2003.

[84] Quoted in Larry Minear: "The Theory and Practice of Neutrality: Some Thoughts on the Tensions", in: *International Review of the Red Cross*, Vol. 81, No. 833, March 1999, p.66.

[85] There are numerous conceptions of neutrality. As Leader (2000:19) notes: "the most significant discussions, disagreements, confusions and conceptual developments have been around the idea of neutrality". In sum, however, it can be argued that the com-mon denominator of all conceptions of neutrality is the principle not to take sides in political struggle (see, for instance, Mackintosh 2000).

ment. For instance, the patron of German Agro Action is traditionally the Federal President of Germany.

The cooperative approach

At an international NGO meeting on humanitarian assistance to North Korea, the neutral perception of aid evidently conflicted with a cooperative understanding of humanitarian action. In the aftermath of the Inter-Korean summit from June 2000, NGO delegates discussed whether aid agencies should publicly support the sunshine policy and include national reconciliation and unification as goals of humanitarian action. The debate centered on the wording of the final report of the conference. Representatives of South Korean NGOs argued that the text should explicitly refer to these objectives. The President of Good Neighbors Korea, for instance, proposed "to move a little bit away from international guidelines" and to include reconciliation and reunification in the wording of the text. The President of World Vision Korea agreed that the notion of political change that resulted from the Inter-Korean summit could not be ignored by aid agencies working in the DPRK.[86] Delegates from Western aid agencies such as Caritas International and German Agro Action, however, adhered to the neutral understanding of aid and argued that humanitarian action should not be mixed with politics. As a result, the meeting's final report does not refer to the political objectives mentioned by South Korean NGO representatives. Western aid agencies successfully pushed through the traditional perception of humanitarian aid as an action that should not take sides in political or ideological discussions.

Notably, an agency's staff employment policy illustrates differences between apolitical, neutral and rebellious traditions. In this respect, US NGOs are particularly close to political institutions. A number of NGO officials, most of them on a higher management level, are former high-ranking State Department or USAID officials.[87] In addition, some US

---

[86] Oral statements made by Yi Il-Ha, President/Good Neighbors Korea and Oh Jae-shik, President/World Vision Korea at the Third International NGO Conference on Humanitarian Assistance to North Korea: Cooperative Efforts Beyond Food Aid, Seoul, 17 to 20 June 2001, author's notes.

[87] For example, James K. Bishop, now Director Humanitarian Response at InterAction, served as US Ambassador in Niger, Liberia, and Somalia; Kenneth Quinones, Director

NGOs maintain close links to members of US Congress. With regard to aid activities in North Korea, the Korean American Sharing Movement (KASM), for instance, reports that "visiting dignitaries of the United States, including Rep. Tony Hall and the Hon. William Perry, graciously carried KASM relief supplies".[88] Amigos Internacionales, a US-based aid organization related to Southern Baptist has strong ties to Senator Jesse Helms. Reportedly, these ties were more than helpful concerning the inclusion of Amigos Internacionales as a PVOC member organization working in North Korea.[89]

The rebellious approach

The fourth view, that regards humanitarian aid as being opposed to politics, is upheld by a group of actors that we described earlier as 'rebellious humanitarianism'. When asked about the differences between US NGOs and French medical relief agencies, the Director of InterAction, a US NGO consortium, answered: "We are non-governmental, they are anti-governmental".[90] In a sense, this is true. Jean-Christophe Rufin, President of ACF, describes the founding idea of the 'sans-frontiérisme' branch of humanitarianism as

> the myth, the idea, that NGOs fight against power. (...) That is, the idea that one has to observe what is happening in the political domain, and that one can only reach the victims by means of a political analysis, by means of engaging oneself. The insolence, and the permanent gap to more neutral NGOs are results of this basic idea. (...) The only course of action for French NGOs is to remain loyal to this spirit, to continue to take their position at the heart of

---

of Northeast Asia Projects at Mercy Corps International, served as North Korean Affairs Officer at the State Department (1992 to 1994).

[88] InterAction, note 44 in this chapter, p.24.

[89] Interview with James K. Bishop, Director Humanitarian Response/InterAction, Washington D.C., 28 November 2001. See also Flake (2003:29): "Despite an apparent outward commonality in mission, there was an underlying tension among the PVOC membership, the result in part of the distrust that mainstream NGOs felt toward Amigos Internacionales, a Southern Baptist-related aid organization with strong ties to the office of Senator Jesse Helms (R-NC). (It was hinted that the inclusion of Amigos Internacionales in the PVOC was a precondition for Senator Helms to allow USAID to provide funding for this operation.)".

[90] Interview by author with James K. Bishop, Director Humanitarian Response/ InterAction, Washington D.C., 28 November 2001.

politics in order to reach the victims. Not in order to make politics themselves.[91]

It is telling to note that organizations such as MSF or MDM politically engage themselves in so far as they seek to influence the policies of Western governments and private companies. Access to basic medical care for immigrants that have no legal status in France, or people's access to HIV medicine in African countries at a price that they can afford are examples of NGO activities that "take position at the heart of politics". MDM's slogan to present its philosophy illustrates this understanding of rebellious humanitarianism: "We fight all diseases. Even injustice".

Importantly, the rebellious view pays highest attention on not getting too close to donor governments. MSF, for instance, only accepts public funds to a certain degree in order to guarantee its strategic independence. Cap Anamur does not accept any governmental funding. On Cap Anamur's policy in regard to governmental donors, the founder of the organization remarks:

> There is a major crisis in the humanitarian community because the boundary between governmental and non-governmental agencies is becoming blurred. (...) I prefer the clear-cut nature of the work in the 1970s and 1980s, when you could be proud to call yourself a non-governmental agency. I remember what it was like when Médecins sans Frontières first started operating during the war in Biafra. It was an obvious counter-offensive against the non-confrontational stance of the International Committee of the Red Cross. I think it would be better for the humanitarian movement if we could go back to that way of working.[92]

From the perspective of 'rebellious humanitarianism', any proximity to political institutions is unacceptable. It is telling to note that MSF personnel see the political career of one of its founders, Bernard Kouchner, as undermining its efforts to stay independent and distant from the French state and government. Agencies such as MSF, MDM or ACF will hardly be prepared to employ government officials as NGO officers. As a result, the proximity of US aid agencies to political institutions is pub-

---

[91] Presentation at *La Responsabilité Humanitaire*. Workshop held by MSF, Paris, 12 December 1996, workshop proceedings, pp.6, 7, 9-10.
[92] See note 51 in this chapter.

licly criticized. Sylvie Brunel, former President of ACF, notes that "charitable organizations are perceived by the North Koreans not as independent associations but as a direct emanation of their respective governments, which is notably true for a certain number of American NGOs" (Brunel 1998:137-138).

Dealing with North Korean authorities: the example of medical aid

The general perception of politics and political actors determines an agency's position vis-à-vis the political authorities in a recipient country. In North Korea, some aid agencies appear to be rather uncritical of the political and ideological system in place, while others are more skeptical and distrustful in their dealing with local authorities as well as with donor institutions. In terms of medical aid and support to the DPRK's public health system, operational consequences of differing approaches become particularly evident. MDM, ACF and MSF argue that it is the task of independent international agencies to carry out, supervise and evaluate medical treatment. This claim, it is argued, derives from medical ethics. An MDM official, for instance, asserts that – in contrast to aid activities in other sectors – "medical relief has a different level of responsibility in regard to the beneficiary".[93] Other agencies engaged in the same activity sector, such as UNICEF and Eugene Bell are more prepared to accept the dominant role of North Korean authorities in dealing with medical assistance. The Chairman of Eugene Bell stresses that "North Korea is not Africa"; he argues:

> North Korean caregivers may not always be as sophisticated as their counterparts elsewhere but capable professionals (...). It is not necessary in most cases for outsiders to treat patients directly. Aid should focus, primarily, on providing them the tools to do their jobs more effectively.[94]

Eugene Bell criticizes Western organizations for ignoring the specific North Korean context and for their intention to implement the aid them-

---

[93] Interview with Nathalie Bréchet, Desk Officer/MDM, Paris, 21 July 1999.
[94] Stephen Linton: *Working With North Korea's Medical System*. Presentation at the Third International NGO Conference on Humanitarian Assistance to DPR Korea. Cooperative Efforts Beyond Food Aid. Seoul, 17 to 20 June 2001. Handout and oral statement, author's notes.

selves. The Eugene Bell Chairman asserts that his participation at international aid agency meetings was "a frustrating experience".[95] Eugene Bell describes its role as a 'donkey' that carries the gifts from donors to the institutions in the DPRK.[96] Eugene Bell tries to link donors and beneficiaries and sees itself as an agent of donors. On monitoring visits, that Eugene Bell calls "dedication ceremonies" in order not to be perceived as a superior or teacher by its North Korean counterparts, the NGO tries "not to appear as Eugene Bell".[97]

Notably, compared to modern methods, the use of the tuberculosis kits delivered by Eugene Bell appears doubtful. German tuberculosis experts assert that, from a Western perspective, some methods that North Korean medical staff applies to fight tuberculosis appear outmoded, questionable and risky. Uncritical support for North Korean practices to fight tuberculosis is therefore, in their judgment, an ambivalent undertaking: "one can accept their methods, but one shouldn't praise them".[98] Eugene Bell is aware of these doubts concerning the methods of North Korean doctors to treat their patients, but continues to fulfil their mandate as a 'donkey'. Agencies such as MSF or MDM were not prepared to leave the treatment of patients and the supervision of the proportional affording of aid to DPRK institutions and authorities.

To sum up, the perception of politics and an agency's stance vis-à-vis donor and recipient government are distinctive features of humanitarian organizations and are closely linked to its tradition and ethical framework. The North Korean aid operation shows that some aid agencies see their work as being distinct from politics, while others accept that their activities are influenced by a political surrounding and by a political struggle in which they themselves seek not to participate. South Korean agencies, by contrast, articulate political goals and, in a way, see the South Korean government and the sunshine policy as an ally. Others

---

95 Interview with Stephen Linton, Chairman/Eugene Bell Foundation, Seoul, 15 November 2000.
96 TV broadcast "Linton hyongje-ui pukhan-deopgi" [The North Korea Aid of the Linton Brothers], *KBS Sunday Special*, 26 September 1999.
97 Interview with Stephen Linton, Chairman/Eugene Bell Foundation, Seoul, 15 November 2000.
98 Interview with Dr. Barbara Hauer and Daniel Sagebiel, German Central Committee Against Tuberculosis/Zentralklinik Emil von Behring, Department Lungenklinik Heckeshorn, Berlin, 24 January 2003.

regard political power as the opponent of the humanitarian movement and see the struggle against political actors as the founding myth of their organizations.

Conclusion: Overcoming Dilemmas?

Humanitarian actors in North Korea have chosen differing courses of action in order to deal with a limited humanitarian space that is being restricted by DPRK authorities and donor governments alike. A number of aid agencies are opting for a course of action that we have named the introvert approach. That is, they seek to minimize or to avoid ethical ambivalence by focusing primarily on their own behavior and standard of action. Consequently, this group of actors endorses common principles of action, and aims to gradually realize these working standards through continued engagement and dialogue. In addition, aid agencies put priority on the humanitarian imperative to provide aid to people in distress. In this victim-centered view, the relationship between helper and helped is of utmost importance. The main focus is on the individual beneficiary of crisis, whose needs and gratitude are being stressed.

A relatively small number of NGOs aims to put an end to moral ambiguity by exerting pressure on the DPRK and donor governments (extrovert approach). These agencies decided to close their programs in North Korea and publicly demanded that political actors review and change their policies. The majority of UN agencies and NGOs in North Korea opts for a combination of victim-centered and introvert approaches. Principles of humanitarian action are perceived as guidelines and longer-term objectives that require a continued presence in North Korea, and that do not justify a decision to withdraw.

Broadly, two conclusions must be drawn from these differing approaches in dealing with a restricted humanitarian space. Firstly, a number of humanitarian actors do not perceive famine relief in North Korea as morally ambivalent. Relatively few aid agencies see themselves as caught in a dilemma situation. The assertion, presented in earlier chapters, that famine relief *per se* is "a process of ethico-political decision" (Edkins 2000:148), is being rejected by most aid agencies engaged in North Korea. In practice, a large number of organizations argues that the moral imperative to provide aid has a higher value than working standards of humanitarian action. Thus, a conflict between two equally important moral principles – that would allow one to speak of a dilemma – is not recognizable.

Secondly, differing courses of action in the North Korean aid effort are linked to the differing ethical frameworks of aid agencies. Explanations given by humanitarian actors to justify introvert, extrovert or victim-centered behavior reveal fundamental differences. Mandate and agenda, the role of proportionality, the view on famine and vulnerability as well as an agency's stance towards politics and political actors define distinctive features of aid organizations that ultimately determine their behavior in the DPRK. Thus, the North Korean experience illustrates that the description of humanitarian organizations as a like-minded, homogenous 'aid community' is misleading. Differences between aid agencies actually "have much to do with organisational culture and philosophy, in many ways they are cultures that never meet" (Leader 2000:42).

Have aid agencies in North Korea successfully "overcome humanitarian dilemmas", as one study on aid work in the DPRK suggests (Smith 2001b)? A humanitarian dilemma, as argued in earlier chapters, emerges whenever the principles of humanity and impartiality conflict, that is, whenever humanitarian action is not able to effectively target the most vulnerable population groups in a given society. It has been shown that, in North Korea, large parts of the population benefit from international aid. Yet working conditions in the DPRK do not allow aid agencies to target the groups of people that are most imminently threatened by death and starvation. However, most aid agencies do not perceive this situation as a dilemma because the principle of proportionality is not an integral part of their ethical framework.

The majority of humanitarian organizations that are engaged in North Korea focus on an introvert strategy. These actors seek to gradually improve their working conditions in the DPRK, which they see as difficult, but, by and large, ethically acceptable. An important tool of the introvert approach are common statements on principles of action. These statements highlight the principle of proportionality and the effective assessment and targeting of the most vulnerable population groups. In a sense, this public insistence on proportionality and impartiality is problematic because aid agencies endorse principles of action that are not essential for fulfilling their mandate. Since most agencies aim to provide longer-term effects in food security, agriculture or water and sanitation they are not morally obliged to rigorously direct their aid to those who are about to starve.

The correlation between course of action and ethical framework is presented in figure 6:

Fig. 6: Aid Agencies' Courses of Action and Ethical Frameworks

Ethical Frame-work / Course of Action	Portfolio and Mandate	Impartiality and Proportionality	Famine and Vulnerability	Stance towards Politics
Victim-centered	- rehabilitation, development - broad mandate (solidarity, peace, conciliation)	- low importance - no integral principle of action	- famine is the result of food availability decline - vulnerability is defined by age and gender	- apolitical (politics and humanitarian action are distinct spheres)
Introvert	- non-medical relief, agricultural rehabilitation, development - broad mandate (alleviation of suffering, poverty reduction)	- medium importance - no integral principle of action	- famine is the result of food availability decline and economic entitlement failure - vulnerability is defined by age, gender and economic resources	- neutral (politics is the surrounding of humanitarian action)
Extrovert	- medical emergency relief - narrow mandate (saving of lives, medical ethics)	- high importance - integral principle of action	- famine is the result of political oppression - vulnerability is defined by political power and social status	- rebellious (politics is the opponent of humanitarian action)

The most effective means of avoiding dilemma situations is the victim-centered approach that, to differing degrees, influences the decision making of all agencies in North Korea. As has been noted with regard to famine aid missions in Soviet Russia or Ethiopia, an exclusive focus on the needs and gratitude of individual beneficiaries can be politically naive. In the DPRK, this view has ultimately undermined efforts of aid agencies that tried to insist on certain working principles. On a number of occasions, aid organizations that accord high priority to the victim-centered approach agreed to work under conditions that other agencies were trying to modify.

The introvert approach seeks to achieve some improvements in terms of working conditions but does not primarily aim to fundamentally change the system of humanitarian aid in North Korea. In this regard, aid agencies have obtained some progress. The number of expatriate staff has considerably increased since the beginning of the international aid operation, aid agencies were given access to counties and institutions that were previously inaccessible, and foreign aid workers can move freely in Pyongyang city. In terms of proportionality, however, in the eighth year after the DPRK's appeal for international aid, the humanitarian space is not fundamentally different from the initial situation. Aid agencies are, by and large, in no position to independently assess people's needs or to directly communicate with ordinary people and beneficiaries.

A further group of aid agencies opts for an extrovert approach in order to put an end to this dilemma situation. These humanitarian organizations are equally bound by the principles of humanity and proportionality, and are thus facing a dilemma in North Korea. However, the withdrawal of aid agencies and the issuing of critical statements on North Korean and donor policies did not have the intended effects on the humanitarian space in the DPRK. Essentially, the extrovert approach faces three obstacles in North Korea. Firstly, the DPRK is less susceptible to lobbying actions and international media pressure than was the Mengistu regime in Ethiopia in the 1980s for instance. Secondly, aid agencies that publicly criticize DPRK authorities have few allies. Neither donor governments nor the majority of aid organizations in North Korea give the principles of impartiality and proportionality the highest priority. Thirdly, aid agencies base their criticism on a political analysis that highlights the role of political loyalty in terms of access to food. Such analysis, as noted above, appears doubtful and has not convinced other aid agencies or donor governments.

Agencies such as MSF and ACF argue that pulling out is ethically more acceptable than the continuation of the aid program in North Korea. This course of action as noted by the agencies themselves, is also morally ambivalent since these organizations do not doubt the existence of massive humanitarian needs in North Korea. Thus, the experience of medical relief agencies in North Korea confirms what has been noted in earlier chapters: the ambiguity of aid is inescapable and, consequently, when there is no coalition between humanitarian and political interests, aid agencies alone cannot overcome the dilemma of aid. They may be able to ignore it, to hope for progress in the future or to withdraw. But neither way solves the dilemma.

Chapter VIII.

Lessons and Conclusions

As noted at the beginning of this study, much has been written in recent years about the ambiguities, failures and dilemmas of humanitarian action, particularly in the post-Cold War era. Most of the analyses and criticisms of the role of aid agencies in humanitarian crises derive from aid missions in war-torn societies where governmental control and public infrastructure had collapsed. The famine relief mission in North Korea, despite its magnitude and duration, has not been focused on by the debate on the "crisis of aid" (Macrae 2001).

A number of authors see international humanitarianism in a crisis because it has been discredited as a result of the changed political order in the post-Cold War era. Fox (2001:288), for instance, argues that the international aid system "has clearly been discredited and has lost confidence in itself". In other words, the ambiguity of aid has increased due to the structural changes in the relationship between humanitarianism and politics. Humanitarian actors now face a reduced space for maneuver, and have to acknowledge that the "Golden Age" of humanitarian action (Vaux 2001:43) is over. The North Korean famine aid operation illustrates the ambiguity of aid because it reveals the aid agencies' lack of means of determining their operational space and of pushing through principles of action. Due to the structural ambiguity of aid, humanitarian actors face the instrument (of donors) and accomplice (of recipient) scenario in North Korea.

We will now discuss in how far the North Korean experience can contribute to the debate on the crisis and on the dilemmas of humanitarian action. In a first step, we will elaborate on the problems and obstacles that humanitarian aid has to face. While most of the discussion focuses on the role of post-Cold War phenomena and the role of human rights, we will argue that proportionality and a lack of consistency lie at the heart of the dilemma of aid. Secondly, we will discuss the suggested solutions to the dilemmas of humanitarianism which are related to the establishment of principles, to enhancing learning and accountability as well as to new coordination mechanisms. In addition, a number of authors argues in favor of 'detaching' humanitarianism from the affective side of aid, that we will discuss in light of the findings of our study.

The famine aid operation in North Korea reveals a number of shortfalls of the debate on the 'crisis of aid' and shifts the focus of analysis on the lack of consistency in humanitarian action.

VIII.1 The Debate on a Discredited Humanitarianism

a) The Role of Post-Cold War Phenomena

Lindenberg and Bryant (2001:76) sum up the debate on the discrediting of aid by saying that "the toughest dilemmas for NGOs working on complex emergencies revolve around whether actions that save lives help perpetuate conflict in insidious ways". As examples for such "dilemmas", the authors mention the support of forced population movements, the diversion or looting of aid, the perpetuation of a war economy, the heightening of conflict and competition by favoring particular population groups (e.g. refugees over residents), and the weakening of local capacities to deal with a crisis (2001:76-77). These situations, it is argued, have occurred more frequently since the end of the Cold War period. In particular, as noted above, aid missions in refugee camps in the Rwanda conflict presented a traumatic experience for the international aid system. Leader (2000:6) concludes that "the lone voices in the 1970s and 1980s that had been accusing agencies of fuelling conflict, feeding killers and of being much more equivocal agents of change than their fundraising or self-image had allowed, became a chorus in the 1990s." At the end of the day, aid agencies were facing a "crisis of confidence" (Leader 2000:6).

At a glance, famine aid in North Korea has hardly anything in common with the dilemma scenarios experienced in civil wars or collapsed states. In the DPRK, no forced population movement or heightened competition between specific groups of people has been observed. Nor does the international aid effort weaken the local infrastructure because the management of the crisis remains a governmental task. Moreover, there is no substantial evidence of systematic aid diversion or looting. Yet the international aid effort in North Korea is one of the most illustrative cases of the moral ambiguity of humanitarianism. It has caused and continues to cause debate and dispute among humanitarian actors. Some agencies are prepared to make the compromises necessary to carry out aid work in North Korea, others are not.

The North Korean case shows that dilemmas of humanitarian aid are not systematically linked to armed conflict, state collapse or direct violence. What aid missions in Biafra, Cambodia, Ethiopia, Rwanda, Sudan or North Korea most essentially have in common is a non-respect for the principle of proportionality. Whenever the affording of aid according to humanitarian needs only is not in line with political interests, the moral integrity of humanitarianism is potentially at risk. This conflict between principles of humanitarian action and political interests is, *a priori*, unrelated to war or violent oppression. Post-Cold War phenomena may be responsible for the more frequent emergence of dilemmas of aid since the early 1990s. But these dilemmas are the result of the ambiguity of aid which is a basic characteristic in the history of modern humanitarianism since the famine relief mission in Soviet Russia in 1921-23. The North Korean experience reminds us of these 'timeless' elements of humanitarian action and thereby helps to put recent developments into perspective.

b) The Role of Human Rights

The assumption that dilemmas of aid emerge in times of civil war and massive human rights violations suggests that aid agencies have to make a choice between their mandate to provide assistance and the incentive to promote peace and respect for human rights. This reasoning does not apply to the famine aid mission in North Korea. Humanitarian organizations were not facing a moral dilemma in the DPRK for the mere fact that they were providing assistance in a totalitarian state that is ruled by oppression and indoctrination. North Korea's poor human rights record, the regime possibly gaining legitimacy or ultimate economic and political survival through the work of international aid agencies do not, in themselves, question the moral integrity of humanitarian organizations. Those aid agencies that consider the working conditions in the DPRK to be ethically unacceptable base their analysis on one major argument: the non-respect of impartiality and proportionality. They do not refer to an obligation to promote peace or democracy.

Human rights play a role in the reasoning of aid agencies only to the extent that access to food and medical care is, in the view of some agencies, being linked to political loyalty. The reality of human rights in North Korea concerns the moral integrity of humanitarian actors only in as far as it undermines the proportionality principle. It is one important lesson of the North Korean case that the dilemma of aid does not result from the competition of humanitarian obligations with other moral incentives but stems from a moral conflict within the humanitarian ethical framework. That is, the conflict between the humanitarian imperative to relieve human suffering and the principle of impartiality. Much of the debate on the dilemma of aid focuses on moral conflicts between humanitarianism on one side, and peace and human rights on the other. In view of the North Korean experience, such a debate largely misses the point.

c) The Role of Impartiality and Proportionality

Proportionality is the sore spot of the moral integrity of humanitarian actors. The principle of proportionality is part of the obligation to provide aid in an impartial manner. As such, this principle is well rooted in the tradition of Western humanitarianism that can be traced back to Henri Dunant and the founding of the Red Cross movement. The analysis of the North Korean aid effort reveals that today's humanitarian organizations do not, or at least not exclusively, perceive their mandate and ethical framework as being determined by Dunant's conclusions from the battle of Solferino and by International Humanitarian Law. NGOs and UN agencies that are engaged in North Korea have a much broader activity portfolio and understanding of their organizational mandate than a traditional concept of humanitarianism suggests. In other words, the diversity of humanitarian actors includes a large number of agencies that pursue other objectives than the immediate alleviation of suffering or the saving of lives through the provision of emergency assistance. The majority of aid agencies working in the DPRK describes poverty reduction, social justice and sustainable development as their guiding ideals. The North Korean aid effort thus confirms what Slim and McConnan (1998) have noted with regard to the values and principles of British NGOs. In their 'values and principles audit' of 15 member organizations of the UK's Disaster Emergency Committee (DEC), the authors come to the following conclusion (Slim and McConnan 1998:3,6):

> the fundamental mission of the majority of DEC member relates to poverty and social injustice. The DEC is obviously not a collection of primarily humanitarian organizations in the strict sense of the term (...). The most obvious conclusion is that the glass slipper of Swiss

humanitarianism finds no perfect fit on the feet of any DEC member with the exception of the British Red Cross, and possibly Merlin (albeit implicitly).[1]

Likewise, the majority of aid agencies present in the DPRK do not adhere to a strict understanding of humanitarianism, neither in terms of activity, nor, most importantly, in regard to the principles of classical humanitarianism. The international aid in North Korea effectively supports the public distribution system, public health institutions, cooperatives, bakeries or other institutions that are essential for ordinary people's food supply and medical care.

Aid agencies that seek to specifically target the people in greatest need, that is, those population groups that are most imminently threatened by starvation, aimed to reach people who have no access to public food distributions and medical care. Working conditions in the DPRK, however, do not allow the targeting of people outside public structures. Consequently, aid agencies that consider impartiality and proportionality as being integral parts of their mandate – namely MDM, MSF as well as ACF – were caught in a dilemma. In North Korea, in their view, the humanitarian imperative collided with the principle of proportionality.

From the point of view of the majority of humanitarian organizations engaged in the DPRK as well as of donor governments, the aid activities achieved the intended effects since the programs effectively reach people in need. From this perspective, no dilemma exists. Whether the famine relief effort in North Korea is seen as a success or as a failure thus largely depends on the understanding of the purpose of humanitarian action: the immediate relief of suffering, or the longer-term improvement of the food and medical supply situation.

In his study on moral dilemmas in humanitarian action, Slim (1997a:248) asserts that "some NGOs will have more moral dilemmas than others, depending on the range and number of their fundamental principles. For example, an organisation whose mission is focused on the main principle of saving life may well have few, if any, moral dilemmas". The North Korean case refutes this assumption and suggests the opposite. An aid agency that principally seeks to save life necessarily aims to reach the population groups most affected by a crisis. Thus, it accords a

---

[1] Merlin is a UK-based, non-governmental medical aid agency, founded in 1993.

high priority to the principle of proportionality and becomes most prone to moral dilemmas.

d) A Crisis of Consistency

Does the experience of famine aid in North Korea confirm the hypothesis of a 'crisis of aid'? When dilemmas of humanitarian action are not systematically linked to post-Cold War phenomena, and when only a few aid agencies are prone to moral dilemmas, why speak of a crisis of humanitarianism?

For two reasons, the North Korean case shows that international humanitarianism is today facing a crisis. The first reason relates to the uncertainties and confusions regarding the ethical basis of humanitarian action. The second argument refers to a lack of consistency in dealing with principles of humanitarian action.

As for the first aspect, the North Korean experience highlights the diversity of humanitarian actors who have fundamentally differing views on the purpose of aid, the stance towards politics and the relevance of impartiality and proportionality. In view of these differences, the common basis of the ethical frameworks of humanitarian actors appears to be very thin. In the first place, the moral imperative to alleviate human suffering, as expressed by the principle of humanity, is common to all aid agencies. In the words of Rony Brauman (1996:38), "to the question 'what is man?', the humanitarian philosophy simply answers that he is not made to suffer". But the answers given by today's humanitarianism to a number of further questions are many-fold. Should humanitarian action seek to provide longer-term sustainable support, or does only the immediate saving of life have the right to be called 'humanitarian'? Is humanitarian action a form of political engagement or is it an apolitical gesture that highlights a common humanity? The debate among humanitarian organizations regarding their aid efforts in North Korea illustrates the confusion surrounding the purpose and mandate of humanitarian action. In other words, the North Korean case suggests that the diversity of and the differences between humanitarian actors have reached a point where it becomes a challenge to define what humanitarian action is actually about. Therefore, international humanitarianism seems to be facing a crisis of meaning.

Secondly, due to this confusion around the mandate and ethical basis of humanitarian action, aid agencies have a differing understanding of principles of action. The behavior of aid organizations in dilemma situations in the DPRK shows that an aid agency's understanding of principles is largely determined by its own organizational mandate and ethical framework. The diversity of actors leads to a diversity of approaches, strategies and interpretations of principles such as impartiality and proportionality. Thus, the definition of principles becomes vague and arbitrary. The result is a lack of consistency between aid agencies' claim and action.

VIII.2 The Search for 'A New Moral Banner to March Behind'

Scholars and practitioners of aid have developed a number of proposals on how to re-establish the moral integrity of humanitarian action in the post-Cold War era. Whereby the main focus is on practice and ethical framework of humanitarian actors. Leader (2000:8) summarizes that "a number of themes emerged during the course of the research to do with the nature and behaviour of organisations that have so far received less attention". The debate on a 'new humanitarianism' seeks to reshape humanitarianism so that aid agencies can better deal with the challenges of the post-Cold War world . Fox (2001:275) concludes:

> There is a 'new humanitarianism' for the new millenium. It is 'principled', 'human rights based', politically sensitive and geared to strengthening those forces that bring peace and stability to the developing world. It offers humanitarian relief agencies a new moral banner to march behind.

The elements of such a 'new humanitarianism' can be divided into two groups. The first focuses on the practice and performance of humanitarian action. The second concerns the ethical basis of aid. The North Korean experience helps assess the potentials and shortfalls of these proposed strategies to re-legitimize international humanitarianism.

a) The Debate on Performance and Practice of Aid

Much of the academic debate suggests that aid agencies should adjust to the geo-political changes of the post-Cold War period. Broadly, in terms of aid agencies' performance and practices, the debate identifies three components of a 'new humanitarianism': codification of principles, enhancing accountability and organizational learning and a better coordination of action. Does the North Korean famine relief mission as the biggest and probably most ambiguous ongoing operation of this kind support such a diagnosis? And, if so, what lessons can be drawn from North Korea concerning the prospect and feasibility of the proposed 'new moral banner'?

The principles debate

Various agreements, protocols, codes of conduct etc. laying out principles of humanitarian action have been drafted in recent years. Some agreements like the Red Cross/NGO Code of Conduct or the SPHERE project aim to generally regulate the activities of endorsing agencies, while others, like the Consensus Statements in the DPRK, refer to humanitarian action in specific aid missions.[2] All statements refer in one way or another to the principles of impartiality and proportionality. Neutrality is primarily mentioned with regard to aid mission in armed conflicts.[3] The agreements on a common set of principles are seen as an important tool to ensure the moral integrity of aid. Leader (1998:290) argues:

> The role of these principles is both to inspire humanitarian action in conflict and guide it in such a way that it is not perverted from its humanitarian mission. In short, they are rules for supping with the devil without getting eaten, or corrupted.

At a time of confusion about the objectives and standards of humanitarianism, the establishment of common principles of action is therefore regarded as "a firm basis upon which responsibilities can be clarified and assigned" (Raynard 2000:13). At the same time, however, the debate has revealed the limits to this principled approach. One weakness is often seen in the fact that the codes do not include any sanctioning mechanism in the case of agencies not fulfilling their obligations: "The extent to which an agency takes these issues seriously has thus been to a large extent up to the agency itself" (Leader 2000:22).[4] Therefore, it could be

---

[2] Other examples are the Code of Conduct for Humanitarian Agencies in Sierra Leone, the Principles of Engagement for Humanitarian Assistance in the Democratic Republic of Congo, the Joint Policy of Operation in Liberia, or the Ground Rules Agreement in south Sudan.

[3] See *RRN Newsletter*, No. 13 (1999), p.12-17; Leader (1999), Leader (2000).

[4] See also Raynard (2000:13) who identifies limits to a code's effect in the following cases: "(a) if they are too vague to mean anything practical in terms of action; (b) when

argued that a code of principles may express a common position of aid agencies. In those cases, however, where there is controversy and dispute among humanitarian agencies, a common statement will have very limited effect.

According to a number of studies, the greatest limit to the effect of codes of principles appears to be their limited application in practice. A DEC evaluation of the role of codes of conduct in the 1999 Kosovo crisis concludes: "The evaluation team found that awareness of the code of conduct and its principles (...) was poor and little attention given to their application".[5] Most generally, however, some authors argue that agreements on principles have a limited positive impact on the moral integrity of aid since they only address the behavior of aid agencies. In view of the Red Cross/NGO Code of Conduct and the SPHERE project, Mourey (2000:318) concludes:

> at the practical level, both the Code and the Sphere Project essentially emanate from the NGOs to guide their work and are of no help against the bad practices of governments, local authorities and warring parties, bad practices which eventually create many disasters.

The role of codes of conduct and Consensus Statements in North Korea illustrates the potential and the shortcomings of agreements on working principles in aid missions where the moral integrity of aid organizations is at stake. The principles mentioned in the SPHERE project or the Red Cross/NGO Code of Conduct were not explicitly referred to by

---

those who have signed up to the code are not monitored in terms of their performance; (c) when those who have not adhered to the code are not held accountable for their lack of adherence; (d) when the agency has not thought through the practicalities of implementing the code".

[5] Disaster Emergency Committee (DEC): *Independent Evaluation of Expenditure of DEC Kosovo Appeal Fund: Phases I and II, April 1999-January 2000*, Vol. 1. London: DEC, p.75. Quoted in ALNAP 2001: paragraph 3.3.4. See also Slim and McConnan who comment on DEC members' understanding of the Code of Conduct signed by all DEC member organizations: "Canvassing DEC members' understanding of humanitarian principles (...) revealed four main factors. First, that most agencies are not specifically aware of and do not use the concepts and language of humanitarian principles explicitly. Secondly, that most agencies are guided by and committed to them implicitly to a great degree and often use different terms to express humanitarian principles. Thirdly, that there is little real knowledge of and reflection on the Code of Conduct in most agencies. Fourthly, that there is very little proper knowledge of international humanitarian law in the great majority of agencies".

aid agencies in their debate surrounding working conditions in the DPRK. The Statement of Humanitarian Principles from November 1998 and subsequent Consensus Statements play a more important role in the reasoning of aid agencies in North Korea. The reference to the principle of impartiality and proportionality contained in these texts aims to describe objectives that the endorsing aid agencies seek to obtain in a mid or long term perspective. It lies in the nature of the North Korean situation that the signatories of these Statements are the least equipped to actively contribute to these goals by their own means. Neither donor governments nor the DPRK authorities are parties to the agreements.

Moreover, the North Korean experience highlights two shortcomings of the principled approach that have not received much attention in this debate on the 'new humanitarianism'. Firstly, the main purpose of codes of conduct in the DPRK is to explain and justify the decision of aid agencies to stay engaged under difficult working conditions. They do not define what is ethically acceptable and what is not. Thus, the agreement on principles does not *precede*, and provide a guide for, courses of action in the DPRK. Instead, the principle statements in North Korea *follow* decisions that had been made in advance. Therefore, the reference to principles of action in North Korea does obviously not provide a 'moral banner to march behind'.

Secondly and more importantly, the North Korean case illustrates that some principles that aid agencies endorse in consensus statements are not an integral part of their respective mandate and ethical framework. This is particularly true in regard to the principle of proportionality. The distinction between 'needy' and 'most needy' may be of utmost importance in the view of classical humanitarianism, which seeks to save the lives of the most severely injured or undernourished. The majority of UN agencies and NGOs operating in the DPRK, however, have a broader understanding of their goals and mandate. Consequently, they are more prepared to make compromises concerning those principles that appear at the top of the consensus statements. Besides issues of application or implementation, the North Korean experience thus points at a further and more fundamental weakness of codes of conduct: their credibility. In other words, as argued above, principles become instruments of an aid agency's strategy more than being guidelines that determine an agency's behavior.

Organizational learning and accountability

Organizational learning[6] and accountability are the second focus of the debate around the 'new humanitarianism'. As early as 1979 Taylor and Cuny, in their study on "The Evaluation of Humanitarian Assistance", concluded that "deliberate and conscious learning from experience is not part of the nonprofit welfare tradition" (1979:37). Criticisms of the learning gap of NGOs and UN agencies engaged with humanitarian action have become redundant since the end of the Cold War. High staff turnover[7], the "hyperactive pace of the relief enterprise"[8] as well as donors' interests in low administrative costs[9] are most frequently identified as being the impediments to organizational learning. As a result, scholars of humanitarianism conclude that "few of the lessons of the past are heeded" (Terry 2000:271), "errors were repeated time and again" (Menkhaus 1996:30), "inappropriate blueprint-type (...) programs continue to abound" (Smillie 1998:53), and "once again 'foreign' humani-

---

[6] Van Brabant (1997) distinguishes between organizational and institutional learning. The former refers to learning mechanisms within an organization, the latter to system-wide learning between and across organizations. He defines organizational learning as follows: "Organisational learning means steering the practice of an organisation on the basis of ongoing, collective and interactive, inquisitive review, by deliberately well-informed staff, of one's own and the available institution-wide experiences and current practices, and their underlying assumptions, models and beliefs" (Van Brabant 1997:7).

[7] For instance, Lindenberg and Bryant (2001:75) note that "many of the operational non-profit organizations complain of high yearly emergency-staff turnover (the Red Cross, 25 percent; CARE, 35 percent; MSF, 50 percent)". Likewise, a study on major French humanitarian NGOs estimates that 40 to 70 percent of the personnel leaves the organization after having worked as an expatriate on one project. See J.M. Davis: *Approche Psychologique de la Médecine Humanitaire. L'Expérience des Médecins Volontaires en Mission Humanitaire à l'Etranger,* unpublished dissertation, Université René Descartes Paris V, 1999.

[8] See Minear (1998: paragraph 49): "The second constraint to learning is the action-oriented nature of the humanitarian ethos. Much has been written about the hyperactive pace of the relief enterprise, borne to the need to respond to rapid-onset crises. In the heat of a crisis, humanitarian agencies and staff can hardly be expected to pause and reflect. The reality that 'crisis x' is often followed by 'crisis y' and 'crisis z' – if not accompanied by them – may shift such reflection more permanently to the back burner. As a result, copies of the multidonor Rwanda study and others like it remain intact in their cellophane wrappers".

[9] See, for instance, Smillie (1996:187): "With very few exceptions, governments refuse to contribute seriously to financing professionalism, insisting on unrealistically low overheads and on putting NGOs through long, inefficient approval processes".

tarian workers arrived ill-equipped in terms of their socio-political and cultural knowledge" (ALNAP 2001: paragraph 3.3.3).

More fundamentally, the lack of organizational learning is closely linked to the fact that humanitarian agencies are not accountable to the people they claim to assist.[10] The debate on the crisis of aid thus focuses on the strengthening of accountability in humanitarian action. According to Lindenberg and Bryant, accountability can be defined as the "answering to stakeholders, including beneficiaries, boards, donors, staff, partners, and peers for the results and impacts of performance and the use of resources to achieve that performance" (2001:212).

Much of the debate surrounding 'new humanitarianism' focuses on the accountability towards donors ("upward accountability", see Edwards and Hulme 1996:8). The primary tool in this regard is the evaluation of humanitarian action and the reporting of the findings to donors or the public.[11] In terms of a "downward accountability" towards the recipients of aid, the debate led to an initiative of British NGOs to consider the establishment of an ombudsman in aid missions. According to the mission statement of the ombudsman project, this new organization within the international humanitarian system "will operate on the basis of concerns raised by the affected population and in response to issues arising from the operation of the system".[12] The accountability of donor institutions, however, is a mostly overlooked "gap in the system" (Raynard 2000:18). One initiative suggests "to channel official donor funds to NGOs and GROs [grassroots organizations] via an independent public institution that can protect them from undue donor influence" (Edwards and Hulme 1996:255). Others argue that donors, like aid agencies, should adopt accountability frameworks.[13]

The North Korean aid mission shows both weaknesses and strong points of accountability mechanisms. Firstly, in North Korea, account-

---

[10] Walkup (1997:51) argues that "unlike market-oriented firms, HOs [humanitarian organizations] are not threatened by the dissatisfaction of consumers (the affected populations)". For in-depth studies on the accountability of humanitarian agencies see Raynard (2000) and Slim (2002).

[11] For greater details see ALNAP 2001.

[12] Humanitarian Ombudsman Project: *Future Directions*. 22 September 1999. Found at www.oneworld.org/ombudsman (21 June 2003). For a presentation and discussion of the project see Mitchell and Doane (1999).

[13] As a model, Raynard (2000:19) mentions the Accountability Framework of the Canadian International Development Agency (CIDA).

ability towards private and public donors primarily means presenting and measuring the effectiveness of aid programs. The effectiveness of humanitarian action, however, is not the greatest problem in North Korea. With only a few exceptions, aid programs in the DPRK effectively meet their objectives. Dilemma situations are not linked to the implementation of projects or to efficiency criteria (neither in North Korea nor in other countries, as the ALNAP study shows[14]). Instead, the uncertainty concerning the proportional affording of aid in North Korea is the primary challenge that aid agencies have to face. No humanitarian agency has left the DPRK because delivered items did not reach the designated institutions. A large number of evaluations undertaken in the DPRK focus on individual project results and does not address the issues responsible for the ambiguity or dilemma of aid agencies in that country. As a result, some evaluations in North Korea confirm the assertion of Edwards and Hulme (1996:13) who speak of "a tendency to 'accountancy', rather than 'accountability', audit rather than learning."

Beyond project evaluations, there have been relatively few policy evaluations that take the broader context of aid into account. Oxfam, the IFRC and Caritas International have let their aid activities be evaluated based on broader terms of reference. The Oxfam and IFRC studies were for internal use only while the Caritas review was published (Smith 2001b). It is interesting to note that the Oxfam and IFRC reviews, though stating that the respective projects were meeting their objectives, were critical of the agencies' policies in North Korea. In view of distribution mechanisms and lack of impact transparency, both reviews recommended not continuing the engagement in the food aid sector. Given the fact that these studies were not addressed at donors, it appears that self-criticism and organizational learning are not necessarily linked to accountability towards donors and have more to do with organizational culture and internal discussion.

The accountability of US-funded aid efforts to the US Congress had the positive effect of refocusing on broader, policy rather than project related aspects of the aid effort in the DPRK. In this respect, the reports of the US General Accounting Office as well as hearings before the House of Representatives played a very important role.

---

[14] The ALNAP study notes (2001:paragraph 2.3.1): "The overwhelming majority of evaluation reports conclude that short-term relief efforts are achieving their purpose and meeting the objectives set for the intervention".

In terms of 'downward accountability', the North Korean case casts some doubts on the feasibility of the ombudsman initiative. Some general doubts have accompanied the project since its inception. Concerning the feasibility of the project, Mitchell and Doane (1999) note that "the most fundamental challenge is to enable beneficiaries to make their voices heard (...). Powerful political and social forces often can hinder and manipulate beneficiaries who seek to make their views known". It goes without saying that, in theory, the direct communication between aid agencies and the North Korean population would allow aid organizations to better assess and target people's needs and, therefore, would most effectively contribute to reducing moral ambiguity and avoiding dilemma situations. In places such as Kosovo, where national sovereignty is being restricted and where international organizations control the local administration, the ombudsman idea appears feasible and promising.[15] However, it is hardly imaginable that North Korean authorities would allow the setting up of an ombudsman which was easily accessible for ordinary citizens and the beneficiaries of aid, and which directly transmitted their concerns and claims to international aid agencies. Thus, the implementation of the ombudsman project largely depends on the specific political situation of a country or region in need of foreign assistance. The more political interests are at stake, and the more local authorities are able to pursue these interests, the more the ombudsman project becomes an illusion. However, dilemmas of aid are most likely to occur in such an environment. As a consequence, the ombudsman project may possibly enhance the performance of humanitarian action in specific aid missions; but it does not provide an answer to moral dilemmas.

---

[15] The Ombudsman Project Steering Committee reports: "An in-depth study of the concept was undertaken in Kosovo, sponsored by CARE-International (UK). Through examination of the activities of agencies involved in the humanitarian response, researchers identified a range of circumstances in which an Ombudsman could be seen to add value and, if in place, could improve immediate performance of agencies on the ground. In consultation with both agencies and claimants in Kosovo, they were able to make concrete recommendations for how the Ombudsman could operate in practice". See note 12 in this chapter.

The role of coordination

Finally, it is often argued that one major weakness of humanitarianism that renders aid agencies vulnerable to manipulation and dilemma situations is a lack of coordination:

> coordination has a well-established reputation for being amongst the most problematic performance areas within the humanitarian system. (...) the extraordinary persistence of the problem can probably only be explained in terms of structural factors such as the large number of separately funded, separately governed agencies typically involved in any single operation (ALNAP 2001: paragraph 4.2.5).

In terms of coordination in the DPRK two observations can be made. Firstly, due to coordination mechanisms put in place by WFP, OCHA and ECHO, information exchange among aid agencies seems to be closer and better organized than in most other aid missions. As a former GAA coordinator asserts: "I have never been more coordinated than in North Korea".[16] The relatively low number of agencies present in the country as well as the fact that all international staff is concentrated in one spot - Pyongyang - further facilitates coordination efforts. Secondly, however, at the request of the DPRK authorities, aid agencies deliberately refrained from sharing information with other organizations, particularly in the early years of the aid effort. A member of the MSF team remarked in 1998: "was it really the Korean authorities who asked organizations not to communicate their reports? People seemed to be very happy with it: absolutely no cooperation, secret kept on activities done or in project. A real shame".[17] In addition, several aid agencies decided not to participate in international NGO meetings in order not to give the DPRK authorities the impression of aid agencies 'ganging up'. In general, and in view of progresses made in recent years, it appears that aid agencies in North Korea exchange information concerning project activities on a regular and institutionalized basis. Unlike in Kosovo, for instance,[18] the role of OCHA with regard to information exchange and coordination is accepted and appreciated by NGOs in the DPRK.

---

[16] Interview with Hubertus Rüffer, former Head of Mission DPRK/GAA, Berlin, 17 July 1999.

[17] MSF: *Kangwon Province – Final Nutritionnal Report. February 98 – August 98.* (Internal report, in author's files).

[18] See ALNAP 2001: paragraph 4.2.5.

Yet the coordination of project activities does not necessarily mean that aid agencies have a common approach in dealing with working restrictions or moral dilemmas. One lesson from the North Korean aid mission is that, in a number of aspects, humanitarian agencies are fundamentally different. In terms of mandate and activity, principles of action, perception of famine and vulnerability and an agency's stance towards politics, humanitarian organizations in the DPRK are extremely diverse. In view of these differences, coordination in the sense of a common understanding of principles of action, of what is acceptable and what is not, is not a technical issue. Coordination mechanisms may have a positive impact upon the performance of aid. But as long as the differences between the ethical frameworks of aid agencies are not addressed, coordination efforts will not be able to minimize the dilemmas of humanitarianism. An Oxfam official concludes: "there is a very pragmatic approach on coordination in DPRK, but no coordination in matters of principle. Due to the disunity on principles, this pragmatism is justified".[19]

In sum, the debate on the performance and practices of the humanitarian actors, by and large, ignores the nature of moral dilemmas. As a result, the proposed solutions to the 'crisis of aid' are hardly appropriate to re-legitimize humanitarian action.

b) Detaching Humanitarian Action? – Reshaping the Ethical Basis of Aid

While much of the debate focuses on the practices of aid agencies, some proposals aim to reshape the ethical basis of humanitarianism. In this respect, the discussion elaborates on three concepts: the insertion of humanitarian action as a political movement, the adoption of a rights-based approach and the integration of peace as the new moral ideal for humanitarian aid.

Humanitarianism as a political movement

A number of authors argue that political consciousness and engagement would reduce the structural ambiguity of humanitarianism. Boltanski (1999:189) notes that humanitarian action – unlike social move-

---

[19] Interview with James Darcy, former Regional Director Asia/Oxfam GB, Oxford/UK, 11 September 2001.

ments such as the trade union movement – does not base its claims on a logic of justice and rights. He argues that humanitarianism follows a framework of philanthropy and does not actively seek to put its claim on the political agenda. By adopting a logic of pity instead of a "politics of justice", humanitarian aid does not have the political weight necessary to push through its claims. Moral dilemmas and the discrediting of aid are therefore the results of the logic of pity. Boltanski (1999:191) concludes: "To take the internal critics of the humanitarian movement seriously thus leads in the direction of a political insertion of the movement". The pressure of humanitarian agencies in France to recognize a right to humanitarian aid and the duty to defend a people against its own leaders *(droit d'ingérence)* serves as a model. Boltanski (1999:191) further notes that "unlike the right to freedom of thought (Declaration of 1789) and social right (Declaration of 1848) which (...) were aimed at States, (...) the right of humanitarian intervention is opposed to States". The politicization of humanitarianism thus provides "a new political bond animated by resistance to government" (Campbell 1998:520). In this regard, the (originally) French school of 'rebellious humanitarianism' comes closest to Boltanski's postulate of the "political insertion of the movement".

A rights-based agenda of aid

The politicization of humanitarianism is intertwined with the concept of a rights-based approach. Slim (2001) argues in favor of a "rights-based humanitarianism and the proper politicisation of humanitarian philosophy". He acknowledges that, given the current ethical framework of aid agencies, the adoption of a philosophy of rights requires "something of a Copernican revolution in philanthropic thinking. It requires humanitarians to reorientate their morality and thought so that they orbit around equality, contract and justice rather than pity and help" (2001:20). The objective of such a 'proper politicization' is to provide a philosophy "which can make political space for itself to challenge, mitigate and even transform the particular politics of violence and war" (Slim 2001:20).

The emotional, affective element of aid is challenged and blamed for being responsible for the discrediting of humanitarianism in recent years. Slim (2001:5) remarks that charity and philanthropy are too often understood as "ends in themselves and left to float free of any serious challenge to power". He argues that

> the virtues of charity and philanthropy, which should have equality at the centre of their meaning, have all too frequently (and often unwittingly) become the means to make the opposite principle of inequality and its resulting suffering morally, socially and politically acceptable (Slim 2001:5).

In short, the perception of aid as an act of a common humanity and thus as an act in itself and the apolitical understanding of humanitarian action as being outside or above politics are seen as politically naive, morally questionable and "self-defeating" (MacFarlane 2000:89). In this respect, the debate on humanitarianism since the end of the Cold War resembles the criticism of "Charity Business"[20] as expressed by exponents of the 'sans-frontiérisme' school of thought in the 1980s.

Peace as a guiding ideal

The promotion of peace, as argued by a number of authors, is a further remedy for the discredited humanitarian action. Instead of the traditional humanitarian focus on the immediate saving of lives, aid should strengthen a society's "capacities for peace". Otherwise there is a risk that it could "do harm" (Anderson 1999). Therefore, humanitarian action should seek to provide structural and sustainable support to a society, and become part of a broader peacebuilding strategy. This 'do-no-harm' approach has gained considerable popularity among scholars, donors and practitioners of aid.[21]

However, with regard to the nature of dilemmas in humanitarian action, the adoption of peace as the moral ideal of aid appears to be the least promising approach. Dilemmas of aid derive, first and foremost, from the non-respect of core principles of humanitarian action. An oppressive regime or a war economy may indirectly benefit from a humanitarian mission that effectively saves the lives of the most vulnerable populations. The only factor that counts from the perspective of classical

---

[20] "Charity Business" is the title of the book of Bernard Kouchner, one of the founders of MSF, published in 1986 (Paris: Le Pré aux Clercs).
[21] For a discussion on the inclusion of humanitarian action into peacebuilding efforts see Michael Schloms (2003): "Humanitarian NGOs in Peace Processes". In: *International Peacekeeping*, Vol. 10, No. 1, pp.40-55.

humanitarianism is the impartial affording of aid in proportion to the needs of a population. The famine aid mission in North Korea - as well as the aid operations in Russia, Biafra, Ethiopia and Cambodia - illustrate that aid agencies that adhere to this traditional understanding are caught in a dilemma when the respect for this principle appears doubtful. Put differently, the question of how to ensure the respect for the humanitarian space lies at the heart of the moral dilemma of aid rather than the economic or war-related effects of humanitarian aid. In this respect, the 'do-no-harm' approach misses the point and provides no answer.

The risks of detachment

The outlined initiatives to change the stance of international humanitarianism towards politics concern the most fundamental aspects of the ethical frameworks of aid agencies. The behavior and reasoning of humanitarian organizations in North Korea has shown that most actors do not perceive themselves as politically engaged organizations. In addition, for a number of agencies, the purpose of humanitarian aid is to bridge political gaps as a gesture of humanity. In that sense, humanitarian action cannot take sides. The politicization of humanitarianism in a rights-based philosophy would thus mean fundamentally changing the ethical framework of aid agencies; as Slim rightfully remarks, it would represent a 'Copernican revolution'. It appears that aid agencies are more and more adopting a rights language and trying not to victimize or patronize the recipients of their aid. However, in view of the ethical frameworks of humanitarian agencies, it is doubtful whether a logic of rights will influence more than just the language of aid organizations. A rights-based approach may be complementary to the ethical orientation of aid agencies, but it will most unlikely substitute it. In addition, a human rights philosophy and a political insertion of humanitarianism one-sidedly highlights the objective side of the humanitarian ethics.

The subjective, affective side that is inherent in the principle of humanity as the prime mover of traditional humanitarianism is being questioned. It has been shown that the victim-centered approach in North Korea and other famine aid missions goes hand in hand with a certain political naivety. Shifting the focus to the other extreme, however, may ultimately undermine one of the moral foundations of humanitarian action. In a way, this would be the capitulation of humanitarianism as an action that expresses the concern, compassion and identification of people who respond to suffering.

Instead of a fundamental shift of the aid agencies' philosophical basis, it appears more promising to accept that the humanitarian ethics contains an affective, empathetic side. As noted earlier, according to Vaux (2001), humanitarianism consists of both 'attachment' and 'detachment'. The challenge is to balance both forces rather than exclusively highlighting one side. We will now discuss in how far the North Korean experience might be helpful in that regard.

VIII.3 Lessons from North Korea: Towards Consistency in Humanitarian Action

The experience with structural ambiguity and concrete dilemmas in North Korea questions a number of views expressed in the debate on relegitimizing humanitarian action in the post-Cold War era. This debate has, by and large, been prompted by the dilemma of aid in civil wars and collapsed states. In a sense, the North Korean case has more in common with the famine aid operation in Soviet Russia in the 1920s than with relief missions in Rwanda or South Sudan in the 1990s. Therefore, the North Korean aid effort helps to refocus on the 'timeless' risks to the moral integrity of humanitarianism that are inherent in modern humanitarian action. As argued above, it appears that the principle of impartiality and proportionality as the sore spot of the humanitarian ethics has somewhat gone out of focus in recent debates.

a) Inconsistency and Its Implications

Aid agencies operating in the DPRK can – under difficult conditions and tight governmental control - effectively carry out their programs. The prerequisite is that they direct their support to the population groups that the North Korean state, according to its own analysis, is first and foremost obliged to help. That is, the large majority of the North Korean population that represent the backbone of the country's agriculture, industry and, ultimately, political stability. The working environment in the DPRK is ethically acceptable to some aid agencies and unacceptable to others. The North Korean case illustrates that the process of diversification of humanitarian organizations has reached a point where humanitarian organizations adhere to differing and even opposite conceptions concerning the purpose of aid, their activism and perception of politics. As a result, aid agencies in North Korea have no common position in dealing with the traditional principles of proportionality and impartiality.

Although an agency's understanding of these principles determines the course of action and the decision to stay or to withdraw, the humanitarian organizations in North Korea did not address their differing perceptions of proportionality and impartiality in the debate surrounding their work in the DPRK. UN agencies and NGOs that continue to work in the country did not comment on the criticism by MSF and ACF of the impossibility of affording nutritional aid according to needs. Essentially, these allegations, based on own observations and, in parts, on doubtful political analysis, were not discussed. The remaining agencies reacted to these reproaches in two ways. Firstly, as in other controversial aid missions in the past, agencies referred to the humanitarian imperative to provide assistance, to the hungry child that would die without foreign aid. Secondly, and more importantly, aid organizations declared their commitment to impartiality and proportionality in common statements on principles of action. In November 1998, aid agencies described the "assurance that humanitarian assistance reaches sectors of the population in greatest need" as a principle of their action.[22] However, it is doubtful whether non-medical aid agencies that are primarily engaged in rehabilitation and development-oriented activities in North Korea consider the principle of proportionality an integral part of their mandate and ethical framework. The public commitment to principles was coined and reaffirmed whenever international organizations and media questioned the sense of the aid mission in the DPRK. These commitments thus appear to be a tool to calm criticisms and doubts rather than an expression of convictions and moral obligations. This lack of consistency between public claims on one side and the reality of action on the other poses three risks.

First, the lack of consistency weakens the role of principle statements as a tool to express a common position in dealing with North Korean authorities and push through common demands. Second, principles of humanitarian action risk only playing a role in the communication between aid agency and donor. The claim of reaching the most vulnerable groups of a society and the presentation of development-oriented proj-

---

[22] *Statement of Humanitarian Principles*, Pyongyang, 25 November 1998.

ects as saving the lives of the groups most at risk may satisfy donors. The risk is that principles thereby become part of a closed system where the formal adherence to principles is a prerequisite for receiving public funds and is not measured or discussed further. Third, the commitment to traditional principles of humanitarian action on paper and the increasing distance of today's aid agencies from classical humanitarianism in reality, poses the risk of self-deception. Instead of discussing the compatibility of modern humanitarian action with the principles coined in the early 20th century, aid agencies may be tempted to argue that, using the terms of Slim and McConnan (1998), their feet still fit into the glass slipper of classical humanitarianism. In sum, avoiding a debate on the consistency of aid poses an even greater risk to the moral integrity of aid than the debate itself.

This lack of open discussion on the principles of action is exacerbated by the heat of controversies and mutual reproaches among aid agencies. Instead of referring to differing mandates and traditions that may justify differing decisions and courses of action, aid organizations presented their analyses as valid for all humanitarian actors and donors engaged in the country. As a result, aid agencies reproached each other for political blindness or for mixing political and human rights engagement with humanitarianism. North Korea thus illustrates the widening gap and the increasing lack of mutual respect between humanitarian actors.

b) Towards Consistency

Due to differing ethical frameworks, mandates and traditions, aid agencies adopted different approaches to dealing with working restrictions in the DPRK. It is neither desirable nor possible to enforce a common approach or to create a homogenous group of actors. However, this diversity is problematic when it amounts to differing interpretations of principles of action. The international aid operation in the DPRK shows that aid agencies interpret principles according to their ethical framework and organizational mandate. In other words, aid agencies are relatively free to define the content and the importance of principles of humanitarian action.[23] A consistent approach to principles of humanitarian

---

[23] See also Leader (2000:48): "Thus the idea of principles of humanitarian action is shifting from something that was intended to regulate agencies, and was thus imposed

action therefore requires the engagement of political actors, namely of donor governments and institutions. In this respect, the North Korean famine aid mission also provides some encouraging signs.

In some cases where there was agreement between NGOs, UN organizations and donor agencies on principles of action, aid agencies were able to push through some demands in negotiations with the DPRK authorities. European agencies report that the permanent presence of ECHO in Pyongyang was helpful in a number of cases. In terms of staffing, project location and program impact control, ECHO-funded agencies obtained some concessions from the North Korean authorities whenever ECHO actively supported their negotiation positions. On ECHO's role in the DPRK, an ECHO Officer remarks that "it's easier for ECHO to be strict, it's a privilege and an obligation to make pressure".[24] Thus, in some cases, the complementary approach of actors with a differing mandate achieved some progress in terms of working conditions for humanitarian agencies.

Furthermore, the US Congress played an important role in initiating discussions on principles of action and the proportionality of aid distributions in the DPRK. The reviews of US-funded aid activities, undertaken by the US General Accounting Office on behalf of the Congress, as well as hearings before the House of Representatives, led aid agencies to explain and justify their policies in the DPRK. These events show that accountability towards donors has a role to play in addressing the lack of consistency and in prompting a discussion on the principles of today's humanitarianism. Other agencies confirm that interventions by donor agencies or UN organizations were helpful in terms of modestly improving some working conditions.

Instead of drafting a new blueprint for humanitarian ethics or reshaping the system of international aid, the dialogue among humanitarian actors and donors may be most appropriate to define a common moral basis of humanitarian action and to find a balance between humanitarian imperative, political realities and aid agencies' own standards and traditions. The result will not be the end of the ambiguity of aid and the eradication of humanitarian dilemmas. As long as humani-

---

by the belligerents, to something agencies are trying to use to regulate the belligerents. This, in effect, is what 'a principled approach' has come to mean".

[24] Interview with Javier Menendez Bonilla, Desk Officer/ECHO, Brussels, 17 October 2001.

tarian action seeks to alleviate human suffering, ethical challenges are inescapable. Instead, the aim would be to minimize the inconsistency between claim and action and to re-establish the credibility of humanitarianism. In North Korea, the opportunity to enter into such a dialogue has been regrettably missed.

Interviewees

a) UN Agencies

Susan DeSouza, UNOCHA
Oliver Lacey-Hall, UNOCHA
David Morton, WFP
Hilde Niggemann-Pucella, FAO
Shahwar Pataudi, UNOCHA
Abdur Rashid, GIEWS (Global Information Early Warning System)/FAO
Jens Schulthes, former Regional Director Asia and Pacific/WFP
Guy Sneyers, FAO

b) Non-Governmental Organizations

Aurélia Balpe, IFRC
James K. Bishop, InterAction
Nathalie Bréchet, MDM
Chang Won-Suk, World Vision Korea
Cathy Choi, ICF
James Darcy, Oxfam
John Feffer, AFSC
Monti Feliciano, CESVI, (e-mail to author)
Elisa Giunchi, CESVI, (e-mail to author)
Hong Song-Young, Korean Sharing Movement
Erica Kang, Good Friends
Lee Ji-Hyun, JTS
Karin Lee, AFSC
Lee Yoon-Sang, Good Neighbors Korea
Nancy Lindborg, Mercy Corps International
Stephen Linton, Eugene Bell Foundation
Christel Neudeck, Cap Anamur, (interview by phone)

Park Chan-Uk, Korean National Red Cross
Park Ji-Hyun, JTS
Jean-Fabrice Piétri, ACF
Hubertus Rüffer, GAA
Pierre Salignon, MSF
Peter Van't Westende, GAA
Wube Woldemariam, CAD
Yeo Joeng-Sun, Korean Welfare Foundation
Yi Il-Ha, Good Neighbors Korea

c) European Commission

María Castillo Fernandez, RELEX
Frank Heske, Delegation of the European Commission in the Republic of Korea
Javier Menendez Bonilla, ECHO

d) US Department of State and USAID

Jeffrey A. Beller, US Department of State
Leonard Rogers, USAID

e) German Federal Ministry for Economic Cooperation and Development

Horst Müller, Division Emergency Aid
Helmut Siedler, Division East Asia

f) Others

Barbara Hauer and Daniel Sagebiel, German Central Committee Against Tuberculosis/Zentralklinik Emil von Behring, Department Lungenklinik Heckeshorn
Dieter Hannusch, Food Security Economist

Lee Won-Woong, Department of North Korean Studies/Kwandong University

Gerhard Michels, Hanns-Seidel-Stiftung

Marcus Noland, Institute for International Economics

Hazel Smith, United States Institute for Peace

Bibliography

Alamgir, Mohiuddin (1980): *Famine in South Asia.* Cambridge, MA: Oelgeschlager, Gunn and Hain.

Alamgir, Mohiuddin (1981): "An Approach towards a Theory of Famine". In: John R. K. Robson (ed.): *Famine. Its Causes, Effects and Management.* New York: Gordon and Breach.

Active Learning Network for Accountability and Performance in Humanitarian Action (ALNAP, 2001): *Humanitarian Action. Learning from Evaluation.* London: ALNAP, (Annual Review Series 2001).

Anderson, Mary B. (1999): *Do No Harm. How Aid Can Support Peace – or War.* Boulder, London: Lynne Rienner.

Appadurai, Arjun (1984): "How Moral is South Asia's Economy?" In: *Journal of Asian Studies,* Vol. 43, No. 3, pp. 481-497.

Arendt, Hannah (1963): *On Revolution.* New York: Viking Press.

Ball, Nicole (1976): "Understanding the Causes of African Famine". In: *Journal of Modern African Studies,* Vol. 14, No. 3, pp. 517-522.

Bennett, Jon (1999): *North Korea. The Politics of Food Aid.* London: Overseas Development Institute, (Relief and Rehabilitation Network Paper No. 28).

Black, Maggie (1992): *A Cause for Our Times. Oxfam, the First 50 Years.* Oxford: Oxfam.

Boltanski, Luc (1999): *Distant Suffering. Morality, Media and Politics.* Cambridge: Cambridge University Press.

Borton, John (1995), "Ethiopia: NGO Consortia and Coordination Arrangements, 1984-91". In: Jon Bennett (et al.) (ed.), *Meeting Needs: NGO Coordination in Practice.* London: Earthscan.

Bouchet-Saulnier, Françoise (2000): "The Principles and Practices of 'Rebellious Humanitarianism'". In: *Médecins Sans Frontières 2000 International Activity Report.*

Brauman, Rony (1995): *L'Action Humanitaire.* Paris: Flammarion.

Brauman, Rony (1996): *Humanitaire le Dilemme. Entretien avec Philippe Petit.* Paris: Editions Textuel.

Brauman, Rony (1998): "Refugee Camps, Population Transfers, and NGOs". In: Jonathan Moore (ed.): *Hard Choices. Moral Dilemmas in Humanitarian Intervention.* Lanham: Rowman and Littlefield, pp. 177-194.

Bronner, Uta (2003): *Humanitäre Helfer in Krisengebieten. Motivation, Einsatzerleben, Konsequenzen - Eine psychologische Analyse.* Münster: Lit Verlag.

Brown, Lester R. and Erik P. Eckholm (1974): *By Bread Alone.* Oxford: Pergamon Press.

Brunel, Sylvie (1998): "Corée du Nord. Une Famine Virtuelle?" In: Action Contre la Faim (ed.): *Géopolitique de la Faim. Quand la Faim est une Arme.* Paris: Presses Universitaires de France, pp. 132-138.

Brunel, Sylvie (2002): "Les Famines d'Aujourd'hui sont des Famine Tolérées" In: *Libération*, 14 June.

Campbell, David (1998), "Why Fight? Humanitarianism, Principles and Post-Structuralism". In: *Millenium*, Vol. 27, No. 3, pp. 497-521.

Chang, Christine Y. (1999): *A Field Survey Report of North Korean Refugees in China*, Seoul: Commission to Help North Korean Refugees (CNKR).

Chung Oknim (2003): "The Role of South Korea's NGOs. The Political Context". In: L. Gordon Flake and Scott Snyder (eds.): *Paved With Good Intentions. NGO Experience in North Korea.* Westport: Praeger, pp. 81-110.

Chung Young-Soon (1996): *Chuch'e-Ideen und (Neo-) Konfuzianismus in Nordkorea.* Hamburg: Lit Verlag.

Clay, Jason W. and Bonnie K. Holcomb (1986): *Politics and the Ethiopian Famine 1984-1985.* Cambridge, MA: Cultural Survival, (Cultural Survival Report 20).

Cox, George W. (1981): "The Ecology of Famine. An Overview." In: John R. K. Robson (ed.): *Famine. Its Causes, Effects and Management.* New York: Gordon and Breach, pp. 5-18.

Cremer, Georg (1999): "Auch Naturkatastrophen sind Sozialkatastrophen". In: *Der Überblick,* No. 1, pp. 52-55.

Da Corta, L. and Stephen Devereux (1991): "True Generosity or False Charity? A Note on the Ideological Foundations of Famine Relief Policies". In: *Development Studies Working Paper No. 40.* Turin: Centro Studi Luca d'Agliano and Oxford: Queen Elizabeth House.

De Waal, Alex (1997): *Famine Crimes. Politics and the Disaster Relief Industry in Africa.* Oxford: African Rights.

De Waal, Alex (2000): Transcript of a Discussion with Alex de Waal. Found at www.bard.edu/hrp/hhrs/dewaal.htm (3 August 2002).

Delorenzi, Simone (1999): *ICRC Policy Since the End of the Cold War. Contending with the Impasse in International Humanitarian Action.* Geneva: International Committee of the Red Cross.

Desai, Meghnad (1984): "A General Theory of Poverty". In: *Indian Economic Review*, Vol. 19.

Destexhe, Alain (1993): *L'Humanitaire Impossible ou Deux Siècles d'Ambiguïté.* Paris: Armand Colin.

Devereux, Stephen (1993): *Theories of Famine.* New York: Harvester Wheatsheaf.

Drèze, Jean and Amartya Sen (1989): *Hunger and Public Action.* Oxford: Clarendon Press.

Drèze, Jean and Amartya Sen (eds., 1990): *The Political Economy of Hunger. Volume I: Entitlement and Well-Being.* Oxford: Clarendon Press.

Duffield, Mark (1993): "NGOs, Disaster Relief, and Asset Transfer in the Horn. Political Survival in a Permanent Emergency". In: *Development and Change*, Vol. 24, pp. 131-157.

Eberstadt, Nicholas, Marc Rubin and Albina Tretjakova (1995): "The Collapse of Soviet and Russian Trade with North Korea, 1990-1993. Impact and Implications". In: *Korean Journal of National Unification*, Vol. 4, pp. 87-104.

Eberstadt, Nicholas (1995): "China's Trade with the DPRK, 1990-1994". In: *Korea and World Affairs,* Vol. 19, No. 4, pp. 665-685.

Eberstadt, Nicholas (1997): "The DPRK as an Economy under Multiple Severe Stresses. Analogies and Lessons from Past and Recent Historical Experience". In: *Korean Journal of National Unification,* Vol. 6, pp. 151-190.

Eberstadt, Nicholas (1999): *The End of North Korea.* Washington D.C.: AEI Press.

Eberwein, Wolf-Dieter (2001): *Realism or Idealism, or Both? Security Policy and Humanitarianism.* Berlin: Social Science Research Center (WZB, Discussion Paper No. P01-307).

Eberwein, Wolf-Dieter and Peter Runge (eds., 2002): *Humanitäre Hilfe statt Politik? Neue Herausforderungen für ein altes Politikfeld.* Münster: Lit Verlag.

Edkins, Jenny (2000): *Whose Hunger? Concepts of Famine, Practices of Aid.* London and Minneapolis: University of Minnesota Press, (Borderlines Volume 17).

Edwards, Michael and David Hulme (eds., 1996): *Beyond the Magic Bullet. NGO Performance and Accountability in the Post-Cold War World*. West Hartford: Kumarian.

European Commission (2001): *The EC – Democratic People's Republic of Korea (DPRK). Country Strategy Paper 2001-2004*. Brussels.

Fisher, H. H. (1927): *The Famine in Soviet Russia 1919-1923. The Operations of the American Relief Administration*. New York: Macmillan.

Flake, L. Gordon (1995): "North Korea's External Economy". Paper presented at the Sixth Annual Convention of the Congress of Political Economists (COPE), Seoul, 5-10 January.

Flake, L. Gordon (2003): "The Experience of U.S. NGOs in North Korea". In: L. Gordon Flake and Scott Snyder (eds.): *Paved With Good Intentions. NGO Experience in North Korea*. Westport: Praeger, pp. 15-46.

Foster-Carter, Aidan (1997): "Ist der Hunger hausgemacht?" In: *Der Überblick*, No. 4, pp. 43-47.

Fox, Fiona (2001): "New Humanitarianism. Does it Provide a Moral Banner for the 21st Century?" In: *Disasters*, Vol. 25, No. 4, pp. 275-289.

Goetz, Nathaniel H. (2001): "Humanitarian Issues in the Biafra Conflict". In: *Journal of Humanitarian Assistance*, www.jha.ac/articles/u036.htm, Document Posted 7 October 2001.

Goldberg, Harold J. (ed., 1993): *Documents of Soviet-American Relations. Volume I: Intervention, Famine Relief and International Affairs 1917-1933*. Gulf Breeze: Academic International Press.

Good Friends (1999): *Report on Daily Life and Human Rights of North Korean Displaced Persons in China*. Seoul: Good Friends/Center for Peace, Human Rights, and Refugees.

Goodkind, Daniel and Loraine West (2001): "The North Korean Famine and Its Demographic Impact". In: *Population and Development Review*, Vol. 27, No. 2, pp. 219-238.

Gore, Charles (1993): "Entitlement Relations and 'Unruly' Social Practices. A Comment on the Work of Amartya Sen". In: *Journal of Development Studies*, Vol. 29, No. 3, pp. 429-460.

Gustavson, Kristin R. and Jinmin Lee-Rudolph (1997) "Political and Economic Human Rights Violations in North Korea." In: Mo Jongryn and Thomas Henriksen (eds.): *North Korea After Kim Il Sung. Continuity or Change?* Stanford: Hoover Institution Press, pp. 132-150.

Harbach, Heinz (1992): *Altruismus und Moral*. Opladen: Westdeutscher Verlag, (Studien zur Sozialwissenschaft 103).

Heininger, Janet E. (1997): "Cambodia. Relief, Repatriation, and Rehabilitation". In: Eric A. Belgrad and Nitza Nachmias (eds.): *The Politics of International Humanitarian Aid Operations*. Westport: Praeger, pp. 111-136.

Hentsch, Thierry (1973): *Face au Blocus. Histoire de l'Intervention du Comité International de la Croix-Rouge dans le Conflit du Nigéria, 1967-1970*. Doctoral Thesis. Geneva: Université de Genève.

Huntford, Roland (1998): *Nansen. The Explorer as Hero*. London: Duckworth.

Jackson, Tony and Deborah Eade (1982): *Against the Grain. The Dilemma of Project Food Aid*. Oxford: Oxfam.

Jansson, Kurt (1990): "The Emergency Relief Operation". In: Kurt Jansson, Michael Harris and Angela Penrose (eds.): *The Ethiopian Famine*. London and New Jersey: Zed Books.

Jean, François (1999): "Corée du Nord. Un Régime de Famine". In: *Esprit*, No. 2, pp. 5-27.

Jonas, Hans (1977): "The Concept of Responsibility. An Inquiry into the Foundations of Ethics of Our Age". In: H. Tristam Engelhardt Jr. and Daniel Callahan (eds.): *Knowledge, Value and Belief. (The Foundations of Ethics and Its Relationship to Science, Vol. 2)* New York: Institute of Society, Ethics and the Life Sciences/The Hastings Center, pp. 169-198.

Jonas, Hans (1979): *Das Prinzip Verantwortung. Versuch einer Ethik für die technologische Zivilisation*. Frankfurt/Main: Insel Verlag.

Kagan, Richard, Matthew Oh and David Weissbrodt (1988): *Human Rights in the Democratic People's Republic of Korea*. Minneapolis and Washington, D.C.: Minnesota Lawyers International Human Rights Committee and Asia Watch.

Kallscheuer, Otto (1995): "And Who is My Neighbor? Moral Sentiments, Proximity, Humanity". In: *Social Research*, Vol. 62, No. 1, pp. 99-128.

Karenfort, Jörg (1999): *Die Hilfsorganisationen im bewaffneten Konflikt. Rolle und Status unparteiischer humanitärer Organisationen im humanitären Völkerrecht*. Frankfurt/Main: Peter Lang.

Keen, David (1994): *The Benefits of Famine. A Political Economy of Famine and Relief in Southwestern Sudan 1983-1989*. Princeton: Princeton University Press.

Kim Jong-Il (1974): *Einige Probleme zum Verständnis der Juche-Ideologie*. After a Conversation with Party Propagandists, 2 April 1974. Found at: www.kdvr.de/texte/jong/juche.pdf (21 July 2003).

Kim Jong-Il (1982): *Über die Juche-Ideologie*. Essay Dedicated to the National Symposium on Juche Ideology on the Occasion of the 70ᵗʰ Birthday of Great Leader Comrade Kim Il Sung, 31 March 1982. Found at: www.kdvr.de/texte/jong/juche.pdf (21 July 2003).

Kim Jong-Il (1986): Zu einigen Fragen der Erziehung in der Juche-Ideologie. Conversation with Officials of the KWP's Central Committee, 15 July 1986. Found at: www.kdvr.de/texte/jong/erziehung.pdf (21 July 2003).

Korean Institute for National Unification (KINU, various issues): *White Paper on Human Rights in North Korea. An Annual Report.* Seoul: KINU.

Kula, Erhun (1989): "Politics, Economics, Agriculture and Famines: The Chinese Case". In: Food Policy, Vol. 14, No. 1.

Kumar, B. G. (1990): "Ethiopian Famines 1973-1985. A Case Study". In Jean Drèze and Amartya Sen (eds.): *The Political Economy of Hunger. Volume I: Entitlement and Well-Being.* Oxford: Clarendon Press, pp. 173-216.

Küng, Hans (2001): *Das Projekt Weltethos.* Munich: Piper.

Kwon Tae-Jin and Kim Woon-Keun (1999): "Assessment of Food Supply in North Korea". In: *Journal of Rural Development,* Vol. 22, No. 2, pp. 47-66.

Lautze, Sue (1997): *The Famine in North Korea. Humanitarian Responses in Communist Nations.* Feinstein International Famine Center, Tufts University.

Leader, Nicholas (1998): "Proliferating Principles. Or How to Sup with the Devil without Getting Eaten". In: *Disasters,* Vol. 22, No. 4, pp. 288-308.

Leader, Nicholas (2000): *The Politics of Principle. The Principles of Humanitarian Action in Practice.* London: Overseas Development Institute, (HPG Report No. 2).

Lindenberg, Marc and Coralie Bryant (2001): *Going Global. Transforming Relief and Development NGOs.* Bloomfield: Kumarian.

Lipton, Michael (1973): "Urban Bias and Rural Planning in India". In Henry Bernstein (ed.): *Underdevelopment and Development: The Third World Today.* Harmondsworth: Penguin Books, Chapter 13.

MacFarlane, Neil (2000): *Politics and Humanitarian Action*. Providence: The Thomas J. Watson Jr. Institute for International Studies, (Occasional Paper No. 41).

Mackintosh, Kate (2000): *The Principles of Humanitarian Action in International Humanitarian Law*. London: Overseas Development Institute, (HPG Report No. 5).

Macrae, Joanna (2001): *Aiding Recovery? The Crisis of Aid in Chronic Political Emergencies*. London and New York: Zed Books.

Maretzki, Hans (1991): *Kim-ismus in Nordkorea. Analyse des letzten DDR-Botschafters in Pjöngjang*. Böblingen: Tykve.

Mason, Linda and Roger Brown (1983): *Rice, Rivalry and Politics. Managing Cambodian Relief*. Notre Dame: University of Notre Dame Press.

McElroy, Robert W. (1992): *Morality and American Foreign Policy. The Role of Ethics in International Affairs*. Princeton: Princeton University Press.

Menkhaus, Kenneth J. (1996): "Conflict, Chaos, and the Social Sciences in Humanitarian Intervention". In: *Anthropology in Action*, Vol. 3, No. 3, pp. 29-32.

Minear, Larry (1998): *Learning to Learn*. Discussion Paper Prepared for a Seminar on Lessons Learned in Humanitarian Coordination. Office for the Coordination of Humanitarian Affairs (OCHA) and the Ministry of Foreign Affairs of Sweden, Stockholm, 3-4 April 1998.

Mitchell, John and Doane, Deborah (1999): "An Ombudsman for Humanitarian Assistance?", in: *Disasters*, Vol. 23, No. 2, 1999, pp. 115-124.

Mourey, Alain (2000): "Follow-up of the Code of Conduct of the International Red Cross and Red Crescent Movement". In: Edward Clay and Olav Stokke (eds.): *Food Aid and Human Security*. London, Portland: Frank Cass, (EADI Book Series 24), pp. 309-325.

Nathanail, Lola (1996): "Small Fish in a Deep Dark Sea. NGOs' Response in North Korea". In: *RRN Newsletter*, 6 November, pp. 6-8.

Natsios, Andrew S. (1999): *Special Report. The Politics of Famine in North Korea*. Washington, D.C.: United States Institute of Peace.

Natsios, Andrew S. (2001): *The Great North Korean Famine. Famine, Politics, and Foreign Policy*. Washington, D.C.: United States Institute of Peace Press.

Noland, Marcus, Sherman Robinson and Tao Wang (1999): *Famine in North Korea. Causes and Cures*. Washington, D.C.: Institute for International Economics, (Working Paper 99-2).

Noland, Marcus (2000): *Avoiding the Apocalypse. The Future of the Two Koreas*. Washington, D.C.: Institute for International Economics.

Pictet, Jean (1958): *The Geneva Conventions of 12 August 1949. Commentary*. Geneva: International Committee of the Red Cross.

Pictet, Jean (1979): *The Fundamental Principles of the Red Cross. Commentary*. Geneva: Henri Dunant Institute.

Piétri, Jean-Fabrice (2002): "Manipulating Humanitarian Crisis in North Korea". In: *Humanitarian Exchange. The Magazine of the Humanitarian Practice Network*, March, No. 20, pp. 13-15.

Rangasami, Amrita (1985): "'Failure of Exchange Entitlements' Theory of Famine. A Response". In: *Economic and Political Weekly*, Vol. 20/21, No. 41, pp. 1747-1752.

Raynard, Peter (2000): *Mapping Accountability in Humanitarian Assistance*. Report Presented to ALNAP at the Bi-Annual Meeting in April 2000. London: Overseas Development Institute.

Reltien, Christophe (2000): "Humanitarian Action in North Korea. Ostrich Politics". In: Action Against Hunger (ed.): *The Geopolitics of Hunger, 2000-2001. Hunger and Power*. Boulder, London: Lynne Rienner, pp. 159-168.

Reynell, Josephine (1989): *Political Pawns: Refugees on the Thai-Kampuchean Border*. Oxford: University of Oxford/Refugee Studies Programme.

Robinson, W. Courtland, Myung Ken Lee, Kenneth Hill and Gilbert M. Burnham (1999): "Mortality in North Korean Migrant Households. A Retrospective Study". In: *The Lancet*, Vol. 354, pp. 291-295.

Schloms, Michael (2003): "The European NGO Experience in North Korea". In: L. Gordon Flake and Scott Snyder (eds.): *Paved With Good Intentions. NGO Experience in North Korea*. Westport: Praeger, pp. 47-79.

Schulthes, Jens (2000): "Is There a Future for the WFP as a Development Agency? Or Does Food Aid Still Have a Comparative Advantage?" In: Edward Clay and Olav Stokke (eds.): *Food Aid and Human Security*. London, Portland: Frank Cass, (EADI Book Series 24), pp. 256-273.

Sen, Amartya (1981): *Poverty and Famines. An Essay on Entitlement and Deprivation*. Oxford: Clarendon Press.

Sen, Amartya (1982): "The Food Problem. Theory and Policy". In: *Third World Quarterly*, Vol. 4, No. 3, pp. 447-459.

Sen, Amartya (1990): "Food, Economics, and Entitlements". In: Drèze, Jean and Amartya Sen (eds.): *The Political Economy of Hunger. Volume I: Entitlement and Well-Being*. Oxford: Clarendon Press, pp. 34-52.

Sen, Amartya (1998): "Pas de bonne Economie sans vraie Démocratie". In: *Le Monde*, 28 October.

Sen, Amartya (1999a): "Democracy as a Universal Value". In: *Journal of Democracy*, Vol. 10, No. 3, pp. 3-17.

Sen, Amartya (1999b): Interview by Doctors Without Borders (MSF), Trinity College Cambridge, 25 May.

Sen, Amartya (2002): "Why Half the Planet Is Hungry". In : *The Observer*, 16 June.

Shawcross, William (1984): *The Quality of Mercy. Cambodia, Holocaust and Modern Conscience*. New York: Simon and Schuster.

Shiva, Vandana (2002): "The Real Reasons For Hunger". In: *The Observer*, 23 June.

Siméant, Johanna (2001): "Entrer, Rester en Humanitaire. Des Fondateurs de MSF aux Membres Actuels des ONG Médicales Françaises". In: *Revue Française de Science Politique*, Vol. 51, No. 1-2, pp. 47-72.

Singer, Peter (1972): "Famine, Affluence, and Morality". In: *Philosophy and Public Affairs*, Vol. 1, No. 1, pp. 229-243.

Sinnott-Armstrong, Walter (1988): *Moral Dilemmas*. Oxford, New York: Basil Blackwell.

Slim, Hugo (1995): "The Continuing Metamorphosis of the Humanitarian Practitioner. Some New Colours for an Endangered Chameleon". In: *Disasters*, Vol. 19, No. 2, pp. 110-126.

Slim, Hugo (1997a): "Doing the Right Thing. Relief Agencies, Moral Dilemmas and Moral Responsibility in Political Emergencies and War". In: *Disasters*, Vol. 21, No. 3, pp. 244-257.

Slim, Hugo (1997b): "Relief Agencies and Moral Standing in War. Principles of Neutrality, Impartiality and Solidarity". In: *Development in Practice*, Vol. 7, pp. 342-352.

Slim, Hugo (2001): "Not Philanthropy But Rights. Rights-Based Humanitarianism and the Proper Politicisation of Humanitarian Philosophy in War". Paper presented at: Politics and Humanitarian Aid. Debates, Dilemmas and Dissension. London, 1 February.

Slim, Hugo (2002): "By What Authority? The Legitimacy and Accountability of Non-Governmental Organisations". In: *Journal of Humanitarian Assistance,* www.jha.ac/articles/a082.htm, Document Posted: 10 March 2002.

Slim, Hugo and Isobel McConnan (1998): *A Swiss Prince, a Glass Slipper and the Feet of 15 British Aid Agencies. A Study of DEC Agency Positions on Humanitarian Principles.* Report for the UK's Disaster Emergency Committee, Oxford, 1 October.

Smillie, Ian (1996): "Painting Canadian Roses Red". In: Edwards, Michael and David Hulme (eds.): *Beyond the Magic Bullet. NGO Performance and Accountability in the Post-Cold War World.* West Hartford: Kumarian, pp. 187-197.

Smillie, Ian (1998): *Relief and Development. The Struggle for Synergy.* Providence, RI: Thomas Watson Jr. Institute for International Studies/Brown University, (Occasional Paper No. 33).

Smith, Heather (1997): *North Korea. How Much Reform and Whose Characteristics?* Brookings Discussion Papers in International Economics.

Smith, Heather and Yiping Huang (2000): "Achieving Food Security in North Korea." In: Paolo Cotta-Ramusino and Maurizio Martellini (eds.): *Promoting International Scientific, Technological and Economic Cooperation in the Korean Peninsula: Enhancing Stability and International Dialogue.* Como, Italy: Landau Network – Centro Volta, pp. 201–218.

Smith, Hazel (2001a): *Five-Year Review of the Caritas Programme in the Democratic People's Republic of Korea (DPRK).* Vatican City and Hong Kong: Caritas Internationalis, Caritas Hong Kong.

Smith, Hazel (2001b): *Special Report. Overcoming Humanitarian Dilemmas in the DPRK (North Korea).* Washington, D.C.: United States Institute of Peace.

Snyder, Scott (1999): *Negotiating on the Edge. North Korean Negotiating Behavior.* Washington, D.C.: United States Institute for Peace.

Snyder, Scott (2003): "The NGO Experience in North Korea" and "Lessons of the NGO Experience in North Korea. " In: L. Gordon Flake and Scott Snyder (eds.): *Paved With Good Intentions. NGO Experience in North Korea.* Westport: Praeger, pp. 1-14 and pp. 111-122.

Taylor, Alan and Frederick Cuny (1979): "The Evaluation of Humanitarian Assistance". In: *Disasters,* Vol. 3, No. 3, pp. 37-42.

Terry, Fiona (2000): *Condemned to Repeat? The Paradoxes of Humanitarian Action.* Canberra: Australian National University/Department of International Relations, (Ph.D. Dissertation).

Thompson, Joseph E. (1990): *American Policy and African Famine. The Nigeria-Biafra War 1966-1970.* New York: Greenwood Press, (Contributions in Afro-American and African Studies, No. 130).

Tugendhat, Ernst (1995): "The Moral Dilemma in the Rescue of Refugees". In: *Social Research,* Vol. 62, No. 1., pp. 129-142.

United Nations Office for the Coordination of Humanitarian Affairs (UNOCHA, various issues): *United Nations Consolidated Inter-Agency Appeal for the Democratic People's Republic of Korea.* New York, Geneva: UNOCHA.

Uvin, Peter (1994): *International Organization of Hunger.* Geneva: Graduate Institute of International Studies.

Van Brabant, Koenraad (1997): *Organisational and Institutional Learning in the Humanitarian Sector. Opening the Dialogue.* Discussion Paper for the Active Learning Network on Accountability and Performance in Humanitarian Assistance. London: Overseas Development Institute.

Van Brabant, Koenraad (1998): "Security and Humanitarian Space – Perspective of an Aid Agency". In: *Humanitäres Völkerrecht – Informationsschriften,* No. 1, pp.14-24.

Vaux, Tony (2001): *The Selfish Altruist. Relief Work in Famine and War.* London: Earthscan.

Von Hippel, David, Timothy Savage and Peter Hayes (2002): *The DPRK Energy Sector. Estimated Year 2000 Energy Balance and Suggested Approaches to Sectoral Redevelopment.* Report Prepared for the Korean Energy Economics Institute. Berkeley: Nautilus Institute for Security and Sustainable Development.

Von Pilar, Ulrike (1999): "Humanitarian Space under Siege". Paper presented for the Symposium 'Europe and Humanitarian Aid – What Future? Learning from Crisis', Bad Neuenahr, 22-23 April.

Walkup, Mark (1997): "Policy Dysfunction in Humanitarian Organizations. The Role of Coping Strategies, Institutions, and Organizational Culture". In: *Journal of Refugee Studies,* Vol. 10, No. 1, pp. 37-60.

Watts, Michael J. and Hans G. Bohle (1993): "The Space of Vulnerability. The Causal Structure of Hunger and Famine". In: *Progress in Human Geography*, Vol. 17, No. 1, pp. 43-67.

Weingartner, Erich (2001): *NGO Contributions to DPRK Development: Issues for Canada and the International Community*. Vancouver: University of British Columbia/Institute of Asian Research (North Pacific Policy Paper Nr. 7).

Weiss, Thomas G. and Cindy Collins (1996): *Humanitarian Challenges and Intervention: World Politics and the Dilemmas of Help*. Boulder, Westview Press.

Weiss, Thomas G. and Leon Gordenker (1996): *NGOs, the UN, and Global Governance*. Boulder, London: Lynne Rienner.

Weissman, Benjamin M. (1974): *Herbert Hoover and Famine Relief to Soviet Russia: 1921-1923*. Stanford: Hoover Institution Press/Stanford University.

Williams, James H., David von Hippel and Peter Hayes (2000): *Fuel and Famine. Rural Energy Crisis in the Democratic People's Republic of Korea*. San Diego: Institute on Global Conflict and Cooperation. IGCC Policy Papers (Working Paper 46).

Woldemariam, Mesfin (1984): *Rural Vulnerability to Famine in Ethiopia. 1958-1977*. Addis Ababa: Vikas.

Woo-Cumings, Meredith (2002): *The Political Ecology of Famine. The North Korean Catastrophe and Its Lessons*. Tokyo: Asian Development Bank Institute, (ADB Institute Research Paper No. 31).

World Resource Institute (1990): *World Resources. A Report by the World Resource Institute in Collaboration with the United Nations Environment Programme and the United Nations Development Programme, 1990-91*. New York: Oxford University Press.

Wronka, Joseph (1998): *Human Rights and Social Policy in the 21st Century. A History of the Idea of Human Rights and Comparison of the United Nations Universal Declaration of Human Rights with United States Federal and State Constitutions*. Lanham: University Press of America.

Young Namkoong (1993): "An Assessment of North Korean Economic Capability". In: Research Institute for National Unification and IFO Institute for Economic Research (eds.): *Economic Problems of National Unification*. Seoul, Munich: Research Institute for National Unification and IFO Institute for Economic Research, pp. 43-64.

Index

Wissenschaftliche Paperbacks

Politikwissenschaft

Hartmut Elsenhans

Das Internationale System zwischen Zivilgesellschaft und Rente

Gegen derzeitige Theorieangebote für die Erklärung der Ursachen und die Auswirkungen wachsender transnationaler und internationaler Verflechtung setzt das hier vorliegende Konzept eine stark durch politökonomische Überlegungen integrierte Perspektive, die auf politologischen, soziologischen, ökonomischen und philosophischen Ansatzpunkten aufbaut. Mit diesem Konzept soll gezeigt werden, daß der durch Produktionsauslagerungen/Direktinvestitionen/neue Muster der internationalen Arbeitsteilung gekennzeichnete (im weiteren als Transnationalisierung von Wirtschaftsbeziehungen bezeichnete) kapitalistische Impuls zur Integration der bisher nicht in die Weltwirtschaft voll integrierten Peripherie weiterhin zu schwach ist, als daß dort nichtmarktwirtschaftliche Formen der Aneignung von Überschuß entscheidend zurückgedrängt werden können. Das sich herausbildende internationale System ist deshalb durch miteinander verschränkte Strukturen von Markt- und Nichtmarktökonomie gekennzeichnet, die nur unter bestimmten Voraussetzungen synergetische Effekte in Richtung einer autonomen und zivilisierten Weltzivilgesellschaft entfalten werden. Dabei treten neue Strukturen von Nichtmarktökonomie auf transnationaler Ebene auf, während der Wiederaufstieg von Renten die zivilgesellschaftlichen Grundlagen funktionierender oder potentiell zu Funktionsfähigkeit zu bringender, dann kapitalistischer Systeme auf internationaler und lokaler Ebene eher behindert.
Bd. 6, 2001, 140 S., 12,90 €, br., ISBN 3-8258-4837-x

Klaus Schubert

Innovation und Ordnung

In einer evolutionär voranschreitenden Welt sind statische Politikmodelle und -theorien problematisch. Deshalb lohnt es sich, die wichtigste Quelle für die Entstehung der policy-analysis, den Pragmatismus, als dynamische, demokratieendogene politisch-philosophische Strömung zu rekonstruieren. Dies geschieht im ersten Teil der Studie. Der zweite Teil trägt zum Verständnis des daraus folgenden politikwissenschaftlichen Ansatzes bei. Darüber hinaus wird durch eine konstruktiv-spekulative Argumentation versucht, die z. Z. wenig innovative Theorie- und Methodendiskussion in der Politikwissenschaft anzuregen.
Bd. 7, 2003, 224 S., 25,90 €, br., ISBN 3-8258-6091-4

Politik: Forschung und Wissenschaft

Hartwig Hummel; Ulrich Menzel (Hg.)

Die Ethnisierung internationaler Wirtschaftsbeziehungen und daraus resultierende Konflikte

Mit Beiträgen von Annabelle Gambe, Hartwig Hummel, Ulrich Menzel und Birgit Wehrhöfer
"Die Ethnisierung der internationalen Wirtschaftsbeziehungen und daraus resultierende Konflikte" lautete der Titel eines Forschungsprojekts, das diesem Band zugrunde liegt. Es geht um die Themen Handel, Migration und Investitionen. In drei Fallstudien werden die Handelsbeziehungen zwischen den USA und Japan, die Einwanderung nach Deutschland bzw. Frankreich und das auslandschinesische Unternehmertum untersucht. Die Ergebnisse des Projekts sehen Hummel und Menzel in den späteren Ereignissen bestätigt: Ethnisierende Tendenzen können sich in der Handelspolitik und der Investitionstätigkeit von Unternehmen nicht durchsetzen, während die Ethnisierung im Bereich der Migration andauert.
Bd. 2, 2001, 272 S., 30,90 €, br., ISBN 3-8258-4836-1

Theodor Ebert

Opponieren und Regieren mit gewaltfreien Mitteln

Pazifismus – Grundsätze und Erfahrungen für das 21. Jahrhundert. Band 1
Das grundlegende und aktuelle Werk eines Konfliktforschers, der über Jahrzehnte in pazifistischen Organisationen, in sozialen Bewegungen und in Gremien der Evangelischen Kirche gearbeitet hat. Ebert breitet in anschaulichen Berichten und doch in systematischer Ordnung die Summe seiner Erfahrungen aus und entwickelt Perspektiven für eine Welt, die mit der Gewalt leben muss, doch Gefahr läuft, an ihr zugrunde zu gehen, wenn sie auf die Bedrohungen keine neuen, gewaltfreien Antworten findet.
Aus dem Vorwort: "Es gibt eine pragmatische Befürwortung des gewaltfreien Handelns in innenpolitischen Auseinandersetzungen durch eine Mehrheit der Deutschen, und dies sollten wir als tragenden Bestandteil der Zivilkultur nicht gering schätzen. Doch die Frage, wie man mit gewaltfreien Mitteln regieren und sich gegenüber gewalttätigen Extremisten durchsetzen kann und wie man sich international behaupten und Bedrohten helfen kann, ist bislang kaum erörtert worden ... Dieses Buch soll klären, was unter

LIT Verlag Münster – Hamburg – Berlin – Wien – London

Grevener Str./Fresnostr. 2 48159 Münster
Tel.: 0251 – 23 50 91 – Fax: 0251 – 23 19 72
e-Mail: vertrieb@lit-verlag.de – http://www.lit-verlag.de

politisch verantwortlichem und doch radikal gewaltfreiem Pazifismus zu verstehen ist, und wie mit gewaltfreien Mitteln nicht nur opponiert, sondern auch regiert werden kann."
Bd. 3, 2001, 328 S., 20,90 €, br., ISBN 3-8258-5706-9

Theodor Ebert
Der Kosovo-Krieg aus pazifistischer Sicht
Pazifismus – Grundsätze und Erfahrungen für das 21. Jahrhundert. Band 2
Mit dem Luftkrieg der NATO gegen Jugoslawien begann für den deutschen Nachkriegspazifismus ein neues Zeitalter. Ebert hat sich über Jahrzehnte als Konfliktforscher und Schriftleiter der Zeitschrift "Gewaltfreie Aktion" mit den Möglichkeiten gewaltfreier Konfliktbearbeitung befasst. Von ihm stammt der erste Entwurf für einen Zivilen Friedensdienst als Alternative zum Militär.
Aus dem Vorwort: "Wer sich einbildet, auch in Zukunft ließe sich aus großer Höhe mit Bomben politischer Gehorsam erzwingen, unterschätzt die Möglichkeiten, die fanatische Terroristen haben, in fahrlässiger Weise. Jedes Atomkraftwerk ist eine stationäre Atombombe, die von Terroristen mit geringem Aufwand in ein Tschernobyl verwandelt werden kann. Wir haben allen Grund, schleunigst über zivile Alternativen zu militärischen Einsätzen nachzudenken und die vorhandene Ansätze solch ziviler Alternativen zu entwickeln."
Bd. 4, 2001, 176 S., 12,90 €, br., ISBN 3-8258-5707-7

Wolfgang Gieler
Handbuch der Ausländer- und Zuwanderungspolitik
Von Afghanistan bis Zypern
In der Literatur zur Ausländer- und Zuwanderungspolitik fehlt ein Handbuch, dass einen schnellen und kompakten Überblick dieses Politikbereichs ermöglicht. Das vorliegende Handbuch bemüht sich diese wissenschaftliche Lücke zu schließen. Thematisiert werden die Ausländer- und Zuwanderungspolitik weltweiter Staaten von Afghanistan bis Zypern. Zentrale Fragestellung ist dabei der Umgang mit Fremden, das heißt mit Nicht-Inländern im jeweiligen Staat. Hierbei werden insbesondere politische, soziale, rechtliche, wirtschaftliche und kulturelle Aspekte berücksichtigt. Um eine Kompatibilität der Beiträge herzustellen beinhaltet jeder Beitrag darüber hinaus eine Zusammenstellung der historischen Grunddaten und eine Tabelle zur jeweiligen Anzahl der im Staat lebenden Ausländer. Die vorgelegte Publikation versteht sich als ein grundlegendes Nachschlagewerk. Neben dem universitären Bereich richtet es sich besonders an die gesellschaftspolitisch interessierte Öffentlichkeit und den auf sozialwissenschaftlichen Kenntnissen angewiesenen Personen in Politik, Verwaltung, Medien, Bildungseinrichtungen und Migranten-Organisationen.
Bd. 6, 2003, 768 S., 98,90 €, gb., ISBN 3-8258-6444-8

Harald Barrios; Martin Beck; Andreas Boeckh; Klaus Segbers (Eds)
Resistance to Globalization
Political Struggle and Cultural Resilience in the Middle East, Russia, and Latin America
This volume is an important contribution to the empirical research on what globalization means in different world regions. "Resistance" here has a double meaning: It can signify active, intentional resistance to tendencies which are rejected on political or moral grounds by presenting alternative discourses and concepts founded in specific cultural and national traditions. It can also mean resilience with regard to globalization pressures in the sense that traditional patterns of development and politics are resistant to change. The book shows the that the local, sub-national, national, and regional patterns of politics and development coexist with globalized structures without yielding very much ground and in ways which may turn out to be a serious barrier to further globalization. Case studies presented focus on Venezuela, Brazil, the Middle East, Iran, and Russia.
Bd. 7, 2003, 184 S., 20,90 €, br., ISBN 3-8258-6749-8

Ellen Bos; Antje Helmerich
Neue Bedrohung Terrorismus
Der 11. September 2001 und die Folgen.
Unter Mitarbeit von Barry Adams und Harald Wilkoszewski
Die terroristischen Anschläge des -11. September 2001 haben die Weltöffentlichkeit erschüttert. Ihre weitreichenden Auswirkungen auf die Lebenswirklichkeit des Einzelnen, den Handlungsspielraum der Nationalstaaten und das internationale System stehen im Mittelpunkt des Sammelbandes. Er basiert auf einer Ringvorlesung, in der sich Wissenschaftler der Ludwig-Maximilians-Universität München aus den Fächern Amerikanistik, Jura, Geschichte, Politik-, Religions-, Kommunikations- und Wirtschaftswissenschaft mit den geistigen Hintergründen und den Konsequenzen des Terrorismus auseinandersetzten.
Bd. 9, 2003, 232 S., 19,90 €, br., ISBN 3-8258-7099-5

Heinz-Gerhard Justenhoven; James Turner (Eds.)
Rethinking the State in the Age of Globalisation
Catholic Thought and Contemporary Political Theory
Since Jean Bodin and Thomas Hobbes, political theorists have depicted the state as „sovereign"

LIT Verlag Münster – Hamburg – Berlin – Wien – London
Grevener Str./Fresnostr. 2 48159 Münster
Tel.: 0251 – 23 50 91 – Fax: 0251 – 23 19 72
e-Mail: vertrieb@lit-verlag.de – http://www.lit-verlag.de

because it holds preeminent authority over all the denizens belonging to its geographically defined territory. From the Peace of Westphalia in 1648 until the beginning of World War I in 1914, the essential responsiblities ascribcd to the sovereign state were maintaining internal and external security and promoting domestic prosperity. This idea of „the state" in political theory is clearly inadequate to the realities of national governments and international relations at the beginning of the twenty-first century. During the twentieth century, the sovereign state, as a reality and an idea, has been variously challenged from without and within its borders. Where will the state head in the age of globalisation? Can Catholic polilical thinking contribute to an adequate concept of statehood and government? A group of German and American scholars were asked to explore specific ways in which the intellectual traditions of Catholicism might help our effort lo rethink the state. The debate is guided by the conviction that these intellectual resources will prove valuable to political theorists as they work to revise our understanding of the state.
Bd. 10, 2003, 240 S., 19,90 €, br., ISBN 3-8258-7249-1

Berliner Schriften zur Humanitären Hilfe und Konfliktprävention
herausgegeben von Prof. Dr. Wolf-Dieter Eberwein und Dr. Sven Chojnacki (Wissenschaftszentrum Berlin für Sozialforschung, WZB)

Wolf-Dieter Eberwein; Peter Runge (Hg.)
Humanitäre Hilfe statt Politik?
Neue Herausforderungen für ein altes Politikfeld
Spätestens mit der Zunahme gewaltsamer innerstaatlicher Konflikte seit Mitte der 80er Jahre ist die von der Generalversammlung der UNO in verschiedenen Resolutionen immer wieder eingeforderte „neue humanitäre internationale Ordnung" dringlicher denn je. Humanitäre Hilfe ist von ihren ethischen Prinzipien und völkerrechtlichen Grundlagen politisch unabhängig, neutral und unparteilich. Doch wie der Kosovo-Krieg 1999 und die Ereignisse in Afghanistan gezeigt haben, droht humanitäre Hilfe immer mehr als Mittel der Außen- und Sicherheitspolitik eingesetzt zu werden. Selbst wenn dies in einer nachvollziehbaren politischen Absicht geschehen sollte, wird die humanitäre Hilfe in ihrer Substanz ausgehöhlt.
In diesem Band, dem ersten in der neuen Reihe „Berliner Schriften zur humanitären Hilfe und Konfliktprävention", werden die Veränderungen,

die sich im Politikfeld der humanitären Hilfe im allgemeinen, in Deutschlande im besonderen, ergeben haben, von Praktikern und Wissenschaftlern analysiert. Insbesondere geht es um die zunehmende Politisierung der humanitären Hilfe, was dazu führt, dass die Bemühungen um eine internationale humanitäre Ordnung unterlaufen werden. Denn die Vermischung von politischer Zielsetzung und unpolitischer humanitärer Hilfe untergräbt langfristig die Glaubwürdigkeit humanitären Handelns.
Bd. 1, 2002, 232 S., 20,90 €, br., ISBN 3-8258-5918-5

Uta Bronner
Humanitäre Helfer in Krisengebieten
Motivation, Einsatzerleben, Konsequenzen –
Eine psychologische Analyse
Die Zahl humanitärer Krisen hat sich weltweit drastisch erhöht. Zunehmend werden internationale Helfer in politisch instabile Regionen entsandt, in denen ihr gesundheitliches Risiko und ihre Überlebenschancen kaum realistisch eingeschätzt werden können. Was motiviert Menschen sich freiwillig in derlei Extremsituationen zu begeben? Schritt für Schritt thematisiert das vorliegende Buch die Motivation und die Schwierigkeiten, auf die Helfer in Krisengebieten stoßen. Gleichzeitig beleuchtet es den Stellenwert der Betreuungsmaßnahmen der Hilfsorganisationen. Die psychologischen Fragestellungen lassen den „Retter vor Ort" in einem neuen Licht erscheinen.
Bd. 3, 2003, 312 S., 25,90 €, br., ISBN 3-8258-6756-0

Friedensgutachten
der Hessischen Stiftung für Friedens- und Konfliktforschung (HSFK), des Bonn International Center for Conversion (BICC), des Instituts für Entwicklung und Frieden (INEF), der Forschungsstätte der Evangelischen Studiengemeinschaft (FEST), des Instituts für Friedensforschung und Sicherheitspolitik an der Universität Hamburg (IFSH)

Friedensgutachten 2001
herausgegeben von Reinhard Mutz, Bruno Schoch und Ulrich Ratsch
Das Friedensgutachten 2001 nimmt sich aus verschiedenen Blickwinkeln der derzeit wohl brisantesten Konfliktkonstellation auf dem Globus an: der Krisenregion Naher Osten. Der Friedensprozess gilt als gescheitert, in den zwischen Israelis und Palästinensern strittigen Fragen scheinen Kompromisse ferner denn je. Die Gewalt dauert an und droht weiter zu eskalieren. Für eine hoffnungsvolle Perspektive lassen die festgefahrenen Fronten keinen Raum. Europa hingegen kann und muss die Atempause der immer noch

LIT Verlag Münster – Hamburg – Berlin – Wien – London
Grevener Str./Fresnostr. 2 48159 Münster
Tel.: 0251 – 23 50 91 – Fax: 0251 – 23 19 72
e-Mail: vertrieb@lit-verlag.de – http://www.lit-verlag.de

fragilen Waffenruhe auf dem Balkan nutzen, um seine friedens- und sicherheitspolitischen Strukturprobleme anzugehen. Die Erweiterung der EU darf die erreichten Integrationserfolge nicht in Frage stellen, Ziele und Mittel einer eigenständigen Sicherheitspolitik sind miteinander in Einklang zu bringen, Osteuropa, einschließlich Russland, braucht glaubhafte Aussichten auf friedensfördernde Einbindung. Im globalen Rahmen stellt sich der industrialisierten Welt die Aufgabe, organisierte Gewalt an ihren Wurzeln zu eliminieren. Armutsbekämpfung und Klimaschutz sind Beispiele. Das Friedensgutachten fragt nach den Ursachen von Bürgerkriegsökonomien und beleuchtet die Bemühungen, das Instrumentarium der UNO zur Friedensvorsorge zu stärken. Ausgewählte regionale Konfliktherde werden gesondert analysiert: Nordirland, Afghanistan, Korea, Irak, Indonesien. Den Abschluss bildet die Thematik internationaler Abrüstung und Rüstungskontrolle, die dem Blickfeld der Öffentlichkeit zu entschwinden scheint. Eng zusammen hängen die offene Frage der amerikanischen Raketenabwehrplanung und das Problem der Ausbreitung von Massenvernichtungswaffen. Die Begrenzung konventioneller Streitkräfte in Europa und die deutsche Rüstungsexportpolitik werden ebenso untersucht wie die Schwierigkeiten wirksamer Kleinwaffenkontrolle.

Von mehr als dreißig Wissenschaftlerinnen und Wissenschaftlern verschiedener Disziplinen erarbeitet, erscheint das Friedensgutachten 2001 zum fünfzehnten Mal. Es wird im Auftrag des IFSH, der HSFK und der FEST sowie in Kooperation mit dem INEF und dem BICC von Reinhard Mutz, Bruno Schoch und Ulrich Ratsch herausgegeben. Es kostet 12,90 €.
2001, 368 S., 12,90 €, br., ISBN 3-8258-5435-3

Friedensgutachten 2002
herausgegeben von Bruno Schoch, Corinna Hauswedell, Christoph Weller, Ulrich Ratsch und Reinhard Mutz
Das Friedensgutachten 2002 kreist thematisch um den 11. September. Die Beiträge erhellen Ursachen und Folgen, die weit über den Krieg in Afghanistan hinausgehen. Was ist das Neue am internationalen Terrorismus? Aus welchen Quellen speist er sich? Wie kann man ihm begegnen? Wie hat sich die Weltpolitik der USA verändert? Welche Rolle nimmt Russland ein? Und wie reagiert die deutsche Politik? Die Anschläge in den USA haben den Massenvernichtungsmitteln, auf deren Kontrolle und Abrüstung wir seit langem pochen, beunruhigende Aktualität verliehen. Und nicht zuletzt verändern neue Sicherheitsgesetze die in der Demokratie immer prekäre Balance von Sicherheit und Freiheit. Zwar hüten wir uns, schon das neue Jahrhundert definieren zu wollen - doch wir versuchen, Tendenzen zu einer neuen Weltordnung oder - unordnung aufzuspüren. Halten die völkerrechtlichen Regeln den Belastungen stand? Brauchen wir eine neue Aufrüstung? Und was hat es mit der Rede von den neuen Kriegen auf sich? - Exemplarisch gehen wir regionalen Konflikten nach: Mazedonien, Serbien und Montenegro, Nordirland sowie dem israelisch-palästinensischen Krieg, der im letzten Jahr im Mittelpunkt des Friedensgutachtens stand. - Nach wie vor ist Frieden weit mehr als Terrorismusbekämpfung. Wir thematisieren diesmal die Teilbereiche zivile Konfliktbearbeitung und plädieren für eine neue globale Kooperationskultur. Den Internationalen Strafgerichtshof bewerten wir trotz mancher Mängel als einen Fortschritt.
Das Friedensgutachten erscheint 2002 zum sechzehnten Mal. Es wird im Auftrag der fünf Institute herausgegeben von Bruno Schoch, Corinna Hauswedell, Christoph Weller, Ulrich Ratsch und Reinhard Mutz. Es kostet 12,90 Euro, im Abonnement 8,50 Euro.
2002, 320 S., 12,90 €, br., ISBN 3-8258-6007-8

Friedensgutachten 2003
herausgegeben von Corinna Hauswedell, Christoph Weller, Ulrich Ratsch, Reinhard Mutz, Bruno Schoch
Das Friedensgutachten ist das gemeinsame Jahrbuch der fünf Institute für Friedens- und Konfliktforschung in Deutschland. Einzelanalysen von mehr als dreißig Wissenschaftlerinnen und Wissenschaftlern aus verschiedenen Disziplinen untersuchen das internationale Konfliktgeschehen und entwerfen Friedensstrategien. Auf diese Beiträge stützt sich die Stellungnahme der Herausgeber. Sie zieht Bilanz, pointiert Ergebnisse und formuliert Empfehlungen für die friedens- und sicherheitspolitische Praxis in Deutschland und Europa.
Das Friedensgutachten 2003 stellt die Frage nach der Zukunft von Kooperation oder Konfrontation in der neuen Weltordnung. Die weitreichenden Folgen des 11. September 2001 und der Krieg gegen den Irak haben nicht nur die transatlantischen Beziehungen und die Zusammenarbeit in den internationalen Institutionen erschüttert, sie machen die tiefer gehenden Asymmetrien des neuen Weltgefüges sichtbar: Das Verhältnis von Macht und Recht in den internationalen Beziehungen steht auf dem Prüfstand; Militarisierung bedroht Entwicklung, Gerechtigkeit, Demokratie und humane Wertesysteme. Auf der Basis einer Analyse dieser grundlegenden Tendenzen fragen die Autoren nach den

LIT Verlag Münster – Hamburg – Berlin – Wien – London
Grevener Str./Fresnostr. 2 48159 Münster
Tel.: 0251 – 23 50 91 – Fax: 0251 – 23 19 72
e-Mail: vertrieb@lit-verlag.de – http://www.lit-verlag.de

Auswirkungen und Alternativen in relevanten
Weltregionen, für das Nord-Süd-Verhältnis und
nach der zukünftigen Rolle Europas: Wie soll
eine Friedensordnung im Mittleren Osten Gestalt
gewinnen, im

Peter Barschdorff
**Facilitating Transatlantic Cooperation
after the Cold War**

ɔublished with

im zerrissene
Konfliktregioɪ
von Gewaltöł
Ressourcen b
von Nordkorɛ
Anti-Terrorkr
Wie müssen ɛ
des Völkerrec
werden?
Das Friedensɡ
Institute herɑɩ
Christoph We
und Bruno Sc
Abonnement
2003, 336 S.,]

DATE DUE

ɑ still allied? After
after the Cold War
ɩde disputes could
ɪs would suffer in
eat (like the one
ɪ Soviet Union).
an acquis atlantique
ɩher. Common
ɩnderstandings
ɡe their views on
ɔeace-making in the
ɑde of agricultural
ɩge over time.
d as a driver of
ɩmain an important

]
Iɪ
im Auftrag
Außen- uɪ
Politische Wi
herɑ

, ISBN 3-8258-5434-5

das Ende des

ɪ Systems auf den

Cornelius Fr
**Der internaɩ
sicherheitsp**
Eine Erkläru
amerikaniscɦ
Dieser Band iɪ
projektes zu iɪ
entstanden. Ziɩ
und US-ameriⅼ
internationalen
und Unterschiɛ
Politiker versu
repressive Maſ
einigten Staate
Drogenanbau-
teilweise unilɑ
kräfte gegen d
Entscheidungst
Transitstaaten
Unilateralismuɬ
des Drogenpro   GAYLORD   PRINTED IN U.S.A.

ɩtionalen Bezie-
ɩspolitik einen
ɩinhaltet Anforde-
ɩme zugleich. Der
ist Symbol für das
ɩnd eine historische
architektur grundle-
eichs Handlungs-
zwischen Auto-
 der internationalen
ɩ verfolgte Frank-
Vereinigung,
hs internationaler
die französische
ɩ die nationale
ɫer Bündnis-
ⅼkreich auf die
ⅼerungen, u. a. die

ISBN 3-8258-5877-4

toren für die unterschiedlichen Strategien sind
unterschiedliche Risikowahrnehmungen, politisch-
militärische Kulturen und Institutionen.
Bd. 27, 2001, 208 S., 25,90 €, br., ISBN 3-8258-5326-8

LɪT Verlag Münster – Hamburg – Berlin – Wien – London
Grevener Str./Fresnostr. 2 48159 Münster
Tel.: 0251 – 23 50 91 – Fax: 0251 – 23 19 72
e-Mail: vertrieb@lit-verlag.de – http://www.lit-verlag.de